MOST PEOPLE I KNOW

(think that I'm crazy)

BILLY THORPE

(think that I'm crazy)

BILLY THORPE

MACMILLAN
Pan Macmillan Australia

First published 1998 in Macmillan by Pan Macmillan Australia Pty Limited
St Martins Tower, 31 Market Street, Sydney

National Library of Australia
cataloguing-in-publication data:

Thorpe, Billy, 1946– .
Most people I know (think that I'm crazy).

ISBN 0 7329 0967 8.

1. Thorpe, Billy, 1946– . 2. Rock musicians—Australia—
Biography. I. Title.

781.66092

Typeset in 12/15 pt Sabon by Post Pre-press Group
Printed in Australia by McPherson's Printing Group

This book is dedicated to my mother who had her ninety-first birthday on 2 April 1998, and to the memory of her best friend and partner for sixty years, her beloved Bill, who was my dad and hero. Mum, your strength and quiet grace have been an inspiration to me all my life, and to all who know and love you. God willing, we'll celebrate your hundredth together . . .

want to thank the love of my life, my wife Lynn, for her love, support and patience with me for the last twenty-seven years, and especially during my many emotional absences while I've been writing this book, when I've been locked away for weeks at a time in 'The Hole' as she calls my debris-laden office. Lynn is the heart and soul of my family which also consists of my two daughters Rusty and Lauren, a family without whose love and understanding I'm positive I would have been locked up or worse years ago. I know you all know it, but I want to say it anyway. I love you.

There are many musicians, some of whom you will meet in this book, to whom I owe a debt of gratitude for their friendship, support and influence on my life and music. But there is one player in particular whose contribution to my music, the bands' success, and Australian rock and blues in general, I must acknowledge. I speak of the legendary guitar player and my dear friend and neighbourhood school mate from Moorooka in Brisbane, Lobby Loyde. Lobby joined my band in 1968, changing my views about music forever. His style and attitude had a huge influence on me and on all who were fortunate enough to play with him or hear him play. Which sadly he hasn't done in over twenty-five years. Lobby Loyde is without doubt one of the most significant, yet uncelebrated and least known of Australia's musicians. His contribution to Australian rock and to the style and attitude of the Sunbury Aztecs, and bands such as AC/DC, is not well known except to those of us who were there, but is nevertheless enormous. His style to this day is unique in every sense of the word. He was a musical force in the burgeoning Brisbane blues scene of the early '60s with the original Coloured Balls and the Purple Hearts. His dynamic influence continued right through that decade to the point where we met again in 1968, and continued through the early '70s. I love ya, Lobbs, and hope for all our sakes you pick up your axe again one day and show some of the young Turks how it's really done.

A very special thanks to Gill Matthews, Paul Wheeler and Warren Morgan for your friendship, talent, and the greatest, most hilarious times anyone could ever hope to experience. Money can't buy the times we shared together. I love you all. It's great being a stamp, ain't it? Jesus, if they only knew! Thanks also to Momma Nene, Kevin Murphy, Jimmy Thompson, Bruce Howard, Michael Chugg, Michael Browning, and our ever-faithful roadie Norm Swiney, Norman E the bad roadee. A big thank you to all at Pan Macmillan, especially to Nikki Christer for her generous encouragement and support with both my books, and to my editor Carl Harrison-Ford for his patience, skill and hard work, and for teaching a green newcomer the ropes. To Mrs Joyce Owens for the cuppa and chat about Banchory Cottage after I knocked on her door, unannounced, at 92 Gipps Street. To Paul McHenry for his book, *Thorpie*, to which I turned many times when I'd forgotten who I used to be, and to Steve Frazer and Ian McFarlane for their dedication to the blues, and for the invaluable information contained in *Freedom Train*.

Thanks to Ansett Australia, Show Travel and Hard Rock Beach Club, Bali for their generous support.

Thanks also to all the many loyal fans who followed and supported the bands and me and who still do. And a big thank you from the bottom of my heart to all those people who bought my first book, *Sex and Thugs and Rock 'n' Roll*, and made it a best seller, and for the hundreds of letters encouraging me to write another. And to all the people I've met at book signings and after my concerts since its release, who have given me so much encouragement.

Without you all my world would turn in a very different way, and this book would not exist.

Contents

Introduction

Several times in my life I've been blessed to have been one of those fortunate riders on the crest of that unstoppable wave called change, and privileged to have felt first-hand the euphoria of the cosmically charged energy pumping directly from its core. In the early '60s I not only lived the rock 'n' roll myth, but experienced the very heart and soul of my generation as it led one of the most significant periods of sociological and cultural change ever to take place on this planet. All things must pass and, sadly, those times and the sense of innocence, freedom, challenge, love and joy they evoked are forever gone. But the spirit lives on and, as you will see, the fickle big toe of fate pointed to me again in the early '70s. And the lunacy started again!

Although *Most People I Know (Think That I'm Crazy)* is set in New York in 1979, it deals largely with the period in Australia between 1969 and early 1971 in which I wrote the song of that name, and with many bizarre and hilarious events that occurred during the rise of the Sunbury Aztecs. As with my first book, this is not an autobiography in the strict sense of the word. It's most certainly autobiographical and an insight into the insanity that seems to surround my life, but it's also a reflection through my eyes of a wonderful and unique period in recent Australian history that will never come again . . . This book was never intended to be a sequel to my first book. However, it is about my life, which I'm extremely happy to say still continues, and is therefore by natural extension an unavoidable continuation of the life I wrote about in *Sex and Thugs and Rock 'n' Roll*. It is, therefore, a sequel of sorts.

There's no escaping the fact that at times my life has been nothing short of an action, adventure, comedy, soap opera with me cast as the unwittingly naive, stumbling and bumbling lead character who somehow manages to scrape through and survive by the skin of his balls. I'm the Jerry Lewis of my movie and it wasn't until writing my first book that I realised it. Like all testosterone-laden males I'd always seen myself as real tough shit, but in writing about myself, and examining me in detail, it came as a bit of a shock to realise I'm really just a funny little fart.

To borrow from the introduction in my first book, 'had I attempted a work of fiction I couldn't have invented characters and situations more bizarre and hilarious than those documented in this book.' Certain names and places have been changed, both out of respect for the privacy of others, and to protect the innocent and guilty alike, including myself. Outside of those changes, regardless of what at times may seem like absolute mania, this book is 100 per cent fact.

The various combinations of personalities in my bands,

and the characters who surrounded us, always produced a special kind of lunacy which was a very large and important ingredient in our music and popularity. It's hard to convey the true level of insanity during our years together travelling Australia, playing every conceivable kind of gig from shit-filled shearing sheds in Queanbeyan to 250,000 people at the Myer Music Bowl in Melbourne. We were shot at, arrested, bashed, run out of towns, barred from television, idolised, locked up, and stoned beyond belief. We got away with absolute murder and offended so many people, it's hard to know why we weren't locked up permanently. But in retrospect it was all just rock 'n' roll fun and nobody ever got hurt. Well, almost nobody!

As you will see, something incredible happened to me in New York city in late 1979. An event so bizarre, even in my life and experience, that it gave me cause to reflect for the first time in many years on the events of which I now write. For those of you who read my last book, here we go again! For those reading me for the first time, welcome to another bizarre episode in my lunatic life and to that magical, unique, mad and crazy world of good times called rock 'n' roll.

Billy Thorpe
Sydney 1998

First Things First

After I relocated from Australia to Los Angeles with my wife Lynn and our four-year-old daughter Rusty in September 1976, it took the best part of a year and a half to get myself into the LA music scene, get a publishing deal with Arista Publishing, and a recording contract with Capricorn Records. The same Capricorn Records that had the Allman Brothers. It was owned and run by Phil Walden, who as a college boy had discovered and managed Otis Redding right up to his death. In 1978 I teamed up with a young hotshot LA producer by the name of Spencer Proffer. Spencer had negotiated himself into his own deal for a label called Pasha Music, which was financed by the German recording giant PolyGram. As luck would have it, PolyGram was also a major shareholder in Capricorn Records and they hooked Spencer up with Capricorn, who were looking for new artists.

Spencer's debut record for his new label was my debut

American album. Titled *Children of the Sun*, the record received all the attention, care and finance a young Aussie rocker like me had only dreamed about previously. To cut a real long story short, the record took off and eventually went to number 1 in about forty states, having broken big time out of Dallas, Texas, on a station called Q102, where it stayed on top of the charts for weeks. What amazed most people was that this five and a half minute sci-fi concept track about the landing of a group of aliens on earth was shooting up the same charts that were being dominated by disco dancin' divas and groups like the Bee Gees. People were boogieing all over the world and here I am with a concept record full of stereo rocket effects and the first guitar synthesiser ever heard on a record. I'm signed with the label that's internationally regarded and respected as the home of Southern, R&B and blues, and I've got a massive science fiction hit in the making. The reviews were like we wrote them ourselves. Capricorn couldn't supply the demand and my first ever live performance in the USA was headlining two sold-out SRO shows at the 5000-seater Maclaren Hall in Dallas in front of a bunch of cheering Texas fans.

Suddenly people wanted me on the cover of *Cashbox* and *Billboard* magazines. Producers from national TV and radio shows were calling about interviews. No-one could work out how this unknown shitkicker from Australia could possibly have a sci-fi hit in the middle of the disco boom. Don't ask me. Charm I guess. After a gruelling sold-out concert tour that took in Detroit, Chicago, Denver, the Carolinas, Georgia, Florida, Texas and Louisiana, I did my last show in Memphis, Tennessee.

Prior to the tour, along with Spencer Proffer and my manager Robert Raymond, I made a quick trip to Macon,

Georgia, for an informal record reception and to formally meet the company. Due to the sudden death of Phil Walden's father the day we arrived, the reception was cancelled and the trip was cut short. Obviously no-one felt like celebrating and it was agreed that I would come back at some stage in the near future. Macon, where Capricorn had its headquarters, is a small town about ninety miles southeast of Atlanta. It's also the home of Little Richard and the town where James Brown made his start. During the tour the title track from *Children of the Sun* was gradually picking up number 1 spots on radio around the country. Seeing I would be ending the tour in Memphis, which was only a hop and skip away, Capricorn organised a record reception-cum-celebration party and scheduled it for two days after the last gig.

Although it doesn't start there, it's on a cold November day in Macon, Georgia, that this story really begins.

Part I

I
Welcome to my Nightmare

'**M**orpheeno . . . Morpheeno . . . Si heee heee . . .
Moorrpheeennno!'

The words echoed off the moon and spun in patterns
that traced the edges of a thousand spiders' webs. Bounced
off solid steel like the scream the fishes heard that night the
Titanic's hull tore like a virgin's hymen below the bone-
freezing Atlantic. Ricocheted off dream-filled eardrums
with a pain that split my head and wrenched me from the
sickening depths of my coma. Eyes fused shut by the arc
welder from hell forced themselves past the steel plate riveted to my skull, squinted through a bolt of lightning white
light, and ventured their first terrified peep at . . .

'Morpheeno . . . Morpheeno . . . Si hee hee hee.' The
words echoed again, sounding like the twisted Mexican bandit in *The Treasure of the Sierra Madre*. Taunting Humphrey
Bogart, 'Baaadges . . . baaadges . . . We don nee no steen-
keen baaadges . . . Morpheeennno . . . haiyee hee heeee.'

Mexican bandits? Welded eyes forced themselves open, slamming images through my brain, pleading with it to get its shit together, take in my surroundings and tell me where I was.

'Morpheeno . . . Si hee hee . . . Mooorpheeeno señor,' Zapata's voice cackled again from the somewhere in front of me. Eyes suddenly found focus on what the brain couldn't compute. Like a graphic on a computer short on memory, an image slowly formed of two moustachioed, shit-eatin' grins beaming at me from across a large, cold, solid white room. The two grinning moustaches lay in chromium-framed beds some twenty feet away. The faces, though obviously Cuban or Puerto Rican, for the moment were blurred. The only discernible features, the tobacco-stained grins that split their faces like knife slits in cantaloupes as they nodded excitedly in my direction. 'Morpheeenoo . . . Si!'

To my left, an empty bed sat against a wall with two barred windows high up near the ceiling. Both slightly open. In the corner to my right a chrome stand holding an electronic machine of some kind. Green sign waves snaked hypnotically from left to right across its six-inch TV screen in perfect sync with the steady beeeep, beeeep of an audio pulse. Moss-green cables from the machine ran across the white floor, under my sheets, and attached to two rubber stickers on my chest. A floor-to-ceiling window stretched from the corner behind the machine to a solid steel door in the centre of the wall. Beyond the door another window extended to the corner next to the grinning cantaloupe opposite me. Both windows were covered on the outside with three-inch, steel-plate mesh bars, and behind one of them sat an Idi Amin lookalike in a dark blue uniform. In his hands a Mossberger, pump-action, 12-gauge, ten-shot riot gun. At first my confused brain deciphered the lettering on the embroidered patch on his sixteen-inch, bicep-bulged shirt sleeve to read New York City Police Department, but it didn't. On closer inspection it read 'Bellevue Mental Hospital for the Criminally Insane. Maximum Security Section.'

Oh shit! said that smartarse in my head. *You've done it this time.*

Clank! . . . Squeak! . . . Clang! The sound of bolts being loosened. The steel door swung slowly open and in strode a big black nurse. And I mean big! This momma put the 'B' in 'Bertha' and looked like she could go twelve rounds with the Hulk, then wrestle Mike Tyson to a standstill for a dozen buckets of the Colonel's best Kentucky Fried. The grinning moustaches went silent. I tried to sit up . . . A searing pain shot up my left side from my elbow to my brain. At that second I realised my left arm was in a sling, covered in plaster from hand to shoulder, and felt like it had been run over by a Melbourne tram. I tried to say something to Bertha but all that came out was 'IIIImmm eerrm caaa . . . bluuuurrrt', which of course in my head sounded like, 'Excuse me, ma'am. Can you please tell me what happened and where I am?', all perfectly articulated and enunciated like old Sir Laurence O. in the middle of *Richard III*.

Bertha came straight at me like a bull at a barrel. Beeep, beeep, beeep, beeep went the heart monitor. She grabbed my right arm, cleaned it with alcohol and slammed a hypodermic needle the size of a chopstick into the mainline. Beeep, beeep, beeep, beeep . . . beeep . . . beeep . . . beeep, the machine responded, and the Mexican grinning squad grinned in unison.

'Moooorpheeeenoo . . . Moooorpheeeenoo . . . Si heeeee heee . . . Aiy yai yaiii!'

'Oohh ssshiiiit. Whaaat hv uuu done nowww?' went the voice again.

The world went into slow motion. Shot-gun-toting Idi Amin rolled his massive frame through the open door yelling in Spanish to the Hispanic mafia across the room. Which I guessed roughly translated into something along the lines of, 'Shut your Spick mouths you greaseball mother-fuckers or I'll put a 12-gauge cap in yo ass.' He positioned himself between their beds, riot gun at the ready, while Bertha administered them the same hit of what I realised was that cotton candied, body clawin', brain padding, lying soul-scratching bitch from hell, Sweet Sister Morphine.

A buzz with a warmth akin to the glow you'd get from the first puff of a cigarette, lying there in bed after a ménage à quatre with Catherine Deneuve, Emma Thompson and Elle Macpherson, slid through my veins like a hot electric snake. I was feeling no pain. In fact I wasn't feeling anything. My brain started to rant. 'This must be heaven. That's it . . . I've died and gone to heaven . . . Car crash or something. Yeeaahh. That's it . . . This is the room at the Paradise Hospital where you get to mend up before being formally introduced to Charlton Heston.' *Hang on. What's wrong with this picture?* asked the smartarse in my skull. '*Ah! It **could** be the steel door, the bars on the windows and the shotgun-toting Idi,*' answered some other voice. Two guys are having a great old rave between my ears like I'm not even on the planet.

'Oohhh fuuuckk off,' I mumbled at the air.

'Watch yo goddamned mouth, boy,' Idi shouted, pointing the riot gun in my direction.

I didn't even blink. I couldn't. I was too whacked. But I wouldn't have moved even if I could have. I might have been doing a slow backstroke in a tank of warm golden syrup but I was compos mentis enough to know I sure as shit didn't want to die at the hands of some six foot three, 300 pound gorilla with a riot gun in the maximum security section of the Bellevue Mental Hospital for the Criminally Insane in New York City, USA.

Yep, that's where I was all right. Smack dab in the middle of Manhattan Island under armed guard in the high security section of one of America's baddest and most notorious houses for the criminally insane. It was Thanksgiving long weekend. November 1979. I didn't have a clue how I'd gotten there.

As the morphine slowly took over, rivers of nauseating pleasure pulsed through my body. My heart slowed . . . Giant steel waves with titanium quills arched their riveted backs and crashed upon crystal glass beaches, pounding my eardrums and reverberating through my head. The room started to spin. To fade. My brain fought for a solid foothold. Teetering on the edge of a bottomless chasm of consciousness. *Got to hold on! . . . hold on! . . . How did I get in here? Help meee!* Screaming the silent scream.

I was slowly drowning in a morphine nightmare. Racking my soggy brain for answers. Abandoning myself to the most despondent reflections. Images spun like painted children's tops. Colours melting into street scenes, into landscapes, into cool blue oceans, Australia, Los Angeles, Georgia, Detroit . . . Back and forth. Up and down. Safe but not safe. Adopting the most extravagant conjectures while frantically rowing a leaking lifeboat through the spume-filled crests of a freezing midnight sea. A distant voice from some far-off shore echoing . . .

How did I get here? . . . heere . . . heeere . . . heeeerrre.

2
Memphis

I found myself drifting. Confused. Images formed then melted into other images. None of them related. The word limousine kept spinning in my head. Why? Did I come here in a limo? And where from? My mind spun out of control. Fighting with itself. Clawing for answers. One minute fixing on how I got there, the next on the unreality of the situation. An armed guard. Why? My brain was packed in cotton wool. Heavy. Thick. Unfocused. No-one driving. Rambling. Grasping for anything that would put it together. No one thought connected to the next. I strained to get back to what I'd been thinking about. Forcing myself to eliminate my surroundings and concentrate on the last twenty-four hours. Limousine? Why limousine? The word 'Macon' came into my head. *What's Macon got to do with this? . . . Macon? . . . Macon, Georgia?* My brain tapped its fingers. *Memphis, that's it! Memphis. The record. The tour . . . The tour! . . . What about the tour? . . . Come on, think. Think!* The room faded around me. Familiar images began to form.

The tour had ended in Memphis, Tennessee. After the Memphis gig I had one free day there before my trip to Macon to meet and greet with the Capricorn Records people. The show had been a 5,000-seater sellout. *Children of the Sun* was number 1 in Memphis, and it was my fifteen minutes in Tennessee. I'd been offered a sightseeing tour as the guest of a radio station that had been one of my first supporters. They'd been playing my record to death in high rotation since the day it was released. Memphis, Tennessee, is hallowed ground to anyone who's into rock 'n' roll and the blues so I jumped at their offer.

Of course there's only one place to go for the first-time visitor to Memphis. It's *the* place. And *the* place I was going that morning was Gracelands. A limousine picked me up at my hotel on Beale Street around 8 a.m. and we went straight to the home of the man who started the whole she-bang. I'd been around, met and known quite a few legends by this stage in my life, and although it's always a pleasure to meet your favourites, I rarely felt like anyone's adoring fan. But as we pulled up outside those famous white double gates with the black cast-iron music notes and the italicised word 'Gracelands', I had a knot in my stomach the size of one of King Kong's cojones.

Elvis's music and persona had been everywhere in Australia in 1956 when I was a young kid of ten squawking out my musical start at rock gigs around Brisbane. His was the cool hip by which all hip was measured. His the untamed male sexuality and style that all tried to emulate, but no-one even came close to. I'd been a generation too young to truly feel or understand the deep cultural significance of Elvis's impact on the teenage world of the '50s, but sitting outside Gracelands it hit me just how big a role his music and influence had played in the direction my life had taken. I owed a lot to the 'Hillbilly Cat'. I also realised at that moment that had I asked some favours from a few heavyweight string-pullers, begged, pleaded and crawled, I most probably could have met him before he died and told him so to his face.

The radio station had called a favour and arranged a visit for a few private minutes before the usual daily throng of pilgrims pressed their flowers and left their tears at the King's final resting place. When we pulled up outside the gate at around 8.30 there were already about 300 people patiently waiting in line. Some sat or dozed in fold-up chairs, wrapped in blankets against the chilly November Memphis morning. Some sat on plastic sheets on the footpath, backs against the wall. They chatted happily to one another while eating donuts and sipping coffee from plastic dixie cups, all purchased from one of the many Elvis concessions directly across the street. Some just stood in reverent silence. Waiting for a dream to come true. Or for some, their worst nightmare to find closure. It was easy to see many had been there all night. Somewhere in the crowd a portable radio wished, 'Gooood mooornin' Memphis. And a special hi ta all you fans bravin' the cold in front of Gracelands. Welcome to Memphis, Tennessee, y'all, the home of the King.' It had snowed a little in the night and although the morning sun left only small patches of snow missed by the street-sweeping trucks, it was still bloody cold. But these adoring punters felt no pain. Only the love and cherished memories of what had brought some of them across the world to be as close as they would ever physically be to the Man from Tennessee.

I had the window of the limo down, taking it all in, when a voice yelled out, 'On ya, Thorpie. Great show last night, mate.' No mistaking that twang. It comes from the real deep south, and after three years away from Australia that unexpectedly incongruous 'On ya, Thorpie' touched me deeply, jetting me home for a nostalgic heartbeat. A few other people yelled hi and came over to the limo asking for autographs. I couldn't believe it. Me signing autographs outside Elvis's house? It seemed irreverent. The limo driver radioed to somebody that we were outside and a few seconds later the huge gates swung slowly open. I heard the DJ announce on the limo radio, 'And here's the number one record in Memphis this week, Billy Thorpe and "Children of the Sun". Welcome to Gracelands, Billy.' A portable radio in the crowd was tuned to the same station and they all yelled their appreciation. As my limo passed slowly through the hallowed gates of Gracelands, 'Children of the Sun' began playing on the radio.

Let me tell you, from the bottom of my heart, that was a MOMENT!

The rest of the day was spent riding around in the limo seeing the sights of Memphis, and eating and drinking with the best bunch of good ole radio boys in Dixie. That night we hit every club on Beale Street, lucking out to hear B. B. King play a two-hour set at one of them, after which he invited me backstage. Good God almighty. A number one record and the two Kings in one day. It don't get much better than that. My tour manager told me there would be a ticket for me at Memphis airport the next day for the 3 p.m. flight to Atlanta. A limo would take me to the airport, with another meeting me in Atlanta for the one and a half hour drive to Macon. *Ah, civilised people*, I thought as

I crawled out of bed at 1.30 p.m. with the worst head known to man. Everything went like clockwork and as my limo pulled into the outskirts of Macon at around 6 p.m. a breathtaking glow slid sensually across the magenta shoulders of the Georgia evening sky like James Brown's golden cape. As we drove through the old southern town, an unmistakable feeling of *déjà vu* came over me. I'd been here before. I knew damn well I hadn't, but it all looked so bloody familiar. The style of some of the buildings, the streets, the scale, the colours, everything. It looked Australian. I'd had that same feeling once before in Savannah, Georgia.

I mentioned it to the limo driver and it turned out he knew the whole history of Georgia. He explained that Macon was one of the very few towns in Georgia which wasn't destroyed by General Sherman during his infamous march to the sea during the Civil War. Legend has it that the locals had paid ole Gen'l Sherman off and, apart from an obligatory cannonball through the church tower just to keep things kosher for the history books, Macon was spared the carnage and looks today much as it did in the early 1800s. He also told me that Savannah was once a British penal colony. Seems that after being elected to the House of Commons in 1722, a certain James Edward Oglethorpe had become interested in prison reform. He formulated a plan for the resettlement of debtors in America, and in 1733 founded the town of Savannah, Georgia, with 116 convicts. This was only fifty-five years before the penal colony at Port Jackson.

Descendants of British convicts. Same state. Ain't that far apart. Who knows? But there's definitely something real familiar about them, I thought as I settled into my hotel suite. I was unpacking my clothes and noticed a hand-written message on the desk by my bed. '*Dear Bill,*' it read:

Welcome to Macon & congratulations. The record's screaming. We went #1 in Chicago, Toronto, New Orleans, Miami, and Detroit today. Sorry I can't be there tonight. Have to be in New York. But y'all have a great time. Speak to you soon. We're going all the way with this one.

A limousine will pick you up at 7.30 sharp.
Stay ready and steady
Phil

3
Think!

Two moustaches and a wombat lay floating in a catatonic stupor. Grins fixed. Eyes stare unblinking. Mouths gape loosely, vaguely, at two large ceiling fans turning lazy circles on a shiny white ceiling. Slowly. Very very slowly . . . Warm cotton wool . . . Alpaca . . . Fluffy . . . Soft . . . Bouncing . . . Giant white sponges on a sea of floating white clouds. No edges. No sides. No sound. No time. Softly . . . Very very softly . . . Shhhhh . . . *That's* where Morpheus lives.

A car tyre squealed, echoing through the barred windows of my cell from somewhere outside, shooting me back. Macon was gone! *Cars . . . Outside . . . Outside what? Where is this place?* Unfocused eyes strained through a dreamy haze. Squinting for a glimpse of something, anything. But there was nothing through the windows but a polluted, solid grey sky. *Must be high up . . . What floor?* I fought to get a bearing on anything, but I couldn't. Unless some activity or sound shot me back into it I had no conscious thought of being under armed guard in Bellevue Mental Hospital. Morphine wasn't consciousness. Not even close. No handles. No parameters. Can't get a fix on anything long enough to hold on. You're just there. No reasoning it. Once you relax and just let it take you, it's terrifyingly safe. No strings. Protected. Real easy to like! Warm cotton wool. Alpaca, fluffy . . . No edges. No sides.

What increased my confusion was the fact that I normally had a 20/20 memory, with pretty near instant recall. For some reason it was gone. I was struggling to bring any order to the events that I presumed had happened in the last forty-eight hours. I was suffering some kind of amnesia. It wasn't total. I knew who I was and my rock 'n' roll past. It was my short-term memory that was the problem. I put it down to the heavy medication. I'd had morphine a couple of times before in hospital and I thought I knew its effects. But on those occasions the doses had been small enough to allow body and mind to function at a semi-normal rate. Only the pain was dulled. A gentle relaxing buzz. But this? . . . I have no idea of the amount Bertha was shooting me up with, but I could hardly move or hold a thought for more than a heartbeat . . . Numb. Every time the morphine started to wear off and some semblance of coherent control returned, the grinning moustaches started back with their demented 'mooorpheeenoo . . . siii!' routine. Sure enough, in barrelled Bertha and Idi and she shot us up again. The Hispanics' clock was hand-wound by Mr Jones himself. They knew within fifteen minutes of their next hit. They'd ridden this train before. Knew the schedule and exactly what time the soul train was due to pull in to the station for a top-up. I began to realise the morphine wasn't just for pain. It was to keep us under control. Immobilised. Subdued. *Why?* I also realised I was in some serious shit.

I couldn't focus my mind on anything for more than a second. Then it was gone. Holographic, 3D, technicolour mega-productions filled my head. I fought them, trying to get back to how I'd gotten there, but the line between fact and morphine fiction blurred with every frame. Old Man Paranoia crept in and out like a twisted brother in a Catholic boys' dorm. The place terrified me. At times when the door opened, dark blood-curdling screams echoed from the somewhere beyond. Long agonising screams. The sounds of the demented planted every imaginable horror in my brain. The other patients? Who? What? And the two grinning beaners opposite? I knew they weren't there for unravelling their grannies' knitting. What heinous act had they committed? My mind bubbled. *Am I safe in this room?* I looked to my right.

There's Idi and his riot gun. If anything happens there's no way he'd miss it. Would he? What if the morpheeno brothers slipped a knife or something . . . Cut my throat before he could get off his chair. Bad-looking bastards. *What if they . . . ? What about . . . ?* My mind spun out a web of sinister possibilities. *Jesus Christ, I could die in this fucking joint and nobody would ever know.* Zipped inside a body bag. Another nameless bum cremated at the city's expense. Who'd know? Does anyone know I'm here? Did someone check me in to this place? *Who? What?* The morphine was definitely doing my thinking.

My room seemed to be at the end of a corridor. There were no windows or doors opposite. Nobody had come past. No activity. Just Bertha, Idi and once a black cleaner in a white orderly's uniform mopping the floor outside.

Who's next door? The paranoia crept back again and again and I couldn't shake it. The boys opposite must have noticed my darting eyes and sweating face.

'Eh, señor . . . Eh ju . . . Pssstt!' the one directly opposite called.

'What?'

'Arggghhhh . . . growwwll,' he went, freaking me out even more. 'Ha ha, ha ha ha,' he cackled, seeing the look on my face. They both laughed. Ranting in a language I didn't understand.

'Ah get fucked you greasy cunt,' I mumbled back.

'Morpheeno . . . morpheeeno,' he grinned.

Beep! Beep! Beep! Beep! . . . My monitor started to boogie across the screen, the little green sign wave pinging like a sonar closing on its target. *Oh shit, relax! . . . Relax! . . . Wait a minute, a **heart** monitor?* I'd been listening to its hypnotic pulse for hours but it had become part of the background underscore to the Boris Karloff sitcom I seemed to be in. It hadn't actually connected, and it wasn't until that moment that the penny dropped. *I've got a heart monitor! . . . What's wrong with my heart? . . . How?* Beep, beep, beep beep beep it started to race . . . *Oh shit, relax. For Christ's sake relax!* I was so bent on morphine that I could hardly move, but even so the shock of this place and my situation had my heart bopping 240. I could only just feel my legs and arms. When I tried to touch my face there was no sensation in it or my fingers. I had to fight to get my good arm up. It felt like a lead weight attached to a body I could only just feel. Like chronic pins and needles when you've slept on your arm. Numb. Useless. Dead!

My arm? My arm's in plaster. Must be broken. But how? Now I know they don't monitor your heart for a broken arm . . . do they? Why? Doesn't make any sense. Nothing made any sense. What happened that put me in here? . . . Think! . . . Try and think! . . . The limousine . . . Limousine to where? . . . Concentrate. Forget the mumbling brothers! Forget the guard. You're just very stoned, Thorpie. You've been stoned before. Fight it! Come on, try! . . . Push everything else out . . . Focus, you arsehole! . . . The Limo? . . . 7.30.

Then what?

4
Georgia on my Mind

The note had read a limousine at 7.30 sharp. And it was right on time. That night I was to attend a dinner party in my honour, the guest list made up primarily of local and southern radio, record and promotional people. Not knowing Macon well, I have no real idea where the house was. I do remember sipping champagne during a forty-something minute drive through light snow before we exited the main highway and continued along a narrow, snow-dressed country road lined by tall trees. An eerie combination of moonlight and the limousine's headlights illuminated the road ahead and the bare fingers of the upper branches of the trees which interlaced high above, creating a stunning natural canopy. Such perfect line. So perfectly formed. A tree-covered conduit to lead any traveller directly to the two large gates that came into view at the end of the long driveway. It was a stunning entrance to a private residence.

The driveway continued in a quarter-mile extension of

the one outside, complete with the canopy of trees, and it culminated in a floodlit circle, at the centre of which was a replica of the Dolphin and Boy fountain from Copenhagen, with water streaming from their mouths. Behind the fountain one of the most spectacular and stately houses I've ever seen was nestled against a lake that rippled silver in the Georgia moonlight. The house, which appeared to be three storeys of solid redwood, was Gothic in design. Thousands of heart-shaped leaves hung from crawling vines, covering the lower walls with a lilac down that crept enticingly up to the huge windows. Through them, I could see the golden flicker of fire and candle light. It was beautiful.

We were greeted at the top of a set of wide stairs, each meticulously carved from a solid piece of wood, by a handsome immaculately dressed black butler who bowed ceremoniously. 'Good evenin', gen'lemen,' he said. 'I am Leon. Welcome to the Shores. We been expectin' y'all.' He escorted us through two twenty-foot glass inlaid doors.

The outside world met the house in a grand entranceway. Its wood-beamed ceiling towered above me in a cathedral dome high above the black and white marble floor. The upper portion of the dome was constructed from glass panels, through which the light from a star-etched moon licked at the upper arches and tree-sized crossbeams, dancing like moon fire down the high red timber walls. Hypnotically casting its silver fingers down into the candle-lit entrance in which I now stood, mouth agape, trying to absorb the splendour of my surroundings.

Southern landscapes, Confederate battle scenes, old family portraits, coats of arms and black marble renaissance sculptures adorned the entrance on all sides. The *pièce de résistance* was an ornate hand painted and gilded antique table which sat in the centre of the room. On it stood a three-foot-tall, glass-encased Rodin sculpture of the Madonna.

Holy shit, I thought. *And this is only the entry!*

Some thirty feet in front of me, the side walls of the entranceway curved enticingly into a high Gothic arch which beckoned me through into the glowing room beyond. All the while Leon the manservant had been waxing eloquent about the 'bildin' bein' constructed entirely from Georgia hardwoods' and its history and the like. But those of us visiting for the first time took no real interest in his valiant attempt at being a polite southern tour guide. Mesmerised by my surroundings, I allowed the splendid design to perform its magic and pull me through the mouth and throat into the belly of the house.

The sight that greeted me as I stood at the top of a grand stairway that led down a flight of red-carpeted stairs to the room below literally took my breath away. At the far end of a long room, a fireplace constructed of large, river-smoothed boulders scaled the centre of the wall to meet a wooden balcony on the second storey, on which I now stood. The balcony ran the circumference of the room, opening up the ground floor to guests who stood at its redwood railings, nursing drinks and laughing together while taking in the action in the room below. In the middle of the room was an enormous dining table, resplendent in white linen and silver candle holders. It was T-shaped with the T end closest to the fire. Its surface covered in china, wine goblets, flower arrangements and silver serving sets of every description. I estimated the number of high-backed medieval banquet chairs to be seventy-five. Around the room, resplendent in white eighteenth-century wigs, stood a number of servants dressed in full blue velvet, knickerbocker livery.

Three enormous Victorian candelabras, each holding a dozen or more tiers of glowing, six-inch candles, hung down the centre of the room, at eye level from where I was standing and some twenty-five feet above the floor below. All were suspended by thick braided chains that were attached to the beams two storeys above. The warm flickering candlelight illuminated the entire room with an enchanting glow. The ground floor and balcony were lined wall to wall with high, redwood, stained-glass French doors which opened out onto decks that ran around the front and side of the house overlooking the lake.

Twinkling yellow light from hundreds of candles mixed with the golden fireglow from within and danced like fireflies around the reflection of the silver moon that floated on the glass surface of the lake. The entire front half of the house was out over the edge of the lake itself. The effect was stunning. The glow from the huge open fireplace filled the warm room. Giving the sumptuous surroundings a medieval air of luxurious, immaculate taste and, above all else, good times. This was one hell of a venue for my first American record reception, and a bloody long way from the Smith's chips, beer, cheese, saveloy and pickled onion receptions in the dreary blue-collar boardroom at Festival Records in Sydney.

My record had first spread in the South, and that's where most of the initial promotional efforts and touring had been concentrated. As a result I'd spent most of the last couple of months meeting southerners. Most of my crew were southern boys and a couple of them, I was astonished to find out, card-, knife- and gun-carrying members of the KKK! I lost track of the southern legends I'd met after Gregg Allman. Always loved that band. One of the greats. And I definitely lost count of all other important southern people I'd met after shaking hands with the supreme good ole boy of his time, President Jimmy Carter. It seems Phil Walden had contributed funds that helped tip the scales on Jimbo's election bid and baaam!—instant big time 'I owe ya one, bo.'

For the most part I like southerners tremendously. They are without doubt the closest thing I've met anywhere in the world to Aussies. This reception, however, turned out to be my first real look at, and social experience with, the grand ole South and what's known as 'southern hospitality'. And believe me, it's no myth. From the hundreds of southerners, male and female, that I've met, never has a people's grace, beauty, charm, pride and nature been more accurately described. As a foreigner and stranger to those parts, it's impossible to put these gracious giving people in perspective with slavery, or with the racial attitudes that still exist in many parts of the South. It just doesn't compute.

From my first nervous minutes that night, pressing the flesh with obviously powerful music people, to the wonderfully relaxed atmosphere that everyone did their utmost to convey, the whole event was a raging success. It can only be described as *the* perfect introduction to an important slice of the heavyweight US music scene of that time and an impressive initiation into southern society. Outside of a short speech and toast formally welcoming me to Georgia, and congratulating me on the success of *Children of the Sun*, I don't remember music or 'bidness' being discussed even once. It was a social event, elegantly done with a charm, flair, loving hospitality and style that can only be described as consummate southern class.

After dinner I was standing talking to a DJ from Charlotte, North Carolina, about the possible convict connection between Georgia and Australia when Leon came over, excused himself for 'intaruptin', and said, 'Excuse me, Mista Thorpe. I bin instructed to tell you that this formal gatherin' will be over shortly but please dontcha leave now, ya hear? There's an informal gatherin' taking place up on the third floor, and as soon as some of these here gentlemen with early planes to catch departs I'd like you to folla me young sir if you'd be so kine.'

A few minutes later, one of the Capricorn people came over and said to me, 'Bill, you were slicker than snot. Shit, son, you're so smooth if a fly lands on ya gonna break its damn leg.' I laughed myself to tears at one of the funniest lines I'd ever heard. 'Like that one, huh?' he laughed back.

'Pretty good, mate,' I said, wiping my eyes.

'Bill, it's bin a grand night. You impressed everyone here. They love your Australian ass . . . We gonna sell a shitload of recerds on this'n, boy. Congratulations. Now I ain't no party-pooper but I gotta take ma leave. Myself and some of my compadres have got some heavy meetins in New York tomorrow and then we're all takin' off for Thanksgivin'. I'm sure we'll party again when the sucker goes platinum . . . Oh by the way, my secatary said to give this to you.' He reached in his jacket pocket. 'She said they look personal and she figured you might want 'em back.' He handed me a slightly battered white envelope. 'OK, Bill, you enjoy yo'self and have a good time tonight. You've earned it, son.'

'Thank you. I'm overwhelmed. I didn't expect anything like this.'

'Our pleasure, son.' We shook hands and he and most of the Capricorn people left.

I looked at the envelope and knew at once that it was mine. The wrinkled corners and crinkles so familiar. One of those pieces that seems to turn up all throughout your life. Stuck away and forgotten for years in some back cupboard or trunk. If you tried to find it you couldn't. Then years later you unpack in a new house and there it is again. I opened the envelope and peeked inside. It looked like a number of old black-and-white photographs and a couple of letters. I was just about to take them out when Leon's voice said, 'Scuse me, sir. Would you to folla me, Mr William, if you be so kine?' I put the envelope in the inside pocket of my jacket and along with about a dozen other people Leon showed me into a brass cage elevator with the inscription 'Made in Kansas City U.S.A. 1885. Capacity 15 adult males' and up we glided to the third floor. So here I am in Macon, Georgia. A record screaming up the charts, a record company that thinks I'm better than sliced bread. I'm at one of the best gatherings of my life. It's in my honour, in one of the grandest houses I've ever seen, and I'm being escorted by Leon the butler to the second party of the night in the same building. Like I've asked myself many times: Where did I go right?

Clang . . . Screech . . . creak! The door opened and in came Bertha and Idi. 'Morpheeno . . . morpheeno,' the maniacs started, shooting me back from Georgia to hell. *Got to hold on to that thought!* my brain screamed. *Leon. The party. Hang on to that for Christ's sake!* Just then a scream echoed through the doorway. The sound of metal doors slamming and chains. Loud male voices. More screaming. 'Aghh! . . . Aghhh!' Somebody on the rack. Burning matches under their fingernails. Eyes being gouged out! 'Aghhhhhghh!' Bone-shilling agonising screams! The door closed behind Bertha and the wailing disappeared. She came straight over to my bed.

Whack! In the needle went. 'Please listen to me. Why am
I here? What's happening?' Nothing! She cleaned my arm.
I was nowhere near off my last shot and I was getting
another. Leon faded like a one-hit '60s rock star. 'Oh, shi-
iiittt!' Warm cotton wool. Alpaca. Fluffy. Soft. No edges.
No sides. Softly . . . Very very softly . . . *That's where Morpheus lives all right.*

Bertha gave the morpheeno brothers a hit. On their way
out I heard Idi mumble, 'Murdering sons o' bitches' and
then, slam! . . . out the door. *Murdering sons of bitches?*
Oh sweet Jesus, what's happening? The poppy juice sluiced
around in my brain. Zonk! Boiiing! Here we go again. No
edges. No sides.

Idi spent most of the time in his chair outside, his riot
gun always at the ready. Moved only to come into the room
with a nurse or doctor or, I assumed, to take an occasional
leak. At which times another armed bull of a guard took his
place. A couple of times Bertha came in with another nurse
and checked the morpheeno brothers' dressings, then
another hit and zonk. The one time they made any attempt
at communicating with me had been earlier that afternoon.
After overhearing Idi's murderers comment I was even
more confused. It wasn't a tough call to work out the morpheeno brothers probably belonged here, but in all the
confusion it just hadn't occurred to me it could be something that heavy. *Murder? Oh shit!* Every conceivable
image of pillage and mayhem raced through my head. I was
staring at them with my nose poking over the top of my
sheet like Foo when the one opposite got my attention with,
'Psst, señor. Whart ju nam ees?'

'What?'

'Ju nam?'

'Billy,' I replied, not sure what I was getting into.

'Que?' he asked, looking at his brother who shook his head.

'Bill,' I repeated.

'Ah . . . Beell. Si si, Beel?' he said, nodding his head.

'Si Beel,' I said. He mumbled something to his brother, then nodded in my direction, saying 'Beel'. His brother nodded to me and grinned.

'What are your names?' I asked.

'Si. Joachim,' answered the one directly opposite. 'Y Francisco,' he added, nodding to his brother.

'Puerto Rico?' I asked.

'Nnnoo señorrrr . . . Cuba!' he said proudly. 'Si, Cuu-ubaaa . . . Whar ara ju frum, eh? Ju spake fony.' They both laughed.

'Australia.'

The brothers looked at each other. 'Que?' one of them asked. 'Que Strala?'

'Not Strala . . . Australia.'

'Si. Que Stralia.'

'It's a big island in the South Pacific, down at the bottom of the world.' They looked at each other again, having no idea what I was talking about. *I* had no idea what I was talking about!

'Ah, whart eet lak, eh? Whart zey av?'

'Ah, a few flying frogs and man-eating galahs, mate.'

'Que?'

'Yeah, and three hundred and fifty pound feather-tailed killer kangaroos.'

They just looked at one another and back at me, mentally scratching their morphine brains. *Scare me, you bastards*, I thought.

31

'The sheilas are all seven feet tall with three tits. And there's deadly spiders, snakes, giant sheep-eating wombats, thirty-foot sharks and crocodiles that come out of the sewers at night and eat little kids. It's a ripper of a fucking place. You'd love it.' I laughed. None of what I said came out exactly like that. Probably sounded more like 'the . . . sheellaasss aaare aaaaalll sevennnnn fooooott taaaall' but they got the gist of it. They both looked at me, then at each other. The one to the left said 'loco', and that was the end of our only conversation.

I went back into dreaming, if that's what you can call it. I was starting to get a handle on how Morpheus played his mind games. Let it take me for a while. Don't fight it. No use. Then it settles. Evens out and something resembling mental coordination returns. I spun around the universe for a while, then the first of a dozen layers of golden syrup slowly dissolved and Atlanta came back. Then Macon . . . Leon. *That's right, **Leon**. Thank God. I lost you for a while.*

5
Thick as Georgia Snow

'**S**'cuse me, sir, would you to folla me Mr William if you be so kine.'

Leon escorted me and some other guests along a mirror-polished hallway of the stunning Georgia mansion. The lights were out when we entered the room at the end, but the telltale sounds of snickering and giggles telegraphed the surprise. As I entered, 'Children of the Sun' hit what sounded like a theatre-sized sound system, nearly blowing me off my feet. The lights went on and I entered a room of more than a hundred applauding people. I had definitely arrived in Georgia. I was formally introduced to the assembly by Leon with a 'Quiet, y'all. Now Billy has just been through the press the flesh part of his evenin'. It's his only night in Macon, so treat the fine young man with yo best southern hospitality and make him feel all at home.'

The whole place applauded. I was stunned. This was a much more informal gathering and although some of the guests from downstairs were present I could tell by the jeans, embroidered and tassled leather western jackets, Tony Lama boots, cowboy hats and 'fuck yeahs' that this was the real party.

People came up to me offering their congratulations and after about fifteen minutes I felt like I'd known them all my life. This room was smaller than the banquet room but it too looked out over the moonlit lake through floor-to-ceiling French doors. A smaller but no less impressive stone fireplace filled the room with a 'welcome y'all' orange glow. This was obviously the party room and I felt perfectly at home from the minute I walked in. One each side of the room there were long, wooden saloon bars with brass rails. Behind each one, bartenders in western outfits complete with waxed moustaches, greased hair and gold card dealers' armbands on their shirtsleeves pulled beer from gold-plated taps and champagne from Crystal bottles. Pretty waitresses in short black western dresses with white bib aprons were taking drinks to guests around the room. Waiters and waitresses were also working the room with silver trays filled with canapes and delicacies from a large table in the middle of the room that was stacked with food of every description. Groups of people stood laughing and cheering in one corner as they played an assortment of pinball and electronic games. I wandered around, talking to people and exploring, looking at the framed photos of celebrities that were all over the walls. The Allmans, Jimmy Carter, Lyndon B. Johnson, John Lennon, the Stones, Willie Nelson, Charlie Daniels, James Brown, Prince Philip, John Wayne, Wolfman Jack, Burt Lancaster and a hundred others. Some of them were with groups of people I didn't know, but all the photos included one man whom I recognised from earlier in the evening. There had been so many names and faces that I couldn't remember his name, but I realised then that this must be his house.

Leon found me again and said, 'Please folla me if yo be so kine' and he led me to a door at the back of the room. He knocked and a voice from inside said, 'C'mon in, y'all.'

I don't really remember what the room looked like because the first thing I saw was a solid oak cocktail table roughly the size of a church door. Covering its top, a two-inch-high, four-inch-wide shimmering albino python wound ominously up and down like a giant snake on a snakes and ladders board. But this was definitely no board game and the snake in question was a PVC-pipe-sized, fifteen-foot winding rail of cocaine that could easily have supported the Santa Fe Express hauling fifty steer-filled wagons, and fuelled the entire first half of a Dallas Cowboys final. I've never seen anything like it before or since. It made that little private stash that Al Pacino stuck his face into in *Scarface* look like a spilled can of talcum powder.

Cocaine was the social flavour of America when I arrived in late '76. Everybody from cab drivers to record company presidents offered me a line within a minute of meeting them, but I'd managed to keep it in perspective. Oh, the odd social line from time to time just for medicinal purposes mind you. But as much as I loved the high, it completely screwed up my sinuses. I've had my nose broken three bloody times, pun intended, and it's left me with a badly deviated septum. For some reason when I tooted coke my nose swelled up like W. C. Fields' and glowed bright red like Rudolph the coke-nosed reindeer. I think that probably saved my life. After the first couple of times spending three or four days trying to see around a swollen nose that

glowed so red you could read by the bastard, the excruciating pain of trying to breathe through a constantly
sneezing honker and a nasal drip that produced enough
mucus to lube a semi, I realised that cocaine, as sweet as she
is, was somebody else's whore.

Now that's not to say the odd occasion didn't arise that
was special enough to warrant the hassle. And this party
was shaping up to be one of them! For some people cocaine
is an instant aphrodisiac, but it always had the opposite
effect on me, leaving me with a willy as limp as if I'd just
gotten out of the Icebergs' pool at Bondi on a freezing July
morning. Still, pure coke is an unbelievable jetstream high.
Not the lip-chewing, mouth-wrenching, diarrhoea-produc-
ing speedy low of the street shit that's been stepped on so
many times with baby laxatives and God knows what else
that the effect is somewhere between speed ranting and taking a dump. All I wanted to do was party hard and leap tall
buildings in a single bound. If the buildings were too tall,
then I had the uncontrollable urge to headbutt the bastards
into submission and bring them down to a suitable leaping
size. And drink! A bottle of Jack just got the oesophagus
lubricated, and with drink came loud. And I was born with
a 500 watt power amplifier for a throat to start with. Like
all coke wankers, I felt perfectly in control of my high—in
my case as perfectly normal as a five foot eight inch hurricane. How the hell can you see what you become on drugs
when you are what you become? I remember being at a
party in LA when I overheard some slimy, coked-out sleazeball trying to con this gorgeous young pair of big tits into
her first line.

'What's it do?' she giggled, wiggling her bum as she
stared mesmerised at the gleaming white powder on the

gold-plated coke spoon the grinning dill held an inch from her face.

'It heightens your personality, babe,' the lounge lizard coolly replied.

'Ooohh . . . reeally? Ooooh gooody.' Snort. Giggle. 'Oooh.'

It heightens your personality, eh? I remember thinking. *What happens if you're a bimbo or an arsehole?* I should have listened to my own logic then, but . . . well, you know. You're only young once and all that.

There was no cocaine in Australia in my road days and I had no experience with it until I got to the States. But after years of brain-cell-ripping abuse playing gigs, tearing up and down the highways and byways of Australia in a van full of a Scotch-guzzling, dope-smoking, road-rocking bunch like the Aztecs and our crew, cocaine wasn't that big a deal. Just another drug. And certainly nothing I could ever contemplate dictating the course of my life. Luckily consumption never got to the point where I went out and bought grams on a regular basis. Now this isn't turning into some Bill Clinton 'but I didn't inhale' bullshit. Inhale! Jesus, I'm an Aries. I can't even spell modarashion. Of course I inhaled. You don't get stoned to get straight, Jack! Like just about everybody I knew in the USA in the late '70s, to me a party was a Bible study without a few grams of the white dynamite! But a party catalyst was as far as it ever went. At some point that I don't even remember, getting stoned no longer occupied any place in my life. It was over. Cocaine, grass, hash, the lifestyle they represented and the people who lived it all became old and passé and that was that. I was just plain lucky.

Now I know I'm a funny little bugger who really belongs in a Disney cartoon, but I have no delusions about who I am. Having been confronted with a lifetime of irrefutable evidence, I know exactly what I become when I get out of it. Although I've never actually *seen* myself ripped to the gills, having been a close mate of mine for as long as I have, and having had to clean up, explain to judges, spend nights in the nick, pay damages, apologise, sever significant relationships and physically fight with people at various stages of my life, I've got a fair idea of who I must have been on the devil's dancin' powder. My guess is something way, waaay, waaaeey to the right of the bastard son from the mating of the Tasmanian Devil and Yosemite Sam, with maybe a sprinkling of Conan the Barbarian, Hunter S. Thompson, Keith Moon and Timothy Leary thrown in . . . And that's a conservative guess!

But for some reason Americans seemed to love my lunacy and encouraged me in it at every opportunity. For the main part, most of the Americans I'd met at that stage, straight or stoned, were pretty staid compared to the company I'd kept for nearly half my life. Most of them had never known an Aussie and had definitely never met a lunatic like I was back then. Apart from the looks of total outrage and disgust I received from most of their women when I started dropping that old Australian term of brotherhood and endearment, 'cunt', with machine-gun rapidity whenever I got into party-induced ranting . . . well, apart from that I was sweet as a nut!

For some unknown reason American women hate to hear that word, and to me that's like a red rag to a bull. Can't understand why they take offence. In the hands of a true Aussie linguistic artiste, it's one of the most expressive words in spoken language. When I've been separated from Aussies for too long the sound of its dulcet tone rolling off some wag's tongue, as smooth and natural as a Coonawarra red, brings tears to this old rocker's eyes.

Anyway, back in Macon, Georgia . . . the area around that coke-laden table was buzzing with conversation. As I entered, a silence fell over the twenty or so grinning people sitting around in front of a blazing fire. Spaced evenly, about a foot apart around its edges, were six-inch-square mirrors on which sat four glass straws. No plastic for these boys. The coke snake was still pristine at that stage and appeared to be undisturbed by human nostril. I was sat next to some southern belle who was probably Miss Georgia that year. If she wasn't she should have been.

'Hi, Bill. Welcome to Georgia,' she giggled, taking my hand and winking.

Down boy, said my dick. *You're married!*

One of the guys stood up and introduced himself as Bo. 'We met downstairs,' he said. It was the guy in the photos, but I didn't recognise him at first. He had shed his dinner jacket and bow tie and was now dressed in an immaculately tailored Confederate officer's jacket, complete with gold braid and epaulettes. I thanked him for what had already been an incredible night. 'Ah, it's great to have ya here, son. You enjoyin' yoself so far?'

I told him I was.

'Well the fun's just about to begin, son.' He smiled, winking and nodding his head. 'As y'all can see ah've set up a little treat for ma guests. Now as ma guest of honour it'd be downraat im-po-lite not to wait for y'all to arrive before partaking of the crystal elixir. Thought you'd like to do the honours before the rest of the house gets amongst it. There's a lotta itchy noses out there been waiting fo yo white ass to arrive, boy.'

I laughed and the room followed with a nervous twitter. 'Er, you do partake don't you?' Bo asked nervously.

You could have bagged the silence as it hung in the air and sold it in LA. Every eye in the room was fixed on my reply. If I'd said no they'd probably have killed themselves or me. I didn't want to be the cause of a mass southern suicide or my own murder, but I took my time, taking in all the bated looks, then shook my head, said, 'You're fucking kidding' and stuck my face in the biggest pile of blow in the state of Georgia. A cheer went up and in no more than ten seconds so too did about two ounces of pure flake. Straight up their noses.

Bo opened the door to the rest of the guests and about half the albino python turned into laughter and inspired conversation. The party took about ten minutes to kick into a space somewhere between backstage of the Sunbury Music Festival and a Greek wedding reception. Kapow! Instant orbit. Out came silver cigarette cases filled with pre-rolled joints. The sound system pounded Lynyrd Skynyrd's 'Sweet Home Alabama' and Crystal champagne corks were popping and falling like miniature mortar shells. Miss Georgia had definitely taken a fancy to me and seemed to be everywhere I was for the next fifteen minutes. 'I jurst lurve yo aaacent, Bill,' she kept saying. Then, 'Why don't we go upstairs? I'd just luuurve to hear y'all talkin' dirty.' My dick started singing Dixie. 'Oh way down yonder in the land of cotton . . .'

'I . . . er, I'm married,' I mumbled. *Get thee behind me Satan, you cunt*, my brain threw in. 'Look, er, miss . . . I don't mean any offence, but I'm married. I have a wife, a seven-year-old daughter and a baby girl sitting back there in LA. You're very beautiful, but this just isn't my thing.'

'Yo ain't queer or nothin' are you, boy?' she asked in all seriousness.

'Are you kidding! Fifteen years ago I'd have done you silly on the table in front of the crowd. But that was another life. I'm flattered by your offer, but why don't you find someone who's interested?' *Oh, give her one*, said my dick. *Lynn's never going to know* . . . No she wouldn't but I'd fucking know and I didn't need that kind of karma.

I don't think anybody had ever said no about anything to this southern fox until then, and by the astonished look on her face her brain just couldn't compute it. With a roll of her big blue eyes, Miss Georgia pouted and then wiggled her tight Levi-covered arse off across the room where she talked to a group of girls who all started giggling in my direction. I guess she told them I was a shirt-lifter because that was the only offer I got that night. About ten minutes later I saw Miss Georgia put a serious lip-lock on some guy, grab his crotch, and then they disappeared.

A little later Bo came over and I could tell by the look on his face what the conversation was going to be about. 'Hey, Bill, that girl wanted to peel yo banana real bad,' he yelled over 'One More Silver Dollar', which was booming through the sound system. 'What's the problem?'

'No problem, Bo. Just not into it . . . I'm married, with kids. There's no problem.'

'Really?' Bo said. Then he took my hand. 'All power to ya, son. I like a man who knows what he don't want. Shit-fire, she must be one hell of a girl!'

'She is, Bo,' I replied, missing her at that moment. The coke had really kicked in. Combined with the six joints I'd helped smoke, and the bottle of Jack, I was flying somewhere between Jupiter and Mars and I really didn't need a rave with a stranger, host or not, about my personal life.

Bo had taken it in but he was flying like me and didn't

need to get down to the psychology of human relationships in the middle of this crazed gathering. So he steered the conversation in another direction. 'Bill, I been looking all my life fer someone ah could care for that much. Congratulations, boy. It's a pleasure to know you. You need anything. A line, something to smoke, a drink?'

'All of the above, mate,' I laughed, and that's how it went for the next fourteen hours straight. At one stage I was down to my underpants in a hot tub with about twenty-five people. Some were half-naked and groping, some fully dressed and some were passed out. I was still raving my idiot head off to anyone who would listen about the nature of the universe, the sekravance of the klakus four on the shnabble deye, rock 'n' roll, comparative religion, and an acid trip I'd taken ten years before. In other words I was fucked-up.

The limo arrived at Bo's around 11.30 all ready for the drive to Atlanta, where I was booked on the 1 p.m. flight to New York. Thank God somebody had gone to my hotel and packed my bags, because when the limo arrived I was still raving at about 60,000 feet and climbing and didn't feel the need for an aeroplane to get me anywhere. Straight out the window and—whoosshh, north-east—I'd be in Manhattan in under half an hour. There were still about fifty crazed people partying hard when I left. The crystal snake still had a bit of a head and tail left, and a sumptuous brunch was being prepared. I really didn't want to leave, but I was off to New York Citaaay, and for a boy from Brisabaine that's still a big high!

If I'd known then what was in store for me, I would have barricaded myself in Bo's magnificent house and never left.

6
Outside

I had no concept of time. Nothing to gauge it by. One moment just slipped lazily into the next. Even if I could have seen the watch that Bertha had on a gold chain tucked into her uniform pocket, it wouldn't have helped. The face would have melted like a Dali clock before my spinning eyes. I was in a void. Eyes fixed on the ceiling fans. Mouth open. Distant. Alienated. No connection to anything real other than the steady hypnotic beep, beep, beep, the needle and 'Morpheeno. Morpheeno'. Sleep and morpheeno. Wake, more morpheeno. No signs of any other activity. Nothing but the room and the needle. The maniacs and the needle. The needle.

I stayed immobilisingly zonked for most of that day. I vaguely remember a doctor examining me, but had no idea what he looked like. Just a blur of a white coat, black hair and moustache. He checked my pupils and heart. Mumbled some unintelligible words to Bertha and scribbled on a chart of some kind. I tried my level best to communicate with him but it was useless. I was so heavily sedated that my lips and tongue felt like half-inflated inner tubes attached to a face I couldn't feel. I couldn't get two words out of my mouth that made any sense. It was impossible to communicate at any comprehensible level. I think a nurse came in a couple of times to check my heart and give me fluids though I'm not real sure. Just flashes. But I do remember Bertha's visits because of her dreaded needle. Most times I came to in the middle of it, then sank help-lessly back into another bottomless poppy dream when the hit took its almost instant effect.

Apart from the spill from the illumination in the hall-way, the only light came from a small barred light fitting above the steel door and bounced off the ceiling, washing the shiny white room in an eerie dull yellow glow that added an even greater sense of mystery to the already bizarre surroundings. My only sense of relief and connec-tion to time that first day came from outside. High up on the wall to my left, the two barred windows yawned like bored gargoyles, vomiting the electric yellow and red of dull flickering neon and dim traffic light onto the walls and across the faces of the snoring morpheeno brothers.

It was winter outside. But wrapped in my poppy cotton blanket, I couldn't feel a thing. Just the echoes from the Manhattan streets far below, which occasionally drifted up into the silence, filling the room like Ebenezer's ghosts. To be caught by my imagination and dance in circles on the walls and ceilings of my mind. I listened, straining for sound. Something! Anything to take my mind away from where I was.

'Baaarrrrp!' The sound of a distant foghorn drifted in.

I must be somewhere near the East River, I thought. *Or is it the Hudson? Water. Tugs. People. Life. Freedom! Out there!* My mind was playing stir crazy games. Don't tell me a full life term isn't a fate worse than death. The chair's a cakewalk compared to the horror of a hopeless, helpless permanent incarceration. This is *it* for the rest of my life? Forever pacing like a caged lion in a cold concrete tomb. Ears and mind filled with screams, beatings, male rape, the clang of electric doors, the rantings of maniacs, and every conceivable evil low-life experience imaginable. Your past your only future. Reliving tattered memories over and over. Fragile fantasies your only connection to loving touch. Hopeless dreams your only reality in the boredom of an endless, mindless routine in a terrifying one-dimensional world. A flicker of life through barred cell windows. A bird turning endless circles in a boundless sky. A jet stream high in the background. Thin white vapour trails at 35,000 feet against a distant sky. A photograph. A magazine. An impersonal, intangible, cold, electric flat image through a cathode ray tube on a TV screen. Your only connection to the world outside. To life! Minute after minute. Hour after hour. Day after day, after year after year after year. Tick! . . . Tick! . . . Tick! . . . Tick! Jesus Christ! Warm up the fucking chair . . . Pleeeeease!

Baaarrrp! Another tug out there. I was starting to lose it. Drifting helplessly away on a sinking boat to some godforsaken who knows where. A thought hit me out of nowhere like a fist in the dark. *My record! Oh shit! What about my record? . . . And the label?* Jesus, wasn't I supposed to be doing something this week? It *is* this week, isn't it? And Capricorn. What the fuck are they going to say when they find out their new golden boy is holed up in a mental ward, high as a kite on morphine? *Oh, it was all a big mistake. Honest!*

'Yeah, right.' Riiip! I could hear the contract tearing . . . My record . . . Macon . . . The reception. I *think* that's how I got to be in New York. But how in hell did I end up in this place?

7
The Big Night Out

My flight from Atlanta touched down at Kennedy at 5.30 p.m. Friday evening. I grabbed a cab and fifty minutes later I was standing in the lobby of the Salisbury Hotel which was diagonally across the street from the legendary Carnegie Hall on West 57th Street, between Sixth and Seventh Avenues, in the heart of Manhattan. Apart from the fact that I hadn't slept in over twenty-four hours and my sinuses felt like someone had driven an eighteen-wheeler through them, I felt pretty good. I was still high but the plane trip and the half-hour layover in Chicago had slowed me down some and I was ready for some dinner and mondo zed-racking. The Macon trip had been a blast to say the least, but it was a long weekend and with those three days off, some fine New York city food and couple of nights' sleep, I knew I'd be fine by Tuesday morning and more than ready for whatever Capricorn Records had set up for me.

My manager Rob Raymond was standing in the lobby when I walked in. 'Jesus, you look like you've had a big one, mate,' he grinned, giving me a hug. 'Jimmy called from Macon and said everybody loved you. Looks like it was a hell of a night.'

'It's still going, mate. Haven't been to bed. I'll tell you all about it over dinner.'

Rob is a Sydney boy, the son of Bob Raymond the author and television journalist who, amongst other things in his notable career, started the current affairs program 'Four Corners' in 1961. This show has run continuously since then on the ABC and become a benchmark in Australian TV journalism, giving many famous TV journalists a break. It became the model for such shows as 'A Current Affair'. Rob junior had cut his teeth in the music business in the early '70s as a promoter successfully touring Australia with such diverse acts as Led Zeppelin, Frank Sinatra, Ravi Shankar and John McLaughlin. We'd known each other to say hi to since the late '60s but hadn't gotten together until 1974 at the tail end of the Sunbury Aztecs. Not long after teaming up we both decided that we should go to the States. Rob and his four-year-old son Sean, my wife Lynn, our four-year-old daughter Rusty and I had all come to the USA together and we all currently shared a big house in Sherman Oaks in LA, high up on Mulholland Drive. The realtor had described it as having a night-time view of the San Fernando valley that 'sparkled like a maharini's necklace'. He hadn't lied.

Rob had flown to New York a couple of days before me to take care of some of our business and for a little pleasure of his own. He never missed a party and he was expected in Macon, but he'd run late at meetings that day and missed the last flight to Atlanta. Back in LA he'd been dating a pretty young dancer with the LA Ballet. Her name was Yvette and she'd recently relocated to the Big Apple to dance with the New York City Ballet Company.

'I'm in suite 819A, right next door to you,' Rob told me. 'Everything's on Capricorn so just sign for it. But don't go crazy, OK?'

'Me . . . go crazy? Craaazee.' I pulled a stupid face. 'Don't worry, mate. I'll be cool.' Rob grinned a knowing grin. We'd been on the road together in Australia and he'd witnessed Aztec lunacy at its peak.

'Good. What do you want to do?' He rubbed his hands. Loved a party did Rob.

I told him I wanted to take a shower and then maybe we'd go to Little Italy for a meal. When I asked him about Yvette he told me she was staying down off Lexington and East 62nd, only a few blocks away, near Tommy Makem's Irish pub. He asked if I minded if she came with us, which I didn't.

'She used to live in New York didn't she?' I asked. Rob nodded. 'Then she'll probably know a great place for Italian. How about we meet in the lobby at 9.30.' A cab to Greenwich Village would only take ten minutes, the snow wasn't that bad and a walk through the Village to Little Italy would be a buzz.

'Sounds good to me, mate. You need a hand with anything?'

'I'm fine thanks, Rob.' I nodded to the bellman, who already had my bags on his little trolley.

'OK. I'll wander over to Yvette's and see you back here at 9.30.'

'Great, mate. See you in a couple of hours.' We shook

hands. Rob turned and went down the steps and out into West 57th. I went over to reception and signed in. The desk guy greeted me with a New York smile that looked like it was going to tear his face if he held it any longer.

'Youra accounta is a all a taken care of, Mr Torpay. Jus a sign for a whatever yu a want.'

'Thank you, er . . . Heinz?' I replied, staring at the name tag on his chest. I chuckled to myself. This guy was as Italian as a Vatican shitter. How the fuck did he come up with Heinz? 'By the way, Heinz, the name's Thorpe. That's T.H.O.R.P.E. Americans usually translate it as Phillips. Fucked if I know how.'

'OK Mister Torpa. Torpa it is.' Either Heinz was convinced he had it right or he was fucking with me. 'An' 'ere is a you key. Please enjoya you stay.'

'I'm sure I will. Thank you, Heinz.'

'You a need a hand with anything, Mr Torrpaaay?' Heinz smiled at me again. He *was* fucking with me! Although he was being very New York polite, with my long hair and clothes he'd tagged me for just another overpaid, zonked-out rock muso.

'No thanks,' I said, nodding to the grinning bellman dressed in his waist-length navy jacket and trousers with the yellow silk piping. Cocked streetwise over his forehead was the customary bellman's box hat with Hotel Salisbury embroidered on it in gold lettering. 'I'll have to tip him for opening my door so I may as well make the bastard work for it,' I said. 'By the way, Heinz, you from that baked bean klakus or what?'

He shook his head, not having any idea what I was on about. I knew how to fix this smartarse *right* up!

'Well, I read in the paper that a stats come down the

four and left a quasseye at the Salisbury to get a slamance in the shnabbledeye for a new book on the New York bandeye. Is that right?'

Heinz sort of nodded slowly back. The New York grin had now become an open mouth.

'Good, mate. Well you see, the article said the Heinz familus naktie maliks carltonfleshled a smeltbum down the brasco and sveltched it through the sakravance into Manhattan harbour, and I thought you might be this quasi. Cuuume oooon, I know it's you, Heinz. Don't be shy. I can keep a scrabble die.'

Heinz thought he'd heard it all until then. *So you want to fuck with me do you, smartarse?* I thought. *I'll have you in tears by the end of this stay!* I walked off, leaving Heinz scratching his head. By the real smile on his face, the bellman was hip to what just went down. He pressed the elevator button. 'Zippy qua for the carltonfleshle, Heinz!' I yelled across the lobby as the elevator doors closed on my grin.

The Salisbury was a grand old New York hotel and the decor still reflected its heyday in the '40s, when the cream of the world's performing artists had stayed there when performing at Carnegie Hall. It had seen better days and was obviously under renovation, but my suite on the eighth floor had been completely redone. I love the older New York hotels like the Plaza and Ritz Carlton. They have a style and flair that's uniquely New York. Even today they smack of the city in the '30s when Mayor Jimmy Walker was scamming the place for everything it had. There's an air of 'we've seen it all' class about the finer New York hotels, and they immediately assimilate their guests into a New York state of mind. My suite was opposite the famed Carnegie Deli, which serves the best Black Forest cake in the city.

The bellman put my bags in the bedroom and I tipped him a fifty. '*Thank* you, sir. If there's anything else you require. Anything,' he winked, 'don't hesitate to call me. My name's Raoul. And by the way, the carltonfleshle was a gas,' he grinned as he backed out the door.

Ah New York. God I love it here, I smiled to myself. OK, what to do? Unpack my bags. Take a shower. Call the operator for a 9.00 p.m. wake-up and take a nap for a couple of hours. I'll be sweet by 9.00. It was 6.40 by the bedroom clock as I unzipped my carry-all. I always carry a couple of changes of clothes and shoes in two different bags in case I lose a game of airport roulette. As I folded back the front flap of my suit carrier the first thing I saw was a clear plastic gladbag with a serious amount of the same flake that had jetstreamed me from Macon to the universe. Inside the bag was a note. I pulled it out and four Texas-sized joints fell to the floor. The note read:

> *Dear Bill, use only in case of emergency!!!*
> *It was a great pleasure meeting y'all. Good luck with the record. Have a great time in ole NYC. Don't be a stranger.*
> *All the breasts*
> *Bo*

I stared at the white powder and joints for about five seconds, then I heard my brain say, 'Oh what the fuck. Fuck your sinuses and . . .' Saanooort! The lunacy began. Talk about instant elixir! I went from feeling like I'd just run two Boston marathons to wanting to run five more. A million gold and silver planets exploded behind my eyes and my head instantly cleared. My sinuses opened so wide I could suddenly smell New York City from the Battery to Broadway, and my brain erupted in a thousand thoughts of what to do in the next thirty seconds. 'Rightgetintheshowerno! Unpackmybags . . . nogetsomefoodno. Going out to dinner. OK OK. Go for a walk to LA . . . No watch TV no. Smoke a joint . . . yeeeeahhh!' . . . Match . . . Strike . . . whoooshhh Puuuff . . . Puuff . . . Ah, hash! 'Here we go again, Billy boy!'

By 9.15 I had done my laundry, ironed every item of clean clothing I had, spit-shined four pairs of shoes, rearranged the furniture in my suite, written four letters, showered, shaved, and polished off a bottle of red and the rest of the joint. I was suffering from the power munchies from hell and floating in midair watching TV when the phone rang. It was Rob, thank God. Five more minutes and I'd have eaten the fucking mattress.

'You ready, mate?' he asked.

'Rob. You in the lobby or next door?'

'In the lobby, mate. Why?'

'Come up for a second. I've got something to show you.'

'OK. Be right up.'

I opened the door and Yvette entered in front of Rob. She looked as gorgeous as ever. Dancers, and particularly ballerinas, have a definite look and style about them. Their delicate beauty, body language and carriage are almost equine. It's as if God has some special mould and every now and then out pops a perfectly formed dancer. In her ankle-length mackintosh raincoat with her ten minutes to two feet sticking out the bottom, her light blonde hair pulled tightly back in a classic dancer's bun, Yvette looked ready to do a take from *Singing in the Rain* with Gene Kelly. She also looked decidedly more New York than she had back in LA. Manhattan does that. The fashion, class, style and mood of the city—from the

MOST PEOPLE I KNOW

Waldorf Astoria to bums in Central Park—are reflected through its image in the elegant dress of the elite of New York society through to the clothes racks in Greenwich Village on Sunday mornings. Whatever the style, it's New York and you take on whichever of the personas best suits your personality or bank account. When I opened the bag of goodies both their eyes bulged and they licked their lips in unison.

'Paarrrdeee,' I laughed and they got into it. I told them the entire story of my Memphis and Macon experiences in about ten seconds while smoking another joint and we floated out into the snow-covered Manhattan streets feeling *no* pain. Rob put his arm out and *ziiiip scareeech!* . . . a yellow cab skidded to a halt in front of us. Only place in the world that happens. I swear there are more cabs than people on that little island. Except at peak hour, that is.

'The Village, mate,' said Rob. The cabbie threw a spinning U-ey and off we skidded. Up West 57th, left on Seventh Avenue and in ten minutes we were standing in light snow giggling like children, staring at the bar and club signs a hundred feet from the corner of Bleeker and Macdougal. So much history in that place. The Blue Note, the Village Voice, Andy Warhol's gallery, all within spitting distance. It's Luna Park for jazz lovers, beat freaks and blues fans and we fell right into those categories. Like most times I've been to the Village, the streets were crowded. It's the hang in New York for locals and tourists alike. Always something happening. Always some legendary musician or band in one of the tiny seventy-five-seater clubs. A great night out by any standards and this was shaping into a ripper. We were all buzzing like cheap electric heaters, feeling no cold and ready to rock.

The three of us walked arm in arm up Bleeker and

headed for Little Italy, the home of the best Italian food in the USA. Well, maybe outside of Chicago, that is. Rob had booked us into a little joint that had been recommended by a friend of Yvette's father and he'd used the guy's name to get a reservation. Rob said from the response he'd gotten when he dropped it, this friend must have a lot of clout. It looked like we were in for a great meal, and we were ready. The hash joint guaranteed that I could eat a tram, a Sherman tank, 4000 hot dogs and sixteen pavlovas. Muncheees!

Guido's was about halfway up Mulberry Street which runs right through the heart of Little Italy. I'd been on there before during the Festival of the Saints, when Little Italy is blocked off and lined with vendors' carts selling the best Italian delicacies imaginable. You eat while sipping a cup of Italian red and strolling to the sounds of Italian opera through the thousands of people who turn out every summer for the week-long festivities. I had also witnessed the famous procession of the saints, when the giant statue of the Madonna is carried through the streets and people pin little envelopes stuffed with cash on her as offerings to her blessing. It's a wonderful and deeply moving experience.

It was getting really cold this night and there weren't that many people on the streets in Little Italy, but the warm, candle-lit glow that shone through the steamy windows of the cafes and bars full of snug and warm grazers made me want to sprint into the first one I saw just for a sambuca by a fire.

From the street Guido's looked quite small, taking up just one store width with a large steamed-up window either side of the front door. The combination of Italian opera playing softly, the mouth-watering odours and the looks on the faces of the diners told us this was the right place. Its

MOST PEOPLE I KNOW

simple but effective Italian decor of red and white table-
cloths, hanging chianti bottles and green plastic vines
strung from the corners and hanging across the ceiling
reminded me of the Spaghetti Bar back in Kings Cross.
There were even Alitalia posters on the walls. Back in 1964
I had spent many a night at the Spaghetti Bar between sets
at Surf City. And one particular night with my girlfriend
Pepper that I'll never forget.

There were about a dozen people ahead of us patiently
waiting to be seated and we took our place in line behind
them. Rob went up to the pretty hostess at the desk, gave
his name and joined us back in the line. Apart from the
great food and service I've experienced in most New York
restaurants, I particularly love the noise and clatter of the
smaller establishments. Aussie restaurants are like that too.
The relaxed, uninhibited ambience of people talking and
laughing with each other adds to the flavour and creates an
atmosphere that's sadly lacking in many restaurants in cool
towns like LA, where people whisper to one another at pre-
mium prices and someone as loud as me sticks out like
dogs' balls. Guido's was definitely my kind of place. Loud.

The line in front of us got smaller by about six people
and we were now almost in the restaurant proper. A large,
round, smiling, sixty-something Italian maître d was
dressed in a roomy white shirt with rolled sleeves and a pair
of baggy brown corduroy pants hitched up by a set of
leather suspenders and a three-inch wide belt that bunched
his pants around his bulbous gut. He was dishing out tables
like a spruiker at a sideshow. 'Devaleen . . . where's a the
Devaleen party? OK, you a gotta the table uppa the back
by a the fisha tank. Eduardo will a take a care of a you.
Smith, are you Smeeth?' he yelled. 'You gotta you table by

a the window. And you miss . . . yeah you with the beeg a tits. Upstairs,' he said to one of a pair of young stunners who didn't bat an eye at his address. 'And a Raymonda. Isa Mr Raymond an a is party ready?'

'Right here,' Rob responded as we went to the head of the line.

'Mr Raymond, ah good, paleased to see you, sir,' he said shaking our hands. 'I'm Guido. Welcome to ma leetle restaurant. Mr Agustino is an old a friend. Nothing but the best for friends of Mr Agustino. Follow a me a pleez.'

We followed Guido through the restaurant all the way to the kitchen in the back, and to our surprise he took us through the swinging doors and into the kitchen itself. The noise and clatter were unbelievable, but the aromas were unbefuckinglievable! The place was bedlam. Waiters in ankle-length white aprons were taking dishes, placing orders and pitching an Italian family-style verbal at full volume with fat Italian cooks in black-and-white chequered pants, white jackets and chefs' hats. The place was steaming hot and I broke into a sweat as soon as we entered. Nobody seemed hassled by us walking through their kitchen and the antics of the staff were obviously normal Italian restaurant kitchen etiquette and an every-night occurrence.

We stepped over a large mess of spilled food that looked like half a dozen full plates of pasta, shrimp, meatballs and salad had hit the deck. It had splashed everywhere from the polished steel stove fronts to the walls on the opposite side. A couple of waiters and a chef were verballing each other in machine-gun Italian over the mess, punctuating their statements as they ranted by stamping their feet and flaying their arms in every direction. Some poor Puerto Rican busboy was on his hands and knees between them, doing his best to avoid the feet and duck the flaying arms while scooping up the red mess into a bucket.

We followed Guido through another door and entered a little room at the back of the kitchen. The room was painted flat white and was empty except for a round table covered with a red and white cloth, a wooden cupboard in the corner, four wooden chairs and a naked light bulb that hung by a twisted cord from the ceiling. 'Please sit,' he grunted. 'I geta some vino. Be righta back.' As soon as he went through the door we all burst into laughter.

'Fuck, what is this?' I asked. It felt like we were in the Godfather's private lair, either ready to negotiate the numbers or be eliminated for not negotiating them in his favour.

Wham! The door flew open and in rolled our friend with four large wine goblets and two big wicker-wrapped bottles of chianti. He swiftly uncorked one and emptied the contents into our three glasses, which killed the bottle. 'That one for a yo soul and a thees a one for a you meal.' Guido grinned and placed the unopened bottle on the table. 'I back in a jeefy with a you foods.'

We all looked at one another and Rob said, 'Excuse me, but we'd like to see a menu please.'

'No menus back ere. You getta my a specialty. Only for you. I already started. I back in a jeefy,' and whoosshh!— back out the door.

'Well mate, I'm sure as shit not arguing with this fucker,' I said. 'He's too big and they'd never find our bodies. He'd probably mince us up and serve us as bolognaise sauce. Fuck, who is this guy, Yvette?'

'Jeesus Billy, I don't know,' she laughed. 'Jimmy Agustino is an old friend of my dad's and I called him about a good place and this is it. Let's just go with it. Looks like fun to me.'

We picked up our wine glasses. 'Salute!' Rob toasted. We clicked glasses and took a long swig. It was great. 'Whoa,' shouted Rob. 'This is fantastic.' I had to agree. Rob was a wine connoisseur and he knew a great red when he tasted one. All I knew about wines in those days were the names on a few favourite labels and the taste of a great one as it slid down my throat. And this was fantastic, with a great nose and rich fruity aftertaste. It exploded against my palate and a pleasant, stinging sensation filled with the taste of sweet oak, pepper, mint leaves and grapes tantalised and excited my mouth and throat. This was the goods and we all looked at each other without a word and took another hit.

Whoosh! The door burst open again and in strode Guido followed by the terrified busboy who must have been on a break from cleaning up the shitty mess. The busboy struggled to carry a huge white serving dish filled with steaming pasta which he nearly dropped when he tripped coming in. But he caught himself just in time and set it down with a relieved sigh in the centre of the table.

'Madonna!' Guido exclaimed, glaring at the kid as they exited. We could hear him verballing the busboy, and the occasional slap 'ow' slap 'ouch' as Guido cuffed the kid behind the ear. Guido came back carrying a tray on which sat a large white bowl covered with a red and white cloth, three large eating bowls, three salad plates, a large green salad covered in green and black olives, two large uncut round loaves of Italian bread, a large block of parmesan cheese, a grater, a bottle of olive oil and balsamic vinegar, a slab of butter, three sets of cutlery and napkins.

'Theesa what Guido start thees little restaurant thirty-five years ago.' He was beaming with pride as he deftly unloaded the contents of the tray onto the table in front of our ravenous, hash-munchied, bulging eyes. 'Enjoy!' He laughed from his gut as he whisked the cloth from the steaming bowl. 'The best a meatballs in alla New York. Allow me . . . I serve.' With the nonchalant expertise of someone who had served food all his life, without spilling one tiny morsel, he filled our bowls to overflowing with about a pound and a half of pasta. Scooped four large meatballs into each of them. Covered them with rich red sauce, then grated a copious amount of parmesan on the top of each pile. I wanted to kiss the big Sicilian bastard but I didn't know him well enough. It looked and smelled fantastic.

'I cook special for a my friends,' Guido said. 'No-one ere ave but a you. Special for friends of Mr Agustino . . . Now enjoy. You wanna anythin' yo joosta holler ina the kitchen. They get for you. Enjoy.' He smiled at us and went out the door.

We looked at each other, looked at the food and did a head dive into our bowls, which were piled inches higher than the sides. All you could hear was 'Ohh shiit . . . Mmmm . . . Fuck . . . Oh God!' as the flavours hit us. Normally I don't like spaghetti and meatballs, but to describe this as spaghetti and meatballs was like calling the *Mona Lisa* a painting. We cut into it like we hadn't eaten for weeks. Every now and then big Guido stuck his head around the door to see if everything was OK. He beamed when he saw our bowls were empty. Filling them to the top again, he disappeared for a second, returning moments later with another bottle of chianti which he placed on the table. He opened the second of the two he'd given us at first and filled our glasses, then opened the other bottle, filled his own glass, raised it to us, shouted 'Saaalute' at the top of his lungs and shot the lot. He held his eyes closed as it went down, then smiled, saying, 'Ah bella vino . . . Bella . . . Bella . . .'

We all returned with a unison 'Saaalute' and skolled ours.

'Now enjoy. Eat . . . eat,' he laughed, and disappeared out the door again. Enjoy? Christ, I was having the time of my life.

Somehow Rob and I managed to kill the second bowl. Poor Yvette was struggling after the first few mouthfuls and sat laughing and drinking while we ate like the characters in that fantastic movie *La Grande Bouffe*, which starred Marcello Mastroianni. In the film he and some friends went to the country to eat themselves to death and succeeded. Now I could always eat but I was *done*. I could hardly move and the wine had knocked my dick in the dust. Next thing, in comes Guido carrying a large bottle of sambuca and four glasses. The busboy in tow with a tray containing four large cups filled to the brim with what turned out to be triple-bypass espresso. When he saw that Rob and I had finished our second bowls he put his arms around us and slapped us both on the back. 'Bella . . . Mucho bella,' he said, proud of the fact that we'd paid him the greatest compliment anyone can pay a great chef. To be honest, if it had tasted like shit I'd still have forced it down. I certainly didn't want to be the one to insult this big Sicilian who'd bent over himself to accommodate the friends of someone named Mr Agustino. This was Little Italy, New York, brother.

'Now, my a friends, sambuca,' Guido said, cracking the bottle of the clear Italian mumbling juice. He filled our glasses and his to the brim, took a handful of coffee beans and carefully dropped three into each of our glasses, because any other number is bad luck. Once again he raised his glass in a toast and bellowed his favourite word. 'Saaa-lute!' and skolled the lot. This was a man happy in his work if ever I've met one. I had the distinct feeling that Guido was like this seven nights a week and wished that God had made the weeks eight days long. This time he sat with us, saying, 'Fuck a them . . . Oh, my apologies, signorina. I mean no a disrespect. They can a do themselves from now on. It's a my time to relax.' We sat like this, drinking and laughing until the sambuca was gone and we were satiated with food and drink. When we thanked Guido and tried to pay him he wouldn't hear of it. The more we pressed the more adamant he became.

'No! . . . no! . . . no!' he shouted, shaking his head and holding both hands up, palms facing us. 'It's a my great pleasure . . . For Mr Agustino, my right arm. Please pay my respects to 'im from me. Now go. No more talk of money.'

We were dumbfounded. *Jesus, whoever Mr Agustino is, he sure swings a big stick in this neighbourhood*, I thought. Guido hugged each one of us and showed us out through the restaurant, which was now deserted and dark. We hugged once more and said a fond farewell to the best restaurant experience I've ever had. You could sell tickets for an event like that.

It wasn't until we got outside that we realised just how fucked-up we were. It was 1 a.m. and freezing, but none of us wanted to go home. Shit it was New York City, an hour after Friday midnight. Only one thing for it . . . another quick nasal nosh and a joint in an alley and grab a cab for a club tour.

By about 3 a.m. we had taken in a set by Maynard Ferguson and his big band at the Bottom Line, had a few drinks watching great blues from Elvin Bishop at another Village club and been to see Irene Cara's solo debut in some club that Rob took us to. We'd also been refused entry to Club 54, which gives you some idea of our state. Shit, everyone from Mick Jagger, Keith Richards and Andy Warhol to the owners regularly threw up all over themselves in that joint, and fell pissed rotten up and down those steps on a regular basis. Well I *was* pretty lit. Perhaps it was my 'You can stick Club 54 right up ya fuckin' arse' comment when the doorman started playing that pathetic 'Let's see . . . who am I going to let in from the freezing cold' power trip on us that did it. Naaah. Couldn't have been that. It was still snowing lightly, freezing cold, and well after 3 a.m. when we decided to call it a morning. We hailed a cab and about halfway back to the Salisbury something caught Yvette's eye.

'Stop!' she yelled at the top of her lungs and the cabbie happily obliged, happy no doubt to be rid of the three raving stooges in the back seat.

'What?' Rob and I yelled in unison.

'There's the 20/20 Club. It's the next best thing to Club 54. Come on, I know the guy who runs it. Let's have one dance before we go home. OK?'

'Okaaayy!' Rob and I replied.

We jumped out of the cab and danced arm in arm across the street like the lion, the tin man and Dorothy. It's amazing but there was still a crowd of hopefuls standing outside the club in the freezing a.m., desperate to get in but being fended off by yet another officious arsehole on the front door. He gave Rob and me the twice-over and was about to give us the bum's rush when he recognised Yvette. He opened the velvet guard rail around the entrance and in we

63

trouped. 'Welcome to the 20/20 club,' said the spunk in the coat check. 'We close at 5 a.m. Have a great time.'

I seem to remember all sorts of chrome, glass, over-made-up faces, gay boys and girls, couples smooching on couches, gorgeous women, too much aftershave and perfume and above all else the hot dance music pumping from an atomic-powered, seriously loud sound system with sub-woofers the size of Boeing 747 engines. The place was packed to the rafters at 3.30 a.m.

We were wobbling around taking it all in and looking for somewhere to prop when, 'Yvette . . . Hey, Yvette.' She looked around and spotted some gay boys she knew who invited us to sit with them. Their chrome and glass table was surrounded by deep padded, purple velvet chairs and a matching curved couch. We joined them, sitting behind a polished chrome railing that ran almost completely around the dance floor, which was sunk about two feet below the bar stations.

After she introduced us to her friends Yvette grabbed me by the hand and said, 'Come on, rock star. Let's see if you can dance.'

Now like I said earlier, how can you possibly see what you become when you're ripped, when you are what you become when you're ripped? And I was ripped to the gills. I hadn't slept in over thirty hours, but what the hell. 'Let's dance,' I shouted, leaping over the railing and nearly flattening a couple of beautiful gay girls who were dancing cheek to cheek to KC's 'Shake Ya Booty'.

'I'm really sorry. I didn't mean, er . . .' I said.

'Just watch it, jerk,' one of them replied.

'Yeah, jerk,' her carpet-munching friend chirped in.

'Ah, go and get fucked, Ralph,' chirped I and moved to

the centre of the dance floor followed by Yvette who was already in hysterics. Well I used to be a dancin' fool when I was a teenager and my wife Lynn loves to dance. I still do now and then. More then than now I must admit. But that's another thing the right combination of the heinous abuses did to me. It turned me back into that dancin' fool. I couldn't control my bloody feet. It's like they had a mind of their own, which at that moment was just as fucked up as my other mind was.

By the middle of the third song we had been joined by some of the gay boys, who were obviously professional dancers. We had a group of about twenty people around us clapping along in time and copying some of the outrageous moves that Yvette and I were making. Yvette of course was cutting it big time with quadruple spins and full splits. I was going at it like a combination of James Brown and a midget snorkeller kicking frantically up to the surface to escape a twenty-five-foot white pointer who was after his dancin' arse. My little feet were burnin' holes in the floor with moves that John Travolta would have sold his momma into slavery to get at in *Saturday Night Fever*. Or so I thought. I do know I was dressed the part that night. All decked out in a full-on club '70s outfit that consisted of black-and-white, houndstooth check, skin-tight flairs with seventeen-inch bottoms, zip-up ankle boots with six-inch heels, a white satin shirt and a black velvet jacket. All hand-tailored for me by the now world famous Richard Tyler, an old mate who started his fashion career in Melbourne in the late '60s. Richard had made clothes for Australian and international stars for years. He'd been making mine since 1969 and had continued making them after he came to the USA in 1977. I had a great collection of Richard's couturier designs. Still have somewhere. Anyhow, I was looking disco smooth in Richard Tyler hand-made originals that night.

So here we are, a ballerina and Thorpie doing a real-life spontaneous dance routine in the middle of one of New York's most famous discos, all sheets to the wind, with the crowd loving every minute of us. I suddenly had this uncontrollable urge to run and leap into the air, which I did . . . Now the leap was a bloody pearler. Rudi would have loved it, but there must have been something wrong with my trim, because instead of landing on my feet I found myself travelling at a blinding speed, arse down, horizontal to the floor, toward the clapping crowd. The crowd had cheered when I took off, but I didn't take that much notice. My attention was riveted on the loud cracking sound my left arm made when I landed on it on the dance floor. It was a bad break and I knew it. Spasms of excruciating pain shot through my arm to my brain. Lights exploded behind my eyes. Whether it was the pain or a combination of the pain and the state I was in, I have no idea, but I knew I was going to pass out. My reflexive reaction was to sprint off the dance floor, grab my jacket, run outside, grab a cab and yell at the driver, 'Take me to the nearest hospital. I've broken my arm!'

The first time I came to I was propped up in a row of chairs similar to the kind you find at airports. But this definitely was no airport. It was a hospital emergency room and it was fucking pandemonium. Now this is Manhattan at approximately 4.15 on a Saturday morning after a New York City Friday night before, if you get my drift. These people weren't there to get splinters pulled out of their fingers. Some were armed robbery and gunshot victims and perpetrators with the slugs still in them. Some still cuffed to coppers. There were stabbing victims, mugging victims, beating victims, rape victims, traffic accident victims, distraught relatives and parents, a lot of blood on the floor, and everyone screaming for 'Almighty Jeeesusss' to save them. And, oh . . . apart from me and some bench bum who had come in out of the cold, the other seventy-five or so people were as black as Mike Tyson's arse. No racial slur intended, but black folks don't have the inhibitions most whites do about voicing their grief and pain. They get a lot louder than most white folks when they're distraught, and don't give a shit who's listening. They let it all hang out, and it was hangin' out big time right in front of me as I came to.

I had no idea where I was and didn't remember getting there. Then a red-hot knife cut through my arm and it all came back. I must have passed out in the cab and the driver must have brought me in. 'Oh shit, my money,' my instincts yelled inside my head. I checked my pants pocket and I couldn't believe it. Not only was it still there, but when I counted it the cab driver, God bless him whoever he is, had only taken about twenty bucks. That was the first miracle of the morning.

Here I am in the middle of a 'M.A.S.H.' episode, surrounded by the walking, bleeding half-dead, and I've got disco elbow! Jesus, how weird does my life get sometimes. I get the strangest karma on the planet. And it's always instant! Disco elbow or not, I could tell it was badly broken and throbbing like an Evinrude. I got up and struggled through the melee to the nurses' station on the other side of the room. A sweet-looking black nurse in her early thirties was doing her best to calm the frantic parents of some teenage girl who had just been gang raped and here I come, dressed like a John Travolta lookalike in the smash follow-up movie, *Saturday Mornin' Elbow*. An orderly came over and helped the couple away and I saw my chance.

'Excuse me, miss, but I'm in real pain. I know my arm's broken bad. Can you please give me something for the pain until I can get someone to look at it?'

She looked at me for several long beats, then screamed, 'Don't miss me yo sweet talkin' English motherfucker. I gots gunshot and stabbing victims dyin' and bleedin' all over my goddamn floor. Now get yo butt-ugly white ass outta my face fore I break yo other goddamn arm and a couple legs to boot. Now go on, git. You'll have to wait yo turn.'

'But nurse, I really am in pain. I . . . I think . . . I'm going toooo paaaaassssouuuuu . . .' The room did several 360 degree pirouettes and so did I. Right before my head hit the concrete floor. The next time I came to I was lying fully dressed on my back on a gurney which was pushed sideways against the wall of a long, dark, curved hallway with the left side of my body touching the cold wall. My left arm was in a sling of some kind but there was no plaster on it. It still hurt like crazy and had obviously not been set. Every time I tried to move an excruciating pain shot to my brain, a million sky rockets exploded behind my eyes and I felt like throwing up and passing out at the same time. Not a good combination. Ask Jimi Hendrix and Momma Cass!

I tried to look at my watch but the pain was too bad. At least I still had the watch! There was a bright glow around the curve in the passage and a dull 20-watt overhead light around the curve ahead, but it was too dark to see very much. When my eyes became adjusted I realised I was on one of about a dozen gurneys that were parked end to end along the wall. I could hear a lot of moaning, groaning and snoring. The loudest and most tormented sounds seemed to be coming from directly behind me. I forced my head back and strained to look over my right shoulder to see where the moaning was coming from. It was from some poor guy with a heavily bandaged head. It was easy to see he was in bad shape because the top of his blood-soaked head was about two inches from mine. *Jesus . . . I've gone from 'M.A.S.H.' to the bloody Crimean War!*

I lay there feeling very sorry for myself, trying to put the evening back together, when a thought hit me between the eyes. I hadn't told Yvette or Rob that I'd broken my arm or where I was going. It had all happened so fast on the dance floor. I leapt, fell, leapt up and sprinted for my coat, disappearing out the door. When I was out of it I was partial to leaping and running around on dance floors or walking around on my knees with my shoes on them like Toulouse-Lautrec and biting people on the arse. Rob had probably thought I was up to my old antics. It occurred to me that I was the only one who knew I was here, wherever here was! I was thinking, *I've got to get a message to the hotel to let Rob know where I am* when a couple of interns came and parked themselves in the shadows against the opposite wall. They lit up a smoke and calmly started discussing everything from the Caribbean vacation one of them was saving for to the size of the tits on the nurse one of them screwed. None of which me or my fellow Crimean sufferers wanted to hear one bloody word about.

'Hey . . . Scuse me. Hey . . . psst. Can you call someone to give me something for the pain. My arm's busted and needs resetting. It's fucking killing me . . . And I need someone to make an urgent call for me, please!' No reply whatsoever. They just kept chatting along, ignoring me. So I tried again. 'Hey guys, I need help. Can you call somebody for me please?'

Not a peep from the low bastards. Not an 'I can't help you, brother' or a 'Keep your shirt on'. Not shit! They just kept talking. Well that's when I lost it and propelled myself full throttle off the trolley in the direction of these two callous fucks. The last thing I remember was the fist coming at me out of the dark. When I came to the third time it must have been later that morning and the first thing I heard was . . .

'Morpheeno . . . Morpheeno . . . Si hee hee . . . Mooorpheeeno!'

8
And the Good News Is

I was awakened Sunday morning by a priest. Father Michael Flaherty. A Japanese chappy. I'm serious. This guy was as Japanese as a sushi roll with an Irish accent. He told me he'd been adopted as an orphan after the Second World War and was raised in Ireland.

'Are you of the faith, William?' he asked.

'Er, no father . . . I'm not,' I answered, trying to clear my head and untie a tongue that didn't want to work.

'Take your time, my son.'

'Well, you see . . . I believe in God . . . But most probably not your God . . . I'm not exactly what . . . you might think of as a religious man.'

'And what exactly do you think that might be, my son?'

'Well . . . you know . . . someone who thinks of God as an all-loving, all-seeing, yet vengeful and wrathful God . . . a God we must love unconditionally and yet fear . . . a supreme male entity sitting on his golden throne in Paradise, dishing out perfect justice to us imperfect mortals down here in our imperfect world. It's the fear part that bothers me most, Father . . .'

'Why is that, my son?'

'Well, how can we love and surrender our lives to something we fear? It's a complete contradiction.' Although I'd just woken up, I felt like I'd had a pretty restful sleep. I don't remember getting a shot during the night and I was quite lucid. But my arm was throbbing like a randy bull's dick and it wasn't easy getting my brain into a serious religious discussion with a Catholic priest. Still, I always enjoyed a good theological rave so I gave it my best shot.

'You see, Father . . . if I accept that God created the heavens and earth and everything, then by extension it follows that he created thought, hate, war, pain, evil, suffering, greed, disease, injustice, and all the things generally regarded as sin. Given the weight of scientific evidence available today, much in the scriptures, such as the seven days and seven nights story, just doesn't cut it. And take Adam and Eve in the Garden of Eden and Original Sin. I mean it's *all* about fear . . . Fear is *the* perfect platform for anyone who wishes to base a religion on blind faith in following a strict doctrine with a central tenet that appeals solely to man's eternal fear of the consequences if he doesn't . . . If fear is the *only* method of getting in touch with a God who can forgive us for the Original Sin that he created in the first place . . . and therefore corrupted the mind, body and soul of man into committing the sins that need your absolution on his behalf . . . well, without that fear, Father, what would be the value of your kind of religious faith . . . and how much real estate would the Vatican own today?'

'Er, may God bless you and heal your wounds, my son. Good morning.'

'Bye, Father Flaherty.'

Father Flaherty left me to burn in the eternal fires of hell and went over to the morpheeno brothers. Their demeanour changed in a heartbeat. From the hard-arsed maniacs I'd observed for the last two days they turned into smiling obedient children. The priest made the sign of the cross and said something to them in Spanish. They both nodded. Placing his purple silk sash around his neck, he knelt between them and they prayed together. He then put his right ear to one of the Cuban's lips and I presume heard his confession, which ended with a murderer's kiss on the body of Christ on Father Flaherty's crucifix. This was repeated with the other brother, after which the father made the sign of the cross over both of them, prayed something in Latin, and left two murderers blissed out on the fact that they no longer had to suffer eternal damnation in the fires of hell. Everything was sweet now. God had forgiven them. And their place at his side in heaven was assured. Just like that. Yeah, right! That's a real convenient rave, that one! *No wonder the world's so fucked up*, I thought, watching Father Flaherty's look of absolute knowing satisfaction as his black smock rustled out of the room.

The routine with Bertha and her dreaded needle went on for most of the day. One time when I was blitzed out I remember some doctor checking my heart but can't recall him at all. A couple of times another nurse came in and gave me sips of what tasted like glucose and water. I can't really recall her either. I was in a pretty bad state and I still hadn't gotten my mind around what was happening to me. It was like a bad dream and I couldn't wake up. I had to

73

find some way to speak to this nurse. *Make* her hear me. I guess it was some time in the evening because I could smell food. Bertha and Idi came in. I hadn't noticed if the morpheeno brothers had eaten or not. I knew I hadn't since I arrived but I wasn't the least bit hungry.

As stoned as I was, I did my best to reason with Bertha and explain my story, but she would have none of it. 'Nurse . . . nurse!' I pleaded as she cleaned my inner forearm with alcohol for another shot. 'I don't belong here! . . . I fell down and broke my arm in a club. That's all. What the hell am I doing here?'

'Sure, sure,' she replied.

'But I'm telling you. That's what happened! I've got to get out of here. No-one knows where I am!'

'Just be quiet and take your shot. I don't want any more trouble from you. OK?'

'Look, I'm not trying to cause trouble. But, please, before you shoot me up again, please talk to me for a minute. What the fuck am I doing here?' I yelled.

'Watch your goddamned mouth, boy!' said Idi, striding over to the bed. 'Any more of that and I'll have them put you in restraints.'

'They'll be no need for that,' Bertha said, showing the first hint of compassion I'd heard since I hit the emergency room two nights before. 'I'm all ears, but make it quick. I gotta give you your next dose. That's my orders. Understand me?'

I nodded helplessly. 'Well, it started Friday night. We went out to dinner around . . . and . . .' It was hard getting my brain to work, but I finally got the gist of it out. 'Look, check my ID.'

'You ain't got any ID, boy,' Bertha said. 'That's the damn

problem! All we found in your jacket were these.' She reached into the drawer beside my bed and pulled out an envelope. It was the one I'd been given at the party in Macon on Thursday. I must have worn the same jacket out on Friday night. I opened it and tipped the contents on the bed beside me. It was a bunch of old black-and-white snapshots and a couple of old letters. On top was a shot of me leaning on the front of my beloved Aston Martin DB4 with a Piper Aztec aeroplane in the background. It had been snapped for me, using my camera, by the photographer during a photo shoot for *TV Week* back in 1965. One of the commercial shots was used as a front cover that year. There was one of my parents proudly holding an apple pie and a bread-and-butter pudding that they'd baked. It was taken outside the little shop they owned in Moorooka in Brisbane during one of my visits home in the late '60s or early '70s.

Another photo had been taken somewhere in Melbourne around 1969 or '70 and had Warren Morgan, Paul Wheeler, Gil Matthews and me standing in what looked like the alley behind the old Thumping Tum. I had my hair plaited in two braids. Another was of us all backstage at some music festival surrounded by hippies, roadies and tents. Maybe Wallacia or Mulwala in '69 or '70, because Kevin Murphy was in the photo and he played in the band just before Gil Matthews joined. We all looked pretty stoned. Another taken in the party room of a house I shared with Warren Morgan and his wife Nene in Toorak in 1970. It was a big group shot with the three of us, Phil Manning and Chain, Wendy Saddington, Bon Scott, Leo DeCastro, Michael Chugg, Kevin Borich, Pete Wells, Michael Gudinski, Lobby Loyde, Kevin Murphy and other assorted heads. And I mean heads. We all looked totally out of it. All falling over each other laughing and clowning for the camera. I still couldn't believe it. I hadn't seen them in years.

I had no idea how these photos had ended up in Macon, Georgia, other than they'd been stashed away in one of my scrapbooks that accidentally got sent to them with some press clippings when Capricorn wanted some history on me. I flashed back and laughed inside. Now I had the bloody Aztecs, half of Melbourne's '70s rock society and my mum and dad with me in Bellevue Mental Hospital. It was ridiculous.

'Who is that?' Bertha said, scrunching up her face as she looked at the photos.

'Look like a bunch of rock star hippies to me,' said Idi.

'Well, they are, sort of . . . Look, that's me there,' I said, '. . . and there. That's who I am. I'm well known in Australia. That's what I've been trying to tell you. I don't belong in here.'

'Jesus, son, you a weird lookin' son of a bitch,' Bertha said, looking at my braided plaits. 'Who's that on the car?'

'That's me too . . . in the early '60s.'

'Damn,' she said.

'Look, I'm here in New York with my manager. His name's Rob Raymond. He's staying at the Salisbury Hotel on, er, West 56th . . . no, West 57th. Yeah West 57th. I'm registered there too . . . Please call and let him know where I am. Please! . . . He'll verify my story.'

''Fraid I can't do that, son. Uh-uh. No can do. No-one's authorised to place outside calls for inmates. That'd cost me ma damn job! Only the head of the ward can do that. It's a long weekend. He won't be back until Tuesday.'

I'm not sure which hit me harder, the word 'inmate' or 'until Tuesday', but I felt sick to my stomach at the sound of them both and the world started to spin in the opposite direction.

'Inmate? . . . What do you mean inmate?'

'Well that's what you are, boy,' Idi chipped in. 'What you thang this is . . . the Plaza damn Hotel? This is the medical intensive care section of the maximum security ward of Bellevue Mental Hospital, boy! And you definitely is an inmate.'

'But what am I doing in a mental hospital? I only broke my arm! What am I doing *here*? . . . All I did was break my fucking arm in a fucking disco.'

'Watch your mouth, boy.'

'I'm sorry, I'm sorry . . . But nurse, can't you please tell me how I got in here? You must be able to find out who . . . Look, I don't belong in here. Do I *look* like a maniac?'

Bertha wrinkled her forehead. Pouted her lips in a half-smile, closed her right eye and bent her head, shaking it. 'Ain't no average look for a maniac,' she said matter of factly.

'Like I told you, I asked a cabbie to take me to hospital and I passed out in the cab. I came to in some emergency room. I had no idea where I was. All I wanted was to get my arm seen to. That's all! I don't belong here . . . Can you please check my file?'

'Oh all right. I'll be back soon as I give them their injections and finish my rouns.' Bertha nodded to the grinning maniacs opposite.

'Who *are* they? I, er, did I hear something about murder?' I whispered, sneaking a look at the morpheeno brothers. '*They* look like they belong here. They're nuts. All they keep saying is "Morpheeno. Morpheeno."'

'That's 'cause they junkies,' she said. 'And they belong here awright.'

'The Severino brothers. Cubans and bad motherfuckers both of them,' said Idi. Seemed to be OK for him to say fuck. 'Last week they killed two people in a house invasion on the Lower East Side. Tied the husband in a chair, then pistol whipped an' raped his wife ta death in front of him before slitting his damn throat. NYPD caught 'em a couple of days later. One of the officers was shot bad . . . Still critical. They had another brother with them that night but he got away. Name's Julio or Juan or somethin'. These two copped to the whole damned thing cause they thought they'd be left to die if they didn't. Doctors took three slugs out that piece of shit and two outta that one five days ago.' Idi nodded at the brothers in turn. 'Shoulda let the motherfuckers bleed to death!'

'*Whaaaat!* I don't belong here with them. They might fucking do me in my sleep!'

'No chance of that!' Idi smiled. 'They locked down secure.'

I looked over at the two killers and could tell by their grins that they'd been tuned in to the conversation. They pulled their arms out from under the sheets, stuck them out of the sides of their beds and rattled the chains attached to the handcuffs on each wrist. They rattled their feet too. 'Moorpheeno,' they chanted at me, grinning and rattling their chains. 'Moorpheeeno . . . Moorpheeeno!' These two crazy bastards were off the planet.

Idi yelled something at them in Spanish. They ignored him, chanting 'Moorpheeeno . . . Moorpheeeno' and rattling their chains. Idi swaggered across the room, pumped a cartridge into the chamber of his riot gun and stuck it in the face of the one opposite me, punching it hard against his cheek. The crazy Cuban just looked at him defiantly and kept on rattling and chanting. Bertha went over and they immediately quietened down. They lay there grinning maniacally at me while she shot them both up. And two scumbag, rapist murderers sank quietly into a morphine dream. In the scuffle I thought Bertha would forget about her promise and I shouted to her to please check my records.

'I'll be back in a while, boy. Gotta finish my rouns,' she said. Idi pulled the heavy bolts across the door and took up his usual position outside the barred window, riot gun at the ready.

My mind raced. *Oh Jesus. I'm an inmate in a fucking mental asylum. I'm locked up with two crazed killers! . . . Get mee out of heeere! . . . It's a mistake!* I turned my head and caught Idi's stare. It was no mistake. Oh shit! Apart from the fact that the Cubans were shackled to their beds and were probably looking at life without parole—or enough current to run a concert PA if the copper they'd shot died—they were happy as pigs in shit. After all, they were alive and being legally shot up with mondo hits of morphine. All free on the state. Outside of the morpheeno rave, the only time they made a peep was when the hits wore off and they mumbled away to each other in Spanish.

The drug had worn off a little and my arm hurt like crazy, but my mind was starting to work overtime. It's crazy how you react to weird situations. You think you're prepared for anything that comes along and then something kicks you right square in the nuts. I started to think about Lynn and the kids. I looked at the photographs and there's Pig, Momma, Rats, Paul, Murphy, Chain, Bon Scott, all stoned out of their gourds grinning at me. It was so ridiculous I started to laugh. 'Jesus, Lynn's going to freak when she hears about this. She'll fucking freak! . . . If only Pig and Rats could see me now. They'd laugh their arses off.' Plenty of people have thought this is where I belong. But I never thought I'd actually end up in one of these joints. The photos connected me to the real world outside and the funny side lightened my situation for the first time in two days. I was giggling away to myself when Bertha came back in with Idi in tow. She caught me laughing.

'So you think all this is funny, do you?'

'No ma'am, I don't. I was just looking at the photos thinking that some of my friends would think it was. That's all.'

'Well, I've got your particulars here. Let's see how funny you really are. Let's seeee . . . You were admitted to this ward from the emergency room at 4.30 Saturday mornin'. Mmmm . . . mmm, yeah, seems you passed out in emergency and gave yourself a concussion when you fell. You didn't have any ID so they admitted you as a John Doe.'

'What do you mean? My name's Billy . . . William Thorpe. I'm not a John Doe!'

'You have no ID of any kind, boy. No-one checked you in and so as far as this hospital is concerned you're a John damn Doe! . . . Now don't interrupt me. I ain't got all day on this. Let's see. Mmmm . . . yeah. It seems that you got violent in the waiting ward and . . .'

'Waiting ward? Waiting fucking ward! I woke up on a gurney with about a dozen bleeding patients. I didn't know where I was and these two fucking . . .'

'Quiet boy,' said Idi.

'Well, says here you attacked a couple of interns and when they restrained you your heart stopped beating . . .' *Heart stopped beating! . . . beating . . . beeeaaatttiiiing!* The words rang in my ears like underwater cathedral bells. Bertha kept talking. 'The interns worked on you until an emergency team arrived and injected adrenalin directly into your heart. And you came back. Seems at one stage you were legally dead for nearly a minute.' *Dead for a minute! . . . Dead for a minute! . . . You were dead for a minute! Whaaat!* Words, images, music, angels, my wife, kids, the club danced a crazed polka inside my head to the music of a calliope. The room spun out of control and I fought hard not to throw up.

'You all right, boy?' Bertha asked. 'You sure you wanna listen to this?' I just nodded, forcing myself back. 'Mmmm, let's see. Seems when they did a blood test on you they found very high levels of cocaine, cannabis and alcohol. All in all, you lucky to be alive, son.'

I couldn't speak. Except for one thought my brain was numb. I still didn't understand how in hell I ended up under armed guard in Bellevue Mental Hospital. 'But, but how . . . how did I get in here? . . . In the nuthouse, I mean?'

'Shit, son, it was Friday night *downstairs*. That's bargain basement time roun' here! The emergency ward would have been jampacked. An' you diiied, son! Your condition was very serious. The only available emergency bed must have been this one. Son, this is the *medical* intensive care section of Bellevue. We have full emergency facilities and staff on this level and you're in good hands. Anyhow,' she laughed, 'you look like you got another sixty years coming on your white ass to me.'

'But I . . . I gotta get out of here.'

'All in good time, son . . . It's Sunday night on Thanks-givin' an' we only got emergency medical staff till Tuesday. So nothing can be done till then. You just gotta sit tight. Chew the fat and get some rest. You're lucky to be here at all.'

'But . . . but . . .'

'Look, I believe you, son. It's too damn crazy not to be the truth. Disco elbow,' she laughed. 'That's a damn first roun' here. Ain't it, Samuel?'

Idi laughed, 'Damn right . . . damn sure is. Disco elbow! He he,' he chortled, sticking out his bottom lip and nodding to himself.

'But this is also a *maximum* security facility, under lock-down twenty-four hours a day,' Bertha said. 'No-one is allowed on or off this floor 'cept for life and death emergencies, inmate and staff changes. And that's all done under strict security procedures and armed guard. What you think Samuel's here for . . . his tan? She laughed, nodding her head. 'No sir, you can't just sign yo'self out like you're in a damn hotel and you din like yo room.' She laughed a big laugh on that one. 'Shitfire, son, we got killers, rapists, rapin' killers, child killers, molesters and worse up here. Jus' look at them two crazy sons o' bitches over there.' Bertha nodded at the Severinos who were blissed out in poppy land. 'An they ain't even in the top ten. Ain't nobody never scaped outta here! Now there's nothing I can do for you right now . . . I'll try and get a supervisor on the phone but it's Thanksgivin' Sunday on a long weekend. I don't like my chances. They're partyin' if they got any brains. We do have emergency surgical staff here on weekends and holidays, but not administration. In the ten years I been here there's never been the need. Now I gotta give you your shot, son. Is that arm of yours still paining you bad?'

After finding out I had died the day before, I was numb body and mind. I'd completely forgotten pain. But as soon as she said the word my arm hurt like a bastard.

'Yes it is,' I said, 'but I don't need to be zonked out with the hits you've been giving me. That stuff is addictive.'

'How's that head o' yours?' she asked. It had a thick bandage around it but with all the confusion and morphine I hadn't given it much thought until then. I reached around with my good hand and felt it. 'Ow!' I winced. It hurt at the back. Must have been where I hit when I fell in the emergency room.

'*See*, boy. With you heart, you busted arm, and you head . . . you a long damn way from fine.' Bertha filled the syringe. 'Maybe you shouldn't be on morphine,' she said, cleaning my arm with alcohol, 'but you chart say morphine and I don't have the authority to change that. Dr Harrison won't be back till Tuesday . . . Ain't *nothin'* I can do for you till then. Now here, give me that arm of yours back so I can get on with my other duties. This will keep the pain under control and calm you down. You'll be fine, boy. Don't *worry* . . . And those two can't hurt you.' Bertha nodded at the flying Severinos. 'Right Samuel?'

'No damned way. Uh Uh. They in tight as white on rice,' he said, nodding his head with his bottom lip out. 'White on rice.'

'Where you say you from with that accent anyway?' Bertha asked as she administered the hit. 'Australia?'

'Yeah . . . Australia . . .'

I didn't feel the needle. Just the fluid enter my arm and cruise like a '56 Cadillac to my shellshocked brain. Bertha and Idi left me lying there stunned. The story she'd just told me had spun me like nothing I'd ever experienced. Ain't everyday you find out you've come back from the dead. Christ . . . I can't go through this until Tuesday. And there's no guarantee I'll get out then. Jesus, I'll be a dribbling wreck by then. Rob must be freaked out. And Lynn . . . Oh Christ! She must be frantic by now. I've fucked up before.

But going missing in New York city is something else all together!

Reality crawled through my befuddled brain like a videotape on slow rewind. The morphine was coming on strong. I was bareback riding that liquid steel horse on a slow-motion carousel and I was starting to panic. Beep beep beep beep. My heart started to race. *Relax. Got to keep it together.* I looked down and there were the photos lying on the bed. I picked one up and stared at it. It was the one with my car. At that moment a police siren wailed fifteen storeys below in the cold Manhattan streets. The poppy juice kicked in big time and my mind floated. Soaring high and free over New York city . . . the country . . . the deep, warm, blue Pacific Ocean. My mind was kicking that can again.

The siren wailed 'your arse, your arse, your arse' like a Persian mother mourning a lost son. I planted my foot but it was no use. What was I going to do, try and outrun a cop car for over a hundred miles to the NSW border? I pulled over onto the gravel shoulder somewhere around Logan Creek about halfway between Brisbane and Surfers Paradise. It was November 1965.

The police car skidded in a blinding cloud of dust and stopped an inch in front of me, cutting off my exit. I watched as a barrel of a copper came storming over to my driver's side window. I put on my best 'Did I do something wrong, officer?' face and waited.

'All right! . . . All bloody right,' said the big Queensland cop. 'Out of the flamin' car.' I got out and stood staring up at his furious sunburnt face.

'You're in a bit of a flamin' hurry! Late for a bloody funeral are ya?'

'Er, no, sergeant. I just didn't notice the speed,' I lied. I'd been doing about 120 mph when he'd first spotted me.

'Yeah, right! . . . What sort of car is this?' he asked, rubbing his hand admiringly over the gleaming, Italian Russo red duco.

'It's an Aston Martin DB4 GT Superlagerra. I believe it was brought out from England to promote a James Bond film. I just bought it.'

'Aston Martin, ey? Many of them about, are there?'

'I think this is the only one in Australia,' I replied, thinking this was starting to go real well. Shit, it needed to. I didn't have a bloody driver's licence.

'Then you must be the bloke I'm looking for,' he said sternly.

'Me? Why?'

'I'll ask the bloody questions here, ya young mug! Now, what's your name?'

'Thorpe . . . Billy Thorpe.'

'Got anyone who can come and get this car?' he asked.

'Get the car? What for?'

''Cause you're bloody gone! That's what bloody for! Bout half an hour ago I 'ad a report of some hooligan in a big red, foreign-looking sports car doin' bloody smokin' wheelies around the quadrangle at Salisbury High School during morning assembly. Wouldn't happen to know anythin' about that would yer?'

'Er . . . Mmmm.'

'Billy Thorpe? Billy Thorpe. You wouldn't happen to be that bloody singer would yer?'

'Yes, that's me.' I smiled. *Aha, a break.*

'Well, why the flamin' 'ell are yer up 'ere in Brisbane doin' wheelies at morning assembly and scarin' half the bloody teachers ta death? Are yer some sort of mug lair or what?'

'Well, it's a long story.'

'I got all bloody mornin', son, and I like a good story.'

He was letting me talk and I figured every minute I wasn't in handcuffs was another minute towards not being in them at all. I took a deep breath and started my rave.

'Well, you see, I used to go to Salisbury High. Did a lot of TV shows and performing up here in Brisbane when I was a kid. I worked a lot at night and didn't get home until all hours, so I was always late for school. My parents always sweetened it up for me but the teachers and head-masters hated it. Especially when I got to Salisbury High School. Bob Mackie, the headmaster, was a real hardarse and he was always giving me a hard time. Even threatened to expel me a couple of times if I didn't quit playing at rock gigs during the week.

'Oh yeah,' the bit copper said. 'I don't bloody well blame 'im! Carry on, I'm still listening.'

'Yes, well . . . you see when I decided to take a shot at the title in Sydney, I went to his office to tell him I was leav-ing. You know what the prick said to me?'

'Watch yer mouth, son! What?'

'He said, "Thorpe you're a degenerate, obdurate malin-gerer and you'll never amount to anything. You'll be back. Mark my words. You'll be back. Now stop wasting my time. I've got work to do." Not so much as a best of luck, hope you make it, or even a kiss my arse. I was devastated.'

'What a low prick! "Degenerate" what?' the cop asked. He pushed his cap back, scratched his head, then patted the car. 'Now what's that got to do with all this? Yer mind if I have a sit in this thing? She's a beauty ain't she?'

It's going real bloody well, I thought. 'Sure, get in.' Here I am, nineteen years old, no driver's licence, about to be pinched for doing 120 miles an hour in a 50 mph zone, and I've got this big copper wanting to hear my life story. *Ah, what the fuck!* He did a once-around the car, checking the lights, colour, tyres and even stuck his big head underneath and checked out the exhaust. I couldn't believe my luck. We both got in and he said, 'Like I told ya, I've got all mornin'. Now I want the bloody truth!'

'Well, sergeant, I suppose it all started the day before yesterday. I was walking down William Street in the Cross when I passed a car dealer called British and Continental Motors.'

'Yer mean Kings Cross in Sydney?' he asked, scribbling it in his notebook. *You're going to need a much bigger book than that, big fella*, I thought.

'Yes that's right . . . Kings Cross, Sydney.'

'And this was the day before yesterdee?'

'That's right.' I watched him scribble that down as well. 'If you don't mind me saying so, officer, I think you might want to hear the whole story before you write it down. Otherwise we'll be here for days. No offence, I'm just trying to save you some trouble.'

He gave me a 'bloody cheeky little bugger' look but nodded and put his notepad on the dash. 'All right, I'm all bloody ears,' he said sternly.

'Well, like I said, I was outside this car dealer's in the Cross when I spotted this car in the window. I went in and some snotty nosed, stuck-up salesman dressed in grey slacks and a navy blue blazer ponced over and told me to leave. "What?" I asked.

'He looked me up and down like I'd just fallen out of somebody's nose and spoke with this put-on plum in his mouth. "I saaid, I'll have to ask you to leeeeave immeeedi-ately. We have some very valuable automobiles, and I can't have riffraff off the streets coming in here and putting their grubby hands all over them." Not that I expected to be recognised, but my face *has* been all over the newspapers and TV. But regardless, how dare this pansy talk to anyone like that? My instinct was to headbutt this puffed-up ponce and kick him in the nuts, but sanity prevailed and I asked him politely if he was the manager.

' "No, as a matter of fact I'm not," he minced. "But what's that got to do with anything?"

'I'd had enough. I came in to buy a car and I've got some prick of an overdressed arsehole treating me like I'm shit. "Listen, you toffee-nosed cunt, I want to buy this car. Now get me the fucking manager. I want to talk to the chicken and not the fucking egg!" His jaw dropped so fast it nearly hit the floor.'

The big copper hadn't said a word. He just smiled and nodded away.

' "Is he here or not?" I asked the car hack. "Excuuuuse me," he smarmed. "Listen sport, you better call him before I have to explain to him how you just lost a sale! By the way, what are you asking for it?" "A lot more than you can afford I assure you." "How much?" "Well if you must know, this exceptional example of a 1964 Aston Martin DB4 is priced at nine thousand pounds."

' "Good," I told him. "Why don't you go and tell your boss I'll give him eight thousand cash for it right now."

'Well, he nearly bloody choked.' I laughed.

'I'll bet he did.' The cop laughed too. *I've got ya*, I thought as I continued.

'The snotball disappeared for a minute and I could hear

bits and pieces of conversation about me coming from the office out the back. About a minute later he came back with the boss, who was dressed almost exactly the same and even had a burgundy silk cravat. I couldn't help but chuckle at the pair of fluffed-up would bes. They looked like they were about to go off to tea and cucumber sandwiches with the Queen on the *Britannia*. "Er, yeees, what seems to be the trouble, young man?" the manager asked, looking at me over the top of his gold-rimmed spectacles.

' "No trouble, boss. I want to buy this car. Your boy here tells me you want nine thousand. I'll give you eight, cash. What do you say?"

' "Well, if I thought for a moment that you were serious, I'd probably bargain you to eight and a half. Do you realise what a superb piece of hand-crafted machinery this is?" More attitude and a giggle at each other. "Well I like the look of it. Looks really fast. And it's just like the one in the latest James Bond movie."

' "As a matter of fact, young man, it *is* one of the . . . ahem, onesssss in the James Bond movie. It was brought to Australia for the purposes of promotion where it was acquired by a local gentleman and then by us here at British and Continental. Now I really can't waste any more of my valuable time educating you about automobiles. I really must ask you to leave."

' "OK . . . thanks," I said and left. As I walked out the door I heard the egg say "riffraff" and they both laughed a snooty "ha ha ha" that sounded like Terry-Thomas putting on his best.'

'Bludgers,' grunted the big copper. 'So what'd you do next?' He was hooked. Back in 1965 eight thousand quid was enough to buy you a small house and car, with change left over for a holiday. It was a heap of dough, but I'd worked my arse off for my money and as soon as I saw that red Aston I knew why. Big money buys really big toys!

'I went straight to my bank, picked up eight thousand quid in one-pound notes, put them in a briefcase and headed straight back to British and Continental Motors. Those wankers were both in the showroom showing some-body the car when I walked in. They spent a good fifteen minutes on the customer without even acknowledging my presence. I just took a chair and sat there grinning, my eight large on my lap. The customer left and they both came striding over to me acting like tough guys. This time the manager copped a real attitude saying, "Now loooook heeeere, I can't have somebody of your type hanging around this showroom. If you don't get on your way, Cyril and I will have to physically remove you."

' "In your fucking dreams you puffed-up piece of parrot shit. Cut the fucking act, boys. You're used-car salesmen not the Queen's guards. Now you want to sell that to me or not?" I pointed to the most beautiful car I'd ever seen.'

'Bludgers,' said the big copper.

' "Now, I've told you for the last . . ." started the boss again.

'I walked over to the desk in the corner of the show-room, opened the briefcase and emptied eight thousand one pound notes onto it. They both shit themselves. "Now here's eight thousand quid. Take it or leave it. If you take it, draw up the papers and hurry up about it! I don't have all fucking day to waste." '

Of course he took the eight large and I was instantly the proud owner of a Russo red, DB4 Aston Martin. What I didn't tell the copper or the salesman was that this was my first car, and the kicker was that I didn't have a licence or any kind of insurance coverage. They were so blown over by the cash stunt that it didn't occur to them to ask until I was halfway to Brisbane that night. They must have shit themselves when they realised that they were still technically liable for the insurance on an Aston Martin being driven to Brisbane at over 100 mph by a maniacal young rock singer with no insurance or driver's licence. I didn't find out till later but they were ringing everybody I knew to try and discover where the hell the car was.

What I also didn't tell the sergeant was that I'd been chased by the NSW coppers doing about 125 mph at 1 a.m. through the canefields near Murwillumbah. I had the car flat as a strap and outran them all the way to the punt on the Tweed River, not far from the Queensland border. In those days there was no bridge over the Tweed. All cars had to be ferried across on a big wooden punt. I came to a screaming halt at the river's edge just as the punt was about to leave and I was the last car on. I was having a bit of a chuckle to myself and when the punt was about halfway across I looked back and saw four headlights rapidly approaching the far bank. Two carloads of coppers came to a helpless screaming halt with no way to get at me until the punt came back a half hour later. I fully expected to be pulled up by armed police somewhere between the Tweed and the Queensland border, but it never happened. To this day I have no idea why they didn't radio ahead and get me, but they didn't.

The copper was sitting there mesmerised. He hadn't said a word in about ten minutes so I just kept on.

'Well I swore to myself that time in the headmaster's office that if I ever made it I'd come back one day and stick it right up his arse. I drove straight out that showroom, got some clothes, drove half the night, stayed at my parents' house in Moorooka, then waited just up from Salisbury High School this morning. At 8.45 on the dot the bell rang and the students started to assemble on the quadrangle. I waited a few minutes while Bob Mackie gave some poor bastard his usual morning power trip, berating him about some triviality or another, then fired up the car and the big V8 baroomed into life. I put my foot on the brake, stuck it in first gear and burned through the school gates. Tore rubber up the school drive. Shot around the buildings at the far end of the quadrangle and did a few smoking wheelies, much to the amazement of eighteen hundred students and the terrified teachers. You should have seen the smoke and the look on Bob Mackie's fucking face when I gave him the finger at 80 mph and shot back down the drive and out the gate.'

'He must 'ave shit 'imself,' the big cop laughed. 'He must 'ave bloody shit 'imself! Ha ha ha ha. Oh Jesus, that's the best I've heard in a long while.' He was holding his gut, shaking his head and laughing a fit, and I was laughing too. 'How far yer goin'?' he asked.

'Straight back to the Cross, sergeant.'

'What, Sydney now? You mean you drove all the way from Sydney just for that?'

'Yep,' I replied.

He grinned and shook his head. 'Now listen. That was a bloody silly thing ter do. What if someone had got 'urt?' I didn't answer. 'Well, it's just as bloody well they didn't. But seein' as it was all in a bit of fun, I'm going to give you a break this time, OK?'

'OK,' I laughed.

'Now yer about an hour and a 'alf from the border at Tweed 'eads. That's legal driving speed, of course.'

'Of course,' I readily agreed.

'I'll call in and say I spotted yer back up the other side of Brisbane headin' north. As long as no-one else spots you, you'll be sweet. Sweet?'

'Sweet as a nut.' I grinned.

'Listen, one more thing. My daughter loves your bloody music. 'Specially that "Over the Rainbow" song of yours . . . Plays the bloody thing to death. That and "Poison Ivy". Can I get an autograph for 'er? 'Er name's Wilma.'

I gave Wilma 'all my love' on the back of a blank speeding ticket and shook the big copper's hand.

'Always good to see a local boy make good,' he said proudly. 'Now, son, bloody slow down and don't let me 'ear of anything like this again.'

'Thanks a lot, sergeant.'

He got out of the car and stuck his head in the driver's side window. 'Don't let me see you around here lairisin' again or I'll lock you up on the bloody spot! You understand me?' I nodded. 'Now piss orf before I change me bloody mind.' He turned and walked away, chuckling to himself. I couldn't believe he'd never once asked me for my licence or registration papers. I put the car in gear and headed home.

Windows down. Beautiful day. Cruising like James Bond in my new Aston Martin. Hour and a half to the border. Ten hours to Sydney and the Cross. All that's missing is a cool beer, a beautiful girl and some music. Get the beer over the border and the girl when I get home. What's on the radio?

The DJ said, 'You're listening to Brisbane's finest, 4BH, and here's our most requested song. The number one record in Australia this week. It's "Twilight Time" by the new Billy Thorpe and the Aztecs.'

Ah, this is the game!

9
BD

I decided to give the main coast road back to Sydney a miss and take the inland route, just in case the coppers I'd endeared myself to the night before put the word out on my car. I didn't fancy spending a night in the nick while some country coppers tooled their girlfriends around in my new Aston Martin so I headed up through Mount Tamborine to Beaudesert. Then it was south along the edge of the Darling Range and hook up with the New England Highway south of Warwick. This would enable me to cross the border at Stanthorpe. From there I'd take the New England Highway down through Tenterfield and Armidale and home to Steak and Kidney and the Irish Moss. There was no way the New South Wales coppers would have posted an alert on me out there, so off I cruised feeling like 007. Until I hit the New England Highway it had been mainly hills and country driving but after Stanthorpe the road opened up and, apart from the occasional eighteen-wheeler, the highway was pretty much mine. The car flew effortlessly along.

It was about 2 a.m. I hadn't seen many cars since Tenterfield and the ride had been one luxurious cruise with me checking myself in the mirror every now and then to see if I looked any more like Sean Connery. I didn't. I'd seen some big lightning on the horizon which I calculated was way to the west of my route south, but I was wrong. The weather changed in a matter of minutes. First light rain and a little thunder and lightning, then Caaaarakkk!—a bolt of lightning struck somewhere up ahead, blinding me momentarily, and suddenly the rain was falling in inch-long droplets and ricocheting off the windscreen and bonnet with the rhythm of a hundred highland drummers swapping fours with Buddy Rich on speed . . . which he often was. After about ten minutes it eased off a little. I began to get the feel of the car in the wet and let it drive. It handled fantastically. Steady as a trapeze catcher's sphincter. It held gracefully around a couple of reasonably long turns and a double S bend at seventy-five miles an hour. *No problemo here. I can do this*, I thought as I sailed along.

My eyes had grown accustomed to the rain and I had no visibility problems. I gave the big triple Webber Gran Turismo her head and let her go like the thoroughbred she was. This car had obviously been built to handle all kinds of conditions, particularly the wet English and European roads. It felt safe as eggs. No slipping or fish-tailing. Just steady, even, controlled grip and tight steering. I was accelerating out of a long left-hand bend doing about 75 mph, feeling like Stirling Moss in the Mille Miglia.

Suddenly out of nowhere there's a horse right smack in the middle of the road about 150 yards ahead! The engine screamed as I changed down, slowing the car a little, but that was it. I had to stay off the brakes or I was a goner. The horse turned to face me, standing stone still just a little left of the centre of the road. Searching my approach. My headlights illuminated him in full. He was big, glistening and black. Looked like a stallion, eighteen hands maybe. No plough horse this. The huge specimen in front of me was a blueblood and I was about to shed a shitload of it on some butt-fuck country highway and probably break both our necks when I did the right thing for both our sakes and tried to avoid him. His huge head and shoulders seemed to float in the headlights, hovering like a 3D holographic trophy. Silver pearls beaded and rolled from his flanks, bursting into stars at his feet. Emerald lasers targeted the car. He didn't spook. Just stood his ground facing me in the rain. I was on the far right side of the road; he was about fifty yards ahead of me. If he didn't move he'd be sweet and we'd both get to live happily ever after. Amen. I could see him clearly now. Three or four more seconds and I'll be opposite him. Close enough to kiss. My eyes were everywhere. The horse. The road. The edges. Trying to see past him. But his stare seemed to be locked in one place. Straight at me. It was spooky.

If he stayed where he was, the road was wide enough to get around him on the right side with a foot to spare. I had no other choice but to go for it. If he spooked we'd both be mincemeat. Suddenly I was on him, hugging the right. I had a clear view. The road ahead seemed clear. Clear that is except for the idiot who shot out of a paddock to my right and ran directly in front of me about 150 feet past the horse, madly waving its arms and a torch in a frantic crazy effort to get me to stop. Holy shit! What now?

I'm abreast of the horse when he's spooked by the idiot on the road and rears up straight at me. Out of the left side of the windscreen I caught a flash of his huge belly, hindquarters and vicious front hooves as he tried to stomp the car while I shot past. I missed him but the left rear of the car started to come round. I eased the steering wheel to the left, trying to correct the slide and avoid a spin, but the tail came around even more. I caught sight of somebody in an oilskin shoot past my left passenger window and I heard a scream. The car careened across the road in a sideways slide, straight through a wire fence and into a big paddock. The paddock seemed clear, thank God. Not a tree in sight. I fought the steering to keep the car sideways and came to a wheel-spinning halt in some mud about a hundred feet from the road. The big engine still screaming. A barn or some farm building only ten feet in front of me. I sat there for a moment, clearing my throat. Trying to get my arse out of it. Then I remembered the person on the road. *Oh fuck, I've killed somebody. Oh Jesus . . . let him be all right.* A million panic buttons went off.

I tried to get the car to move but the wheels just screamed in a whining wet spin. The car was bogged up to the axles and when I scrambled out I fell flat on my face in the mud. Feeling my way around the back of the car I felt something hanging off the left back bumper. It was a big piece of oilskin. 'Oh shiiiit!' I stumbled through the rain and mud in the direction I thought I'd come and after falling into a gully in the dark I finally found the road.

'Are you all right?' I started yelling. 'Can you hear me?' No answer!

I found the road and was sort of half running through the rain in the pitch black. I was about to yell again when

I ran right into the fucking horse. It scared the shit out of both of us. *Naaaaayyyeee!* the bloody thing screamed. I took off one way and it another. I fell face down in another gully full of water and when I climbed out I was soaked to the skin. I took a step, tripped and fell arse over head over something. Reaching out I felt a cold wet face and realised it must have been the person I'd hit. Next minute the horse was over the top of me, rearing up. Trying to stomp me into the road. I rolled away into the gully again. I was frantically clambering and slipping up the muddy sides when the horse appeared at the top and reared up, wailing an ear-splitting Naaaaayyyeee! It was then I realised it was protecting the person on the road! *What the hell can I do?* I thought. *I've got to help this person but this thing could seriously hurt me by killing me stone dead!* Then I heard a moan.

'Are you okay?' I called out. 'Can you hear me? The bloody horse won't let me near you. If you can hear me, call it off so I can help you. Can you hear me? . . . Can you . . . ?'

'Stop yelling! I can hear you, you blasted idiot. Stop yelling. You're spooking BD. Easy, BD, eeaaasy.' The horse settled instantly.

'Are you okay?' I asked. 'Can I come out?'

'Oh, stop whining.' It was a woman's voice. 'Come and give me a hand. I think I've busted my ribs. Ooohh, blast!' I got out of the gully and cautiously made my way towards the voice. Through the rain I could just make out the horse with his head down, licking the face of a girl who was sitting up in the middle of the road. 'Where's my torch?' she yelled. 'Can you see my torch? I had it in my hand when I went down. It's over there somewhere near you I think.' And the horse spooked at me again!

'Whoa . . . whoa, BD,' she calmed and he settled again.

'Can't yell. It scares him . . . It's over there somewhere near you. Feel around,' she half whispered as I groped in the wet mud. I found it and turned it on. 'If he spooks, shine it at him. Bright light frightens him and he'll stand dead still . . . OK?'

'OK,' I replied.

Let's see, loud noise and bright light spooks BD. *Better not fart,* I thought as I shone the torch in the direction of the voice. The narrow beam was broken by a rain-soaked young girl in a Drizabone with a hood pulled over her head. I crawled over to her. She was on her knees, holding her ribs and glaring at me.

'What the blazes do you think you were doing?' she spat.

'I was just coming around that bend back there and the bloody horse . . .' *Naaayyeee!* the bloody thing went 'Er, BD . . . BD was standing in the middle of the road. If I'd braked I'd have killed us both. We were both doing fine until you came leaping out of the fucking bushes and nearly fucking killed us all!'

'Watch your mouth, sport,' she admonished.

'Sorry, miss. I'm a little freaked out too. It was an accident. Look, there's no point in arguing here in the middle of the road. Christ, we could all be minced by a semi any minute. Where do you live? My car's in a bog over there but I'll walk and get some help or help you get to wherever you want to go, whatever you want to do. Can you walk?'

'Yes, I think so. My parents' farm's about half a mile down the road. There's no need to go for help. It's just my ribs. Anyway the nearest hospital is in Armidale and that's miles away. Look I'm, mmm, okay I think. Come on . . . help me up.'

Armidale! I couldn't believe it. A few years before I'd been driving this same road, going in the opposite direction with Colin Baigent, the drummer from the first Aztecs, and we'd hit a bunch of bloody cows in his '38 Hudson, nearly killed some silly old fart on his pushbike and slid into a barn. Jesus Christ, what is it with this fucking place and me? I lifted her carefully up and got her somewhat steady on her feet. Her ribs were obviously bad and she had a slight limp, but seemed, well, alive and almost chirpy considering. Bloody BD got agitated every time I touched her. Her continued soothing and my torch flashing kept him calmed and off we limped towards her farm with BD snorting an inch behind my head. A few minutes later we came to a pair of paddock gates.

'This is iiitttt,' she moaned and passed out. I caught her before she hit the ground and picked her up in my arms, managing to get the torch in my mouth at the same time. Braaayyyee, went BD.

'Nor net buckt,' I managed through the torch and he shut up. The girl was about my size and hard to carry but I managed to get the gate open and in we trudged with BD still right behind me. He wasn't going to let me out of his sight. I closed the gate behind me, fumbling to get the chain loop over the hook. There were house lights about 300 yards ahead and I staggered down a muddy driveway, reaching what looked like a perfectly kept front lawn and garden. The girl was still out cold so I made for the front door of the little farmhouse and carried her inside. BD tried to follow me into the house but I kicked the door closed behind me. Braaaayyee!

This horse is a definite bloody nut case, I thought.

It was an old bluestone country cottage, immaculately

decked out in period country furniture and with a huge fire blazing in a stone fireplace. The room was lit in a fairytale glow from a combination of the firelight and the yellow flickering light from several antique kerosene lamps. It was beautiful. A large wooden Biedermeier style sofa sat to the right of the fire by the hearth and I gently eased the girl onto it, carefully lifting her legs up.

'Is there anyone home? Hello. Anybody here?' I yelled, but no-one answered. I scouted the house for a phone but couldn't find one anywhere. I wasn't sure what to do. Make her comfortable. That's it . . . See if she's hurt. I removed her boots and managed to get her Drizabone off. It had a big piece torn from the front. In the firelight glow I got my first real look at her face. She was maybe twenty-two years old, soaked to the skin, with long, mud-splattered, light blonde hair which was stuck to her face, but I could see she was beautiful. She wore a pair of R.M. Williams boots, old jeans and a faded denim shirt buttoned to the neck. She was still unconscious. I didn't know what to do next but decided to get her soaked and muddy clothes off. I unbuttoned the jeans and pulled them off from the ankles, then unbuttoned her shirt and carefully slipped it off, hanging it with her jeans on the large brass fire screen. I was so caught up in getting her things off without hurting her that I hadn't noticed at first. She wasn't wearing any undies! And she was beautiful all over. Hey I'd be a lying bastard if I said I didn't look. I'm no perve, but looking was unavoidable. Here I am miles from anywhere in some farmhouse with an unconscious naked young beauty in front of a fire. *Christ, if anyone comes in now the locals will lynch me for sure.* The thought made me nervous and for a minute I considered dressing her again but realised that was idiocy. There was a bathroom at the end of a short passageway, so I went and got a couple of towels and took a bedspread from a bedroom on the way back.

The girl was still out cold on the chaise and I covered her with the bedspread. She looked like a wet child, deep in a peaceful sleep, and I didn't want to disturb her. I felt her pulse and it seemed steady. I dried her hair off as best I could and got all the mud off her face, then felt her legs, ankles and arms. Nothing was broken. Apart from some light grazing on her left hand she seemed fine. I didn't want to touch her ribs while she was out, so I sat on the edge of the chaise and looked at her for a minute. *What to do now?* I wondered. *What if she has a concussion or has gone into shock?* I knew I had to try to bring her around. I looked around the room and noticed a collection of spirit bottles on what looked like a Georgian mahogany serving table on the far side of the room. Sitting next to the bottles were some crystal goblets and decanters. This was one upmarket farmhouse. I found a bottle of cognac and poured a couple of glasses. My hand shook so badly I nearly spilled the lot, but I shot one of them straight down and steadied myself for a second or two. I took another shot and started to feel better. I took a glass over to the girl, put my hand under her head, lifted it, and tried to get some brandy into her mouth. Half of it went down her front but some must have gotten into her throat because she woke up coughing and gasping for air.

'Oh Goddd, cough cough, er . . . what cough . . . splutter . . . cough . . . what happened?' she whimpered, looking around. Trying to focus, she gave me an astonished look and said, 'Who are you? What the hell are you doing here?'

'There was an accident,' I explained. 'I nearly hit you

and your horse out on the road. Don't you remember? Are you OK?'

She looked at me blankly for a few beats, then her eyes focused on mine. 'Oh . . . Oh yes, I remember now. Oooh, God, my ribs hurt like crazy.' She winced as she touched her side. 'Hey . . . Hey, where are my clothes? I'm naked!' she yelled, pulling the bedspread tight around herself. 'Where are my clothes? What are you up to? You . . . you dirty . . .'

'Heyyy, wait a minute. I had to get your things off. You were soaked to the skin and I wanted to see if you had any broken bones. You were out cold and I didn't know what the fuck to do. Your clothes are by the fire. Look, I didn't mean any . . .'

She looked across at her clothes on the fire screen. 'OK. OK. I'm sorry,' she said. 'But I thought . . . you know.'

'It's fine. Are you all right?' she felt her ribs again and winced, the pain from the movement contorting her face. 'My coat got hooked on your blasted car. It whipped my legs out from under me and threw me onto the road.' She felt her ribs again. 'Oh God, it hurts to touch them.'

'Do you have a bandage or something I can bind them with until you can get them looked at? Some strong cloth will do . . . anything to keep them in place. I only checked your arms and legs while you were unconscious but I can have a look if you want. I've had mine broken and I know what to feel for—'

'I bet you do.'

'No, seriously. You need to get them taped if they're broken and it's not going to be pleasant. Can I get you some dry things to put on? What can I do for you?'

'Could you run me a bath so I can get cleaned up? I'll see to my ribs after a good soak. You'll have to empty it first. I was taking one when the thunder spooked BD and I just threw my jeans and a shirt on. That's why I wasn't wearing any undies. I don't want you to think that I'm that sort of girl or anything.'

'What sort of girl?' I grinned.

'The kind that goes around without without any knickers on . . . you know.' She blushed and I got my first smile. It lit up the room.

'What's your name?' I asked. 'Do you live here or what?' Neither of us had any idea who we were talking to.

'Jill. Jill Farnsley. This is my parents' country place. I come up here sometimes to ride BD and be alone. I'm from Sydney.'

'What's BD short for?' I just had to ask.

'Oh, Brain Dead,' Jill said matter of factly. 'My father bought him to breed, but all he ever did was bite the mares. I'm the only one who can ride him these days.'

Brain Dead, I thought. *Jesus, I'm lucky to be alive. Brain Dead?* There was a silence and we sat looking at one another.

'Don't I know you?' Jill said. 'What's your name?'

'Billy . . . Billy Thorpe.'

'Oh my God. Oh Jesus! Billy Thorpe! I thought you looked familiar . . . Oh Christ, I love you!' She grinned. Her whole persona changed and so did the relationship. 'Oh God, I've got all your records. Look, go over there . . . Go on!' She pointed across the room. 'In the top drawer of that cupboard. Go on, open it.'

I went over to a cupboard against the opposite wall and opened the top drawer. Sure enough, sitting on top was my latest album. Pulling it out I saw a whole pile of clippings and magazine covers of me and the band. I looked across at

Jill, who was sitting up with the bedspread pulled around her, a grin on her beautiful face. 'Come here. Bring them over and sit here beside me . . . Here.' She patted the chaise beside her.

For the next half an hour the accident and our situation went completely out of mind. I poured two more cognacs and we drank them as she told me the shows of mine she'd seen and this article and that, and asked what's this person like and had I met the Beatles and why did the original Aztecs break up and . . . did I have a girlfriend or anything? I answered all her questions and then the reality of where we were came back.

'Hey, let me run that bath for you. And then you need to get some rest. It's got to be 3 or 4 a.m. We can talk about the music business in the morning.'

What are you saying? yelled my dick. 'Ah shut up. Can't you see the girl's hurt?' I said to myself. *Come on, let's help her forget it*, my dick whined. 'Down boy!' *Oh, okaayy . . .*

'Oh, God, Billy Thorpe,' she kept saying. 'Billy Thorpe. I can't believe it . . . Billy Thorpe.' Like I wasn't there. Then she winced. 'Ooh, my ribs. Can you take a look?' she asked.

The bedspread dropped to her waist. It was no accident. It was a deliberate 'and how about you take a look at these while you're at it!' The formalities were over but I made a serious attempt at examining her ribs. Feeling around them. They all sat evenly and I couldn't feel any breaks or bumps, but they were obviously very tender and her whole right side had started to turn a bluish red. It's hard to tell with ribs. There could have been hairline fractures for all I knew, but they were probably just badly bruised or torn ligaments which can be just as painful as a break. Every time I touched her she squirmed and a couple of times it wasn't from pain. Her nipples came up like two puppies' noses and she was giving me the look. This injured young spunk was definitely coming on strong. See, my dick is rarely wrong. That's why I don't argue with it any more. Picked it right away, the astute little bugger.

Jill took my hand and put it on her breast. 'Why don't you see if this is OK?' she meeowed. It was perfectly all right, a perfect thirty-eight D, and I ran my hands all over both of them just to make sure. 'Oooh ... I feel better already,' she purred and then she kissed me. She had big soft moist lips and her tongue instantly found the inside of my mouth. Talk about turning from a turd into a rose. *Shaayyit, boy ... we got the luck of the fucking Irish or what!* chortled my dick. Her hand went down to my crotch and that's when I realised I was soaking wet and shivering cold. From the rain I mean. And regardless of whether I'd just been handed the key to the golden gate, I wanted to be warm and dry when I entered.

'I'm soaked, Jill,' I said. 'Look, why don't we get cleaned up? There's plenty of time for this if you're up for it when we're clean and dry. Let me get that bath together first.'

'OK,' she pouted. 'Oh God, Billy Thorpe ... Billy Thorpe,' I heard her repeating as I walked down the passage and ran her bath. *Ah, the price of fame*, I laughed to myself.

'It's ready,' I yelled. 'Hang on, I'm coming out to help you.'

'No need,' she said. 'I'm ready.' I turned around and Jill was standing at the bathroom door, naked as a babe. She was gorgeous. Five seven, long legs, a curly blonde bush, big green eyes, and a perfect set. Her dishevelled appearance made her look even sexier. I must have been ogling. 'See anything you like?' she purred.

'All of it!'

'Well my parents won't be down until tomorrow,' she grinned. She walked slowly over to me, her eyes fixed on mine, holding her ribs with one hand. She threw her left arm around my neck and had her tongue in my mouth again. My hands moved over her body. She began to squirm and purr.

'Into the bath first,' I told her.

'Oh, all right,' she said and I helped her get in. 'I'll be back when you're finished.'

'Oh nooo . . . you bathe me. I'm hurt. I can't reach anywhere with these ribs,' she faked. 'Here, take the sponge. I want you to wash me.'

So I did and spent the next half hour sponging every inch of her. Christ, how do I get into these situations? I wondered. I nearly killed you less than an hour ago.

I got Jill out of the bath and towelled her from head to toe. She went to her bedroom and I ran myself a bath. A minute later Jill was back. She wanted to wash me but I wasn't up to it. I insisted my ribs were fine and had my bath alone. I needed to relax a minute myself. That had been a close call on the highway and I didn't want to even think about the damage to my new car. My hand shook as I washed myself and I realised I was shaken up more than I'd thought. I soaked for a while letting the hot water soothe me, then I dried myself and headed to the living-room.

Jill was lying on a rug in front of the fire, wrapped in a towel. 'Come here,' she whispered and opened her towel. I lay down beside her and started to kiss her. 'Do it to me,' she whispered. I gently got on top of her.

'Oh! God, my ribs! . . . My ribs!' she moaned. 'Oh get off me, please . . . Oh, that hurts too much.' Jill rolled slowly over onto her stomach. 'This way,' she whispered, bringing her knees up under her, exposing herself to me. *Oh, if you insist,* said the voice. I stood there looking down at her in the firelight with a hammer that would have given BD a complex. Then I knelt behind her, pulling her gently to me, and eased myself in.

'Oh God,' she moaned and . . .

'Morpheeno. Morpheeno. Sii heee . . . heee heee!'

'Come on, boy, stop moanin'. It's time for your shot,' said Bertha.

10
Bellevue in the a.m.

Bombers flew around the concrete room, engines droning like giant bees in an empty corrugated-iron water tank. But at least the murdering bastards were asleep and I didn't have to listen to their morpheeno routine for a while. Finding out the truth about them had whipped the crusted dung from my mental blanket and shot it right off the stage and into the wings with a resounding zing! That first day and night there had been a touch of absurd cartoon innocence about the Severinos. A kind of Felliniesque quality that the morphine had manipulated into the only humour in my situation. But in the blinding light of truth, Fellini dived straight out the window like a sprung lover and Nosferatu crept in and went straight down on his girl.

Morpheus is a devious bastard. Likes to screw with you. Takes your pain upon his velvet back and lifts you effortlessly to a soft quiet cloud. Comforts and caresses you. Strokes your aching body with his down-covered hands.

Then plummets head-first into an invisible pit crammed with the vipers of your own subconscious design. No escape but another cloud. No way there but on Morpheus' velvet back.

But the photographs brought me back. Confirmed my own identity. Tangible doses of pleasurable comfort in what had become an even more insane, frightening and helpless experience. Entire sections of my life came back. Time had no meaning. There was no order of chronology, just vivid images from my past. Beyond the mania that was taking place with Bertha, Idi and the Severinos, the room started to take on its own surreal proportions which distorted distances, angles, sounds, light, colour and smells. A fourth dimension in which it became increasingly harder to separate the real from the fantasy. I wasn't sure if it was the morphine stone or I was actually starting to succumb and settle into the routine, but the scariest part was that I was actually starting to look forward to Bertha's shots and Morpheus' dark world of technicolour entertainment. No matter how I cut or sliced it, regardless of the circumstance, I was stoned as a maggot. And it was good. Too damned good. That's how the habit starts. It's just too good. That's why people get hooked. Inviting as a pretty girl lifting her skirt and offering you the first bite. Morpheus creeps up on you from behind and you don't know he's stuck his knife in your back until the sweating pain of that first Jones. Too late then, brother. You gone! That was the big worry. 'Until Tuesday . . .'

We stumble through life thinking there's no real order to it. That things have happened at random. Although someone like me can point to different moments in time and see their significance in terms of a developing career, even then they seem to be random. Lying hopelessly in the Bellevue ward with no connection to the real world other than some photographs, I had nothing to do other than think. I guess the morphine was plugging into some real old stones. Reactivating brain cells that had been hammered into submission years before by a million miles on the road with the rock 'n' roll circus. Lying there trying to put my life together I went back to the Cross in the '60s. To my ménage à trois with Pepper and Natalie. To the original Aztecs. It all seemed to meld into one continuing adventure, the spaces between the significant moments erased. It occurred to me for the first time that when my life and career had taken leaps forward the significant events occurred over extremely short periods of time and at an almost blinding speed. My early success in 1964 had come about in less than twelve months and the significant changes I had gone through since the '60s, changes that had irreversibly headed me in the direction my life had subsequently taken, all pretty much occurred between 1969 and 1971. All were represented in one way or another by the photographs. I had been born again, not in the Jesus religious sense, but physically, mentally and musically, when I got to Melbourne in the late '60s.

Melbourne? I went for two weeks and stayed eight years. *Eight years!* How the hell did I go to Melbourne for a fortnight and stay eight years?

'Hello, is that Billy Thorpe?'

'Yes it is. Who's this?'

'Actually, we have never met. Vince Maloney suggested I give you a call when I got to Sydney. This is Robert Stigwood. Do you think we could meet some time this week before I go back to London?'

111

Robert Stigwood! My mind did a quick double-take. *The* Robert Stigwood who managed Eric Clapton, Cream and the Bee Gees. *That* Robert Stigwood? Can't be! Someone's geeing me up here! 'Yeah, right! Who the fuck *is* this?'

'Billy, I er . . . ahem . . . assure you this is Robert Stigwood. Vince Maloney has been playing guitar with Barry and the boys and when he heard I was to visit Sydney he suggested I give you a call. I'd like to talk to you about London if you have the time.'

'Oh I'm sorry, I thought it was someone having me on. Sure, any time. Where are you staying?'

'I'm at the Chevron Hotel, up at Kings Cross. Are you far from here?'

'No, I'm in Double Bay. With a good wind I could hit you with a shanghai from here.'

'Oh dear boy, I assure you that won't be necessary. How about tomorrow? Say two o'clock in the p.m.?'

'Two o'clock in the p.m.'s fine by me, Mr Stigwood. I'll see you then.'

'Good . . . By the way, it's Robert. I'm in suite 816. Buzz me when you get here . . . Bye.' Click.

It was 18 June 1968. Robert Stigwood, Vince Maloney, Barry Gibb and the Bee Gees? Christ, what a small world. After my first band had split, Tony Barber and Vince Maloney had gone out as a duo. They monikered themselves Vince and Tony's Two. What a godawful name. There was initial media interest and celebrity that stemmed from the hysteria that still surrounded all of us who had been a part of Billy Thorpe and the Aztecs, but Vince and Tony's duo effort didn't work musically and after a few months they went their separate ways. Tony moved to Melbourne and recorded a number of innovative novelty hit singles as a soloist in 1965 and '66. He had a couple of top 10 hits and was very popular for a time. Being the true embodiment of Mr Bean, Tony's act was as out there as he was, but extremely entertaining and at times hilarious. His stage antics were particularly weird and one night I saw him on national TV dressed in a chicken suit, sitting on a pile of huge eggs, miming one of his hits. God knows why but it evidently made perfect sense to Tony. But chicken suit or not, eventually the novelty wore off and Tony faded from public view.

I hadn't seen or heard of Vince Maloney until he turned up in a *TV Week* photograph with the Bee Gees, some time in late '67 I think. After he and Tony had split Vince had made his way to London. To cut a long story short, the Bee Gees decided they wanted to be a band and not a vocal trio. Christ knows why. They recruited Colin 'Smiley' Petersen on drums. Colin had played the title role of the quintessential Australian bush child in the successful film *Smiley* back in 1957. And who should they recruit on guitar? None other than Vince Maloney from the Aztecs. What makes the circle even smaller is that the Bee Gees, Barry, Maurice and Robin, had all grown up in Brisbane in the late '50s at the same time as I had. We'd been show-biz brats together and had all started performing at local dances and on kids' TV at the same time. Barry and I are the same age and I can remember our first TV show together. We'd have been about eleven or twelve years old. Robin and Maurice just knee-high kids. They all wore white tennis shorts, white T-shirts and, are you ready, long white knee-high socks and white tennis sneakers. They looked like the junior chipmunk tennis squad. Funnier than shit, but as they always have, they sang their little arses off. Their national success in Australia had come quite a bit before mine and they had preceded my move to Sydney by a good three years. Now through that old connection and Vince Maloney, Robert Stigwood is calling me about London.

I arrived at the Chevron at 1.50 sharp. Nothing anal, I just like being right on time. I walked up the steps to the Chevron Hotel. Brendan the concierge was on duty, resplendent in his blue uniform with the gold flashes on the shoulders, spit-polished black brogues and—the universal sign of a concierge from New York City to the Irish Moss—a military-style officer's cap with a flat top and a gold-braided brim. Brendan not only looked the part, he was one of the best and world renowned. He could be trusted to get anything together and had personally handled the needs of people like Judy Garland in his capacity as one of Australia's top doormen.

'What's doing, me ole?' he asked with his ever-welcoming smile. 'Me ole' was Sydney street slang, short for 'me old china plate', or mate. 'Everything sweet?' he asked, shaking my hand. He slid the forefinger of his left hand conspiratorially along the side of his nose, shooting it off into the air as if flicking a bug from the tip, in the universal street sign for Eetswa . . . Looking good . . . The girls are sweet . . . Everything's cool . . . whatever the streetwise needed to convey at the time.

'Sweet as a nut, Brendan. Couldn't be better, mate,' I replied, returning the gesture.

'I saw in the kite that you got done.' He smiled, cocking his head down to one side in a 'Come on, come on, give me the shit' look.

Sydney street slang was not only rhyming but sometimes double-rhyming. Such as the word 'kite'. A kite touches and scrapes the sky and is therefore a skyscraper, which rhymes with paper. So when Brendan saw it in the kite he read it in the newspaper.

'Yeah, mate, somebody didn't like my top notes and threw a bomb down the stairs of the Hawaiian Eye. Blew me and the band through the bloody wall and showered the joint with a mixture of beer, Chinese food, wood and plaster. The joint was almost empty and luckily nobody was hurt. I got my nose broken again. That's twice now!'

There had been a story and photo of me in the paper sitting in a hospital bed with my broken nose heavily plastered. Turns out the attack had nothing to do with us. Just an incident in an underground club war. Right place wrong time. That's all.

'Jesus, me ole, they get the bludgers or what?'

'No, mate. But they figured it was something to do with some bad business. I just happened to be playing there that night. I had Reg Melaney as my bodyguard for the next three months. We both felt like a couple of real hoons. But knowing Reg had his shooter ready made me feel a lot better.'

'So what are you all smiles and spit polish about today, my son? Got a spunk inside eager for some pop star attention or what? You're looking too sharp for anything but Ted,' He winked, shaking his lapel. 'Ted' or 'Theodore' was street slang for pussy.

'No, mate. No Theodore. Got a meeting with someone who's staying here.'

'Yeah right. Just how many sheilas have you had in the last few years anyway?'

'Oh, thousands, Brendan, bloody thousands,' I laughed as we turned and walked up the marble stairs and through tall brass-trimmed glass doors into the Chevron Hotel lobby. Brendan held the door open for me as I passed. 'This way, sir, you dirty little cunt,' he whispered. 'You still with that young spunk Jackie Holme, me ole?'

'Yeah mate, still together.'

'Jesus, she's bloody gorgeous, you lucky little bastard.' We both laughed. 'Haven't seen you about lately. You workin' or what?'

'Well, I've been doing five straight at the Whiskey for the last three months. It's been great. You know, the R&R crowd. Fantastic vibes. The US soldiers really get it on and it's Saturday night every night. Best time I've had since back in the Surf City days.'

'Yeah. Great fucking times, eh?' We both went silent for a few beats. 'A lot of the American big brass stay here,' Brendan said. 'Crazy as loons some of 'em. Bloody good blokes though, most of 'em. They paid off my mortgage in tips last year. Hope the bloody war never ends.'

'Well I'm getting itchy feet, Brendan, and this meeting might just scratch them. Where's the house phone, mate? I need to call the room.'

We shook hands and he gave me another nose salute which I returned. It was 1.29 and 30 seconds when I asked the house operator to put me through to room 816 and at exactly 1.30 a voice said, 'My my, we are prompt aren't we? Come on up. I've ordered lunch in the room.'

I got into the open elevator and pressed 8. It started up, then stopped on the mezzanine floor where the bar over-looked the lobby. The doors opened and in staggered two genuine, pissed-rotten cowboys. I should say two genuine, pissed-rotten and very famous cowboys. It was none other than Roger Miller of the 'Dang Me' and 'King of the Road' fame. With him was the legendary country picker Thumbs

Carlisle. I'd noticed Roger's life-size blow-up in the lobby but I hadn't thought that much about it. Now here I am in the lift with two very pissed, very loud, extremely well known and talented good ole boys in search of somethin', and it weren't the word of the Lord.

'Dang, boy,' said Roger. 'Ya see the bodaaayycious ta-tas on that little blonde gal?'

'Surer than shit, hoss. She wants to dangle my lariat, boy. Lawd what an ass.'

'She's gonna dangle both our lariats and the goddamn horse too, Roy. She's coming up when she gets off.'

'We'll all be gettin' off when *she* gets *off*, Roy.' They both went into a gut-wrenching laugh, slapping each other on the back and dangin' and shit-yeahin' like I wasn't in the lift.

The last time Roger Miller had been in Sydney in the early '60s, Roger, Tom Jones and I had done the legendary George Street crawl together. That's drinking a pony of beer in every pub up George Street, from the Sydney Harbour Bridge to Broadway. In those days it seemed like there was a pub on practically every corner for twenty city blocks. By the time we got to King Street we were very happy. By the Sydney Town Hall we were pissed. By Chinatown uncontrollable. And by the time we hit Broadway we had an entourage that consisted of Jim Oram from the *Sun* newspaper, may he rest in peace, a couple of toothless old winos who couldn't believe their luck, four of the ugliest sheilas in Sydney, a couple of them middle-aged hookers, two off-duty coppers from the Darlinghurst nick and about half a dozen like-minded, cheering punters. It was outrageous to say the least and a pile of us ended up shit-faced screaming drunk in the back of a paddy wagon, only to end up drinking with the crown sergeant at Darlinghurst and getting laid by some of the best looking girls in town. All on the local coppers. Ah, the price of fame.

The best thing was, as well known as I was around Sydney at that time, in the company of a maniacal Welshman and a crazed, shit-faced cowboy, nobody took that much notice of me. In fact I was practically invisible. That was until it came time to get locked up. Then it seems my invisibility shield melted. If there's a stink or a ruckus, regardless of guilt or innocence, I always seemed to be the one that got thrown in the nick. Story of my life. Well, story of this part of my life.

'Been in the back of any police wagons lately, Roger?' I asked, patting him on the shoulder. He spun around, not recognising me at first, then a huge grin came over his face and he threw his arms around me.

'Goddamn. If it ain't the goddamn Braffer,' he yelled. 'Thumbs. Thumbs, this is the Braffer. This boy got an asshole that belongs in the goddamn London Philharmonic. Thumbs, this is, er . . .'

'Billy. Billy Thorpe, Roger. How's it hangin' mate? . . . Hey Thumbs, great to meet ya.'

'Like a goddamn baby's arm with pomegranate in it, son. How the hell are ya?'

'Great. I didn't realise you were playing here. You on tonight?'

'Yuuuppp! Nine-thirty and midnight. Gotta get the edge goin' first. You wanna come up for a coupla drinks or three?'

'Can't mate, thanks. I've got a meeting. Maybe I'll swing by for the late show. You want to put my name down? OK if I hang backstage?'

'Sure, Braffer, sure. Be ma plaaeesssuurrre, son.'

The elevator reached the eighth floor and I said goodbye to the two drunkest cowboys south of the Pecos. As the doors closed behind me Roger let off an enormous ripping fart and the last thing I saw of them through the crack in the closing doors was Roger on the floor holding his gut and Thumbs frantically fanning the air. 'See ya, Braaaffer,' I heard Roger scream as the lift went up. They had no idea what floor they were on and probably went up and down a dozen times before heading back to the bar for another couple of bottles of Jack Black, no ice.

I don't remember who gave me the enchanting name, but in the early '60s I was known as the Braffer by half the Australian music business. 'Braff' is an old Australianism for fart, and at one time in my life I was world class. The original Aztecs called me Braffer and so did some of the fans. After a while the name sort of wore off, thank fuck, but Barry Gibb immortalised it on the Bee Gee's first English album in a song entitled 'Harry Braff'. Now there's an important piece of rock mythology. Another piece of the circle. Vince Maloney, the Bee Gees and the Braffer. There just has to be a cosmic connection.

When I knocked on the door to 816 it was opened by a distinguished-looking gentleman in this thirties, dressed in an immaculate black mohair Savile Row suit. When he welcomed me he spoke with an educated Australian accent and I hadn't realised until then that one of the most powerful entertainment managers in the world was an Aussie. In fact he was from Adelaide.

We had a delightful lunch of fresh lobster and champagne and Robert put an offer to me to go to England in a couple of months to see if he could get my career off the ground. Since Vince's comments he had checked on my success and gotten hold of some of my records. 'You've got a great voice, Billy,' he said to me, 'and if we can find you the right song I think you can have a successful start in the UK. What do you think?'

'Great! When do I leave?'

'About six weeks. Would that suit you? Are you able to get away at such short notice?'

'I'll be there. Just give me a place and time.'

So that was the plan, Stan. England in September. Record some tracks and see if I had what it took to crack the scene.

The Cross was beginning to wrap itself in a warm, golden evening glow as I walked down the Chevron steps and crossed Macleay Street. Long shadows draped themselves from the tops of buildings, falling like giant velvet theatre curtains, signalling the end of the matinee performance of yet another beautiful Sydney day. The trees lining Macleay Street were thick with orange, yellow and red leaves. Alive with tiny, singing, chirping sparrows that rose up in their hundreds at the sound of a loud car horn. The traffic was light and I hailed a cab back to Double Bay to think about the future. As I turned into Bayswater Road the neon door opened in a burst of electric reds, yellows and greens. The night shifters came on. It was show time in the Cross for another night.

Jackie was home early from an all-day fashion shoot for *Australian Vogue*. A stunningly beautiful New Zealander, she and I had met in early 1966, fallen head over heels in love and had lived together ever since. I had proposed to her not long after we met and gave her a diamond engagement ring on her twenty-second birthday, but she could never quite commit. Her parents had had some sort of trouble in their marriage and I think it stuck in the back of her head. Anyway, we lived together and thoughts of marriage just seemed to slip away. 'Jack', as she liked to be called, was Australian model of the year and bore a slight resemblance to English model Jean Shrimpton, but in my opinion Jack was way more beautiful.

She was also full of life. A real thoroughbred with absolutely no ego about her striking beauty and modelling success. She didn't give a shit about modelling and told me she wanted to quit about twice a week. We had been photographed a lot together and were sort of *the* young pop couple for a time. Jack's modelling image and my pop star persona were perfect visual fodder for the personality pages of the day. Jack and I were living in the top half of a duplex just up from the Double Bay shopping centre, and sharing the place with us was a hundred-pound purebred boxer dog, Sonny, who had also been a twenty-second birthday present for Jack. We'd had the place for about a year and for all intents and purposes lived as husband and wife. And that was a large part of the tension that had started to grow between us. Her fiery Leo personality was gasoline on my Aries fire. And vice versa. In good times it made for an exciting, no holds barred, loving, sensual and caring relationship. In fact we adored each other. Still do. But on a bad day . . . Shiiiitfiiire! And sadly there were starting to be more bad days than good.

We were drifting away from each other and both too young to recognise what was happening or how to deal with it. My regimen till 4.30 a.m. at the Whiskey and some of the strenuous touring I'd been doing earlier in the year, combined with Jack's heavy, up at 5.30 a.m., sixteen-hour modelling days meant we spent less and less time together and when we did a lot of it was disastrous. Both incredibly strong-willed, neither of us would ever give in to the other and we fought like cats and dogs. Sometimes physically. Especially when we drank. And we drank a lot of champagne! A break-up was inevitable. For all that, there was still a strength to our partnership—a place in which we both still found a combined strength, camaraderie and love—a unified position from which to deal with the heady worlds we both lived in. So like the stubborn, psychological masochists we both were, we bit the bullet and stayed together.

'How did your meeting go?' Jack beamed as I walked in. Regardless of the negatives developing in our relationship, we were always interested in each other's careers and supported each other at every opportunity and level, including financially.

'Oh, nothing much happened.' I grinned and went into the bedroom.

'Oh come on, Bill. Come on . . . Tell me. Tell me what happened,' she purred, following me and pouting in the little-girl voice she always used when we were alone.

She leapt onto the bed. The black crepe de chine minidress she was wearing from the modelling shoot flew up, revealing her black lace panties. She was always a turn-on. Jack was one of the most beautiful and sexy girls in Australia. She was sex on a stick and I was the envy of every male model, photographer and young boy in the country. I think one of the strongest elements in our relationship at that time was the sex. It was always incredible. Unlike many beautiful young girls I'd known, Jackie didn't flaunt her beauty and sexuality, at least in public that is. In fact she'd been hassled so much by lecherous Romeos and dirty old men as a teenager in Auckland, where she'd grown up, that she'd developed a kind of defence mechanism that conveyed an almost cold, defiant personality in public. But in private . . . Bingo! In private she was an uninhibited sexual dynamo who loved it all, and our lovemaking was always light years beyond anything the word satisfying can ever convey.

Even at that time we made love every day or whenever we could. Even if it was in the few minutes that we saw each other between when I came home and Jack got up for work. In a nutshell, good sex kept us together. Neither one of us was interested in sleeping around. It just wasn't part of our make-up and personality. I'd had just about all the stray slash I could handle in one lifetime from my pop star early days in 1964 and '65.

'Come on, Bill, what happened? Tell me, you bastard!'

'Ah, he wants me to go to England, that's all. Where are we going for dinner?' I teased.

'Come on, Bill, tell me?' she cooed, seeing me eyeing her naked thighs. 'You can tell meeee,' she vamped, slipped her panties off erotically and sliding down the bed onto the floor at my feet. 'Get down here and tell me all about it. There's a good boy,' she whispered, pulling me between her legs. 'You won't regret it, I promise.'

I didn't have the strength left to go and see Roger Miller that night.

I decided to set up two weeks of solo gigs in Melbourne before I left for England as a way of putting some extra cash in the coffers. I had no idea how long I'd be away and asked Jack if she wanted to come with me. She had done some very successful modelling work in London in 1966 and could easily have had a great career there. Part of the reason she'd come back to Australia was me, and I owed it to her to ask. Like her I also didn't want it to just end but we both knew that with me in England for months, and her in Australia, it surely would. Nothing was really decided and the day of the Melbourne gigs came up with Jack and me making a loose plan to hook up in London when I got settled. I was going down to Melbourne for two weeks, then back in Sydney for four days . . . then London.

My band at that time was a four-piece. Paul Wheeler on bass, Mick Lieber on guitar and Jimmy Thompson on drums. With me occasionally playing rhythm guitar. We had planned to meet at the airport at 9 for a 10 a.m. flight to Melbourne. Mick Lieber was a young English blues guitarist from the Peter Green school, and he could play his arse off. He was a funny character with a strong East End accent and was well known in England. He later went on to play with Ashton, Gardner and Dyke who had had a hit with 'Resur-rection Shuffle' in 1971. Mick had only been in Australia a short time and was playing around Melbourne with Danny Robertson's Python Lee Jackson when they came to Sydney as a guest on my television show, 'It's All Happening', which was the top national live music show of its day. We got talk-ing. When Mick came to live in Sydney I offered him a gig.

But Mick was bit of an unpredictable character. Liked to hang out with some of the heavy American R&R dopers. Don't get me wrong, he was a great bloke and I liked him a lot. It never affected the way he played, but there was an air of unreliable 'I don't give a shit about the music scene' about him. Standing at the airport five minutes before the flight took off I knew Mick wouldn't show up. My instincts were spot-on. His phone rang off the hook, his girlfriend hadn't seen him in a couple of days, and I flew off to Melbourne with a drummer and bass player but minus a guitarist to play two weeks of sold-out gigs.

Like so many other weird acts of fate in my life, that event set the course for what at the moment can be described as the rest of my life. The Melbourne gigs were sold out. We had to go on so I had to play guitar on the few songs I knew. I filled the set out on guitar with old rockers like 'Be Bop A-Lula', 'Whole Lotta Shakin'' and a few blues songs like 'Rock Me Baby'. After a few boos and walkouts that first night for not playing many of the old hits many of the crowd had come to hear, the audience ended up going berserk and that was not only the end of my pop-star, singing-only, front-man persona, but the beginning of my permanent guitar playing on stage. The beginning of a whole new career. For a while there was a lot of aggro and fights at gigs caused by the fact that I'd stopped playing all my old hits but it slowly subsided and audiences began to warm to the new music. Some of the old fans drifted away. Some stayed and we picked up a lot of new followers who were into our new brand of rocking blues. I learned one of the most valuable lessons of my life during that period. Reinventing yourself is the key to longevity. I was knocked out with the Melbourne scene and the reception we'd received. We had obviously given them something that they hadn't heard before and there was no doubt in my mind that I had to explore it further. The first two weeks became a month, then two, and Paul, Jimmy and I rented an apartment on the beach in St Kilda. When I decided to stay Jackie came down to Melbourne and we looked for a house where we could all live.

*

That piece of land containing 6 perches and 2 lengths of a perch or there of would being part of Crown Section 21 at Melbourne East Parish of North Melbourne, County of Bourke at East Melbourne, in the city of Melbourne, Victoria, Australia with dwelling house thereon known as 17 Gipps Street East Melbourne.

Such was the description in the title deed for the property containing a small dwelling which in 1880 became known as Banchory Cottage and in the 1940s as 92 Gipps Street when the street numbers were reallocated to coincide with the growth of population in Melbourne. Built in 1874, Banchory Cottage was one of a number of cottages and houses built at that time in East Melbourne, many of which are still standing in immaculate shape more than 120 years later. In the later part of the nineteenth century, under the sponsorship of an organisation known as the Female Middle Class Emigration Society, a number of women left Britain to seek a better life in one or other of the colonies. This emigration scheme, which operated between 1862 and 1882, existed primarily to allow single, educated, genteel and unemployed young ladies the opportunity to migrate to Australia in the hope of finding suitable positions with well-to-do families as governesses and the like. In August 1862 a group of eight governesses arrived in Melbourne aboard Her Majesty's Frigate *Result*. Among the party were Isabella MacGillvray and her sisters Margaret, Christina and Wilhelmina Craigie MacGillvray. Their brother the Honourable Paul H. MacGillvray, MA, MRCS, had lived in Williamstown near Melbourne for some years and not long before the sisters' arrival had accepted appointment as resident surgeon in the goldmining township of Bendigo. He had kept his Williamstown house, into which the sisters moved upon their arrival in Australia. Margaret, who was the youngest of the sisters, gained employment as a governess. At some stage she and Wilhelmina moved to Melbourne and with the help of their brother purchased the cottage at 17 Gipps Street for £910. The sisters named the house Banchory Cottage after the small Scottish town of Banchory, from which the clan MacGillvray hailed. It was on the River Dee, not far from Aberdeen.

Wilhelmina MacGillvray died, a spinster, on 27 April 1886 and willed her half interest in the cottage to her sister Margaret, who also died a spinster in the house a short time later, having willed her interest in equal shares to her niece and nephew Imina MacGillvray Tuplis and James William Tuplis of Mildura in Victoria. The tiny cottage passed through a number of owners until it was purchased by the Barton family some time in the early 1960s. I rented it with Paul, Jimmy and Jackie in December 1968 and it became the house of lunacy. Wilhelmina, Margaret and Imina MacGillvray must have turned in their graves when they saw the mania that took place inside its durable walls. It was in that house that a million brain cells died and the Sunbury Aztecs were born.

According to the hip press, the good times had ended forever at Altamont speedway on 6 December 1969 when the Rolling Stones and the Hell's Angels got together for a night in hell. But what did we know? Altamont was a bloody long way from Gipps Street, East Melbourne, and seeing nobody had been killed at any gigs around Australia lately, and the vibes were definitely happening as far as we and everyone else were concerned, so was the world! Just because the Stones' ego trip to do a free concert on the coat-tails of

Woodstock shot them in their own arses, why the hell should we be on a bummer? After all, this's Strayia, mate!

Just like every other night, and for the last twelve months, the little cottage was packed to the rafters with the usual contingent of musos, club owners and stoners. Jack and I had a bedroom just inside the front door off the street. The house had become such a popular hang it seemed like we had someone knocking on the door every five minutes, day and night. I wasn't getting much sleep as it was, but with the endless knocking next to my window, I wasn't getting any at all. It got so bad I started timing the knocks and I wasn't too far out. As a result I completely lost it and nailed a four-foot-square, hand-painted sign to the front door, which stopped the traffic for a while. But some old lady saw it and called the coppers. They made me take it down and the traffic started all over again. The sign read:

To those about to knock. About ever 8 minutes DAY and NIGHT some arsehole knocks on this door and I'm going fucking insane! My bedroom is the front window to your right and I haven't slept in 6 fucking months. Regardless of what you've been told this is not the Melbourne Salvation Army, the Hilton or the Thumping Tum East, IT'S OUR HOUSE. We don't save souls, take confessions, serve breakfast, arrange marriages, sell cars, arbitrate disputes, find lost dogs, supply inspiration, give spiritual guidance, sell drugs, bust virgins, counsel lost teenagers, or need your stimulating conversation. Therefore:-

If you're not bleeding from every orifice and about to die.

If your gear hasn't blown up and you need to borrow

an amp.

If you didn't leave your clothes here last night and you're naked in the street.

If you're not a philanthropist with a million dollars to give away.

If you're not a record company that wants to give us a deal.

If you're a debt collector.

If you haven't called so we know you're coming.

Or if you're a copper without a legal search warrant then;

FUCK OFF!!!!

Peace and love

Another night of gigs ends. Another party started. 'Honky Tonk Women' was blaring for the fifteenth time in an hour. Heavy beverage and much heinous substance were being consumed and the quaint little cottage was rocking its doors off. Number 92 Gipps Street was happening big time and so was Melbourne that summer of '69. Things were shifting again. Another phase was starting. Just like it had back in '64. I felt it coming then and had been fortunate to have been right in the middle of Australia's experience of a cultural upheaval that shook the planet. 1969 was a different space, but I could feel something new happening all over again. After the initial excitement generated by R&R in 1966 and '67 the Sydney live music scene slowly sank back into its lifeless self. Once again I'd been privileged to experience the peak of a significant cultural event from the core. This time it had been at the Whiskey Au Go Go. But by mid-1968 US servicemen and their vibe were just another stitch in the fabric. The Whiskey was still rocking every night but the glow was gone. The excitement faded and by 1969 it was just business as usual. As far as local music was concerned, Melbourne was the only scene at that time and it was taking off like no other in Australian history.

There were somewhere around forty live music gigs in and around Melbourne every week. Local town halls in suburbs such as Mentone, Coburg, Moorabbin, Preston, Box Hill, Kew 'Q Club', Ormond Hall 'Opus', Glenferrie, Brighton, Camberwell and Dandenong were regular weekend live gigs, as well as clubs such as Bertie's, Sebastian's, the Thumping Tum, Catcher, Traffik, That's Life. Humpty Dumpty's, Garrison and Teazer. This doesn't include pubs such as the White Horse, Village Green, Waltzing Matilda, Mathew Flinders, Beaumaris, Frankston, Southside Six and a dozen others that Bill Joseph, the Godfather of the Melbourne live music scene, had opened. We took the first production into pubs when the drinking age laws changed, opening them up to rock 'n' roll and creating Aussie Pub Rock. These mainly city gigs also don't include pubs like the Sundowner in Geelong and gigs in other Victorian country towns like Ballarat, Bendigo, Warrnambool and Shepparton, and beach towns like Torquay and Lorne. Many featured four or five local, original young bands a night, Thursdays through Sundays, playing to packed-out crowds of up to fifteen hundred rabid local music fans. Very few of them had record deals. It was all on the strength of the live playing! It was Surf City all over again, but this time on a much broader and more significant scale. It embraced all styles of music from blues, pop and country to the newly emerging 'hard rock'. Many a Saturday we would play five packed-out gigs. Five different gigs in one day! At an average of two one-hour sets per gig, we were playing live ten hours a day, and that was the norm for us and a number of other hot young bands around Melbourne in 1969 and early 1970.

The Melbourne band line-up at that time is too large to list in detail but some of the most successful were Daddy Cool, the Aztecs, Zoot with Rick Springfield, the La De Das with Kevin Borich, Spectrum, the Carson County Blues Band, Company Caine, the Twilights with Glen Shorrock, then Axiom with Glen Shorrock and Brian Cadd, Max Merritt and the Meteors, who were huge, Chain, Healing Force, the Loved Ones, the Valentines with Bon Scott, then Bakery with Bon, the Masters Apprentices, Buffalo with Peter Wells, Pirana, Madder Lake, Campact, Red House Roll Band, Kahvas Jute, Levi Smith Clefs, the Captain Matchbox Whoopee Band, Leo [De Castro] and Friends, Doug Parkinson in Focus, Greg Quill's Country Radio, the Adderly Smith Blues band and that's just a few. All working in a town of one and a half million people. By comparison with today's radio-inspired, lacklustre scene, it's mind-boggling! You can see why I stayed. By contrast, Sydney, with a population of over two million, had only one half-decent legitimate live venue, The Here in North Sydney. Sydney was stone dead, and a far cry from the magic that had taken place there only five years before.

One typical five-gig day started at the Village Green Hotel, a packed-out, thousand-capacity pub that was a Saturday arvo bastion of rockingdom, where we played three sets starting at 2.30 p.m. As usual the afternoon turned into rock 'n' roll mayhem. I got a jug-skolling contest going with the crowd and the whole joint got into it big time. By the time we were ready to leave the publican was pressing bottles of Johnnie Walker Black Label into our hands and begging us to play a couple more sets. He'd never sold that much grog in his life. After the Green we went into the city to play Birtie's, a three-storey club on the corner of Spring and Flinders Streets in the heart of the city which had once been the home of the Public Schoolboys Club. It was run by Tony Knight, the son of a very successful catering family. A handsome flamboyant character who sat at the front door four nights a week dressed to the nines in velvet and lace, Tony embodied the elegance of the 'Mod' Edwardian style that had become so popular in Carnaby Street in the late '60s. Birtie's was without doubt the best live music club Australia has ever had. Unlike the Whiskey, which was Australia's most successful licensed nightclub, Birtie's—like all Melbourne venues except the pubs—didn't sell alcohol. Birtie's was all about local live music and people came in droves simply because of the bands and the vibe. We started our night-time line-up of gigs at Birtie's with two one-hour sets starting at 7.30. The third gig was at Sebastian's, which was also run by the Knights, at 10 p.m. Sebastian's was a converted grainery, quite a bit smaller than Birtie's, and it too was packed Thursdays through Sundays. What's particularly impressive is that it stood about half a mile up the street from Birtie's and was just as popular. Next we headed to the Thumping Tum in Little Lonsdale Street about half a mile away for two forty-five minute sets starting at midnight and then literally around the corner to the Catcher for a one-hour set at 3.30 a.m. Melbourne's inner city was alive with music in 1969 and 1970. Apart from the Village Green, which was a twenty-minute drive out of town, all the other gigs that night were within the same square mile in the heart of Melbourne's inner city. All featured at least four hot bands a night. All packed to the rafters. All raging.

All an absolute pleasure to play. In my experience and travels, the scene this produced was the equal of any in the world. Never before or since have that many quality live clubs and venues operated successfully and simultaneously anywhere in Australia and their very existence is an indication of just how vibrant, current, exciting and stimulating the Melbourne scene that I'd discovered on my way to England really was.

As soon as Norm Swiney—Norman E our bad roadee—had packed the gear at the Catcher, as usual it was straight to the International Club for Scotch and Cokes and schnitzels with many of the other bands and crews that had been on the same treadmill of rock 'n' roll lunacy that night. The International Club schnitzels were huge, two bucks, and the drinks a dollar. It was owned and run by a couple of Greek guys and obviously a front for something, but at those prices with that vibe who gave a shit! They loved the bands and it was the one place in Melbourne that catered for musos till dawn. It was a party every night. Bands, roadies, band molls, girlfriends and mates hung there together. Pool, the occasional fight, laughter, tears, dope-smoking, Scotch-drinking, story-swapping, good-natured, healthy free-thinking and harmless lunacy until way past dawn. Then armed with sufficient supplies of Scotch and whatever else seemed appropriate, people headed home to party, and we wheelied it a short half mile across the Botanical Gardens, past Captain Cook's cottage, to Gipps Street, just to put a little edge on it in case we came down from the night's festivities. Which rarely happened unless someone screwed up real bad with the supplies. Hang the bastard!

The party usually wound down around 9 or 10 a.m. on

Sunday morning and it was time for a few hours' rest. Now by rest I don't necessarily mean sleep. Rest meant no indulging for a significant period of time. No partying until the sun went down. Well, maybe the odd joint just in case. Either way, from what was still in your system, you'd be raving your head off, ranting maniacally about the nature of the universe, or the coagulants of the variable dioxins within the nature of the crysosis, that generates the sekonix, that turns the shnabble driving the crash malik through the bandeye or something equally as important to the future of mankind. Ranting like a rabid bat to anyone who'd listen, and even if they wouldn't. Anyhow, with some rest, a massive dinner of vegetables . . . Oh, we were vegetarians. Meat-eating was a disgusting, unhealthy habit that definitely polluted the mind and body and shortened the life span, maaan. Hey hey. Then several cleansing ales, a couple of joints of Buddha, and Baabaaboom!—we were well and truly fitted up for another night of insanity at the three gigs we'd be playing that Sunday night. Such was life around the clock, week after week at Aztec Manor. Life was rocking its tits off!

Money was no problem. We were dead broke. No problem. Fuck money. Money was the 'tool of the devil', 'root of all evil, maann' and all that shit. The logic may have been a residue of the hippie dripping shit so many of us had been spouting, but the sentiment was absolutely pure. We lived to play music and in between got ripped to the gills and actually talked to each other. Communicated with each other. The dope broke down all the barriers and opened up the libido and people got to one another at a level that mattered. No matter if it seemed to the outside world like a bunch of whacked-out degenerate, long-haired hippie musos. Fuck the outside world. This was the only world. Music was the world. Gigging every night of the week and getting people off was the world. The crowds felt it every night in the energy and uninhibited force that came from the bands. No hype. Pure put your arse on the line jamming, rocking, kick-arse rock and blues. Good or bad we all meant it and the audiences knew and respected us for it. The atmosphere, attitudes and fashion of these young Melbourne audiences, although reflective of what was happening in the UK, had their own flavours and styles. They weren't a copy of something from overseas. We had moved on into new things and it was once again happening in Australia, simultaneously for the same reasons. It was all new. Experimental. Fresh. And a far cry from the boring sameness of the reality of the pop schlock that television and radio was trying to sell, and a far cry too from the daily grind of Bob and Joan's unreality of the 'real world'.

For musicians and music fans, these were real times. Times worth writing about nearly thirty years later. The kind of times I'd heard about when jazz and blues were taking shape in the bars, barrelhouses, honky-tonks and juke joints of Mississippi, Chicago or New York. The great escape. People were digging music for the right reasons. Because it was fresh, an outlet, and invigorating, and for a few hours a night we were totally free. They flew wherever we flew. Sometimes we all crashed and burned, but at least we tried to fly. There was a definite tangible scene taking shape. Not some hype-induced product of some trend-oriented promotion company arse-wipe's imagination. This was happening for real and we all knew it. Dozens of great bands. A community of young, original, talented, like-minded creative individuals who lived and breathed the music. An extended family who for the most part were real good friends. We shared digs, gigs, women, and everything in between. Nothing was sacred and no social mores were safe.

The sense of 'US' was once again undeniable. That same vibe I'd witnessed back at Surf City in 1964, in what seemed like another life, was happening all over again. Back then the first Billy Thorpe and the Aztecs had racked up six top 10 hits between June 1964 and June 1965. The second line-up, another five top 10 hits by September 1966. That's eleven top 10 hits in two years. Not a bad run, all things considered. You know . . . things like the Beatles and Stones and about fifty other heavyweight overseas acts hitting the radio every other week. Even then we were thought of as just 'local talent', which for the most part was regarded as inferior to anything from overseas. Ain't too easy being a local in an international world. In 1969 there was still a giant void between the Australian music industry's and the media's perception of the standard, value and relevance of international and local talent, but the Melbourne music fans didn't give a shit about it. This was their music. By their undying support they helped create it, and that same interactive energy and need that had spawned so much creativity and the unstoppable force of change back in the early '60s was happening all over again.

The baby boomers were on the move again. Same demographic, different time. Five years later. No longer teens. Early to mid twenties for the most part. Been there, done a bit. Felt the boot in the balls and the pleasures of life for ourselves. Entitled to be individuals. Earned the right. Tastes and imaginations well honed. 'To hell with Vietnam, national service, America,' said we. 'This is not our bloody war. Stay the hell out of it! To hell with the domino theory, a job, money, sleep, coppers, popular opinion, right, wrong. Back to the nitty-gritty! It's my party and I'll die if I want to!'

Quiet, historic, prim, puritanical old Melbourne town, with its self-proclaimed image as the classical and cultural centre of the universe, was being violated every night of the week. Dr Shakin' J. Feelgood had taken over, and there was nothing anybody could do about it. Pure force of numbers. In the old converted granaries, warehouses and livery stables that dated back to original settlement, and in what had been the gentlemen's clubs, bars and pubs of the '20s that had become home to the Melbourne blues and rock scene, silent, lonely spirits sentenced long ago to walk the chain-clanging walk of the restless dearly departed eagerly awaited each new night's lunacy to commence. To be young and alive again. To join the dance of life. To wail and scream unfettered and unnoticed in the company of mods, sharpies, skinheads, rockers, acid heads and maniacs who now inhabited their once lonely domains from sundown till dawn. Melbourne was an eclectically original melting pot of fashion and style and the undisputed centre of Australian original popular culture. It was undeniable. Unfortunately the rest of the country had no idea it was happening and just ambled along in their ignorant bliss, listening to or watching the pabulum that TV and radio spewed out as popular Australian culture.

I lay there in Bellevue thinking about it all. What had brought me to Melbourne for two weeks before going to England. And why I'd stayed. I relived it all. That piece fits there and that piece . . . The room was almost dark. I figured it was some time in the early a.m. I looked over and the morpheeno brothers were snoring like a pair of chainsaws. My arm throbbed and an excruciating pain shot through me every time I moved. *Screw* the pain. No-one had come in in a while and there was no way I was going to call for a shot. This was the first real lucid moment I'd had. A dull green glow pulsed from the monitor to my right. Faint red neon licked the walls, slid like electric teardrops down an oily window and kissed my face. No movement. The steady beep, beep, beep of my monitor. As the neon continued its robotic dance the sound of the monitor became hypnotic. My mind started to ramble. Wander. Idly kicking a battered tin can along an endless windy beach.

11
Canberra Rocks

inding out how I came to be in a ward at the Bellevue Mental Hospital for the Criminally Insane didn't change the fact that I was locked in a nuthouse and couldn't get out. It did, however, help take a little edge off the absolute psychological helplessness of my situation. At least I knew how I got there, but it didn't help overcome the shock of coming so close to biting the big one. It would be a while before I came to terms with that. I hadn't thought to ask how bad my arm was. I remembered how much it had hurt when I broke it, and it was in plaster from my shoulder to my hand, so I figured I hadn't just broken a bloody fingernail. I also knew that my body throbbed from my shoulder to my big toe when the morphine wore off. I definitely needed something for the pain, but surely something like codeine would have done the trick. I wasn't going to argue with Bertha about medication to keep me calm for my heart's sake, but I was starting to sweat between shots and knew only too well I'd be scratching like a twenty dollar whore when I came off it. If I got out of there on Tuesday that still meant I'd be on over seventy-two hours of continual shots of morphine. That was more than enough time to get me a sniffling, body-scratching, marrow-aching Jones that would take more than a couple of coffees and a hot shower to shake. I had the permanent dries. My tongue felt like the felt on a pool table in some outback beer garden. I downed bottle after bottle of water only to piss it back into a banana-shaped stainless steel bottle. And that isn't real easy with a plaster cast from hand to shoulder. Especially when you're as whacked as a maggot. A couple of times Bertha had to hold the bottle for me and I felt like a helpless three-year-old going pee-pee.

The lights were still off when I woke. I still had no idea of the time. No idea what day it was. Was it yesterday that Bertha told me I'd died? Or the day before? Dead! Holy shit, did that really happen? One look at the green beep, beep, beep, beep on the monitor screen beside me answered that question quick smart. I tried to put some order to the events but couldn't rationalise. I took in the room. The wall-to-wall iron barred windows. Some other guard I hadn't seen before sat in Idi's chair. Riot gun on his lap. The two murdering rapists were still snoring like a Spitfire and Messerschmitt in a dogfight. Diving and climbing in a steady buzzing rev of their nasal engines. An occasional burst of machine gun fire from the backs of their claggy throats. Apart from the beep, beep, beep from my heart monitor, and the Battle of Britain taking place opposite me, the only other sounds were a faint ocean breaking through the air duct on the ceiling that I hadn't noticed before and the occasional haunting bark of a car horn speeding by and echoing through the window from the streets below. The red neon continued to pulse a slow 'Come and get it' . . . off, 'Come and get it' . . . off from somewhere outside, slapping the walls and ceiling with the back of a giant magenta hand in a rhythmic slap, ouch . . . slap, ouch. Morpheus was back in control.

I didn't remember it, but somebody must have shot me up while I slept because I was zonked again. I tried to move my hand. It was heavy, thick, seemed to push the surrounding air clumsily aside. Slow motion. My jaw itched and when I raised my hand to scratch it I saw my arm come slowly up and touch my face but I couldn't feel anything. My head was playing games with itself. The itch psychosomatic like an amputee still feeling the itch in a leg that's gone. My legs! I couldn't feel my legs. *Oh shit!* Oh, they're still there. Christ, I thought for a minute they were gone! Ah, the demon Morpheus. It was a bizarre feeling. A bit like opium only more of a chemical buzz. More metallic tasting. Less colourful. But the fog was just as thick. I'd smoked opium in a den in Macau in the late '60s. Spent a day and a half there as a matter of fact. Bit like this drug experience except when the ancient looking Chinese amah stopped packing my dream pipe the stone eventually wore off. I straightened up and left. No such luck here. Even if they let me out now I'd have to be carried like a baby. Walking was so far out of the realm of my unreality it wasn't funny. Neither was this joint.

I felt like a helpless babe lying in my metal cot in Bellevue Mental Hospital, wired to a heart machine, waiting for Bertha to come feed me another hit of mumbling milk from her steel-tipped tit. No way out. Nothing to do but freak and dream. No connection to the world. No psychological bearings other than six old dogeared black-and-white snap-shots from different periods in my life. How did they come to be here? No idea. I reached over in the half-light from the corridor, almost dropping the photographs from a numb, throbbing hand which felt like a twelve-inch-thick pingpong bat on the end of a 200 pound rubber arm. I looked at them, not sure of who the morphine faces were that grinned back at me across a million years. I didn't realise it but many of the significant changes I had gone through were in one way or another right there in my hand. Who *are* these people? My brain tried to put names to faces and picture the circumstances in which they were taken. Let's see . . . This one is of Lobby, and . . . Paul and . . . that's Jimmy Thompson and me . . . and who are those huge guys in the background? The look like coppers. *Cops?* When *was* that? Jimmy was still on drums. Must be 1969. Maybe '70. Where was that taken? I *know* that place. Come on, think! Canberra? . . . No not Canberra . . . that little joint near there? . . . Queanbeyan, that's *right*. Fuck I'd forgotten all about that. Jesus, we were nearly killed!

'Roll another joint . . .' the battle cry echoed again from somewhere deep down in the murky depths of the back seat. In a sturdy Bedford dual-wheel beast packed to the gills with band gear, six merry travellers sit mesmerised by the world flashing by in two hypnotic, solid, unbroken, parallel lines of greens, yellows, reds and browns. The upper branches of giant ironbarks that have stood guard, bemused by the antics of generations of travellers on this highway since the long trek south in the gold rush of the 1850s, swayed high above our heads in the light wind. Refracted sunlight from magic flame trees shines like fire in the morning sun as they dance seductively past. Heads buzz, minds fly, enthralled by the ever-changing visuals being channelled to grey matter through highly tampered visual receptors. We're stoned as wombats.

Much cheering followed the heralded arrival of a new batch of Thai Buddha sticks into the little house in Gipps Street, East Melbourne, the morning of our departure. For a time six forlorn, tormented souls sat with furrowed brows and heavy hearts, incredulously contemplating . . . Oh God, it doesn't bear thinking about . . . Far too horrible . . . Contemplating having to make the 350 mile drive from Melbourne to Canberra. Ooh it's painful to say it . . . Straaaight! But once again the Gods have favoured our gallant cause. Justice has prevailed and the righteous survived.

It was a glorious, crisp, sunny spring day in September 1969. The countryside glowed with the unparalleled and divinely inspired beauty of nature just being herself. No Dobell, Gainsborough or Van Gogh can touch her. Surely we had been put there at that time and moment simply to witness and admire. To give lasting testimony to the unique power and majesty of the extraordinary Australian bush as it unfolded before us with every mile. A van load of happy pranksters on yet another rock 'n' roll adventure.

The band had formed in December 1968 when Lobby Loyde joined Paul Wheeler, Jimmy Thompson and myself and we had clicked. In less than six months we were one of the top draws around Melbourne and we were picking up new fans and gigs as the weeks went by. It was firing. Every week we played, the crowds grew by another hundred. It was obvious to all that something special was in the making. A couple of times over the past four months we'd been playing this regular gig in Canberra at the rather swank for its day Canberra Park Royal Hotel. The Young

Qantas Club had a regular monthly booking for the Park Royal ballroom on Saturday nights. Various bands performed for the airline club which consisted of about 1500 Canberra yuppies. It was a very different audience from the suburban kids who filled the Melbourne clubs night after night and the fact that they loved our music gave us more confidence in the fact that we were onto something with more potential than just local club appeal. It was a fairly upmarket, fully licensed affair, with many of the punters decked out in suits and ties or evening dresses. But the response had been great and they instantly embraced our new brand of balls to the wall rock. They loved having this bunch of long-haired rockers playing for them, and as a result we found ourselves in Canberra roughly every six weeks, enjoying the hospitality of the hotel for the weekend, and all on Qantas. It was a gig from heaven. A thousand happy punters, great money, all the food and Scotch we could consume, all gratis, and we always looked forward to the booking.

Darryl Cavanaugh, our roadie at that time, arrived at Gipps Street around 7 a.m. with the old Bedford van packed with our stage gear, and at 7.30 we hit the highway. This trip we had also been booked to play in Sydney the following week at the Here disco on the North Shore, which was another favourite of ours. The last couple of times we'd played there we'd sold it out.

This trip turned out to be the start of the first significant period for the band. We were booked solid over the next few months and recorded our first ever single. It was a crowd favourite, 'Rock Me Baby', with 'Good Morning Little School Girl' as the B side. The band was starting to get national recognition and we slowly began making inroads in other states. Just over two months later, in January 1970, we headlined our first major event at Australia's first outdoor rock festival, the Pilgrimage of Pop at Ourimbah, which is approximately an hour north of Sydney on the way to Newcastle. Also on that bill were Tully, Leo and Friends, and Chain. The festival was run by a bunch of genuine California hippies who had a band called the Nutwood Rug and the festival site was on their farm. Theirs was *the* genuine California acid, blues rock sound and we'd played quite a few gigs together. These guys were living the dream in their little piece of paradise, miles from anywhere in 1969. We got into more than our fair share of the heinous goods, but Nutwood Rug's consumption of acid and smoke made us look like amateurs. Christ, they had come halfway around the world and bought a farm just to be left in peace to get high to their hearts' content. They loved us and had invited us to headline their festival, which we knew would be a blast.

The drive to Canberra was uneventful. Oh, lots of the usual farting, swearing and laughter to whittle away the miles, and as usual on long trips—or even a trip to the corner store—we fired up a few joints, opened some cans of Coke, filled them with Dimple Haig and, sound system blaring the blues, we blitzed our way across country in grand rock 'n' roll style, stopping only for a leak, a quick graze or an ice-cold draught beer or three in some country pub with the sweetest pipes on the planet. I loved the road and the unfettered freedom of racing off to some far-off destination to play a night of blistering music to enthusiastic crowds of fans. There's a sense of freedom to that gipsy lifestyle unequalled by any other in my experience. Especially when you get to do it across a country as big, ballsy and beautiful as Australia. To me, that's what being a musician is really all about. Not the accolades, money and fame, but the blood and guts of being a player. That's all it's ever been for me. Music and the people. The blues were starting to pick up new enthusiastic fans outside of Melbourne and we found the punters who had liked us the time before inevitably brought along several new friends the next time, and on and up it went.

We arrived in Canberra about 5 p.m. and headed straight to the Park Royal. Darryl and I went to check us in and Annette the bleached blonde front-desk spunk, who had given more than the room key to the odd band member, greeted us with, 'What are you guys doing here?' We looked at each other, then at her.

'We're here for the gig tonight. It is tonight, isn't it?' I asked, thrown a little by her question.

'Oh yeah,' she replied, 'but there's been a bit of a screw-up with the ballroom this month. It was double-booked and the Qantas Club is having the do somewhere outside Queanbeyan. Didn't you know?'

Somewhere out of Queanbeyan! I thought. Where the hell around Queanbeyan are they going to have a gig that holds more than a thousand people? Queanbeyan in 1969 was a farming, horse-racing and training town some ten miles south-east of Canberra. Apart from the odd local dance, about the only thing that happened there on a Saturday night was sheep-fucking, dick-measuring and bar fights. And that was on a big night! But if that's where the gig is then what the hell! The Qantas Club had always been super-organised and there was no reason to suspect tonight would be any different. Annette wiggled her tight little bum, gave me a suggestive flutter of her eyelashes with the directions, and off headed the happy pranksters to sunny downtown Queanbeyan.

We drove around Queanbeyan for about half an hour trying to find the gig until we'd had enough of 'It's that way' . . . 'No it's not it's that way' . . . so we pulled into a service station to ask the locals. Everybody in a country town would know where the big gig was at. Sure enough, as soon as I got out of the van a couple of big country cockies who looked like they were on a break from tractor trailer tossing, came rambling over to me, stubbies in hand.

"'S Thorpie isn't it?' one asked.

'Yes it is, mate. Do you know where we're playing tonight?'

'Mate, they got you in a fuckin' shearing shed 'bout twenty fuckin' miles from here. Just go through the fuckin' town fer about five fuckin' miles and follow the fuckin' highway out of fuckin' town. About fifteen more fuckin' miles you'll come to a fuckin' left turn. There's only one fuckin' turn on the whole fuckin' road fer twenty fuckin' miles, so yer can't fuckin' miss it. Take that fer about a fuckin' mile and yer can't fuckin' miss the bastard.'

'Thanks mate. Much obliged. You and your mate coming tonight or what?'

'Aw,' the other one answered, 'those flamin' Qantas Club bastards from flamin' Canberra aren't letting any of the flamin' locals in. Me an me mates tried to buy some flamin' tickets this arvo, but they told us that it's a flamin' private do for flamin' members only.'

'Thats a bit rough, mate. Sorry about that. We don't have any say in it. See you next time then, and thanks again,' I said shaking their hands.

'No fuckin' worries, Thorpie. We'll see yous tonight

anyhow. Fuck those fuckin' Canberra fuckin' debutante poofters. It's not their fuckin' town. Me an' me mates are going down the fuckin' pub fer a few, then we'll fuckin' head over fer a fuckin' listen. They'll need a fuckin' army to keep us fuckin' mob out.'

Oh boy, I thought.

About forty-five minutes later we turned down the dirt track to the 'fuckin' shearing shed' and five minutes later we were banging, bumping and 'oh shitting' our way across a field to a group of battered-looking wooden buildings. It wasn't the fact that this normally upscale gig was taking place in an old, wooden shearing shed with no stage, which meant we had to set up on the floor, that bothered us. This wasn't the first time. It was more the stench of the stale sheep shit that some local lads were scraping off the floor, sweeping into piles and tossing out the window that was the bummer. The joint reeked worse than a Bombay shitter. This was about as far as you could get from the elegant, well-appointed ballroom at the Park Royal. But a gig's a gig and we made our way around the piles of sheep shit and set our gear up in the corner where the power cords hung from the walls like vines. Maybe a hundred feet wide by sixty feet deep. No ceiling or lined walls. Open beams under a grey cantilevered corrugated-iron roof. Bare untreated timber walls with rough studs that stuck out like the rib cage of a rusting whale. Shit-caked timber floor cut and scraped by the hooves of a million terrified animals. One door at each end with another door behind the stage area that probably led to the holding pens.

Darryl and Pete did their best to create a stage area against the back door. The local lighting guy had set a couple of rows of spots to the left and right of it and once the gear was up it looked like a stage. We were almost finished doing a raging sound check when in waltzed six of the biggest coppers I've ever seen. They looked like the combined front row of Manly and St George on stilts. They strode straight over to us, blinking furiously with their hands over their ears, and the biggest one, a six foot six, 280 pound, barrel-chested curly-headed blond bull of a copper screamed, 'Qviet pleaze. Qvieettt!' gesturing wildly with his hands for us to stop playing.

'Jeezus Chritszt dat ist blooty loudt,' he yelled, tilting his head and patting his ear with his hand like he had water in it. The other coppers did the same. 'Ve hert ju a blooty mile avay! Ju always play dat lout?' I felt like saying, 'That wasn't loud, mate. Wait till it fires up tonight' but nobody said a word. 'Vitch vun ist Billy Torpe?' We all looked at each other and fought back a big laugh. He sounded exactly like Colonel Schultz from 'Hogan's Heroes'.

'Er . . . I am,' I answered nervously.

Now I've always gotten on famously well with coppers. They've always treated me with the utmost respect. It was always a sort of comedy show with the police and me. It reminded me of the Road Runner cartoon where Ralph the Sheep Dog and the Coyote walk together to work, lunch pails in hand, chatting happily about the weather. Then the whistle blows and the game's on! It was like that with the police. When I was being arrested or on the way to the nick, it was always 'Sorry to have to do this, Thorpie, but me sergeant's got a bee up 'is arse about yer' or 'The last time I saw you was at some show or another with me missus. You were bloody great.' Polite and friendly as you please. Then as soon as we got to the station the same coppers were all 'the party of the first part in the first instance' and much serious officious formality. Even when they were locking me up for obscene language with such regularity that I thought there must have been some sort of contest to see who can lock Thorpie up the most times in a week, there was obviously no real problem. Just misdemeanour stuff. Bloody annoying, that's all. The problem here was it was 1969 and we were holding big time. I had a block of hash the size of half a Cadbury's bar of fruit 'n' nut in my pocket, and when I looked around I could tell by the strained look on Lobby's face that he was trying his level best to mentally suck the block he had in his right through his jeans and up his arse without the coppers noticing.

'I am Schultz. Sergeant Alfie Shultz, but du can calls me Alf. Ve are de security fer der nacht.'

It *was* Colonel Schultz! All of a sudden the band got really busy rerolling leads and slipped off one by one, leaving me half-ripped, dick in hand, in the middle of the Queanbeyan police force, with a block of hash that would have gotten me two years in the nick back then.

'Pleased to meet you, Alf,' I shook his hand. 'Ermm . . . So, had many shows up this way?'

'Ach, not for a vile. Ser last vos ein contry and vestern show and zum locals tries to get into free, unt ve hat to close ert down. Beent noboty play 'ere in six monts. Zee only reason zis is tonacht is ze Qvantas Club donate five hundret dollar to local polize fund und dey pay us to look after tings.'

'Oh great,' I said, knowing the answer before I asked the next question. 'Do you expect any trouble tonight?'

'Oh jah. Der alvase zum trouble vis booze, but it vill be goot. Zis ist un priveat turn . . . Don't vorry, ve take care off ju.'

'What kind of trouble?' I asked.

'Vell, der lokal boyz are pizzed dye don't get in and dere's verd zey come out anyvay. But ve handle dem OK.'

'OK. Look, we can handle ourselves too, Alf. But keep an eye on us. I don't want the gear trashed.'

'Ve be shveet, Billy. Don't vorry non. Listen, I lak ju ter meet der boyz 'ere. Billy zis Bob, Ken, Ralphy, Charly unt Gazza. Zey know zere vay around a shtink too. You in goot hants.'

'Pleased to meet you,' I said, shaking hands with about a ton of six foot six inch grinning, solid country beef.

I could see these boys were the real thing. Big, friendly country coppers who were as tough as they looked. These blokes were big ole farm boys. No bullshit here. They looked like they each ate a steer and a gross of eggs for breakfast, washed it down with a keg of beer, then ran to work towing the car with their teeth just to help the digestion. Each of their hands was the size of both of mine together and a couple of the hand shakes rattled my balls and made my teeth ache. I vos in goot hants, all right. Alf took us out back to a caravan that had been set up for our dressing-room and we waited as the punters rolled up for the big night in Queanbeyan. I told the guys what Alf had told me and nobody was particularly fazed. We'd seen plenty of trouble before, our crew could go like thrashing machines and we'd never found ourselves in the middle of anything that we couldn't get out of. One of the organisers brought some hamburgers, Scotch, Coke and beer and we settled in to wait for the crowd to turn up. Carloads of people began arriving and by 8 o'clock the gig was starting to rock inside. The place was packed with about a thousand upscale Canberra yuppies and they were already laughing and dancing to the sounds of 'Honky Tonk Women', 'Polk Salad Annie', 'Spinning Wheel' and other current favourites that were pumping through the PA system.

When we entered for our first of five forty-five minutes sets that night, a huge cheer went up. We made our way through the shoulder to shoulder crowd getting the usual 'G'day Thorpies' and 'On yas' as we passed. The same thing was happening that had happened with the original Aztecs. The crowds were starting to consider us as mates. Many of them had seen us so many times that we knew them by sight and sometimes by name. A personal relationship beyond band and audience was starting to develop, just like at Surf City. Some nights during breaks we would hang out with the crowd and wherever we played lately it seemed like the first six rows were old mates.

The lack of a stage made things a little weird, because at five feet eight all I could see was the first row and the heads of some of the taller punters around the room. But they didn't seem to care and they began clapping and yelling enthusiastically for the night to begin. I went over to the mike and yelled, 'So how are ya?'

'Great' . . . 'Bloody oath' . . . 'Let's bloody rock', came back the enthusiastic replies.

'Well the Park Royal has seen better days,' I laughed and the crowd laughed with me. This Qantas Club crowd were always right with us, and shearing shed or not, it was obvious from the vibe that we were in for a great night. 'So what do you want to hear?'

'Rock Me Baby' . . . 'Be Bop A-Lula' . . . 'Momma' . . . 'Gangster of Love' . . . 'Granny's Got the Biggest Flaps in Town' came the shouts back. No kidding, we had named an instrumental by that last memorable moniker.

I counted in 'Rock Me Baby' and off we went. The first set ran like clockwork. The shearing shed started to feel like a million dollar club and it was rocking by the time we took our break. I knew we had them for the rest of the night. The band had started to hit its stride since Lobby joined back in December. We'd spent a year mainly in the Melbourne clubs honing, refining and redefining our style and it had developed into a fresh, high-energy, original style and sound. There was an undeniably new power to the music, and an energy that none of us had ever experienced before. The trio with Paul, Jimmy and me had been a fantastic experience and very popular, but playing three-piece, my singing had been restricted a lot by having to play guitar all the time. But with Lobby's knowledge and experience in the blues, his phenomenal arsenal of technique, powerhouse chording and soaring melodic driven solos, songs that we'd played as a trio took on a new life, meaning and energy.

The first set ended with enthusiastic cries of 'More... More' and we took a break. Alf and a couple of the boys came back to the caravan and assured us the music 'Vos too blotty lout, but zey luff you bastards and eet real goot.' We drank a few beers and after they left we snuck outside in the dark for a couple of sly joints while Darryl kept a lookout, then went back on for the second set. We were about halfway through the second song in mid wail and Vaawhoomp! The power went out, freaking everybody out because it went pitch dark. It's always freaky when you're in the middle of a great song and the vibe stops dead in its tracks. Particularly at a gig like this where all the power is tied to one line so that when it goes, everything goes off at the same time. Lights, PA and amps. One second you're soaring at 150 dB of head-splitting rock, then ... deafening silence and pitch black.

Nobody said a word for a second or two, then the inevitable mumbling from the crowd and the band. I had no PA so I cupped my hands and shouted, 'Everybody hang on. Don't move. It must be this shitty shearing shed's power. They'll change the fuse and—' Vaawhoomp . . . sizzle . . . squeeeell . . . feedbaaaackk! The power came back on, scaring the shit out of everybody a second time. I counted the song back in and we went right back into Lobby's solo at the point we left off. The crowd let out a mighty cheer and a minute later we were back rocking like nothing had happened . . .

Vaawhoomp! Off it went again. Total darkness. I was shouting something to the crowd when I heard a scuffle break out. Then the unmistakable sound of punches connecting and what sounded like a full-blown fight. The locals had obviously arrived and were the cause of the power cuts. They'd come to fuck the gig up and it was working. Except for the odd flicker from torch beams the whole place was pitch black and we just stood against the gear, waiting for what was going to happen next. I could hear punches connecting and girls screaming, but it sounded like it was coming from my right at the back of the shed. Then I felt somebody next to me and heard 'Whaaackk. Urgghh. Crash! Someone had decked Lobby, who had been standing to my left facing the crowd. I heard him fall and hit his amp. I turned, straining through the dark to see what was happening and got smashed in the shoulder by a full-on punch which sent me back into the drum kit with a loud cymbal crash but didn't knock me down. Somebody was king-hitting us and luckily for me they'd missed my face and caught me in the shoulder. I pulled myself out of the drum kit and Caarashhh!

'You bastards,' Jimmy yelled from behind me and the drums went over. I heard Jimmy wrestling with someone on the floor behind the kit.

I couldn't see a thing but the noise was enough. People were screaming at the top of their lungs and the fight had started to spread into a ripper. Then Smaaack! right in the mouth and down I went. A torch beam hit me in the face and Darryl and Frank picked me up, torches in hand. In the dim light I saw that the stage area was surrounded by pissed-rotten farm boys, all hell-bent on a Saturdee night fight and breaking as many Qantas Club heads as they could in the bargain. It was easy to pick them by the way they were dressed. A big frame came up behind Darryl with a mike stand in its hand. I grabbed Darryl's torch off him and shone it in the big mug's face. I couldn't believe it. It was one of the blokes who'd given me directions at the service station in Queanbeyan. Just as he was about to hit Darryl, I swung the steel-cased torch over Darryl's head and hit the big bludger on the jaw as hard as I could. He went backward over the drums and I heard Jimmy laying into him as he went crashing through the drum kit. Someone grabbed me from behind and I swung the big heavy metal torch over the top of my head as hard as I could with both hands. It connected with a dull wet thud as bones and flesh parted company and whoever it was let go with a scream, collapsing behind me. I spun around, shone the torch down into a dazed face. It was the other guy from the service station. *Jesus, what the hell did we do to offend these bastards?* I wondered. Blood streamed from a deep gash in his forehead and he looked up at me like a helpless dog that's about to be shot. I lifted the torch as high over my head as I could and brought it down on the exact spot I'd hit him before. He grabbed at the torch as it came down and the force of the blow broke his fingers and went through them to catch him on the right collarbone with a loud crack as it broke. Darryl came from behind and smashed him with a crashing downward right hook to the side of the face. The guy was out before he dropped.

Lobby had his guitar by the neck and I could hear Whooosh, Urgghh, Whooshhh as he laid it upside any head he could reach. Lobby was normally a very gentle, quiet bloke, but he'd grown up with a hard crowd in Brisbane and could go with the best of them. In the torchlight I caught a maniacal gleam in his eye just as twenty pounds of solid Fender Jaguar guitar bounced a perfectly tuned unamplified E chord right off some poor bastard's head.

The coppers were nowhere in sight and we were in the middle of a hard-core brawl in the dark, trying to keep from being king-hit and protecting our gear at the same time. We were being grabbed and hit at from every direction and in a way the dark was helping because we had the torches and they couldn't see us. I think we all had the 'bugger the gear, this is dangerous' thought at the same time because Paul grabbed my arm, I grabbed Lobby by his, Lobby grabbed hold of Jimmy and we sort of dragged and stumbled our way through the dark, heading for the nearest wall. I was swinging the torch with my left hand and it connected a couple of times. I have no idea who I hit but this was getting dangerous. There was no time for 'Excuse me, are you on our side, sir?'

We had almost reached the wall when a number of guys jumped on us, breaking my grip. I heard Lobby belt some guy behind me and when I shone the torch ahead I saw little Jimmy hanging off another's back, riding him like a

mule and belting him around the face from behind . . .
Then a pair of big arms pinned my arms to my sides from
behind and somebody stared doing speedball practice on
my upper body from the front. I couldn't get loose and the
torch dropped to the floor. I was helpless. Whoever they
were they were big and the guy behind shouted in a
drunken voice, 'This'll teach you bastards to play for them
poofters!'

For a second my mind flashed back to Surf City five
years before when Mulatto Mick and his boys and about
500 people, including the original Aztecs, had been in an
epic John Wayne sized brawl that ended up with Tony Barber in hospital for six weeks. This time I was the one getting
the hiding. I was seeing stars every time a punch landed and
the pain of the blows was starting to dull. I just hung there
between two unseen thugs taking one hit after another to
my body, and one or two to the face. I'd tucked my chin in
close to my chest and weaved my head, which was the only
thing I could move. I tried leg sweeping the big bludger
behind me but his feet were set as firmly as the pylons
under the Sydney Harbour Bridge. Luckily it was pitch
black and whoever was delivering my hiding couldn't see
me either. He was just throwing haymakers in the dark and
catching me on top of the head, on the forehead, shoulder,
wherever the punches happened to land. I was just about
out when I felt the grip around me loosen. Torch beams
converged around me and I heard the unmistakable sound
of bones breaking. The next second my feet were three feet
off the ground and somebody was carrying me upright
from behind and pushing me through the brawling melee.

'Hank on Billy. Ju be OK,' shouted the voice from
behind. 'It Alf unt Charly.'

The cavalry had arrived.

Alf got me over to the side of the room and the next minute I was flying through the air . . . 'Arrgghh fuuuck!' Spaloosh, I landed outside in the fucking trough full of stinking sheep shit. I was trying to get it out of my mouth and eyes and—'Arrhh shit', thud, then 'Holy shiiiitt', spalosh!—Paul and Lobbs landed beside me. It was pitch black and the container we were in was at least five feet at the sides. It stunk like the Hulk's jockstrap and we were all trying hard not to throw up. We clambered out over the sides and I split the arse of my jeans in the flurry of elbows and arseholes. We sprinted around the front of the building just in time to see Alf carry Jimmy out and shoot straight back inside.

'Jesus, you guys stink. Somebody shit themselves in there or what?' laughed Jimmy.

'Ah, get fucked,' we all said, trying to brush the damp sheep shit off our clothes, faces and hair.

A lot of people had left the shed and some were already screaming off in their cars, but inside the brawl was growing and the screams were sounding more desperate. Young blokes, couples and hysterical young girls were falling out the door and down the steps beside us. It was like a fire had erupted inside and they were fighting their way out for their lives. It was pandemonium and just as dark outside as inside the hall.

All I could hear was the sound of screaming and things being smashed, which I guessed was our gear. Then Spriiizzzttt! Crackle! Buuuzzzz, Hummm . . . the power suddenly came back on. Screaming yahoos came crashing out of windows and through the door like somebody had yelled free grog outside. Some were being helped by their mates and I caught sight of the prick whose head I'd split with the torch. He was a mess. 'You're fuckin' gone, Thorpie,' his mate yelled as they ran past. Before Alf or any of the other coppers could get to them the cowards were in their cars and off into the night in a squeal of burning rubber and dust. Gone!

People clambered over one another to get out the door. Some were trampled in the press and others flung themselves out the tiny windows, landing on their faces on the damp grass below. Some of them, male and female, had obviously taken a belting. Evening gowns were ripped off to the waist. Some of the guys were covered in blood, shoeless and shirtless. All were hysterically shouting and screaming. It was like a war zone. Now we were miles from butt-fuck nowhere. No chance of ambulances arriving at any minute or police reinforcements here. This was a bush dance and Alf unt der boyz ver it! Christ, if the power hadn't come back on when it did, God knows what would have happened.

Slowly the screaming, swearing and crying started to subside and an eerie quiet came over the scene. A pregnant silver moon fell from behind huge nimbus clouds, casting a melancholic glow across the sky, lighting the old shearing shed and surrounding paddocks of outer Queanbeyan with a magic worthy of a Hollywood movie. A few groups of young guys got their courage together and jumped into their cars with shouts of 'Let's get the bastards' and 'We'll kill 'em' and similar bravado, but the thugs were long gone. Probably sitting in a barn somewhere by now. Drinking a few cool ones and laughing their drunken arses off over the heads they'd split. Licking their wounds and buggering a few sheep just to put an edge on their big night out. The low mongrels.

Then all was quiet. Eerily quiet. Just gentle sobs from young girls and the whispers of lovers consoling each other in the open air. One by one people started to drift away. Couples hugged and half carried each other to their cars, and in what seemed like seconds, the band, Alf and der boyz and the totally freaked-out young promoters were the only ones left. We all got into the caravan.

'Jesuz, ju boyz shtink bad,' was the first thing Alf said. 'What da fuck happen?'

'You threw us out the fucking window into the sheep trough, you crazy bastard,' I laughed.

Alf looked at us for a moment scratching his head. 'No shit,' he laughed.

'No Alf, lots of fucking shit. That's vy ve shtink, you dopey big prick.'

'No shit,' he said.

'No Alf, lots of fucking shit.' I laughed, rubbing it out of my hair. Everybody broke up and it cleared the bad vibe in a flash.

We got cleaned up and I changed my pants. Then we mixed some drinks and the usual after-fight post-mortem took place. Alf said he recognised a couple of the mugs who'd started it. Apparently they weren't locals after all. From Queensland, he seemed to think. Just in Queanbeyan looking for work. Anyhow, he was going to nab them first thing in the morning and it wouldn't be a polite lecture they'd be getting from Alf and his mates. These blokes would be lucky if they didn't end up back in Brissy with their heads torn off at the waist and rammed permanently up their arses. Alf was 'Pizzed richt orf' and we weren't that bloody jubilant ourselves. Christ, an eight-hour drive, all the gear wrecked and a kicking for the pleasure. Ah, there's no bidness like show bidness! I'd like to strangle the prick who wrote that. He'd obviously never played to a brawling crowd in the dark in a shit-stinking shearing shed.

We checked ourselves out and none of us were badly hurt. My back felt like I'd been run over by a train, I had some bruising around my eyes and a badly split lip, but nothing serious. Lobbs had a ripper of a black eye, Jimmy a couple of bruised ribs and Paul had a big stoned smile on his silly face. Darryl and Peter came out to see if we were OK. They loved a stink and by their faces we could tell they'd been belting mugs to their hearts' content. Neither of them had a scratch on them. They told us that some of the drums had been destroyed and the cymbal stands were bent in the shape of Queensland heads and beyond repair. The amps had gone over but they were OK. Luckily the boys had retrieved the guitars. The promoter came good and, apologising profusely like it was his fault, paid me in cash for the night. We waited until the crew packed the van, said our goodbyes to Alf and the boys, and hit the road for Canberra about 11.30 p.m.

The van was electric. There's nothing like a stink to get the buzz going and we went through the usual 'Did ya see that' . . . 'What about when that guy this . . .' and before long it was another rock 'n' roll memory. Just another rock 'n' roll night.

We were cruising along at about 80 mph, about twenty minutes out of Canberra, laughing and joking about it all, when a car came hurtling out of the dark in front and straight at us. Darryl pulled the van to the left and the car shot past us at about 90 mph, missing us by no more than a couple of inches. Another pulled out of nowhere from the opposite side of the road and got in behind us. The car that had come straight at us did a wheelie and shot past the passenger side. Smaaash! . . . a bottle smashed through the passenger-side window. The window shattered and Jimmy's face was cut by flying beer bottle and window glass. I was sitting in the back, directly behind him, but I saw the bottle coming. I ducked and covered my face and the shattered glass hit my arms without cutting me. One of the cars locked in in front of us about three inches from our front bumper, trying to slow us down. Darryl was fighting the wheel, trying to avoid it, when the rear car came along my side. The moon cleared the clouds for a second and in that silver instant I saw the unmistakable glint from a gun barrel sticking out of the window not two feet from my face.

'Look out!' I yelled. 'They've got a gun.'

Darryl slammed on the brakes and the car shot past us then, bang! . . . bang! . . . two shots split the air but missed and went over the top of the van. I'd grown up in Queensland and spent quite a bit of time around Stanthorpe as a kid. I'd been around and handled quite a few guns from handguns to big-bore rifles. No mistaking the sound I'd just heard. It was a .303 rifle. These boys weren't fucking around. A .303 bullet can tear half your arm off at that range. The car sped past and fell in beside the other car, blocking the road ahead. That was it! Without any prompting Darryl flattened the van to full battle-cruiser speed and rear-ended the car to our left at about 80 miles an hour. The combined weight of the old Bedford van, all our gear and us, hit the back of the beaten-up FE Holden like a battering ram and it shot off the side of the road careening into a ditch. The rifle barrel came out the right rear window of the car in front and another barrage of bullets hit the air.

Lobby was sitting in the middle front between Jimmy

and Darryl and this time one of the shots had hit the target. It entered the lower front of the van in the grille, somehow missed the block and passed upward through the dash, missing Lobby's head by no more than half and inch before exiting through the roof just above my head. I heard the bloody thing whistle past my face. We all heard it, especially Lobbs. We all lost it and started screaming, 'Kill the bastards! Run the bastards off the road!' Darryl didn't need any prompting. He flattened the van and rear-ended the other car, sending it into a spin and off the road into the bush. We gunned past them and took off down the highway at about a hundred miles an hour. In about ten minutes the lights of Canberra became visible ahead and the gun-toting mugs seemed to have dropped off. Everybody was in shock, Jimmy was badly cut and Lobbs was really shaken.

We pulled into the centre of town at the roundabout with about two miles to go to the hotel. Lobby shouted, 'Hey Thorpie, aren't the Valentines playing at the Centrum tonight?'

'Yes mate, I think they are. Why?' I asked.

'Well, I don't feel like sitting in my room after that. Why don't we go and have a beer with Bon and Vince?'

Everybody thought that was a great idea and Darryl parked the van outside and ran in to see what the deal was.

The Valentines were a cabaret-style band out of Perth who became very popular around Melbourne in 1968–69. The band was fronted by two lead singers. One was Vince Lovegrove and the other, none other than the legendary Bon Scott. The Valentines were a sort of variety show band whose usual tonsorial adornments consisted of plumped hair with thick jaw-length sideburns topped off by orange tuxedos, frilly shirts with frilled cuffs, orange bow ties and white patent leather shoes. Get the picture? Bon and I had been good mates since we'd met in Perth in 1967. Although he fronted this variety show band he was a hard-case nutter and a rocker at heart. That's all he ever wanted to sing.

Bon was a massive fan of our band and came to gigs to hang and have a few beers whenever he could. Ours was the kind of balls to the wall rock that he really wanted to play and of course he eventually did. A few years later our manger Michael Browning started managing this young rock band, two of whom were the younger brothers of George Young from the Easybeats. They became known as AC/DC, Bon soon became their lead singer and a rock legend was born. AC/DC opened for us at a few gigs and we played on shows together a lot when they first started happening in Australia. Small world, ain't it?

Bon was a wiry little bugger who loved a smoke, a drink and a stink, so we got on famously from day one. The Valentines' roadie, Mick Christian, was an ex-butcher, boxer and as roadie-come-security he rarely went on the road without, amongst other things, a razor-sharp butcher's knife about twelve inches long and a gun. And Micky would fight the *Queen Mary* when he was on speed, and Mick was always on speed. But I have to say, like most of the streetwise heavy blokes I knew at that time, Mick was a good bloke. He was staunch and would do anything to help a mate and we were all good mates.

'I'll run in and see if it's happening. You guys hang here. I'll only be a sec,' Darryl said. He jumped out of the door and sprinted up the stairs to the club which was on the second floor. Darryl and Mick had been boxing mates who trained together and busted a few heads from time to time. I knew he couldn't wait to tell Mick about our big night.

Thirty seconds later Darryl, Mick and Bon came bounding down the stairs.

'G'day Thorpie, Lobbs, boys. Everything sweet? Where are the mugs?' Bon smiled, jumping in the back next to me. 'Where's the fuckin' bullet hole? Jesus Christ, Thorpie, that was bloody close, mate.' Bon and Mick checked out the holes in the dash and roof and we ran down what had happened. 'Who were the bastards, Thorpie? We gonna flatten 'em or what?' Bon was ready.

'No, mate, they dropped off,' I told him. 'Where are you guys staying? You want to come and have a few beers?'

'We're at the Park Royal, same as you,' he said. 'Thought we'd catch up with yers after the gig for a smoke. Anyway we've finished for the night. No point in goin' back in that joint. It's dead.'

Downtown Canberra on a Saturday night was deserted after 9 p.m. and there wasn't a car in sight. I asked Bon where the punters' cars were. 'Aw, the pricks all took off at 11 o'clock on the dot. The fucking place was packed for the first two sets, then it emptied like a flushed shitter. There's only a couple of ugly tarts and some drunks left upstairs, mate. They've all gone 'ome for some sleepybyes. We packed up a while back. Me an' Mick was just 'avin a couple of cool ones. Can we get a ride back with you blokes?'

'What about the others, mate? They coming back?'

'They've hooked up with a bunch of ugly sheilas. They had a few leg-openers and they've gone to a party at one of their houses. It's gonna be an all-nighter by the looks of 'em. They got our van so they'll be sweet.' He turned to Mick. 'What do you want to do?'

Just as Mick was about to answer, a car came screaming

around the corner. It was one of the maniacs from Quean-beyan wanting some more of us. Without a word Mick opened his leather bag and pulled out a sawn-off .303. Its stock had been reshaped like a target pistol grip. I didn't see any magazine in it but even at one shot at a time we had a .303 war about to erupt. We all leapt out of the van and five sets of elbows and arseholes took off in eight different directions behind posts, flower pots, pillars . . . anywhere that was protection from a bullet, but none came. Mick and Darryl didn't move. They just stood there, Clint Eastwood style. Feet apart. Mick slammed the bolt shut on the .303 and pointed the gun at the big mug who had jumped out of the car as it screeched to a halt. The other three doors opened and out piled another six half-pissed idiots. The first guy walked straight up to Mick and stood about a foot in front of him. This guy either had the balls of an elephant or the brains of an ant because Mick had the loaded .303 pointed at his chest and the big mug didn't bat an eye.

'What're ya gonna fuckin' do . . . shoot me, you fuckin' cunt?' he yelled defiantly at Mick. Now Mick definitely wasn't going to ask him for a dance. 'Go on, pull the fuckin' trigger. You haven't got the fuckin' balls.'

It was definitely the ant brain that was in command. Christ, this idiot didn't know who he was screwing with. I'd seen Mick nearly kill a bloke in a fight once and the guy he maimed for life was twice his size. Mick was a double for a young Hunter S. Thompson, but what Hunter had in journalistic prowess Micky had in street fighting skills. He was a bad motherfucker and the last person you tell he hasn't got the balls to shoot anyone. Mick didn't give a shit and would have shot a nun if she'd gotten far enough in his face. Darryl stepped towards the other four and stood his ground in front of them. One by one we came out from behind the posts and they all took a step back. I saw Mick's finger tighten on the trigger and the big guy lunged at him grabbing the short rifle barrel with both hands. They were wrestling with it and waving the bloody thing in all directions. Everybody except the two of them hit the pavement. Then Baaaang! Tiiingg! . . . aang! aaangg! aaang! aangg!—an ear-splitting shot ripped off, echoing through the silence of the Canberra night.

Time stood still for a second and in that instant Mick threw a perfect right hook and decked the big bloke in one. Darryl jumped straight into the others, catching one with a left rip to the ribs and we all got stuck in. In the meantime Mick is trying to get another round in the chamber and I swear he was going to finish the guy off then and there. All of a sudden Billy Thorpe and his band are about to be accessories to murder and the whole complexion of the situation changed. Regardless of what had happened out on the highway, killing somebody with a sawn-off .303 was deep shit.

One of the guys came straight at me yelling, 'That was my fuckin' mate you bashed with the torch, you cunt.' He lunged at me, both feet off the ground. I sidestepped him and caught him across the face with a backhand and heard his nose snap. Bon had grabbed one of them, head-butted him, and was giving him a terrific hiding. He dropped the guy with a savage kick to the nuts and was inventing some new stage steps on his head. From the way the country boys fought it was obvious none of them had any training or could really fight. All haymakers and huge unfocused swings in the air that were easily slipped. Darryl had dropped another one with no effort at all and the situation was pretty much under control. Except for Mick that is. I looked back and Mick's reloading the gun, still pointing it at the yobbo he decked. The cockies were all down and it was time to split, not kill one of them. Bon saw Mick as well and yelled, 'Mick . . . Mick . . . Don't do it, mate. It's not fucking worth it. Let's get out of here.'

'Ah, fuck him. I'll show the sheep-fucking cunt about fucking balls!' He snapped the .303 round in, slammed the bolt, and the shell entered the chamber.

'No mate, stop!' I yelled as Bon and I leapt at Mick, grabbing him from behind so he couldn't get the gun in the air or his finger to the trigger. He struggled yelling, 'Let me go, you bastards. I'll kill yers! Let me fucking go I said!' But the two of us had him tight. I had my face buried deep into his back with my arms around his, and Bon was on the side doing exactly the same. Mick couldn't move. Gradually his rage subsided and he stopped struggling.

'Mate, let's get out of here!' I yelled at him. 'They would have heard that gun shot in Melbourne. It's got to bring the coppers, mate, and you need that less than we do. Come on, get in the bloody van and let's get back to the hotel.'

We all piled in. It wasn't until that moment that I realised Lobby had been sitting there in the front of the van through the whole thing. He was ghostly white.

'You OK, mate?' I asked him.

He didn't say a word, just pointed to a second hole in the dash and roof above my head where Mick's bullet had passed. It must have been no more than an inch from where the other bullet had entered and exited. Jesus, Lobby had come within a gnat's pube of biting the big one twice in one night and he was understandably mortified.

Darryl flattened the van. We turned on the main road

towards the hotel as another car load of mugs came to a screeching halt next to their mate's car. They jumped out, got their mates up, then into the cars and after us. The chase was on all the way back to the Park Royal. No guns this time, thank God. A couple of bottles were thrown at the windscreen but they both bounced off the bonnet. Micky wanted to kill them all of course, but we stopped him from getting at the gun. We were six and they were eleven, but by the lame way the others had fought these odds were OK. As long as we made it back to the hotel without being rammed, we would be fine if it came to another fist fight. We all came to a screaming halt outside the Park Royal at the same time and they were on us again.

Mick was smart enough to know that a sawn-off .303 outside our hotel was not a good idea and he stuck it under the back seat. Jimmy jumped on one of them and was hanging on for dear life while the guy tried to get him off. Bucking and kicking like a crazed horse trying to lose its breaker, Jimmy kept throwing punches around to his face and they both went down in a heap on the pavement. Darryl and Mick got straight in and dropped two of them and Bon and I were sparring with two more like a couple of bare-knuckle prize fighters. 'Come onnn, you sheep-fucking cunt . . . Come onnn,' Bon was goading. Bon was even smaller than me and the sight of him sparring with this big country cockie and calling him a cunt had me in hysterics. The bloke I was with was big and I threw a straight right, catching him on the chin. I think one hair on his head said 'What the fuck was that?' He didn't even feel it. 'Argh shit!' I yelled and took off with him chasing me. We were running around in circles like the Marx Brothers when I turned and kicked him in the nuts. He went down, throwing up all over himself as he hit the pavement. Not a pretty sight. Paul and Lobbs belted a couple of blokes then ran into the hotel to get some help and pretty soon some of the staff were out front yelling for it to stop. One of the staff yelled that the police were on their way. I got Mick's attention and mimed shooting a gun. He got the hint in a flash and ran to the van, grabbed the gun and sprinted around the back of the hotel. Nobody noticed him in the hassle.

We all saw the opportunity to get into the hotel and sprinted for the giant glass doors. Lobbs and Paul held them open and we barrelled into the lobby. The bloke behind the front desk started screaming like a sheila the second we came sprinting in. He was as camp as the Albury Hotel and I wasn't certain if he was screaming out of fear or excitement at seeing this bunch of bloody, long-haired young boys.

The doors to the hotel were each about fifteen feet high, six feet across, and made of four- or five-inch glass. Standing outside on either side of them were a pair of huge white ceramic pots about six feet in diameter and four feet high. Each containing a large palm three. We were standing at the front desk just inside the doors when Jimmy yelled 'Look ouutt!' and Caaraaash!—one of the pots sailed through the air, palm tree and all, shattering both doors. We were struck dumb and stood there staring at the giant upturned pot, still intact, and sitting upside down in a pile of dirt. The broken palm tree sprawled gracelessly like a fallen dancer amongst a million diamonds of shattered glass. We're standing there with our mouths open. The gay guy is screaming at the top of her lungs and the pissed cockies came storming in through the gaping hole and over the debris like commandos at the Normandy invasion. It was on again in the Park Royal lobby. I got hit and went down and so did Paul. I was biting the shit out of the calf of the guy that hit me and he was screaming like a banshee. I had a huge bite of jeans and leg and I was literally trying to bite it off. He's yelling and screaming while dragging me around the floor trying to shake me off like I was a dog dry-rooting his leg. He finally shook me loose and went hopping out the front door. Bon belted one of them over the head with a chair, Texas style. Mick Christian came hurtling down the stairs, trusty sabre in hand. He was swinging his razor sharp butcher's knife at them like Errol Flynn when I heard the wail of sirens. the country boys heard it too and bailed over the pile of dirt and palm tree and out into the street.

They got to their cars and were about to pull away when three carloads of coppers and two paddy wagons screamed to a halt in a semicircle, blocking their exit. The coppers grabbed everyone. They pulled the local boys out of the cars and came in and dragged us all outside. I couldn't believe it. They wouldn't listen. No chance to explain who was who. I got thrown face first into the wall and Jimmy hit the wall beside me with a slap.

'Hey . . . hey, we're staying here. It's them you're after, not us!' I yelled. Whaackk! I got a backhand in the back of the head for the trouble. When Jimmy saw that he went bananas and started screaming in some language we'd never heard before. He did that sometimes when he got real excited and we had nicknamed him the Bluey Rooster because he looked and sounded like a chicken with a blue face when he did. His screaming got one copper's attention.

'All right. Calm down, son. Calm bloody down.'

The same one, a big grey-headed sergeant, said to me, 'You're Billy Thorpe aren't you?' I nodded. 'Let him go, constable,' he said to the copper that still had hold of me. 'Now what in the name of flamin' tarnation's goin' on 'ere eh?' he asked me.

Everybody started shouting at once. Jimmy started screaming his head off again and it looked like we were all headed to the Canberra nick for the night to sort it out in the morning. Then, Screeech!—another car pulled up. Alf und der boyz jumped out. Alf came over to the sergeant who'd been talking to me and told him what had gone down in Queanbeyan. 'Dees boyz are OK,' he shouted, pointing to us. 'Dose are der bastards dat started the shtink and hurt all der people.' He walked over to the big mug who looked like the ringleader and kicked him square in the balls, then gave him a couple of pile-driver punches to the face as he collapsed holding his crushed nuts in agony. Alf was giving us all an inspired performance of his favourite German folk dance on the mug's face when the sergeant shouted, 'All right, all right. That's enough, Alf. We'll take care of it from here,' Alf backed off immediately.

No-one, us or them, said a word about guns. They'd have pinched us all on the spot. The coppers carted the Canberra boys away in the paddy wagons and Bon, Mick, the band, me and Alf and der boyz went into the hotel and had a couple of beers in my room. We'd been there about forty-five minutes when Alf politely said, 'Okaay, boyz, go pack jor shtuff. You're leafing.' He was polite about it but there was no doubt what it meant—'The next stage out of Dodge leaves in five minutes. Be on it.'

We were in the van and on the highway in nothing flat, Alf's police escort in front. Fifteen minutes later we reached the NSW border. Alf waved for us to stop and we got out. 'Vel, boyz, it's been a gas. Ju are all righcht. Dose fuckin cunz. I see dem in jail, der bastards. But ve don't vant to zee ju in Canberra for a vile, OK? Shtay out of town fur un vile. It not helty fer you ere. Undarshtant?'

We undershtoodt, all right. We'd been run out of town. Oh well, it wasn't for the first time. Another rip-roaring week in rock was off to a big start and we still had five more gigs to play. The van began to roll.

'Roll another joint,' echoed around the van from somewhere deep down in the murky depths of the back seat. Match . . . puff . . . puff . . . drink . . . buuuurpp! . . . farrrrrt! . . . peeewwww! . . . 'Hi ho, hi ho, it's off to Sydney we go.'

Part II

12
Detective Jack Cirello

Arghhh! . . . Agh! 'Where is he, you motherfucker?' *Argh . . . No . . . Arrrgh!* 'That hurt, you piece of shit? How about this?' *Arghhhhhh!* 'Where is he?' *Argh!* 'You grease-ball piece a shit.' *Argh . . . Arghhhh!*

I thought it was another morphine mambo. A freakish nightmare. But as the haze cleared I realised it was coming from in the room.

Arghh! 'Give it up, you fuck'n slimeball. What's amatta? Can't take a little pain, you scumbag?' *Argh . . . No . . . No . . . Argh.*

'Where is he?' another voice cut in.

There were two hospital screens around the Severino brothers and the moans were coming from behind them. I looked for Idi but he was gone. My eyes darted around the room.

Argh . . . Argh! 'I want your greaseball brother. You scumbag! Where's Julio? How about you, you want some

177

of this?' *Arghh . . . Argh!* 'Come on, where is the mother-fucker. I've only just started on *you.*' *Argh . . .*

'Come on, Jack. That's enough,' said the second voice. 'This ain't the way to go! If one of these fuckers dies we're both in the shit. This ain't the way, Jack.'

'Let 'em fuck'n croak. I wanna see it! Motherfuckers.' *Arrghh! . . . Arghhh!*

'That's enough, Jack. I said cool it! We ain't gonna get nowhere but trouble like this. Let's see how they do after a day on the wagon.'

'OK, OK. I'm cool . . . I'm cool.'

'Jack, they'll be so strung out they'll give their goddamn mother up. Come on, leave it man.'

'You're gonna fry, you fuckers!' the first voice yelled.

The screen shot open and out strode two real tough-looking dudes. Obviously cops. One mid-thirties. Five ten or so. Handsome. Italian. Romany nose and dark eyes. Blue jeans, leather jacket and a black pork-pie hat with the brim turned up all around. Black shoulder-length hair hanging out the back. The other much older. Late fifties. Over six feet. Big man with thinning grey hair and a wrinkled dark blue suit. They both looked like they were from central casting, straight off the set of *The French Connection.* But I could see these guys were the real deal. No play-acting here. They didn't sit down at night and learn the next day's lines while they took off their make-up. Their insane New York reality still stared them in the face when they eventually closed their eyes. Tough-looking bastards both of them. Low painful moans came from behind the screens. They saw me looking and came over.

'Who the fuck are you lookin' at? Who are you?' the smaller of the two spat at me.

'Er, Billy . . . Billy Thorpe.'

'You been tuning in, scumbag?'

'Hey, easy man! My heart stopped in emergency. There were no beds in general so they stuck me in this fucking joint.'

'Oh yeah?'

'Yeah. My arm's broken and I've been listening to these fuckers for the last two days. They're out the window. So take it fucking easy . . . Check with the sister.'

The cop was furious, ready to kill somebody. His eyes flashed, darting around the room. A cobra ready to strike. His breathing heavy. *I wouldn't fuck with this guy*, said my arse.

'You got some ID?' the cop asked.

'No, that's my problem. I was admitted as a John Doe.'

'I'm listnin',' the cop said, pushing his hat back and scratching his forehead.

'Look, I'm stuck here, man. I can't get out of this joint until administration comes back on Tuesday and sorts it out. I'm an Australian musician . . . just visiting New York. I don't belong in here. It's a mistake!'

He looked at me for a second or two, then the rage slid from his face like water pulled down a windscreen by a squeegee. He tried to smile.

'OK, sorry man. Sorry,' the older cop said. 'Hey, Jack, he's cool. Ease off, man.'

'Sorry brother . . . sorry,' the younger one said. 'Those low-life motherfuckers killed my partner and I want their goddamned brother's dick on a string around my neck!' Big tears welled in his black eyes. He shook them away and took a deep breath. 'I'm sorry, man.'

We all looked at each other in silence. 'I'm Detective

First Class Jack Cirello. Homicide Division, Queens,' the younger cop said. 'And this is Detective Moore.'

'Pleased to meet you,' I said, shaking their hands. Christ, I was having my first conversation as a human being in three days and it was with two homicide detectives who had just been leaning on a couple of murderers. And I mean leaning literally. All the while I could hear the brothers moaning.

'You been in here a couple days you said?'

'That's right.'

'You hear these motherfuckers talkin'?'

'Sure, they're always mumbling away to each other. Mostly in Spanish or Cuban or something.'

'You picked up on anythin' they been talkin' about?'

'Well I've heard some. Didn't make any sense to me, though. They're whacked on morphine most of the time anyway. They just rant.'

'We'll soon fix that. Let's see how the junkie mother-fuckers do when they don't get their next fix. You look a bit strung out yourself, kid. You a junkie or somethin'?'

'No I'm fucking not! They've got me on heavy doses of morphine too. I'm spinning out most of the time. The sister won't take me off it until she gets authority on Tuesday. My arm hurts bad but I'm starting to scratch, man. Listen, can you help me?'

I quickly told them my story and asked him if he could try and contact Rob Raymond. This was an opportunity I couldn't miss.

'Shit, brother, you're in more shit than a midget in a sewer,' Detective Cirello said. He leaned over and whispered in my ear. 'Listen, brother. If you hear those two scumbags talkin' about anythin' that makes any sense to you, let me know. I'm gonna be back later and hang out for a while. I'll be in and out over the next couple days. They gonna be movin' those motherfuckers to a prison hospital sometime this week and I want to watch the scumbags sweat.'

'Christ, I hope I'm out of here before then.' I tried to laugh.

Cirello looked at me with a crooked smile. Pursed his lips. Nodded his head. Straightened his pork-pie hat. 'Be cool, brother,' he said and patted my leg.

'See ya, son,' said the other cop.

They pressed a buzzer I hadn't noticed before by the door. Idi appeared in a flash. Opened it. And they were gone.

Holy shit, I thought. *What have I done to deserve this?* Stuck in Bellevue, shot full of morphine. Can't get out. And I'm in the middle of a triple murder now the cop they shot died! These two are facing the chair. I looked over but the screens were still around their beds. Apart from the moaning, I had a private room. I wish!

I lay there for some time putting it all back together. It took me a while but I figured out it was Monday. *Only Monday!* It felt like I'd been there for months. For the first time my chest ached. Not my heart, my chest and ribs. I pulled back my gown and my whole chest area was a dark bluish yellow. At first I couldn't work out what had happened, then I realised it was probably from the workout they gave me in emergency when they'd brought me back. My brain had been so active with morphine-induced dreams I was exhausted. My arm hurt bad. My head ached. My chest hurt. But my heart seemed to be fine. I hadn't experienced any heart pain or even a hint that a hypodermic full of adrenalin had been pumped into it two nights before. It still hadn't sunk in fully that I'd died and come back. How do you come to terms with that. I *died*? Jesus! I closed my eyes. 'Thank you, God,' I whispered. 'I owe you one.' I guess he wasn't ready for me. Hey, it was Friday night. Maybe he was snowed under too. Who knows? But I was still here and, regardless of the circumstances, very bloody happy to be alive.

Some time later, Bertha and Idi arrived. She went over to the Severino brothers first. They'd been moaning the whole time and the 'Morpheeno por favor . . . morpheeno' had started some time ago. This time they sounded like they really needed it. Bertha went behind the screen. 'Oh shit!' I heard her say. She rushed out the door with Idi in tow and reappeared about a minute later. This time they had another nurse with them, carrying what looked like fresh bandages. She was mid-twenties, Latino of some kind. About five six. Very pretty with creamy olive skin. Her hair hung in a long black plait from under her white starched nurse's hat. She glanced at me without a smile and they all went behind the screens. 'Cut that dressing, Angelina. I'll get this one.' The murderers moaned as the nurses worked on them. 'Those goddamn cops,' I heard Bertha say. *Moaann . . . arghhh . . . moan.* 'You're OK? . . . Just a little bleeding.' *Moannn . . . Arghhh!* . . . 'Stop moaning, boy. You're OK. *Okaay?*'

Jack Cirello had leaned where it hurt the most. Couldn't blame him, I suppose. These weren't people. They were animals that had murdered two innocent people and killed a cop. Bertha knew that too, but I guess her nursing responsibilities superseded her personal feelings. I didn't really see the point in keeping them alive and getting them back fighting fit so that they could go through the motions of a trial. When you killed a cop in New York in 1979, you died. That's capital murder. No ifs, buts or oh shits. No 'There are extenuating circumstances, Your Honour. My clients had an unstable childhood . . .'

'Ladies and gentlemen of the jury, have you reached a verdict?'

'We have, Your Honour.'

'Is it unanimous?'

'Yes, Your Honour.'

'Will the defendants please rise. Foreman of the jury, please read the verdict to the court.'

'Fry the motherfuckers!'

'Morpheeno . . . morpheeno por favor?'

'Not today, boy,' Bertha said.

Cirello must have had permission to interrogate them and the withdrawal of the morphine had obviously been sanctioned from someone higher up. I knew there was no way that Bertha would make that decision on her own. She was too old a hand at this game to get her arse in a sling over these two maniacs. The treatment the Severinos had received from Cirello could have been spur of the moment, but I doubt it. When one of their own dies in New York, the force closes ranks and it's fair game.

'Morpheeno . . . morpheeno,' the brothers continued.

'I said no! . . . Now shut your damned mouths.'

'Morphee . . .'*Aarghh!*

'Shut you goddamned cop-killin' mouth, or you'll need more stitches!' spat Idi.

'Samuel, that's enough. Now get out of here or I'll report your black ass.'

'Fuck 'em,' he said and stormed out from behind the

screens and out the door. Slamming it. He took up his regular seat outside the window.

'Morpheeno . . . por favor . . . morpheeno.'

Bertha and the nurse pulled the screens back against the wall and there were the Bobbsie twins. They looked completely freaked out and very sorry for themselves. 'Morpheeno,' they kept on. Bertha ignored them and came over to me. The young nurse carried the old dressings out.

'You didn't see or hear anythin' did you, son?'

'No ma'am.'

'That's good. 'Cause if you did and this got out you gonna find yourself subpoenaed as a witness for the defence. You got enough problems, ain't *ya*?'

'Yes ma'am.'

'Now these two suckers are gonna be moanin' and groanin' for a while. Somebody thinks they been getting too much morphine, so I'm gonna hold out for a while. Don't take any notice. They chained down and fine. How 'bout you? Did you sleep?'

'Sleep's not the problem, Sister. Staying awake and getting out of here's the problem. Can't you hold off on my morphine too?'

'Can't do that, son. I told you already. Only Dr Harrison can do that. Look, I know this whole thing's weird but let me tell you somethin' for your own good. You had your heart stop on you for a full minute. You were critical there for a few hours, could have gone either way according to your file. If I cut your dose against Dr Harrison's orders and you go and die on me, it's my ass! I can't take that responsibility. They didn't prescribe your medication by accident. Now stop hasslin' me 'bout it and let me do my damned job! I know you got a problem, but it'll get sorted out.'

'What about them?' I nodded towards the Severino brothers. 'You're cutting their dose.'

'Oh they got a different doctor today.'

'Who is he? Can't you ask him about me?'

'Oh no.' Bertha grinned, cleaning my arm with alcohol. 'Dr Kokorobasure lookin' after those boys today.'

She didn't know it but I knew exactly who Dr Kokorobasure was. I'd been in New Orleans plenty of times. I'd heard that expression from Cajuns I've worked with and Dr Kokorobasure is their expression for fun and games. Bertha gave me my shot.

'Morpheeno,' the Severinos yelled, seeing the needle go in. 'Seeester, por favor. Morpheeno.'

'Arghhh . . . morpheeno ai yai yai, you dickheads,' I growled at them. The one opposite me spat at me and it landed with a splat in the middle of the room. 'Morpheeno,' I laughed again and they started jabbering to each other.

'Don't you get them riled, son,' Bertha yelled. 'I got enough shit on my hands as it is. Understand me?' I understood. 'OK, you done. I'll see you this afternoon.'

I felt the liquid whore sliding through my body and all pain left. It felt good and I realised that I was starting to enjoy the buzz. And that scared the shit out of me!

'Sister, did . . . did you manage to get . . . er, get through to anyone?' My speech was already starting to go.

'No I couldn't. I'm sorry. But like I said they'll all be gone for the Thanksgivin' weekend. Dr Harrison will be back tomorrow afternoon so you be cool, OK?' Bertha smiled. 'You gonna be fine, son. Your heart's beatin' and you alive, so don't fret. The morphine's for the pain and to keep you relaxed and stable. We don't want no more heart problems, now do we? So just relax. Say, you hungry?'

I hadn't even thought about food, but as soon as Bertha mentioned it, I was. 'Erm . . . yes . . . yes, Sister. I . . . I think I could . . . er, eat something.'

'OK. I'll get them to bring you somethin' a little later. Now you rest up.'

'Thank . . . thank you . . . sister.' I slowly drifted off. Don't remember the dream but I woke up with a hammer you could demolish the Empire State Building with. Something woke me and I came around to see an orderly pushing a wheelchair into the room. Whoever this guy was he was in a bad way. Both arms were in plaster and sticking straight out in front of him. His entire head and face were wrapped in bandages so he only had a mouth and two eye holes. They got him into the bed and he lay down moaning, but pretty soon he was asleep. I looked at the Severino brothers. Their eyes were as big as saucers and darting every which way around the room. Both sweating hard.

'Morpheeno . . . seester. Morpheeno por favor,' they pleaded with Bertha, rattling their chains. She ignored them and left. They were obviously starting to Jones. And scared as a sheep at a Kiwi picnic. They knew what was coming and it hadn't even started to hurt. These two were going on a hell ride in about four hours and I was sitting front row. I drifted off again.

When I woke, Detective Cirello was sitting on a chair by the door, staring at the Severinos with hate-filled eyes. The brothers were both in bad shape. Moaning. Sweating. Eyes darting. Looking everywhere except at Cirello.

'You awake, man?' Cirello asked with a half smile.

'Yes. Sort of. The morphine just whacks me out. Can't keep my eyes open.'

'So you're a musician, huh?'

I nodded.

'What brings you to New York City?' He was trying to be friendly and there was no reason not to go along. I needed someone to talk to and was grateful for the conversation. I told him what I could remember about getting there and asked if he'd made a call to Rob. He said he called a couple of times but it was engaged and promised he'd call again when he got off duty.

'The sister says you were high on cocaine,' he said, switching from Jack back to Detective Cirello. 'I thought you weren't into that kind of shit.'

'Well I'm not, usually. Just got caught up in it all I suppose. I can tell you now that's the last fucking time, detective. It nearly killed me.'

'Call me Jack, brother. You mind if I bring my chair over?'

'Not at all. I'd be glad of some company. It's been a hard three days.'

Cirello slid the chair over to the side of my bed and sat down in front of the heart monitor. I noticed the steady beep . . . beep . . . beep. I'd all but forgotten it. It was just part of the maniacal underscore by now.

'So . . . You from Australia, huh?'

'Yes. I live in LA but Australia's my home.'

'What brings you here?'

'Ah want to take a crack at the big title. Not much left for me to do down there. I've pretty much done it all. It's a huge continent but a small country. Been real lucky there. Just time to get out before I turned into a hack.'

Cirello sat patiently listening. By the changed look on his face I guessed that he was grateful for the conversation as well. Anything that took his mind off *his* reality. I was dying to know what had happened but I didn't ask. I figured if he wanted to tell me about it he would.

'These friends of yours?' he said, pointing to the photographs on the bedside table. 'Mind if I take a look?'

'No, not at all. They're just some old shots got sent to Georgia by mistake. I just got them back.'

Cirello picked the photos up and started flicking through them. 'Jesus, that you?'

'Which one?' I asked.

'Sitting on the car, man. Shit, you looked different then. You in Sydney in '66 or '67?'

I told him I was.

'Then you remember R&R?'

'Very well indeed. Why?'

'I was there, man.'

'No shit. I don't believe it, Jack. I was workin' in a club owned by my manager. Thousands of you guys hung out there. They were fantastic times . . .'

'The Whiskey?' he asked.

'How the fuck do you know that?'

'I went there every goddamned night, man. Shit, I knew I'd seen you before. You had a band that played downstairs?'

'Yes I did.'

'You ain't gonna believe this.' Cirello smiled and shook his head. 'We had a goddamned drink together one time, man.'

'You're kidding! When?' I looked at Cirello, trying to take years off his face. Trying to get back.

'You remember Pam Redding?' he asked.

'What, Pam Redding the stripper?' I couldn't believe my ears. Pam used to work at the Pink Pussycat where I'd had so many great times when I first arrived in the Cross back in 1963.

'Yeah, Pam Redding. We hung out together when I was there the last time. She was a friend of yours, wasn't she? I remember her taking me downstairs at the Whiskey one night to meet this big pop star and we had a drink together. Fuck man, I don't believe it.'

'*You* don't believe it! Here I am stuck in the Bellevue nuthouse talking to a New York cop that used to date Pam Redding and we met at the Whiskey nearly fifteen years ago. Christ! What do you think the chances of that are?'

'Big time, Billy. Big fuckin' time!' He laughed. 'Is this a small goddamned world or what? Put it there.' Cirello held out his hand. We looked at each other for a minute without saying a word, both straining the memory banks. Cirello broke the silence. 'I was in Nam twice. First time, '66 and '67. Second time '68 and '9. Air Cav. The 7th.' He smiled the smile of a man with memories, a lot of them real bad.

'Seventh Air Cavalry. Choppers. I heard all about you guys.'

'You in Nam?' he asked.

'No, not me, thank God. I missed out somehow. I thought I'd be the first to go as the poster boy for Australian youth but they got another singer called Normie Rowe. Poor bastard!'

'All power to you, son. It was living hell.'

'Seventh Air Cav, eh?'

'Yeah, 7th Cav.' He nodded slowly as the horrors came back.

My experiences with US servicemen on R&R had been one of the changing points of my life. Of a lot of people's lives. After my national television show 'It's All Happening'

189

ended I took a break from the business, but it was short-lived. I missed it all too much. American servicemen were hitting Australia, and primarily Kings Cross, at the rate of about 10,000 a week. Business was booming. Every bar, coffee shop, armpit, strip joint, brothel, church, restaurant and urinal had worked out a way of separating the young, shell-shocked, terror-crazed, teenage American servicemen from their R&R pay, and the town was raging day and night. The day the first contingent arrived, the bohemian Kings Cross that I'd been privileged to experience the tail end of in 1963 and '64 was gone forever. In its place the beginnings of the hard-core, smacked-out, cocaine and crime-ridden red-light shithole it is today. The gutter-level equivalent of any on the planet. In a few years Surf City was no more. That grand forty-year-old 5000 capacity theatre at the top of the Cross where so much had taken place was torn down. The Kings Cross underground railway station sits directly under where Surf City stood, and above it one of the greatest pieces of ill-conceived, butt-ugly, cheap architectural shit ever built. The Crest Hotel, now the Capital. Tell me money didn't change hands to make that sort of thing happen. Ask Juanita Nielson!

Gone too Surf City's equally successful sister club, The Beach House in Elizabeth Street in the city. Times had changed and so had the gigs. I was still managed by John Harrigan, who had leased the Kings Cross Theatre and converted it to Surf City in the early '60s. He had put me together with a young surf band called the Aztecs and the rest of it is Australian music history. Surf City had been our home and headquarters for a phenomenal two years. From total obscurity and 250 people a night the band went orbital and drew 60,000 people to the Myer Music Bowl in

Melbourne just one short, incredible year later. Surf City became the hub of Sydney's and eventually Australia's new music scene and the unquestionable birthplace of the new music of the '60s. John Harrigan was a hustler and as swift as a fart. But above all else he was a believer in the scene and in me. He and Dennis Wong, who owned and ran the infamous Chequers nightclub, joined forces and opened two new clubs. First the Hawaiian Eye in the heart of the city, which as the name conveys had an Irish theme. Then Australia's most successful club ever, the multi-levelled Whiskey Au Go Go on William Street, just down the hill from the Cross. Both buildings are gone today. Many of us Cross night shifters, those of us who lived and worked in the Cross of the early '60s still lived and hung around its dubious domain. It was a magnet and hard to tear yourself away from. Something, someone, was always happening.

By the time of R&R many of the successful Australian bands and records and singers of the early '60s, myself included, had started to sound square, even passé. Popular culture changed overnight and much of the early '60s music just didn't translate. It seemed almost quaint and infantile in comparison to the hard-edged realities of what was now happening in the world, politically, musically and culturally. The innocence and teenage-oriented naiveté that had spawned '60s popdom and the resulting attitudes had been hyped into a sad submission that gave way to a quasi peace and love movement mentality. Crossbred with a harder edged hippie drug culture, it produced a demographic with very different influences, attitudes, needs, wants and tastes from those that existed less than five years earlier.

Like no other decade before or since, the '60s were unique in that each year was radically different from the one that preceded or followed it. I say 'were' in the plural because the '60s were a 'were'-plural and not a 'was'-singular decade. Attitudes, tastes, trends and fashions were invented and rendered obsolete at an incredible pace, only to be replaced and superseded by equally original, stimulating and mind-boggling alternatives that instantly satisfied, then faded as fast as those that had preceded them. Under the umbrella of the Beatles and later the hippie movement's free love and peace, the '60s have been lumped into one cohesive, conveniently marketable decade by some experts, but nothing could be further from the actuality. The ten years from 1960 to 1970 were more than a decade. They were some kind of subconscious, cerebral warp, consisting of a series of ten separate, evolving, time/cultural spaces, connected only by the will, desires, needs, achievements and failings of that increasingly powerful, continuously evolving, all-demanding demographic—the baby boomers. With the addition, of course, of a number of insignificant little events contributed by the straight old farts of the day—like putting a man on the moon.

The swarm of US servicemen who hit Australia in their tens of thousands in the mid to late '60s were 99 per cent baby boomers, and with them came their own musical tastes and wants. These 'boys' referred to the USA as 'the world'. In Vietnam they lived in hell and Billy Thorpe's 'Over the Rainbow' or Normie Rowe's 'Shakin' All Over' just didn't get 'em off. No siree. To the street- and rice-paddy-wise young soldiers who had just spent an endless lag in some netherworld ducking incoming and stitching their best buddies into body bags while listening to the riffs, soul and funk of the likes of James Brown, the Doors,

Booker T. and the MGs, Rufus Thomas and Jimi Hendrix, much of the successful Australian pop of the early and late '60s must have sounded like the virgins' chorus. The US servicemen wanted to get high on booze, skank, speed, morph, dope and pussy, and hang it all out in funky bars listening to the sounds from back in the world. Like, 'Don' play me none o' that local shit, son. Gimme somethin' frum back in the worrrl fo' me and ma lady ta dance to.' You get enough guys with a grand a night in their pocket telling the managers of clubs, 'None o' that local shit, man. Give me some music from back in the world!' and that shit starts to stick in people's heads. Before you knew it, a lot of Australian music suddenly became 'local' and many of the inroads into the cultural cringe we'd made, as young Australian musicians, went straight down the shitter like everything else associated with the Vietnam War. Especially self-respect.

So here I am working downstairs in the Whiskey. Five sets a night. Wednesday through Sunday. I was still very successful. But when I compared what I did with the cultural vibe that R&R had brought with it, and looked at the 'local' mentality that had started to take hold in radio and in the industry in general, I was starting to believe the negative local bullshit myself. One day in 1967 I bought an album by some English band I'd never heard of called Cream. After hearing Eric Clapton's solos on 'NSU' and 'I Feel Free' I came close to ending it all by jumping out the window. *What the fuck was that?* . . . What kind of music is this? . . . How does he play like that? . . . How can you get those sounds? . . . Where did that come from? . . . Who else plays like that?

I was turned around from that moment and there was

no turning back. So into the Whiskey Au Go Go for five nights and twenty-five half-hours a week, playing Sam and Dave, Otis Redding, Joe Tex, Muddy Waters, Howlin' Wolf, Son House, Robert Johnson and any other blues, funk and R&B music I could find. Screw 'Over the Rainbow' and 'I Told the Brook', and screw anyone that got in my face when I didn't play them. And too bad if my whiter than whitebread pop voice didn't suit a lot of the new material I was trying to do! This was learning time and I was learning fast. The first thing I learned was that in the real world of music, in that world of musicians who really mattered, regardless of how many hits I'd had, on that playing field I was still the orange boy. I asked as many questions as I could, getting down with young US servicemen, black, yellow and white, from Chicago, New York, Alabama, Mississippi, Arkansas, Georgia . . . you name it. Trying to get a handle on 'the world'. Their world as opposed to mine. And some of these guys could play their R&R arses off. Many were professional players from all walks of musical life and for the first time in Australia there was a period in which Australians could get their influences first-hand. Not just at an occasional international concert or from recordings. These guys were the real deal, and happy as pigs in shit to show us.

Most of the black guys were still niggers where they came from, but they bled red like everybody else when they were blown to bits. Being thrown into that living hell of a war had fused every neuron in their brain. But here they were in Sydney, 'Orstralia', free as birds in paradise, with gorgeous young white bitches clawing the walls for some of their company, their money, cocaine and especially their black dicks. These boys were in heaven and a fantastic audience to play to every night. The Whiskey Au Go Go was like a war zone bar. The kind you see in the movies. Although the battles were 6500 miles to the north, from the US military presence in the streets of Sydney the front line could have been in Bondi.

You name it . . . it was happening. You wanted it, someone could get it. Everyone was flush. Everyone was on a twenty-four-hour pass. The smell of terror and rage oozed from their pores. These were human beings teetering on the edge, and many had fallen off a long time ago. They spooked at the slightest noise, could snap at the drop of a hat, and yet the high-voltage tension that surrounded them was addictive, palpable, euphoric. Life was a ritual of pleasure. So much to be had here in paradise and so little time until they were back in hell. Theirs was the epitome of the 'live hard die young' ethic that so many of us pseudo-hipsters tried to emulate. The difference was they were living it for real and the mindset it produced was addictive. It may sound sick but I think we were all high on the fear that they'd brought with them from Vietnam. Like Johnny Rotten later said, 'anger is an energy', and he's right. This was a mass high or maybe even high mass, I don't really know. All I know is that it was like nothing I'd ever experienced. These young American soldiers, black, Asian, Hispanic and white, were like nothing I'd ever encountered and I was so high on it all I needed a stepladder to scratch my arse! Now here I was almost fifteen years later lying in the nut slammer at Bellevue talking to a New York cop I'd met at the Whiskey Au Go Go on R&R! Strange world, ain't it?

Jack Cirello and I reminisced for a couple of hours about Sydney, the Cross, the Whiskey, Pam Redding and the strippers at the Pussycat. It was stimulating conversation and exactly what I needed. Every now and then the Severino brothers would moan through their pain-filled, withdrawal-induced sweat. 'Morpheeno . . . por favor . . . morpheeno.'

'Tell me where your brother is, you greaseballs, and you can have all the shit you want,' replied Cirello.

Not a word from the beds opposite.

'These are all you?' Cirello had the photos in his hand. 'With the long hair I mean?'

'Yep.'

'Look like acid rockers to me.' He laughed. 'You get into acid much?'

Now this wasn't the kind of conversation I wanted to have with a New York City detective. I could see me getting back to my hotel and finding it searched. 'Well, I, er.'

'That's cool. Man, we got into everything in Nam. That Vietnamese weed was deadly. And acid . . . I first tripped in Nam in '66. Me and my buddies got into it big time. Helped keep us sane, man.'

'Me too, Jack.' I smiled.

'Yeah,' we both said, unconsciously shaking back the velvet curtain.

Practically everybody I knew in the late '60s was taking LSD. Almost overnight it became acid rock and liquid light-shows, patchouli oil, hippie velvet, butterfly patches, embroidered bell-bottoms, frayed denim shirts, ban the bomb and peace signs. I wore my hair in two plaited pigtails, Cherokee style, predating ole Willie by fifteen years. I'd been dosed with LSD at a party in 1967 by some visiting US marines and I loved the experience. So much so that, being the naive young idiot I was, I thought I should tell the whole of Australia about it. I organised to go on television and be filmed taking it under clinical supervision. I mentioned it on

Sydney radio and the Minister of Health happened to be listening to the show on his car radio and nearly ran off the road. He threatened the ABC and me and sent some Federal boys around to see me. After a heavy berating I reminded them that LSD was not an illegal substance in Australia at that time, which it wasn't, and politely asked them to leave. But the event never took place. It wasn't until acid became prevalent around the Melbourne scene that I tried it again.

I don't remember the circumstances, but like millions of people all over the world we were experimenting. After a couple of trips I discovered that it didn't send me insane and make me want to kill babies and my parents. Quite the opposite. Oh, it definitely bent my brain. But we weren't bothering anybody, so why not play? For a while the band and I took it on a regular basis and I had some amazing experiences. For the most part, no-one in the straight world whom I came in contact with ever knew. I'd gone from being Billy Thorpe the pop singer to a long-haired maniac seemingly overnight, and most people thought I *was* crazy. But I assure you I wasn't. Sideways maybe, but definitely not crazy. We must have seemed weird at times, to say the least. But to the straight world in Australia in the late '60s everything about the flower-power pop culture was alien and weird. It was an amazing experience and one I'll never forget. I did TV shows, rock festivals, radio and press interviews, you name it, completely blissed out. And although this period is the one that gave rise to the 'Most People I Know Think That I'm Crazy' state of mind, it turned my head around forever.

Now, I'm not advocating the taking of LSD for pleasure or as a cure for anything. In today's fucked-up world, acid is a dangerous drug. I haven't taken LSD in over twenty-five years. They were very different times from today and acid was definitely one of the catalysts behind the social stance that many of the millions of baby boomers adopted, world-wide, in the free-thinking, free-loving, 'it's all possible' state of mind that was so prevalent. 'Nothing by accident,' and LSD was *the* perfect social drug for the time. All who took it experienced the Divine at one level or another, whether they realised it or not. The mind-expanding experience dovetailed perfectly with the psychology behind various Eastern philosophies and opened up undeniable psychological alternatives to the religious, governmental, dictatorial attitudes that had existed, for the most part unabated, for centuries. Everything in its place and a place for everything. Well, screw that!

It forced us to look, to question our lives and those of the people we realised controlled them. Suddenly I knew that we, our parents and our parents' parents had been lied to for generations. In our minds, the Establishment was crumbling before our flower-powered eyes. The corruption of church and state became all too obvious. For the first time the authoritarian world was being questioned by millions of young people in a way that couldn't be ignored. People were asking questions and the Establishment and the world they controlled were starting to rumble. The attitudes the acid subculture produced changed the way a generation of people saw each other, church and state, and there was no way to reverse it. It peeled back a veneer that had been carefully and calculatedly applied, and vigorously maintained, by generations of corrupt and self-serving politicians, religious leaders and the military. And straight or not, only the ignorant, or those terrified of the truth and what it meant, couldn't see what lay underneath. The change had been made.

'Free love' and 'Freedom' weren't just some hippie flower-power concepts. Free love wasn't about LSD-induced free sex in mass orgies. Free love was the concept of the freedom to embrace all things. Not just those people, ideas and things we were told were politically correct and socially acceptable. Freedom was the fundamental right that all human beings had regardless of birth, religion and social rank—the right of choice to act out of their own conscience. Not simply because society, and in particular the church, said that's the way it is. It was time to shake the cage. Freedom, peace and love weren't just catchphrases invented by a blissed-out generation with nothing better to do than smoke grass and chant and march against the evils of the Vietnam War, the shootings at Kent State and the injustices suffered by the Chicago Seven. If you consider the weight and strength of the Establishment's stranglehold on society at that time, the acid generation's very existence represented a destabilising threat to the status quo. Even though we hadn't realised it at the time, this was one of the few unified affirmations of our generation's solidarity. We demanded the right to choose. We wanted a say. This new and powerful generation was no longer just going to go along with 'big brother's' mind and physical control . . .

I can't speak for anybody else, but in my case the mind-expanding experience gave me a social conscience. Forced me to take a look at the world, my place in it, my relevance or irrelevance, in ways that hadn't even occurred to me before then. I'd had everything on a silver plate for as long as I could remember. A wonderful childhood with fantastic loving parents in a stable environment. I'd been famous since I was a kid, had one of the most successful careers in Australian music history, and was buzzing along nicely as the embodiment of the boy-next-door, cleaner than Kleenex pop star, singing my cleaner that Kleenex number one hits. Well, my acid experiences changed that forever. I became a frequent visitor to the Melbourne Theosophical Society, where I was introduced to the Eastern writings and teachings of some of the greatest minds ever to set foot on this or any other planet. Minds whose philosophies had been suppressed through their exclusion from any school library or classroom in Australia. I discovered at first hand that there were alternatives. Like millions of others I started to think, and that was the genesis of the change that occurred in me both physically and psychologically almost overnight in late 1968. A change that put my feet on the path forever.

If all this sounds deep, it was. It's from the heart for those of you who weren't fortunate to experience those magical times when we felt connected to everyone on the planet and shared a goal, unified by the belief that all men, women and children were indeed brothers and sisters. Connected by something far greater than race and creed. God, whoever or whatever he or she is, wasn't the unquestionably exclusive property and domain of the church, but existed everywhere in the fields of nature's divine existence and in the cathedral of the heart and mind . . .

'Where was that taken, man?' Jack Cirello pointed to a shot of me and the Aztecs backstage at a festival when Kevin Murphy was still in the band. 'You all look *spaced*,' he laughed.

'Well I guess we were,' I laughed too. 'Let me see. That was at the Wallacia Music Festival, sometime in early 1971 I think. Yeah, it was called Odyssey.'

'You guys ever play on acid?'

I smiled and nodded my head. 'Once or twice . . . yeah, once or twice.' Then I laughed.

'What was that like? I can't imagine standing up in front of thousands of people on acid. What a fuckin' freak-out that must be. What's it like? Scary?'

'No Jack, quite the opposite. Wanna hear a funny story?'

'Shoot man,' Cirello said. 'I ain't got nowhere to go.' He looked across at the shivering Severinos.

'Okay, Wallacia was . . .'

13
Wallacia

It wasn't the divine that put Pig, Murphy, Paul, Norman E, Rodney, my boxer dog Buster and me into a stripped-out, dual-wheeled Ford transit van with mattresses on the floor, heading blissfully off to the Odyssey Music Festival in Wallacia, NSW, on an overnight 600-mile drive from Melbourne. We had started to experiment visually with our performances around this time. All with the help and genius of our creative director and lighting designer, Rodney Currey. Among a hundred other things, Rodney was working with the Australian ballet as a lighting director when we met. A total eccentric, complete with an Albert Einstein shock of blond hair, Rodney had never had a drink or smoke in his life. He had ideas and design concepts that were years ahead of their time and wanted to do a film on us and our adventures, the first instalment of which was to be our performance at the Odyssey festival. Rather than just film the band in concert, it was agreed that he would come with us on the trip and shoot the whole experience, documentary style, including the drive up. We took the passenger seats out of the van, bolted a a racing car seat facing backwards behind the driver's seat for Rodney to film from, filled the back with mattresses, all dropped a trip—except Norman E and Rodney of course—and at 6 p.m. on a Friday evening off we blissed to Wallacia.

It's hilarious being with a group of people who have all dropped a trip at exactly the same time, particularly this maniacal lot. Acid comes on with predictable timing regardless of the individual. It's usually about an eight-hour experience but the course it takes is always pretty much the same. For the first half hour or so the van was abuzz with laughing happy talk of our adventure. Then it slowly sank into silence as the lysergic acid began to do its stuff. Colours shifted into sounds, sounds into colours. That metallic taste hits your mouth and a deep purple aura starts to form around everything. Particularly the seemingly disembodied, beaming faces floating ethereally in the flickering half-light of the darkened van which had slowly started to animate into a living breathing organism with six happy Jonahs in its stomach. Lights from Melbourne's outer suburbs bent towards our approach and away as we passed. Lasers beamed through the van's windows, dancing provocatively across our faces in a kaleidoscope of colour, all perfectly synced with the rolling rhythms of a steel beast that galloped gallantly forth into the great unknown, effortlessly devouring mile after mile of bitumen. Nobody spoke. We were all lost in our personal, psychological metamorphosis and rapture as the sound of Rodney's camera grew louder . . . *louder* . . . *louder!* Without realising it we had all slipped down and were lying on our backs on the mattresses. All transported, zooming the universe in our own private reveries. I looked up and saw a giant yellow, liquid moon dripping light through the window. The edges of it melting and reforming, melting and reforming, dripping golden droplets that turned into fireflies on the mattress beside me. The vibration made them dance in time to the breathing sound the van now made. The van was alive! Every mechanical sound, every bump of the road, was an anatomical reaction from the giant steel beast in which we were now orbiting the universe. I was lost in the firefly dance.

'You see that, Thorpie?' said Paul

'See what?'

'That . . . ummm . . . that was great.'

'What?' said Murphy.

Silence.

'Can you see that?' Pig asked. 'Look, a star meeting. Out the back window. Look.' We all crawled our way to the back door and peered into the night-time sky. Four faces and a dog nose pressed against the back windows and the universe beyond. 'Look, they're all gathering at the centre of the sky. It's a star meeting.'

The Milky Way was alive. Its outer edges spiralling inward, creating a swirling, conical, three-dimensional sea of light that drew the heavens towards the glowing white heart pulsing hypnotically at its centre. At that moment a shooting star rocketed across the heavens, eager to join the billions already gathered for another cosmic celebration in the great hall in the sky. It was beautiful. LSD-induced autosuggestion or not, we all saw it and sat there like little children with our faces against the window. Emotions began to ebb and flow. Flashes of situations, people, places, flowers, shot through my mind's eye. I was away. Slowly the personal silent experience gives way to animation and conversation about things deep. The beauty of the experience we were having. A new song. How much Pig wanted the whole world to feel what he was feeling right now. No-one could disagree. In our minds it was the warmest, most loving feeling in the universe, and if the whole world took acid there'd be no more wars. No more anger. No need for money . . . No heaven . . . No hell . . . All those sorts of LSD-inspired, illogical, impractical things.

I was a time-traveller. My destination forgotten. My reason for going irrelevant. All consciousness of being in a van had gone. I simply was. 'Where are we, Norm?' somebody asked, shaking me back to reality. It took my mind a second to get its earthly bearings and I realised I had no idea where we were or how long we'd been on the road. 'Just the other side of Seymour,' Norm replied. I crawled to the back door and looked out the window. From the deep blue star-encrusted canopy of sky that hung like a painted backdrop outside the window of our travelling stage, I knew we were well into the countryside. One by one we all came back to earth. The trip had come on full-bore now and the van became a metaphysical, humanitarian think tank, full of universally beneficial ideas. At some stage it just about always came down to peace and love, sharing and caring, but of course your acid-induced experiences are tempered by your own demons, real or imagined. The ones that usually live way down in the subconscious, buried for the sake of your sanity and well-being. I never once had a bad trip or a freak-out on acid, but plenty of people came face to face with themselves and their demons during a trip and couldn't handle what they saw. When I looked at Murphy I could see he was on a bummer. He looked terrified.

Kevin Murphy was six feet two and our drummer. Muscular, sinewy, with an angular, craggy face, a long Romanesque nose and big sad eyes, he always took on the persona of a great big bird when I was tripping. Others saw it too and he had acquired the nickname El Condor. In the little turn-of-the-century cottage in Gipps Street, with its thigh-high windowsills and doorknobs, El Condor was a giant. On acid he seemed to touch the ceiling. His favourite acid trick was to put a rubber band around his forehead, run into a room full of blissed-out strangers and yell 'El Condor sees all'. Then he'd wrinkle his brow and the rubber band shot up over his head, pulling his hair up into a foot-high Samurai pigtail that stood straight up on the top of his head. It was hilarious to us, but to the uninitiated the giant El Condor and his vertical hair stomping around was a terrifying sight. Guaranteed to freak some poor bastard on his first trip so far out he would never touch the demon LSD again. This night, El Condor was crashing and burning big time.

Having done it real hard in London with a heavy habit at one stage of his life, Murphy had some serious skeletons in the closet. He'd kicked and was pretty much straightened out by the time we met, and for the most part his skeletons stayed locked away. But tonight the closet door came flying open.

'Something's not right, man,' he said. 'I can feel it . . . Something's not fucking right.'

'Everything's cool, Murph' . . . 'We're just on our way to Wallacia, mate.' . . . 'Yeah just relax, Murph' . . . our combined reassurances attempted to quell the growing beast we'd witnessed a couple of times in the past. But Murphy's eyes darted from side to side. Out the front windscreen, the rear door, the windows, then back at us, Rodney and his camera. He was like a feeding bird watching for predators.

'Something's not right, man,' he kept repeating. 'Something's going to happen, man.'

Fear was just as addictive as laughter, especially in our heightened state of awareness, and the paranoia hit us all. Whether we admitted it or not, we were all waiting for the unexpected . . . like a meteor to end its 10 million mile journey through the back window of the van or something equally logical. Then it really started.

'Cops!' Murphy yelled. Eyes darting around the van.

'Where?' in paranoiac unison.

'There . . . there . . . Behind us . . . That car . . . They're cops . . . I can feel 'em, man!'

We all tried to melt into the walls and peep out of the back window at the same time. Any kind of freak-out on acid was bad, but having to deal with cops, especially country cops back in the *Easy Rider* days, was definitely the worst freak-out of them all. After the shock of the film *Easy Rider*, all law was the devil. The night Paul and I went to see it in a packed movie theatre in Melbourne, the entire audience just sat there stunned for about half an hour after it ended. The whole place was silent for about ten minutes and then strangers actually began to talk to each other, discussing the film and how it had affected them. I've never seen that happen over any other film. It totally freaked out the Melbourne drug culture. Paul and I saw it that night tripping and it affected us big time, let me tell you. That was a very significant film for its day.

To use the oft-quoted description, LSD is a mind-expanding drug in as much as every sensation, thought, sound, taste, smell, touch and sight is intensified to uncontrollable proportions. But as much as it can heighten one's experience of beauty to a sense of the divine, it can also have the completely opposite reaction and the mind could become lost in the living hell of some private paranoia. To some, the most benign occurrence could become a negative trigger that produced a physically sickening fear. That's the dangerous side of LSD, and paranoia had El Condor by the balls.

'They're cops!' shouted Murphy, starting to panic.

'No they're not!' came Norm's reassuring voice from the driver's seat. 'I passed them about two miles back. It's a couple of young girls. They've been behind us ever since.'

'Undercover cops,' said Murphy. Now we're all blitzed. They could be undercover cops. It's logical. Then, zoom!— the car overtook us, speeding off in the distance. As relieved as we all secretly were, Murphy had started the paranoias going good and once it starts on acid it can stick like shit to your blitzed-out psychological blanket. The van got noticeably quiet and everyone drifted back into their own little dreams or nightmares . . .

'Cops! Oh shit, it's cops!' yelled Murphy again. There was another set of headlights behind us. Once more we all went through about five minutes of the same routine. Peering out the window, listening to Murphy's logical-sounding assessment of the situation. 'It's cops. They're following us. The girls were cops, just checking us out. They . . . they radioed these cops.' Nobody said a word. *Could be*, said the trip. We're all back peeping out of the back of the van. Not realising how ridiculous four tripped-out, freaked-out longhairs and a boxer dog must have looked if you were in the car behind. But we were invisible, maaaan! Paul had told us so a while back.

'Just think yourself away, man, and no-one will be able to see you,' he said in a moment of LSD-induced genius. I closed my eyes and gave it a real good try. I even went up the front of the van.

'Hey Norm . . . Norm.'

'What, Thorpie?'

'Hey, man, can you see me in the rear-view mirror?'

''Course I can, you silly prick. Now sit down before you hurt yourself.'

I crawled back. 'Hey, Paulie.' No answer . . . 'Hey Paulie, Paulie. It doesn't work.' Still no answer. 'Pauleeeee!' I yelled, freaking everybody out and making Norm clutch the wheel and send the van sideways.

'Shhh,' whispered Paul. 'I'm starting to fade, man.'

I concentrated on him, waiting for him to disappear but he was still there. 'No you're not, Paulie. I can see you plain as day.'

'Sshhh . . . sshh . . . it's starting,' he whispered. 'I've got to concentrate. My hand's disappeared, man. Won't be long now until I'm gone!'

I looked for a minute. 'No it's not, Paulie. You're sitting on it.'

He looked down. 'What? . . . Ahh shit!' He sounded disgusted. 'I thought I was starting to fade.'

We all broke up.

'Cops,' Murphy whispered. 'They're coming up on us!' He pointed excitedly at the pair of blinding headlights that were closing in on us from behind, looking like two anti-aircraft spots to our pinpoint pupils. 'Quick! Throw the shit out the windows,' he yelled. 'Get rid of the grass and booze, maaan!' Like if it *is* the cops they're not going to see cases of beer and about four ounces of grass come flying out the van in front with all our faces pressed against the window. Without warning Murphy slid the side door open and kicked out four cases of beer, then two bags of grass. To this day I have no idea why he thought throwing the beer out was going to save us.

'Crazy bastards,' Norm mumbled. We didn't say a word. The anti-aircraft lights hit high beam and the car was right on our back bumper, beeping its horn. We all waited for the flashing light and the wail of a siren. Then, whoooosh, around the right side of the van . . . it's alongside.

'They're pulling us over. Stop, Norm! It's resisting arrest!' yells Murphy.

Norman the Wise doesn't say a thing, but we're all convinced that this is the first step in a long chain of events that will end with us breaking rocks and a lifetime of buggery at the hands of depraved, vicious guards in some God-forsaken penal colony that makes Devil's Island look like the Club Med.

Suddenly Pig says, 'It's a caravan, man. It's a family car with a caravan. They've got kids in the back.'

I crawled over to the window and, sure enough, it's just a family in a car towing a caravan. The driver honked and shook his fist. Must have been the cases of beer. Murphy crawls over and ventures a peep.

'It's cops, maan. Oh shit!'

'Murphy, they're pulling a bloody caravan, man,' I yell at him. 'It's not the cops.'

'Yes it is. It's . . . it's . . . it's cops on holiday!'

Well that was it. The whole van, including Norm and Rodney, burst into hysterical laughter. 'Cops on holiday,' Paul screamed, holding his ribs. I'm pissing myself. Pig's laughing so hard that no sound's coming out and tears are streaming down his cheeks. Norm's trying to keep the van in a straight line. Rodney's on his knees crying with laughter. And Murphy . . . Murphy hasn't taken his eyes off the holidaying coppers with their wives, kids and caravan.

'The beer! The beer!' shouted Paul.

'And the dope,' yelled Pig. 'Oh shiiittt. Norm, turn around, man. Turn around. We've got to go back and get the stuff. It's not far!'

Norm dutifully slowed the van and threw a U-turn in the middle of nowhere, without a word of complaint. He's heard this all before and way worse. Norm was the best. Without him we probably would have been dead or worse long ago. We headed back about half a mile and there in the middle of the road was a busted case of beer, the cans scattered all over the highway. We gathered them, threw them in the van and began walking back down the road with Norm driving slowly behind, the headlights on high beam.

It was a beautiful night in the last days of January 1971. In the majestic panorama above floated the electric white band of the Milky Way. Alpha Centauri pointed its cosmic beacon toward the ancient Crux, or Southern Cross, which floated at 7 o'clock on the celestial dial. There at 12 o'clock, the mighty Orion and to its right Aldebaran in Taurus. There Virgo, Leo, Gemini, Sirius, Hydra. Billions of diamonds dancing around a silver moon from which the Gods played their magic games with the earth, tides and minds. A sky so clear, deep and inviting that I reached up into it, took a handful of dripping diamonds and put them gently in my pocket. Cosmic lovebeads to bring us luck at the festival the next day. The heavens were alive and talking to us with light. We stood mesmerised, feeling so small and humble in that presence, drinking it all in, trying to will ourselves off this planet and into the great unknown, or waiting for some passing alien to pick up on our peaceful vibes, whoosh down and take us all for a cosmic ride. But none came. Bummer!

'Hey, get off the highway,' yelled Norm, who'd been watching our cosmic reverie. 'You'll be road kill if a truck comes.' The moment passed and we continued our search and found an intact case of beer in a gully beside the road. We walked for about another hundred yards, with Buster panting happily beside us, and that's when we saw it. No, not an alien spacecraft, but something just as way-out in the middle of nowhere. A beaten-up, bright yellow Volkswagen kombi van, covered on all sides and top with cosmic paisley motifs, peace signs and medieval inscriptions. It was parked just off the road to our right. Next to it, stacked neatly by a fence, the other two cases of beer. We wandered over to check it out and a voice from the nowhere of the dark of a nearby field said, 'Hi, brothers . . . Peace, maaan.'

We all took off in different directions, including Buster.

'Wait, brothers,' said the voice. 'Don't leave.' Out of the paddock floated a genuine hippie couple. Both resplendent in burgundy and yellow crushed velvet bells, embroidered ugg boots, embroided Afghan sheepskin fur-collared coats and floppy black velvet hats with big feathers in the band. Their faces were decorated in bright green and orange day-glo make-up like Red Indian warriors'. 'Peace brothers,' the guy said again. 'I'm Gadriel, maan.' His beautiful young girlfriend just sniffed a bunch of wild somethings she had in her hands while Buster happily sniffed her crotch. We might have been tripping but these two were off the planet.

We stood there looking at them like a bunch of kindergarten kids with stage fright. In the security of the van, with the people you loved and trusted, the acid trip was fine. But day-glo Gadriel and his lady floating out of a field out here in the night . . . Whooaa!

'Peace,' Gadriel said again.

'Peace,' said Paul, who had always been the closest thing to a hippie amongst us and, truth be known, was a hippie at heart.

'Peace be with you all,' the guy said again. 'Hey, you're Billy Thorpe, maaan? He focused his spinning beams on me. *Whoa . . . Freak. Gadriel's speaking to me! . . . Handle it . . . Handle it.* 'Hey man, cooool. Me and Moon Girl are on our way to Wallacia, man, to see you guys. Cool, maan. Say hi to Billy Thorpe, Moon Girl. And that's the Aztecs, maaan.' Gadriel slipped the band another peace sign. 'Cool, maaan,' he said, slowly nodding his head in agreement with some cosmic thought he was having. Moon Girl floated herself over to me about three feet off the ground, a completely blissed out smile on her face and Buster's nose an inch from her arse. She gave me a flower and a peace sign which she repeated to all the guys without saying a word.

'Hey, maan, coool . . . cooool. Look what the Gods gave us, man.' Gadriel gestured to the cases of beer by the fence and our gladbags of grass that he had in his hands. 'Me an' Moon Girl were dancing with spirits of the field, maan, and they fell like manna from heaven. Landed at our feet, maan. You want some?'

We all looked at one another.

Gadriel pointed to the cases of beer by the fence. 'You take that. Me an' Moon Girl don't imbibe of the devil alcohol. And here, man, the Gods sent this for you too. They knew you'd be here before you did. Take this peaceful offering of the sacred weed, maaann, and have a safe journey.'

He handed me one of the gladbags of dope. 'There's a cosmic bond between us forever, maaan.'

'Hey, I threw that.' Murphy started to say.

'Thanks man,' said Pig. 'That's very gracious of the Gods.'

'Peace be with you,' said Paul.

We all gave Gadriel a peace sign, headed back to the van and drove off, leaving Gadriel and Moon Girl dancing to some cosmic symphony that was playing only in their heads. As we drove away half a dozen day-glo, velvet-clad moon-trippers joined them in their dance beside the road. They must have been standing in the dark silence all the time. Too blissed out or paranoid to get into a conversation with a group of mortals by the side of a country highway.

'Hey, that was cool,' said Paul and we all agreed.

'That guy really believes that this stuff fell from heaven,' Pig said. 'He was being very gracious in sharing with us, so let's not insult his loving gesture. Let's roll some up and have a beer. It's only fitting.'

Roll, roll, roll, light, puff, puff, puff. Open beers. Gulp. 'Hi ho, hi ho, it's off to Wallacia we go . . .'

'Morpheeno, por favor . . . Morpheeno . . . por favor, señor,' the Severino brothers pleaded, shooting me out of the story.

'Where's your goddamned brother, you spick motherfuckers?' Cirello strode over to the brothers. Their eyes were wide with terror. I almost broke up at the sight of these two maniacs peeking terrified over the tops of their sheets like two kids who had just heard a bump in the night. 'You talk to me you can have all the shit you want. No talk, no stuff. Understand?'

They didn't reply. Just stared at Cirello as he came back

over to his chair by my bed. 'Motherfuckers,' he spat. 'They'll roll over. Where were you?'

'What?' I asked. I was still looking at the loons opposite.

'Wallacia. You were telling me about Wallacia.' For a second it was gone and I racked my brain. 'The hippies at the side of the road. You were talking about the . . .'

'Oh yeah, right. Well . . .' I continued my story.

The rest of the trip was fairly uneventful except for an enormous fart that Buster dropped which freaked everybody out so much we had to stop and jump out for some air. And an eighteen-wheeler that threw one of its rear tyres which caught fire, spinning straight at us in the blackened night. An 80 mph spinning fireball headed straight at us, bounced off the road in front, sailed over the top of the van and danced off into the distance behind us. Nobody said a word for about a stone freaked minute, then we were 'Oh shitting' and 'Whoa, maaning' about that for the next fifty miles.

We arrived at the festival site at 2 p.m. the next day. All still flying and ranting from the acid high. And all buggered. Standing at the front gate was our old mate, ex-roadie and Wallacia festival organiser, Lee Dillow. Lee had been an acquaintance of mine since back in the Cross in 1964 and for a while in 1969 he had been my road manager. He, Norm and Norm's brother John had grown up together and had been mates all their lives. Lee's an incredibly funny guy, with a natural speed-ball repartee and a sense of humour as dry as a sand sandwich. Everyone loved him and in another life he could easily have been a successful stand-up comedian. For a while he was aide de camp to Paul 'Crocodile Dundee' Hogan and worked as his assistant through that movie and the sequel. He spent a lot of time in LA, where we hooked up again after many years. I had a couple of hilarious nights with Hogan and John Cornell, aka 'Strop', when they were renting Joan Collins' house in Bel Air. As we drove through the gates, Lee stuck his head in the passenger-side window.

'Morning, William my son. Norm. Morning, gentlemen. Ah-ha! Long night, eh boys?' He laughed knowingly.

'G'day, son,' said Norm. 'Everything sweet?'

'Ah, there's a bit of a shitfight going on.' Lee rubbed the bridge of his nose between his thumb and forefinger. Lee's eyes looked like piss holes in the snow and there was no doubt he'd been up for a week. I asked him what the problem was. 'It's the local council,' he said. 'They're hassling us about not having enough portable dunnies. And the wombat fucking contractors doing the fences are as slow as an elephant fart. We can't let anyone in until the council approves the shitters and the fence is done. So it could start a bit late.'

'Oh yeah. How late?' I asked. We were one of the headliners but the best spot on an outdoor concert is not always closing the show. For me the top spot was always just as the sun went down and you got the best of both worlds, with a cosmic light show followed by the stage lights. It was always *the* magic moment.

'You guys are supposed to be on at 9. It'll probably be more like midnight, but that's cool. Nobody's got to be anywhere.'

'What time's Daddy Cool on, mate?' Norm asked. I believe that this was Daddy Cool's first performance outside Melbourne.

'They're right before you guys,' Lee replied.

'Looks like a big crowd,' I said.

'Yeah, it's great. The problem right now is we've got 30,000 excited punters out there waiting to get in and they won't let them in until they've approved the whole fuckin' thing. But we'll be sweet.' Lee slid the tip of his right forefinger the length of his nose, from bridge to tip, in the old street sign. 'Zippy qua with a naktie, son,' he said to me. It was an old street phrase that went back to the Cross in the '60s. Everything's sweet.

'Where to?' Norm asked.

'Backstage area. Your suite is reserved.'

We drove through the gate, acknowledging the smiling faces, waves and 'Onya, Thorpie. Onya, Pig. Paulee . . . Pauleee' from the passers-by. I always get an adrenalin rush when I'm pulling into an outdoor festival. Everyone's there for one reason and it's a great feeling to know that you are a big part of it. Passing an endless array of panel vans, camper vans, tents, caravans, trucks, motorbikes and cars, we reached the backstage area and the full view of the site met our eyes. It was expertly picked and perfect for a three-day outdoor festival, with the stage and backstage area at the bottom of a long sloping valley. Tents with flags, coloured ribbons, teepees, cloth gunyas and other makeshift abodes were dotted on the hillside and behind the fences on three sides like futuristic medieval villages. The stage was about eighty feet across and high up, so it dominated the site. It was the biggest stage I'd seen up to then and the PA in front of it gave me a boner. This was going to be great. Bless you, Dillow my son. Bless you.

Buster had slept most of the way, but as soon as the van door opened he took off like shit out of a shanghai. I guess he wanted to put some distance between himself and the maniacs he'd been locked up with for the last twenty hours.

But he could look after himself and I let him go. Hey, dogs like festivals too. Apart from the bands that had already arrived and the crews that swarmed like ants over the stage scaffold and grounds, the place was eerily empty. It's people that make a festival, not the music. We had a caravan to ourselves and moved in.

The hassle with the dunnies and fence went on all day and finally the local authorities had to let the 30,000-plus crowd in before they rioted. But the hassle continued. No music could be played over the PA and no bands were allowed to perform. Only emergency public address messages were permitted and the event started to get weird. It was getting dark and the natives were getting restless, to say the least. Suddenly, as if some mass subliminal message had been transmitted through 30,000 minds, the whole place went tribal. Many people had travelled hundreds of miles to be there, only to be left standing in utter frustration outside the gates for hours. When finally let into the site they had been left to their own devices to entertain and amuse themselves. Sitting around with no music and nothing better to do, they started to get into their festival stashes. I could hear the ground swell and buzz, changing in pitch and intensity. By 6 p.m. a low ominous moan began to float from the crowd. It told me they'd obviously taken a serious slice of their three-day stash in one hit. The psycho corroboree began.

Forty-four-gallon drums that had been placed all over the festival site for refuse were piled with wood, debris, anything that burned. Suddenly they burst into blazing life, setting the sky on fire in a rainbow of licking flames and a million glowing sparks. Thousands danced in hypnotic, chanting circles around a hundred raging fires that dotted every part of the hillside. As they danced they started banging the burning drums with planks of wood and branches in a percussive cacophony of tribal rhythms. With every blow a thousand Roman candles of floating golden sparks exploded into the night sky, illuminating the primordial mass in one mesmerising, spontaneous ancient primal ritual. The audience was no longer 30,000 individuals but one tribe venting its anger and frustration. Chanting an ancient prayer to the Gods for the festival to begin. A hundred fires blazed like burning shrines. Holy beacons in an ancient rite. Guiding spirit and prayer to the star-studded heavens. The chants grew louder, merging slowly into one soul-stirring drone of human emotion. We stood there mesmerised, in no doubt that we were witnessing the human race in its natural, uninhibited, primal state. A glimpse of something from millenniums past, it was both incredible and scary.

The police got the message in a heartbeat and fifteen minutes later the festival began. The original schedule had the first band on stage at midday, but it was now 6.30. Although the organisers had cut some of the smaller bands off the shortened bill, it didn't look like we'd be going on until at least 1 a.m. so we all joined the primal party that had now spread to backstage. Kerosene lamps were lit in the tents. Barbecues flamed. Joints and wine casks went round and the party really began. I wandered around talking to people I hadn't seen in a while and about half an hour later I ran up on stage to watch Fanny Adams play. Fanny Adams was Doug Parkinson's new band and it featured Vince Maloney, Johnny Dick and Teddy Toi, all ex-Aztecs. They were great!

Pig, El Condor and Paul were already there. All grinning out of their trees. In fact they looked ripped to the gills. I couldn't work out why. I'd been with them all evening and I knew they hadn't been into anything much. In fact we'd all talked about how this was an important gig and that we were here to play. We'd have the whole weekend to party afterwards, but they were blitzed and could hardly talk. I asked Paul if he was OK. He just grinned at me like a lovable leprechaun. And Pig! Dear old Piggy had turned into a living, spinning Sitting Bull, resplendent in a red and white American Indian blanket and black felt western hat with the crown punched out and a huge eagle feather standing a foot from the brim like some sort of antenna. I went over to him. 'Ug,' he said. I didn't even ask!

It was about 7 p.m. We had plenty of time before we went on so I decided to go on a hunt for Buster, who had vanished when we arrived. I can remember being out at the back of the crowd when whatever it was hit me and—baaadoiiiingg!—something came on like gangbusters. I knew instantly that some lowlife had dosed me. It took the top of my head clean off! I had slept for a while in the afternoon and woke up refreshed and ready to rock. Apart from a few beers I hadn't had anything. I racked my spinning brain, trying to work out what was happening.

It must have been the bloody cake! Earlier, after we had eaten, one of the promoter's girlfriends, a beautiful young Californian hippie dressed in a squaw's outfit, brought us some coffee and cake. Unsuspectingly, we all ate it. In fact I had about three pieces. It must have been laced big time with God knows what.

I came to about five hours later. I had no idea where I was or what I was doing there. The sound of my name was sort of familiar but that was it. I sat up to find myself in the arms of some young girl out in the crowd, in the middle of

30,000 screaming maniacs. They were yelling for the band and me.

'So who's on next?' a voice yelled through the PA. 'Thorpie and the Aztecs!' the crowd replied in a cheer. 'Thorpeee . . . Thorpeee . . . Thorpeee . . .' they chanted.

'Well they'll be here in ten minutes so get yer arses into gear. It's time to rock!' . . . Yeahh . . . whistling . . . yelling.

I had no idea what was happening. I was completely whacked. The crowd's cheers came at me in nauseating tidal waves that broke on giant steel drums inside my head. I felt like throwing up. I put my hands over my ears, trying desperately to shield my brain from the sickening sounds. I looked at the girl and she started to melt. I looked around me. I was sitting in the centre of thousands of terrifying creatures, with liquid limbs and fire eyes. Their moaning heads and faces were a grotesque blur of twisted dripping flesh, morphing before my eyes. I was ratshit and on a major bummer. 'Who are . . . wha, what's happening?' I tried to ask the vibrating blonde who was stroking my hair. She just rocked back and forth, humming without a word. I don't think anybody had recognised me in the ripped crowd. For all intents and purposes I was just another one of the thousands of blissed-out people there that night, enraptured or suffering from the tribal stone that had occurred some hours earlier. I tried to get up and fell on my face. I tried again. Same thing. My legs wouldn't get in sync with my head. Whatever I was on was seriously strong. It felt like mescaline but I wasn't sure. I tried to get my mind around it but couldn't. It was too bent.

'Billy Thorpe . . . Has anybody seen Billy Thorpe?' Thorpe . . . Thorpe . . . Thorpe . . . ricocheted the echoing voice around my skull. 'Thorpeeee . . . Are you out there

Thorpeeeeee?' It echoed again. I lay back on the cool grass, hyperventilating. Too gone to move, let alone sprint up and say 'I'm here . . . I'm here.' I definitely wasn't there. I was starting to space out on the sky diamonds and the chanting when I was lifted full body off the ground and carried like a babe in arms through the crowd which melted and scamelshed in a blur of colour and sound as I passed. A voice said, 'You'll be right, mate. I've got you.' Then somebody else dripped alongside and the voice said, 'He's cool. Looks pretty out of it, though. I'll get him backstage. Tell them to put an acoustic act or something on.' I couldn't speak. I looked at the face that was carrying me and the blur morphed back into Bobby Jones.

'Oh Jesus, Bobby, is that you, mate?' I managed to get out.

'Yes, mate. Be cool. I'll look after you.'

'Where's the door to get out, mate? I . . . I've got to get out of here! Somebody's dosed me with something . . . I'm gone!'

'There's no door, mate. We're outside at a festival,' I heard Bobby giggle.

Festival? . . . What's a festival? I thought.

But the moment I knew it was Bobby, I immediately felt safe. Bobby Jones was the toughest guy I've ever known, and I've known and seen some serious tough in my time. I'd known him since the early '60s in Melbourne. Back then he had a troupe of loyal young devotees whom he trained regularly in the park in Beaconsfield Parade, Saint Kilda. Bobby was now the most respected and feared martial artist in Australia and the sensei of the many Go Ju Kai karate schools that he had developed and now promoted and managed. I'd done a lot of judo and jujitsu as a kid and was always interested in martial arts. I joined Bobby's personal club on Elizabeth Street in Melbourne and I went to the regular public night classes. He had shown me incredible respect, and as well as the public classes I had been privileged to train with Bobby and his black belts during their private daily training sessions. Bobby and his black belts also looked after the security at most of the major events and were the regular security at many of Melbourne's dances and clubs, including Birtie's and Sebastian's. Bobby later went on to work as personal security for all the major international acts that came through Australia in the '70s and '80s, including the Stones. He did the exclusive security worldwide for Fleetwood Mac in their heyday. One of his black belts, Dennis Dunstan, stayed with Mick Fleetwood for ten years and eventually managed him. It was Dennis who hooked me up with Mick and the relationship turned into our band, the Zoo, which was successful in the USA in 1992–93, having the second most played single, 'Shakin' the Cage', on US AOR radio that year. Bobby's organised security methods had changed the face of the Melbourne scene and kicked the arse of just about every sharpie and skinhead who had the misfortune to have come across him and his boys when they started stinks in the gigs.

'Take him to his caravan,' I heard a voice say. The next minute I was lying in a bunk with Sitting Bull opposite me, which freaked me out even more.

'That you, Pig?' I asked.

'Ug,' he grunted, which is all he said for the next two days.

I managed to explain that I'd been dosed to Norman E and the process of trying to get me straightened out enough to play began. I must have drunk fifty gallons of black coffee.

It didn't straighten me out but the familiar faces stopped melting and my brain started to get some sort of control. I'd played ripped many times and the thought of going on stage in front of 30,000 people didn't faze me that much. Time, talking, laughing and numerous 'Ugs' passed and I eventually found myself in the dressing-room below the stage, surrounded by the concerned faces of the band and crew. Norm was fussing over me like a mother hen.

'You all right, mate?' he asked. I told him I was and asked when we were on. 'As soon as you're ready, son.'

'Well, now's as good a time as any, mate.'

'Here's your guitar, Thorpie,' he said, putting the strap over my head and leading me out of the tent.

Paul said, 'See you at the end, Thorpie, Murphy, Pig.'

'Ug,' went Pig.

The stage was at least forty feet from the ground and to get to it I had to climb what seemed like a thousand steps. My guitar neck felt like it was made of rubber and the strings were rubber bands. I knew I was about to play but really didn't know what was happening around me. All I could hear was 'Thorpeeee . . . Thorpeeee.' I was almost at the top when I took a major wrong turn and stepped out into midair, high above the crowd. Everything went into slow motion. I had my left hand on the guitar neck. I felt it hit something, breaking it clean off about halfway down the neck and leaving it hanging by the strings. I looked at the crowd. Looked up and saw Sitting Bull, Murphy, Norm and Paul's beaming faces over the front of the stage checking out my trim . . . It was surreal and in no way frightening. Somehow I knew I wasn't going to hurt myself and I just floated down. Or so it felt. I expected to land gracefully on my feet and climb back up on the stage. I looked down again and landed in the soft cushion of a hundred gentle hands that were reaching up to break my fall. Not a scratch, a break or even a broken fingernail. When I looked up I realised just how lucky I'd been. It was a hell of a long way up to Sitting Bull's grinning face.

Bobby and some of his boys got me backstage. The band were all there, staring at me like I'd returned from the dead. They were still as whacked as I was.

'Whoa, Thorpie, that was really fucking cool,' laughed Paul. 'Can you do it again?'

'Ug!' said Big Chief Pig.

Apart from my guitar neck, I was fine. Not a scratch. Norm got me another guitar. This time when I went up the stairs Norm and Bobby walked either side of me and I made it to the stage. The whole crowd must have seen me fall and when I reached the top a deafening roar rose up into the star-encrusted dome above. The sight from the stage was incredible. For as far as I could see a sea of faces danced in an eerie combination of fire and starlight. Liquid . . . Flowing . . . Moving and swelling like some great rainbow-coloured ocean driven by a slow wind. Every colour imaginable drifting and floating in choreographed waves, conducted by some unseen hand. Back and forth. Side to side. One floating, heaving, chanting mass. It was beautiful.

Norm plugged me into my stack and Lee came over to me. 'You right, son? Feel like a big pipe of opium or what?' he said jokingly.

'You're fucking kidding, mate. Let's get going before I sprout wings and fly away.'

I looked at all the guys and they were all looking at me. We were ready. Lee went to the mike and said, 'Well, looks like he's been enjoying the festival to meeee. Are you ready?'

Yeahhhhh! . . .
'Are you sure?'
Yeahhhhhhh!
'Then here they are . . . The one and only Aztecs!'

The crowd roared as I counted in a slow blues and the band took off at brain-melting level. I felt that indefinable, electrifying magnetic energy that charges the air and connects it to the force that drives the cogs that turns the wheels that get me off. It's the drug of drugs. So bloody addictive. One hit and you're hooked for life.

Now, when I say I counted in a slow blues I mean a real s-l-o-w blues. This song was so slow you could have washed your car, eaten dinner, gone to the movies and mowed the lawn between offbeats. I freaked myself out. I was ripped to my toe tips. My guitar still felt like it was made of rubber with my fingers growing out of it. The crowd was melting. I was sitting on the wing of a Flying Fortress at 65,000 feet. And I was loving every bloody second of it. I looked around at the band and they were all up there in the stratosphere with me. Rocking hard. The feel was incredible. The crowd was wailing. So I kept it going and it lasted for fifteen of the longest minutes of my life. But the crowd loved it and it finished with a deafening cheer. I don't remember too much after that, but Lee Dillow told me the next day that we'd killed them. And evidently I was having such a great time they had to get a hook around my neck to get me off. Like I said, it's addictive. You can never get enough of that high.

About 3 a.m. I found Buster. Or I should say somebody else found him and put him in our caravan. I was still ripped and wobbled in to find him stretched out on my bunk. He was lying on his back, as stiff as a board with his legs straight out and his tongue hanging from the side of his mouth like a roll of athletic gauze. 'What's the matter, boy?' I asked, stroking his big head. He didn't move and I thought he was dead. Then he rolled his bloodshot eyes. I tried to find somebody to help me and Lee told me there was a medical tent up the back of the crowd. The festival was still raging and nobody could be spared to help a freaked-out rocker and his spaced-out dog so I struggled up through the crowd, out of my brain and with a stiff ninety-pound boxer in my arms. Chain were raging on stage and no-one took any notice of Thorpie and his catatonic dog. No-one that is except for some of the security. Ten minutes and a dozen hysterical laughs later, I was standing outside the medical tent.

Just then the door of the adjacent caravan opened and out poured half a dozen big coppers. I was standing outside the police command post! Oh shittt! Maintain . . . maintain. Coppers. You're whacked . . . maintain! I'm still spinning big time. I've got a stiff dog in my arms and I'm standing face to face with a bunch of melting coppers!

'Jesus, your sheila's a bit of a dog, Thorpie,' the big sergeant laughed, breaking up the rest of them.

'I . . . er . . . um . . . well . . .'

'Haven't been getting her pissed, son?' another comedian copper asked.

'Looks a bit young to me, sarg. Better check her age.'

They all broke up. I'm seeing stars and lightning bolts shooting out of the top of their heads. Um . . . dinggg . . . oh shitttt . . . padoingggg! My eyes were spinning like two raffle wheels but the coppers hadn't picked up on it in the half dark of the caravan and tent lights.

'Well he's um a bit . . . I'm, er . . . spoinggg . . . just taking him . . . into the medical tent.' Talking was hard enough, but talking to the law . . .

'Mary's on duty,' said the sergeant. 'I'll introduce you to her. She's a big fan.'

Oh joy. In I waltzed, Buster in arms, coppers in tow. Spoing . . . badoing . . . breathe in, out . . . in, out. Maintain . . . Maintain.

'Look who we've found, Mary. His girl's a bit crook, luv,' the sarge laughed.

'Oh my, Billy Thorpe! I was going to ask someone to get me your autograph,' she said excitedly. 'Will you sign one for me?' She hunted around for a piece of paper, not taking a blind bit of notice of the fact I had a bloody stiff dog in my arms.

The medical tent was just that—a tent with a canvas floor. A couple of St John Ambulance guys who looked like they'd just come from twenty schooners at the pub sat in a corner chatting. They nodded their heads to me as I came in. Around the room were a number of stretchers containing some very out of it looking people, all contemplating a life that in their minds was coming to a rapid end at any moment. Obviously there as the result of a freak-out.

Mary was a big country nurse. Late forties, five foot ten, with curly blonde shoulder-length hair parted down the centre. She had a ruddy complexion, huge boobs and a broad beam. In my ripped state she looked like Mae West in a nurse's uniform. Mary's getting some paper. The coppers are all grinning at me and I'm holding a stiff dog and doing the oh shit shuffle. Heeeelp!

'Er, can I put him on this table?' I asked Mary.

'Yes, go ahead,' she smiled, coming back with the paper and pencil. I put Buster down. He was still rigid, with all four legs sticking straight out and his big pink tongue distended. 'Can you sign one to me with love to Mary and the other to my husband Bob. Say something to him like "get rooted". He'd love that from you.'

The coppers all broke up and so did she. Boing . . . pirouette . . . maintain . . . maintain . . . I signed Mary's with love and told Bob to get fucked. She took them, thrilled as a schoolgirl, and gave me a kiss on the cheek. *Oh Jesus, how do I get into these things?* I thought, Maintain . . . maintain!

'Now let me see,' Mary said, examining Buster. 'Do you think somebody may have given him something?' She looked at me and must have been able to tell I was out of it but she didn't say a word. I just smiled.

'Er, I . . . I don't really know. He's been gone all day.'

'Looks to me like he's in shock.' She checked his heart, felt his legs and stomach. Checked his eyes with a pencil light. 'Well, he *seems* OK. There's been a few spider bites but I don't think that's it.' She felt around his groin and when she touched Buster's dick it shot up, looking like a frayed wet carrot, and quivered like a throwing knife in a wall. It was red raw. 'Well that part's still alive,' she laughed. 'He's going to be fine. I'll give him a little stimulant to revive him. OK?'

I nodded. She got a bottle of spirits of ammonia and waved it under Buster's nose. His eyes shot open, his legs relaxed, his tongue went back in and he started panting and thump-thumping his stubby tail on the table. It was a miracle. Back from the near dead. 'There there. Good boy,' Mary said, patting his silly big head. His eyes rolled, loving the attention. 'Now let's have a look here.' She got a long-stemmed cotton bud from a tray beside the table, opened Buster's legs and touched his quivering dick. Aiy kai yai . . . yai ya yai . . . yai yai! He shot straight up in the air, landed

MOST PEOPLE I KNOW

on all fours on the table, shook himself and took off around
the tent like his arse was on fire. Straight out the door and
gone.

'Shit, Mary!' said the sarge. 'That hit the bloody spot!'

'Oh oh!' she said.

'What?'

'It's exhaustion. I reckon he's been rooting himself silly.
There must be a bitch on heat out there somewhere. You
better find him quick before he roots himself to death.'

Great! I could see me wandering around in the crowd all
night, whacked, saying, 'Excuse me, has anybody seen a
couple of fucking dogs?' I just let it go. I was too gone and
exhausted to be tromping around in the dark looking for
Buster. He could be anywhere. Anyway, if he wanted to kill
himself over some bitch, so be it. Must be some extra fine
pussy. I'd write a blues about him one day.

I didn't find Buster until the next night when one of the
crew brought him to the caravan in a truck. He was stiff as
an ironing board and stayed that way until we got back to
Melbourne more than twenty-four hours later. It was nearly
a week until he could walk. And they say dogs grow to
resemble their owners. I mean, really.

Jack Cirello was laughing his head off. 'Jesus Christ!' he
said at last. 'You *do* belong in here.'

Right then Bertha and Idi came in and she gave me my
shot. I didn't argue. After her last rave to me about my
heart, I'd stopped protesting and did as she said. Kick back
and relax. Kick back? I was so far back they'd need to send
a search party to find me. The Severinos tried the morpheeno rave on Bertha as soon as they saw her fixing me.
Cirello stared them down and Bertha was out the door,
leaving them shivering and sweating like a couple of turtles

230

on an LA freeway. Cirello tried to get me back into conversation but Morpheus had me and it took some time until I could speak again.

'Jesus, man,' he said, 'that shit sure knocks your dick in the dust!'

'What?'

'You went out like a goddamned light.'

'What do you mean?' I said, staring at him, bewildered.

'You been out for two hours.' He smiled. 'You OK?'

I looked at the Severinos, then back at Detective Cirello. 'Sure, Jack, sure. Right as rain. On top of the world!' Beep, beep, beep, beep.

14
Cirello Loses It

The Severinos were sweating pineapples. Ferocious sunken black eyes darted in oily wet stubbled faces. Lips swollen red from constant biting. Scratching, snorting, moaning and thrashing around in their beds. The eerie sounds of rattling chains. They looked like doomed patients in some twisted Boris Karloff movie. Meanwhile, I guess you could say that Jack Cirello and I had hit it off. Finding out that we had been in the Cross and the Whiskey together so many years before and then meeting again under these ridiculous circumstances had blown us both away, and the kind of bond that exists between people who have shared a special event, time and place started to form. We discussed the Vietnam war, the state of America, music, cars. You name it. Bertha had hit me up once during the day and I'd conked out for a while, only to come to and get straight back into it with Detective Jack Cirello who was still sitting next to my bed, eyes fixed on the Severinos.

'Won't be long now,' he said. 'They're starting to Jones bad. Look at the miserable fucks. Hey, greaseballs. Hey . . . Feeling a little uptight?' He laughed. 'Motherfuckers!'

'Argh, morpheeno . . . por favor, morpheeno,' they moaned.

'Fuck you,' Cirello said and went back to talking to me.

'Hey Jack, do you mind if I ask you something?'

'What?' he asked.

'With them. You know, your partner . . .'

Cirello looked as me for a moment and his eyes teared over. 'Oh man,' he said in a long sad sigh. 'It's 'cause of me Bobby joined the force. He was like my kid brother. Came up through the ranks fast. Thirty-one years old. Thirty-fuckin'-one, man. Second week on the job. Wife and two young kids . . .' He looked away for a second, shaking back his composure.

'We traced them to an address in Queens. Staked it out and went in at 2 a.m. Younger brother wasn't there. I told Bobby to hang back but he was gung-ho. Young. Bullet-proof.' Cirello gazed vacantly at the air above my head, focusing on some distant image that only he could see. Tears bounced off his flushed cheeks. 'Those fucking animals cut him down when he ran through the door. Cut him to pieces with a pump-action. Didn't have a goddamned chance. Took him five days to die. You fucking animals!' he screamed at them.

I lay there watching and listening. Not saying a word. He calmed and started to speak again.

'They staked out a young couple. Young Jewish couple. Just married a couple months. Ran a small jewellery business down in the diamond district.' Cirello was breathing heavily. Veins swelled and pulsed on his neck like blue vipers. His eyes were glued to the Severinos as he spoke. From their faces, they knew exactly what was happening. 'There were three of the cocksuckers. Those two and their scumbag brother. Been high on base and smack for a week. Followed the couple home. Waited until they were asleep and broke into the joint. They wanted diamonds . . . thought they had them stashed in the house. They beat them. Gun-whipped them. The husband kept denying they had any so they took the wife . . .' He hesitated for a second. He'd seen it, I could tell. His mind flicking through images as he spoke. 'They tied the husband to a chair and the wife to the bed. Took turns raping her over and over in front of him . . . Forced him to watch . . . Did horrible things to her. Even used their gun barrels. Tore her to pieces . . . Coroner said she died from shock . . . Fucking animals!' he screamed, spitting at them. They both winced.

'Must have forced the husband to watch the whole thing. Only a little guy. The poor helpless bastard. Can you imagine, man?'

Yes I could! My mind flashed to Lynn and the kids back in LA, alone. No idea where I was. 'Oh God, get me out of here,' I prayed under my breath.

Cirello continued. 'Tried to terrorise him into telling them where the diamonds were and getting their rocks off at the same time. Kick is, there weren't any fucking diamonds. They worked for her parents. These pricks wouldn't believe it. They ransacked the house. Left the husband tied and gagged in his own bedroom looking at his beautiful young wife, raped, naked and dead in a pool of blood on their bed. When they couldn't find anything they gun-whipped his face to a pulp and slit his throat. Even got at her again after she was dead.'

Cirello swallowed hard, trying to get his mind around the picture of her that was indelibly burnt into his soul.

'Neighbours were woken by the noise. Caught the numberplate on the car as they sped away. They were so fucking high they'd parked right outside the building, the dumb fucks. I was on the scene ten minutes later. Jesus Christ, it was a fucking war zone. Blood everywhere. Fucking horrible what they'd done. Especially to her. Bad as anything I saw in Nam.' He gazed off again. 'I . . . I got a wife and kid too man.' He tilted his head to one side and nodded, sighing a long sigh at the thought of them.

'Me too,' I said.

'Their wedding photographs were by their bed. Happy young Jewish couple. You know, full of life and hope. Just starting their life together. Smiling at the camera. Happy. In love . . . She was really beautiful.'

Cirello shot up, grabbed a bedpan from my table and threw it full bore with a backhand that sailed it across the room and crashed it into the face of the one directly opposite me. 'You fucking scum!' he yelled. 'I want your fucking brother or I'm going to slit your mother's fucking throat. I'll fuck your little sister in the arse just like you did to that woman! Comprende, you fucking animals? I'll shoot her fucking tits off and shove them in her mouth, you fucking pieces of shit!'

They heard him all right. They weren't even breathing for fear of death. Cirello was shaking with rage. He went over to their beds and stood there for a minute, glowering at them, then reached for his gun. But the holster was empty, thank God. Must have had to check it when he came in. Otherwise he would have put a bullet in them then and there. He was crazed with rage. Tears streaming down his face, his shoulders racked, sobbing. The Severinos saw him go for his holster and pulled the sheets up over their heads, terrified, rattling their chains. Like the cotton sheets were going to protect them from a .375 magnum in the balls. They shook with fear. The sheets rippling from their shaking bodies.

Beep, beep, beep, beep . . . My heart monitor took off like the reverse signal on a truck backing up. Bertha and Idi appeared at the window to my right. She took in the situation in one glance and came straight in the room with Idi in tow. I guess she must have been able to monitor my heart from outside. I felt like throwing up. The room was turning slow revolutions around the ceiling fans. My heart pounded in my ears in time with the beeping from the monitor and I wanted to be anywhere but in that room.

'I'm sorry, man. I didn't mean to—'

'What the fuck is going on in here, Detective? This is a goddamn hospital,' Bertha yelled. 'And this is an emergency room. Regardless of who's in here. You wanna kill this boy?' She came over to me.

'No, Sister. I'm sorry. I lost . . . I'm sorry. I'm—'

'I think you need some air, detective.'

Cirello hesitated.

'Now!' Bertha screamed. Cirello looked at me for a long beat, then left the room. Idi stood there like a raging black bull but didn't say a word. He pumped a shell in the chamber and stood by the door, glaring at the Severinos.

Beep, beep, beep, beep . . . 'Calm down, boy. Get that heart of yours under control. Come on, give me your arm.' The needle went in. Beep, beep, beep, beep, beep . . . beep . . . beep . . . beep . . . beep . . . beep . . . beep. The morphine started to shut me down.

'What the hell happened here?' Bertha looked from my monitor to the Severinos, who were still shaking under the sheets.

'It's, um . . . partly, partly my fault, Sister.' I could scarcely get my mouth around the words. 'I made the . . . the mistake of asking . . . Detective Cir . . . Cirello about the murders and his . . . his partner. He . . . he just lost it.'

Bertha went over to the Severinos and pulled their sheets back. They looked fifty years older. Expressionless, blood-less skin hung from their faces like slack chicken flesh. Lifeless. Grey and twisted like sun-rotted inner tubes. Black lizard eyes jammed open. Not blinking. Sweat-soaked black hair smeared on their heads and faces. They made no sound. Just lay there shaking. Bertha pulled their sheets all the way down.

'Oh, Jesus!' she said, turning her head in disgust. 'They've pissed and shit themselves . . . This ain't right. This just ain't right. No goddamned way. I ain't taking responsibility for this shit!'

She took out two fresh needles and gave them what they needed more than air itself. The terror left their faces and the blood returned. Their reptilian eyes glazed over and they slowly drifted back into the grinning blitzed-out brothers I'd come to know and love. Bertha left and returned with the young Hispanic nurse who had come in earlier. Angelina. She was carrying fresh linen. They pulled the screens around the beds, changed the shit-filled sheets and cleaned the brothers up. After they were done the nurse left with the dirty laundry and Bertha came over and checked me out.

'You OK, boy?' she asked, checking the monitor. 'That heart seems nice and steady now. You experienced any heart pain at all?'

'Er no, sister . . . I haven't. None . . . at . . . a-all . . .'

'That's good. Now you get some rest while I straighten out the detective's Eyetalian ass. This shit is over or I'm reporting it. It just ain't right. Even they got a right to care in here.'

Bertha and Idi left, Idi taking up his usual position. I was lost somewhere between terror and ecstasy. Cirello had freaked me out to the point I felt physically sick. It wasn't just the horror story of the young girl and her husband. Cirello's rage was demonic and I had no doubt he would have offed them both then and there. I looked at the Severinos and then at the plaster-covered patient in the bed beside me. The screen had been pulled between us for most of the day and I'd forgotten all about him until that moment. Through the right peephole of his bandaged face I thought I saw a wink! 'Get it together son, you're losing it again,' said the voice in my skull.

Cirello had left some magazines on the bed and I tried my best to get into them. Anything to take my mind away from what had just happened and where I was. The colour photographs danced around on the pages like reflections on a windy lake. The pages zoomed in and out, I couldn't get my eyes to focus on the print and I found myself re-reading paragraphs I'd already read. I glanced over and noticed the photographs on the table where Bertha had put them. I pulled myself up with my good arm on the trapeze above my head and reached over. The past was the only sane thing about this place. The first shot I saw was of me standing on the steps of my parents' shop in Moorooka in Brisbane. The photo was rippling like a polaroid that's been rubbed while it's developing, but even through the ripples there was no mistaking my mum and dad. They stood proudly holding a bread-and-butter pudding and an apple pie that they had baked for me on one of my visits home. Looked like the late '60s or early '70s by my ponytail but I couldn't place it. When was that? Mum and Dad. Brisbane. I drifted in and out of the photograph, then off into a blissful half sleep. It felt good. My parents' smiling faces spun slow cartwheels on my eyelids, calling to me across the years.

15
Strike me Lucky

'**P**lease stow your tables and bring your seat backs to their upright position. We will be landing in Brisbane in ten minutes. Thank you for travelling TAA. I hope you've enjoyed your flight and in future when travelling you'll choose to fly with us again.'

I woke up with my head jammed against the window. It was 2.30 on a Friday afternoon in November 1970. After the release of our first album, *The Hoax is Over*, on 2 November, we had gone on tour to promote it. The line-up then still consisted of Kevin Murphy on drums, Lobby Loyde on guitar, Paul Wheeler, bass, and Warren 'Pig' Morgan on keys. The tour criss-crossed four states playing every conceivable gig from pubs to country barns. Anywhere that we could get punters to come and see us. Ninety per cent of it we had travelled in Pig's faithful old blue beast 'The Valiant' with Pig driving and Norman E following with our gear in the van. The tour had flattened us and we decided to take a couple of weeks off after it ended.

During this period I was staying with Pig and his wife Nene in a little flat in St Kilda and we got on great. It was small but most of the time we didn't see that much of each other, except for dinner. Pig and I would head off to work around 8 and wouldn't be back until around 2 the next morning. There'd be the usual post-gig drinks and we'd sleep late into the afternoon, get up, have dinner, and that was the routine. When we didn't work we were at loose ends. After a couple of days bumping into one another around the flat I thought it would be the right thing to do to get out of there for a while and let them have some privacy. I decided to go to Brisbane and see my folks for a couple of days, then head down the Gold Coast. Just hang out for the week.

I loved my parents and sometimes they loved me back a little too much. Whenever I went to stay with them my mum just couldn't relax. She'd be, 'Billy, you look so thin . . . Here, Billy, eat this . . . Come on, it'll do you good . . . Here have some more. Got to keep up your strength.' Or, 'Are you sure you don't want to sleep in our bed? That couch is so uncomfortable. Go on, take it.' Sometimes it was fine but if I wanted any real rest it was impossible. So, lately I'd book into a hotel and just spend the days with them. This trip I'd booked into Lennon's in Roma Street. It wasn't the greatest pub in the world and a long way from its former status as Brisbane's leading hotel. I'd stayed there a lot when the original Aztecs were firing and I knew it well. There were better digs, but I liked the staff and I always got a great suite whenever I stayed there. So Lennon's it was.

A blast of steaming tropical air hit me as I walked out the

terminal doors and took my breath away for an instant. I walked over and stood at a cab rank, wiping the dripping sweat from my face. Some TAA hostesses came bouncing across, all dressed up in their blue flight uniforms and little hats. They all looked really pissed off but one of them, a pretty young blonde with a great little body, gave me a big smile as they passed. I'd noticed her noticing me during the flight. She'd stood on the little footrest on the side of the seat in the adjacent aisle and reached up into the lockers on both sides just a couple of times too many. First time I got a glimpse of her tight little arse. The second a full-on grinning snapshot of her white-lace-panty-covered Theodore. *Mmmm . . . either this pretty young thing is real clumsy or we're getting the come-on*, I thought. She didn't look too clumsy as she wafted past me now. 'See ya, sailor,' she winked. I was up there to see my folks that afternoon and I couldn't be bothered with the old chat-up routine, so I let it slide. 'See ya,' I smiled back as a line of six bouncing young hostie butts disappeared into the parking lot. *Hey, what are you doing?* whined my dick. *She was a walk-up start.* I was going to belt him in the mouth, he was always getting me in the shit. But punching myself in the nuts outside Brisbane Airport was not the right thing to do. Besides, people had recognised me.

I got a cab and was at Lennon's twenty minutes later. I checked into my suite and called my mum. 'Yes, I'm in Brisbane. What's that? . . . No, I won't be staying the night. I've got some business while I'm here and I have to be up early in the morning . . . Excuse me? . . . Oh, Lennon's. Listen, I'm just going to take a shower and I'll be over in an hour and a half . . . You too, Mum. See you soon . . . OK, I won't eat anything before I get there. I promise.' Just as I thought, I've got to eat a whole roast dinner, half a plate-sized apple pie and a bread-and-butter pudding that she and Dad have baked for me. Even then she won't be convinced I've had enough to eat, and I'll have to wrestle with her not to take a hamper of food. Near loved me to death, did my mum. Still does.

It was just as I thought. The table was set ready to go and as soon as I was in the door Mum had a roast lamb dinner on the table. They ate two mouthfuls and I had to eat the rest. There was no worse insult than not cleaning my plate. They'd both come up the hard way in the Depression and you always cleaned your plate. Wasting food was a mortal sin. 'Just think of all those little children starving in Africa, Billy.' Don't get me wrong. No-one makes a roast like my mum. And Mum and Dad's apple pies and bread-and-butter puddings were the stuff of legend. It was the amount that was the problem. There was no way I could tell her that this is it, I'd stopped growing. Mum was convinced if I hadn't left home I'd be six feet by now. She was right, but it would be six feet around!

Mum was all ready to serve up the pies but I needed a week's rest from the dinner. There was no way out of eating them so we talked for a bit. They were always interested in what was happening with my career and a few of the various band members had kept in touch with them over the years, sending them clippings and such. I told them we had just recorded *The Hoax is Over* and that it was at number seven on the Melbourne charts. What I didn't tell them was that we recorded and mixed the album in one night tripping and it was hilarious. At one stage in the lunacy I dropped my only guitar pick, which was green, on the green paisley carpet. Lobby only had one pick so we spent a ridiculously hilarious hour on our hands and knees 'whoa man-ing' at the carpet which we couldn't separate from the pick.

Before eating the pies I took my parents outside to the front of their little store on Fegan Drive and took a shot of them proudly holding their creations. Six servings later I kissed them goodnight. 'I'll be back in a few days . . . Yes, I'd love a roast chicken, Mum. And a pudding, Dad.' I waddled down the drive, fell into the cab and belched and farted my way back to Lennon's.

My folks were in their mid-sixties at that time, so the nights with them were always early. It was about 9 p.m. when I rolled into Lennon's and crashed for the night.

I was awakened about 2 a.m. by a noise. I had no idea what it was but it woke me from a burping coma. I was sweating like a turd in a vinyl handbag. Music was playing. It sounded like it was right next door, but it wasn't that loud. Anyway, after the hotels the Aztecs and I had terrorised how could I possibly ask somebody to keep it down? When I checked the air-conditioner it wasn't working. I called the front desk. 'Oh yes, Mr Thorpe. We're terribly sorry . . . Yes we know. All the air is out at the moment. This heat has shorted something . . . Yes, we're onto it. Good night, Mr Thorpe.' I was just about out again and, *buump!*, there it was again. This went on for about half an hour. Every time I was nearly asleep, *buumpp!* Wide awake by now, I put a wine glass to the adjoining door and heard the muffled sound of people partying. Not heavy, but the unmistakable sounds of laughter and dancing feet shuffling on the carpet. *Buumpp!* Well, bugger this, I've got to say something. Party all they want, but enough of the bumping on the wall. I put on my robe and went and knocked on the door. The party inside went silent. An eye came up to the peephole and then the door flew open.

'Hi, sailor. You lost?' It was the TAA hostess from the

plane. Wrapped in a towel! 'It's OK, girls, it's a friend.' She turned back to me. 'Come in.'

I walked in and the music started again. I turned into the suite, which was a mirror image of mine, and walked into every man's wet dream. Six young girls dancing around in bare feet, panties and T-shirts. 'What . . . I . . . it's . . .' I mumbled.

'A maaannn!' one of them shouted.

'And it's a young man, too,' said another.

'It's OK, come on in,' said the girl who answered the door. 'Don't take any notice of them. They won't hurt you. My name's Vanessa.' She shook my hand. 'We're all hosties.' I recognised a couple of them from the flight.

'What are you all celebrating at two in the morning?'

'We're just relaxing. It's too hot to sleep, and there's a bloody strike on. We're all stuck here for the weekend.'

Holy snapping arseholes, Batman! yelled my dick. *Six girls and we live next door.*

'Hi Vanessa . . . I'm Billy.'

'Oh we know who you are, Billy. Don't be coy. Girls, look who I found wandering around lost.' I was introduced to the others. Kim. Pat. I didn't catch the others' names at first.

I didn't know what to say. Here they are having a rock 'n' roll slumber party in their undies and not giving a flying fuck that I've just walked into it. In fact they seemed over-joyed to see me. They were all a bit pissed and giggly but the vibe was great. All in their early twenties. All big smiles and very relaxed. Their room was stifling hot and the windows were open, but there was no air. They were dripping wet from dancing and their T-shirts were stuck to their tits. Vanessa was a killer five-six natural light blonde with a round Irish face, milk-white skin, big hazel eyes, a perfect body from what I could see beneath her towel, and a cheeky grin. A couple of the other girls were also beautiful. The others attractive but not outstanding. But at 2 a.m. in their wet T-shirts and undies they all looked like Miss World to me.

Vanessa went to the bar fridge. 'Oh shit,' she said, 'we're out of beer. Have any of you girls got any left in those cans? Come on, the sailor's thirsty.'

'No. Look, why don't I go next door and get some?'

I went back to my room. *Oh boy, six girls, six girls*, sang you know who. My fridge had six beers, a half bottle of Moët and assorted soft drinks. I decided to phone room service.

'How can I help you?'

'Can you send a dozen bottles of champagne, a dozen glasses and some ice to 1006 and charge it to my room? What's that? . . . Yes, I know I'm in 1004, but I want it next door . . . What? . . . Oh, just getting to know the neighbours, mate.'

I went back into their room. 'Listen, there was nothing in the fridge so I've ordered a few drinks. They'll be up in a minute. OK?'

'Oh great,' Vanessa vamped, kissing me on the cheek.

'So what are you girls going to do all weekend? Do you know anyone up here who can help you or is this it?'

'Well we're pretty broke, Billy. Only got about a hundred bucks between us and there's not much we can do on that. The only clothes we've got are our uniforms and these T-shirts TAA gave us. So we're a bit fucked really.'

My dick didn't say a word.

'What are you doing up here?' Kim asked. 'You're a

Sydney boy aren't you?' Kim was a big one, maybe twenty-two or three and stunning. Easily six feet, cut like a racehorse, long slim legs, jet-black hair in a Cleopatra style, large firm boobs and big green eyes.

'Originally from Brisbane,' I told her. 'I've been on the road for two months. Need a bit of a break. I'm up for a couple of weeks to hang out. See my folks . . . You know. I might head down the coast for a few days.'

'You married, Bill?' one of them asked.

'Er no, er . . .'

'Janelle,' she replied.

'No Janelle, I'm not.'

'Girlfriend?'

'No, no girlfriend. Why?'

'Oh, just checking,' she said. Janelle and Kim were the two girls who gave Vanessa a run for her money.

'Let your hair out,' said Kim, out of the blue.

'What?'

'Your hair. Let it out. Go on, I want to see what you look like.'

'Why?'

'Aw just because,' she purred.

'Come on, we all want to see it, don't we, girls?'

'Love to see it,' one of them giggled.

'Behaaavve!' Vanessa scolded.

'Come on, sailor. I'll undo it for you.' Vanessa pulled the rubber band off my ponytail. It fell over my face and down my back.

Kim came over. 'Let me brush it . . . Can I?' she purred.

'If you want.' I smiled, a bit embarrassed by the whole thing. I couldn't tell if they were taking the piss or not.

'Oh I want,' purred Kim. 'I love long hair on a man and

you have beautiful hair.' I sat in one of the armchairs. Kim got a hairbrush from the bathroom and started to brush my hair. My dick shot to attention, bulging my undies and the front of my robe.

'I can see Billy likes having his hair brushed too,' Vanessa laughed. They all broke up in a fit of laughter. I went scarlet.

'Oh, you've embarrassed the poor boy,' said Kim. 'Don't be embarrassed.' She kissed me, putting her tongue straight in my mouth. 'You're amongst friends. Ooh, you taste good.'

'Let me taste,' said Vanessa, kissing me. 'Mmmm, sailor,' she said.

'Me too,' said Janelle, and one by one I was tongue-kissed by six half-naked hosties. My dick had so much blood in it it's a wonder the weight of it didn't pull me off the chair.

There was a knock at the door. Room service. I wiped six flavours of lipstick off my mouth with the bottom of the towel that Vanessa was wearing.

'Here take it,' she said, pulling it off. She had on a white lace bra and panties. I thought I was going to cark it right there. 'You keep it. I'll get another.' Her tight little arse wiggled off to the bathroom.

Kim opened the door. 'Whoopee!' she shouted. The poor old room service guy nearly had the big one when he pushed the trolley full of champagne into the room. He must have been seventy and he was mumbling to himself. His eyes darted from one set of wet tits to the next.

'I'll sign for that, mate, thanks,' I said.

'Th-thank you, Mr Thorpe,' he said, his hands shaking as he eyed the girls and did the slowest reverse exit in history.

When Vanessa saw the champagne she said, 'Oh my God, a dozen bottles. Oh, sailor, you do know how to treat a lady. Come and get it, girls.'

The corks were out before the old guy was out of the room and for a second they forgot I was there. I watched them. They were like kids on Christmas morning. I've always enjoyed the company of women, and I don't mean just sexually. I like to watch them. They're not another sex. They're another species. It's a great privilege to see them in a group being themselves. When they're by themselves they're funny, intelligent, amusing, entertaining and uninhibited in a way that most men never get the chance to see. Their guard is usually up when we're around. Amongst themselves they tell dirty jokes and they fart and belch. In a group, *sans* men, women are far more interesting and much better company than just about any group of blokes I've ever been with. And make no bones about it, they're all dirty little things at heart. They've got us by the balls and deep down they know it. Bless their little hearts!

The dozen bottles of champers went down quicker than the *Titanic*. We were laughing and dancing and I was being passed around faster than a backstage joint. My gown was gone and I was in my underpants. Vanessa had her bra off and I was wearing it like Mickey Mouse ears, bouncing off chairs and leaping around like a fool. Kim's T-shirt was off. Janelle's too. And the others were thinking about it, it was so bloody hot. 'Hi, you're listening to Brisbane's finest on radio 4BC, and here's a blast from the past. It's Billy Thorpe and the Aztecs with the number one hit of 1964, "Poison Ivy".' The record hit and the girls all hit the floor jiving. God knows why we weren't getting any complaints from other guests, but there had been none so it all was sweet. After one particular massive group dance we all fell on the floor in a sticky, sweating, laughing heap.

'More shampoo,' I yelled.

'More shampoo,' they volleyed.

I got on the blower and ordered another dozen. The room service guy couldn't believe his eyes when he brought them up. I was lying on the bed being back-rubbed and massaged by Kim and Vanessa.

'Oh a, Ja-Jesus,' the old boy said as he pushed another trolley in. He brought the slip over to me on the bed and tried to give me the pencil, but his hand shook so much it shot up in the air and landed on one of Vanessa's tits.

'Here, I think this is yours,' she said, grinning.

The old bloke could hardly hold onto it. I signed the docket lying face down on the bed with Kim and Vanessa's tits jiggling in his face as they massaged me. He'd never forget it as long as he lived and my legend in that hotel was assured for life.

'You got a key to that adjoining door to my room?' I asked.

'Er, yes, Mr Thorpe. Why?'

'Well, would you open it please? These girls are all sharing this suite. There's six of them in here. I've got some spare beds they can have.'

He took about a minute to get the key in the lock. It's hard to find the keyhole when you're shaking like a shitting Eskimo with the first hard-on you've had in ten years, and perving over your shoulder at the same time. He left mumbling to himself, holding his heart and shaking his head.

'Anyone wants to use my room, go ahead. There's plenty of space. I can use the pull-out bed.' Two of the girls had started to fade and one asked if I was sure. 'Yeah, go ahead. I'll be fine. Night, girls. Don't be bad.' They grinned and off they went. The rest of us got into the shampoo again and the party kicked on with Vanessa, Kim, Janelle and Pat. The dancing and laughing continued but the champers had hit and we were sweating hot. We talked for a bit, then went out on the balcony for a drink.

'God I'm having a good time,' Kim said.

'Me too . . . Yes, thank you . . .' said the others.

'It's sweet . . . My pleasure. I needed this.'

'So did we,' smiled Vanessa.

'Listen, do any of you smoke grass?' I asked. Kim and Vanessa were keen. 'What about you two?' I asked the others. They'd never tried it. I went into my room to get the readies. One of the girls was passed out on the bed and the other was coming out of the bathroom, naked and wet from a shower.

'Oh, excuse me. I . . . I just need—'

'That's OK, mate . . . go ahead,' she said, not batting an eye as I squeezed past her into the bathroom.

I went back next door, rolled a joint that would have killed the Rolling Stones, lit it and passed it to Vanessa. She had a big hit, then handed it to Kim and she pulled it back. The other two looked at it like it was a smoking turd.

'Want some?'

'Oh, I don't smoke cigarettes,' said Janelle. 'I'll cough my heart out.'

'Here,' I said, taking a big hit. I went over to Janelle, put my lips on hers and gently blew the smoke into her mouth.

'Do that to me,' said Pat and I did.

'Me too,' said the others and I ended up smoking the whole thing, blowing it into their willing mouths. We sat for a while, not saying anything, just enjoying the high and looking at the Roma Street neon. What there was of it.

'God I wish we had some clothes so we could all go out

to a club,' said Janelle. Nobody else said a word. They were all lost in the buzz from the joint.

'Anybody got any cards?' Kim asked. 'We could play strip poker.'

'Be a bloody short game,' laughed Vanessa.

Silence hit and we all drifted off again.

'I know . . . Let's play spin the bottle,' said Vanessa. 'One sailor and three girls. It'll be a laugh.' Everyone seemed to agree with her.

We went back inside and I grabbed an empty Moët bottle and the five of us sat in a circle on the floor. 'Turn the lights out, Kim,' Vanessa said. 'There's plenty of light from outside.' She did and we began to play. I'm whacked, half-pissed and happy as a Kiwi on a sheep farm.

'You spin first,' Kim said to me.

'Well how are we going to play this?' I asked. 'What are the rules?'

'No rules here, Billy,' giggled Kim.

'I mean, how do we win? What happens when the bottle points to you?'

'Well,' Vanessa answered, 'whoever the bottle points to can dare any one of the others to do anything and they can't refuse. If they refuse they're out and they have to go next door. OK?'

'Fine by me,' I said, spinning the bottle. It landed on me. 'Anything?' I asked Vanessa.

'Anything, mate,' she said.

'Okay, Kim, take off your panties.'

'Ah, that's a bit ordinary, sailor,' giggled Vanessa but Kim stood up, no hesitation. She started humming the stripper's theme and slowly slipped her black lace panties down. Spinning them in the air and casting them over her head like a stripper, revealing her heart-shaped trimmed jet-black bush. She had no inhibitions at all. She was opposite me in the circle and sat down, her long legs out in front of her, slightly apart. Sweat was running down her boobs and she was grinning like a Cheshire cat.

'Mmmm,' she purred as she wiggled her bum on the cool carpet. 'OK, your spin, Billy.'

The bottle landed on Vanessa. She looked around the circle. Her eyes stopping on mine. 'OK, sailor. You take my undies off.' She grinned. I had a boner you could have changed a tyre with and there was no camouflaging it as I crawled over to Vanessa. She stood up in front of me pushing herself into me. I put the forefinger of my right hand in the elastic of her undies and slowly dragged them off, my hand brushing her curly blonde bush as they came down. She smelt so good. *Oh God, give me strength*, said my dick. I crawled back.

'Your spin, Vanessa,' Kim said excitedly. The bottle landed back on Kim.

'Ooo goody,' she said. 'Vanessa, you take Billy's undies off with your teeth.'

Oh shit, I thought as Vanessa crawled over to me. When I stood up, my hard-on was sticking out like the turning signal on an old Morris Minor. There was no hiding it and no point trying. She put both her hands around my butt and pulled me into her face, nuzzling me. She got her teeth in my undies and slid them down, her nose brushing the tip of my old boy as she went. *Dadoiiing!* There it was in all its glory. Vanessa crawled back. The others didn't say a word. Just stared at it. I tried to cover up.

'Uh aahh,' said Kim. 'We want to look. We're not covering up are we?' She opened her legs slightly and pointed her toes in the air. Vanessa did the same. She was right. I took my hands away and sat down.

'Oooh, bon Napoleon,' said Kim and they all giggled. We were like seven-year-olds playing 'you show me yours'. Except the seven-year-olds I remember didn't look anything like this group of young spunks.

Kim spun next and the bottle landed on Pat, whom I'd almost forgotten was there. She hadn't said a word but just stared wide-eyed at what was happening.

'Oh I can't . . . I can't,' she said and ran into my room.

'Pussy,' said Vanessa.

Funny, that's what I was thinking, said my dick, which was ready to have the Union Jack tied on it. I was doing my best to hide it but there was no use.

'Shut the door, Janelle,' said Vanessa. Janelle went and closed it.

'I'll spin,' said Kim. The bottle landed back on her. 'OK. You take Janelle's panties off, Billy.'

As I crawled over to her I wondered if dicks have the same fascination for women that pussy does for men. No matter how many you've seen you never get sick of looking. Funny world, ain't it?

Janelle lay on her back and lifted her legs and bum obligingly as I slid her panties off. She had a beautiful curly blonde tush. I crawled back over to my place and we sat looking at each other. Naked as babes. All checking each other out. All perving.

'Tell me something, girls.'

'What?' said Kim.

'Do women like looking at dicks as much as men like looking at pussy?'

'Until they go blind, sailor,' laughed Vanessa.

'Where are you all?' Kim asked. 'I can't see a bloody thing. I'm blind. I'm blind.'

We all screamed with laughter. It was great.

'OK, my spin,' said Kim. The bottle pointed to Vanessa. 'Billy, come over here and kiss me anywhere you like.'

'Whoa,' the other two laughed. My heart started thumping like the bass drum outside Jimmy Sharman's boxing tent. I looked around the circle and they were all grinning.

'Go for it,' purred Kim.

Crawling over on my hands and knees, I gently pushed Vanessa backwards. I kissed her boobs and worked my way down. She lifted her knees and opened her legs. I put my face between them. Oh, the sweet taste! There is no other like it in the universe. And no two taste alike. If you could bottle it women would be in big trouble.

Vanessa moaned and rubbed her tits as I kissed and gently bit her. 'Don't stop,' she moaned. 'Please don't stop.'

I heard Kim say, 'Ooo you naughty little girl,' and laugh. 'Come on, Ness, just one kiss. The morning's still young.' Vanessa moaned.

I crawled back and Vanessa spun. It landed on Kim.

'Kim, go over and kiss Billy anywhere you like,' she said to herself. We all laughed. Kim crawled towards me on her hands and knees like a big cat. Her big boobs swaying from side to side, her eyes glued to mine. She pushed me back. I knew she wasn't going to kiss me on the lips. I put my hands on the floor behind me and leaned back and she kissed my old boy. The excitement of the sexual game had me so high I nearly came. Kim kept kissing it and then took it in her mouth, working it like a professional.

'Hey,' said Vanessa. 'You said kiss.'

'I aaammm,' mumbled Kim.

'No you don't. Just one kiss. We've got more spins yet.'

'Oh all right,' Kim said, bringing her face up to mine. She had this lecherous smile on her face and licked her lips, then turned around and crawled over to her place with her legs wide open. Showing me what was coming, pun intended. The sexual tension in the room was electric. Waves crashed in my head. My teeth were buzzing and I was humming all over. I swear I could hear myself. I looked at the girls and they were all wiggling and shifting, trying to ease the burning that we all felt. It was a fantastic feeling. There was nothing sleazy about it. We all knew where this was going. It was the time it was taking to get there that made it so exciting.

Kim spun again and it landed on Janelle. 'Vanessa, come over here and kiss me wherever you want.' I nearly fainted and fell back on the floor with a gasp. They all laughed. Janelle lay back in anticipation, seductively rotating her hips. Vanessa crawled over. She licked Janelle's toes, then slowly worked her way up her thighs and put her face between her legs. Janelle let out a loud moan and grabbed Vanessa's hair, pulling her face into her. Kim crawled over to me and started kissing me passionately, rubbing me with her hand.

'Hey, not yet. There's more spins yet,' said Vanessa.

'Oh shit,' Kim moaned as she crawled back. 'I'm going to explode.'

Vanessa got up from Janelle and moved back to her spot. As she passed me she winked. 'Having a good time, sailor?' she whispered. Janelle sat up and spun the Moët bottle. It landed on Vanessa.

'Okaay,' she said. She looked at all of us in turn and

licked her lips. 'Okaaay. Billy, you take my hand and kiss me wherever you want. Kim, you take my other hand and kiss Janelle wherever you want, and Janelle you do the same to Billy. No breaking hands.'

We took each other's hands and pulled in closer, sitting almost face to face with our legs entwined, our naked bodies touching. We each kissed our allotted partners wherever we could without breaking our hands. Then Kim kissed me as Vanessa kissed Kim and Janelle kissed us all.

'OK, enough fucking around,' I said at last. 'Let's all get into bed!'

The moaning I heard when I woke up the next morning was me. We'd gone at it until around 7 a.m. and fallen asleep, exhausted, in each other's arms. I learnt combinations that I never even knew existed. Although the girls loved entertaining each other they also wanted something other than a face between their legs. Seeing I had the only one in the room . . . Jesus, they nearly killed me. Kim was a maniac. There was no satisfying her. The more she had the more she wanted. I woke up the next morning in the middle of them with Kim going at me under the sheets like a squirrel storing nuts in a tree. It was infectious and that's how Saturday started.

Talk about the breakfast of champions. The other girls got another room and the four of us hung together the whole weekend. It wasn't a forty-eight-hour orgy, but close. At one stage or another I ended up in bed with them one at a time, and a couple of times with all of them. It amazed me to find out that none of them had ever been with another girl before. And only Kim had been with a couple of guys one time. It was the mixture of champagne, grass, the spirit of fun and the irresistible spontaneous urges that started it.

None of them had ever done anything remotely like this and they loved it. I was in and out . . . of the hotel, I mean! I let them use my room as their own. Saturday and Sunday I made a few calls during the day but we mostly hung out, watching TV. At night we sat around drinking and laughing, discussing everything from flying to politics. But it always came back to sex. We played sex games like children. They told me their whole history and they were amazed by some of my old road stories. Saturday night I shouted them dinner in the hotel restaurant. It must have blown the Lennon's restaurant staff away when I trooped in, arm in arm with three gorgeous TAA hosties in full uniform. The word would have gone around from the room-service guy and the smirks I got from the staff in the lobby confirmed it. They would have shit themselves in the restaurant if they'd known that none of the girls were wearing any panties under their skirts and what was going on under the table during dinner. Ah, the follies of youth!

They wanted to know all sorts of things from a man's point of view. Like what it was that men found so exciting about women in garter belts, suspenders, stockings and high-heels. Now I'm an expert on that but still found it hard to explain. I'd sort of gotten used to seeing them in their undies and T-shirts. It was all very relaxed. Oh, I was still looking but the initial excitement had gone. So they paraded around nonchalantly in panties and high-heels to see if it would turn me on. It did. They wanted to know where a man's sweet spot was. And I wanted to know all about their G spots. They willingly showed me what they liked. They were fascinated when I told them about living with two girls in a ménage à trois in the Cross in 1963, and all the fun and games we got up to. It went from talking to touching and back to talking, then more touching. Sensual massage. Kundilini tricks. Extended arousal. All the fun and games imaginable. My knees were red raw from praying the strike would never end!

I'd read a book on Red Indian mythology. According to it, women's vaginas fall into a number of distinct categories and shapes. Six, I think, all represented by an animal. Each category is representative of their individual and sexual personalities. For instance the 'horse' likes to ride hard, the 'doe' soft and gentle and so on. Now we got right into that. At one stage they were all on the bed with their legs spread, examining each other and letting me check them out. I was in heaven playing doctors and nurses with real big girls. And there was no chance of Mummy coming in and spanking us! And the Indians were right. The girls asked me if the same was true for penises. I assured them that mine was *the* perfect example of the bionic helmet and the true prototype for all the great cocks of our time.

The strike ended on Monday and we said our goodbyes. Kim had a camera and got the bellboy to take a snap of us on the front steps of the hotel. We all exchanged numbers, promising to call each other. I spent a couple of days with my folks, stuffing my face, and then took a flight to Coolangatta, where I spent the rest of the week lying on the beach, reading and doing bugger-all. No girls. Light booze. Lots of zeds. I booked myself on a flight back to Sydney the following Sunday and as I walked on board, standing in the forward galley were Vanessa and Kim. They went scarlet when they saw me. Didn't say a word. All during the flight they went about their duties as if that weekend had never happened. They paid me no special attention, treating me like the rest of the sheep.

The flight landed. I was about six people back from the door in the galley and just about to walk off the plane, when someone tugged my sleeve from behind. A voice whispered in my ear 'Haiy yai ya ya. Haiy yai ya ya,' like a Red Indian. I turned around and there were Vanessa and Kim, grinning from ear to ear.

'We'll never forget ya, sailor,' Vanessa whispered and they both winked. I did see them again, but that's another story!

16
Dr Harrison

I was awakened Tuesday morning by the smell of food. Under normal conditions the sight of watery scrambled eggs, hard bacon, overripe oranges, dry toast and warm milk would have left me cold. But I was so bloody ravenous I pulled myself up with my good arm and woofed it down. I felt a lot better. Apart from the menacing grins and the occasional laugh when they said something I couldn't understand but which was obviously aimed at me, the flying Severinos were pretty quiet. Today was *the* day. Long weekend gone. Business as usual in the nuthouse, which meant the full complement of staff was returning. Detective Cirello came in for a while after breakfast and I asked him if he'd called the Salisbury Hotel to get hold of Rob. Cirello said he had but Rob wasn't in. He'd left his name and number but hadn't heard from him as yet. At least it was a start. I was beginning to get some communication to the world outside. I was still bleary-eyed and out of it but I felt more up than I had since I arrived. Cirello took a phone call and didn't come back for a while.

The Severinos were sitting up waiting for their morning hit. No more 'morpheeno' bullshit. It was the chair for them and they knew it. Cirello's presence had them completely freaked and most of the time they lay facing away from him, quiet as murdering babes and looking anywhere but in his direction. It sounds strange, I know, but I'd kind of gotten used to them. Murderers or not. They couldn't hurt me and there was no getting rid of them, so I might as well roll with it. All in all, it was pretty peaceful in the nuthouse. A sort of routine had set in and here we were just one big happy freaked-out family. My morphine dreams were taking me around the universe. The images in my head were the most vivid I've ever experienced. I'd shoot awake in a cold sweat from the middle of one bizarre episode after another. One minute I was back in Australia, the next at Cedars Sinai Hospital in Los Angeles waiting for my daughter Lauren to be born. And at times the dreams were really erotic. I'd come to with a woody solid enough to hit a 90 mph baseball clean out of the ballpark. I had no choice but to lie back and let Morpheus drive. Apart from the menacing grins when Cirello left the room and the occasional laugh when they said something I couldn't understand, the mumbling morpheeno brothers didn't hassle me and I tried my best to ignore them. Impossible! In between stones they mumbled away in Spanish. Most of the time they completely ignored me and it was just me, my heart machine and a swirling brain. I didn't need a brain surgeon to tell that I was an idiot for putting myself in this place. *Never again*, I thought. Regardless of their reality, the morpheeno brothers still looked like something out of a cartoon and now and then the whole thing felt exactly like that. If it wasn't so scary it was funny and I kept having this funny thought about that old rave between old lags in the joint.

'What you in for?'

'Axe murder. Four families,' the guy replies.

'What you in for?'

'Raped my mother.'

'What you in for?'

'Bank robbery. Killed three guards.'

'And you?'

'Er, disco elbow.'

What a bloody riot!

It must have been about half an hour after Cirello left when a smiling Sister Bertha came in accompanied by a doctor I hadn't seen before, and of course Idi, who must have worked seven days a week. Ah, there's nothing like being happy in your work.

'How are you this morning?' she asked.

'When can I get out of here?'

'Well I might be able to assist you there,' the doctor said. 'I'm Dr Harrison. I'm in charge of the medical staff in this section. And you are?' he asked while he checked my pulse and eyes.

'My name's William Richard Thorpe, but most people call me Billy. I'm an Australian living in Los Angeles with my wife and family. I'm only visiting New York for a few days and somehow I ended up here.'

'Yes, well Sister Beatrice has told me all about you and I've checked your file. It seems you don't belong here. But unfortunately the intensive care section of the Bellevue

General Hospital is still full. But I'm not empowered to release anyone from this facility. That has to go through channels and even then you'll need a qualified professional from outside this facility who is willing to take medical responsibility for you in writing.'

Oh shit! I thought.

'You seem to be making a rapid recovery,' Dr Harrison continued, 'considering you've had a heavy concussion and a near fatal heart attack. But from a medical standpoint I'd like to hold you at least another couple of days. Also from an insurance point of view we don't want you released prematurely, then you suffer another heart attack and sue us for negligence.'

'I assure you, doctor, I'd be glad to sign any waiver you wish to draw up. I just want to get out of the place.'

'Well, I'll convey that to my superiors and see if I can get the ball rolling on this.'

'Doctor, about the morphine. I'm going to end up a junkie at this rate. My arm's still very painful but surely you can give me something else. I'm getting the cold sweats.'

'I'll put you on codeine,' Dr Harrison said. 'That should keep you relaxed and the pain down. It will also help you with any withdrawals you may experience.'

'So I can expect withdrawals?'

'Oh yes, but not severe. You'll probably experience some anxiety and tension at first. And some difficulty with your bowel movements. But that should all pass. What has Mr Thorpe's dosage been, sister?'

'Here are Dr Mason's instructions,' said Bertha, handing him her clipboard. He read it and the look he gave her said, 'Jesus H. Christ, sister, that's enough to sedate a fucking horse and ease the pain in a quadruple amputee.'

'Well, er, in that case . . . mmm . . . we'll stop the morphine immediately. How about we see how you fare for the next hour or two and we'll start administering codeine as your needs require?'

'Fine by me, doctor.'

'Right, I'll get onto this right away. Nice to meet you, Mr Thorpe.'

'Same here, doctor, and thank you. Oh, before you go, my manager has no idea where I am. In fact as far as my family and friends are concerned I've been missing since 4 a.m. on Saturday morning. They must be frantic by now.'

'Good Lord,' he replied.

'Could you please phone my manager and he can let my wife know I'm OK. I hope he's still staying at the Salisbury Hotel on West 57th. His name is Robert Raymond.'

The doctor wrote it down and my brain cheered. 'I'm not empowered to make calls on behalf of anybody in here, but I'll pass it on to the appropriate people.' He patted my leg reassuringly and then left.

Bertha went over and gave the bruise brothers their normal shot, changed their dressings, and then she and Idi left.

By the end of the first hour my arm was throbbing like a pile-driver but I decided to ride it out. An hour later my whole left side felt like I'd been head-butted by a buffalo, and a half hour after that I was shaking uncontrollably from head to toe, my teeth ached, the hurricane blowing in my ears got louder and louder and my head pounded, signalling that it was about to explode. I had a feeling in my bowels like I'd swallowed a watermelon and I was sweating like the proverbial turd in a fog. I was also seeing little green ants all over my bed and seriously thinking about eating my way through the bars, tackling Idi, and making a run for it down the hall and out into Manhattan with my arse hanging out of my back-to-front gown. Every movement, every sound spooked me. My eyes darted from the morpheeno brothers to the windows, to the door, to Idi and back again. I was about to give a rebel yell when I heard the door being unbolted and in came Bertha and Idi on their normal rounds.

Right away she saw where I was at. She pulled a hypodermic from the tray beside the bed, filled it with codeine and—whack! Straight in the mainline. Instant relief. Some other doctor entered and did the usual tests on me. He and Bertha conferred and there was a lot of head-nodding before he smiled and left. Bertha shot up the Cubans again, then came back over to me. 'Feel a little better?' she asked. The codeine was a lot different from the morphine. Not as dense-feeling. But there were still no edges. No sides. The warm cotton wool wrapped itself around me and I felt the best I'd felt in days. It was like a lead weight had been lifted. I picked up my photos and went through them.

'God, if you all could see me now you'd shit yourselves laughing,' I said to myself and laughed. And wouldn't the Aussie press have a field day with this. Jesus Christ, how do I get myself into these situations? It's un-fucking-real. Talk about instant Karma! I flicked through the snapshots. Such great times, such fantastic people, I smiled to myself. Such great friends. I've gotta stay in better touch when I get out of here. It's funny you don't put that much importance on things like how you meet people. You just meet and that's that. You either have a relationship or you don't and if you do the relationship usually eclipses your meeting until years later it's just a faded memory.

Lying there, I started to mull over the faces. All of them

contributed in one way or another to my life and success and I started to think about them. Paul, Pig, Momma, Murphy, Lobby, Rats. *Rats! Jesus, what a fucking maniac!* I thought. And Warren 'Pig' Morgan. How did we meet? How did those two maniacs end up together? God, remember the house that Pig and Momma shared with me in Toorak. The parties. The dope plant . . .

17
Pig, Paul and the Rat

first met Warren 'Pig' Morgan in Perth in 1967 when I performed there as a solo artist after my TV show, 'It's All Happening', closed. It seems to be the pattern of my life that I go somewhere seemingly for a short visit and end up staying years. I went to Melbourne for two weeks and stayed eight years, went to LA for twelve months and stayed twenty years, and that trip to Perth in 1967 I went for a week and stayed nearly a year. I loved the place and for the most part Perth loved me. I had an enormous following from the original Aztecs days and it was only two short years earlier that we'd been greeted at Perth airport by thousands of screaming fans. I didn't get there that often, so my visits were always a blast and the crowds huge.

I was treated like rock royalty by just about everybody I met and as a result got to enjoy Perth and everything it had to offer a twenty-two-year-old rock star. I was out every night at parties and clubs and one night ended up in this jazz bar called The Hole in the Wall. It attracted a decidedly gay crowd from time to time so it was known around town as The Backs to the Wall Club. The first thing I heard as I entered was this soulful Jimmy Smith-style Hammond organ. On the small stage was a five-piece combo called the Beaten Tracks. They were good but the keyboard player was great. They acknowledged my presence during the set and in the break I invited them over for a drink. I shook hands with them in turn: Dave Hole, the guitar player; Ace Follington, drums; Murray Wilkins, bass; Ross Partington, vocals.

'G'day, Billy, Warren Morgan,' said the keyboard player with a huge smile. He shook my hand with a vice-like grip as he sat down. Warren was a little older than me. Maybe twenty-eight or so, about five nine and as fit as a bull with the broad chest and the muscular body and arms of a surfer. He was dressed in the usual jazzer's outfit of black pants and a roll-neck sweater. Black hair framed a big angular face, large square jaw, big lips, doe eyes and a large smiling mouth filled with big white teeth. 'How you enjoying Perth, Billy? You're still killing 'em, eh?'

'Looks like it.' I smiled, instantly liking this big friendly bear. 'So you play here often?'

'Oh, a couple of nights a week.'

'That Mose Allison song was great, mate. You do a lot of that kind of stuff?'

'So you're into Mose, eh? I'm impressed. Thought it would be Jerry and the Pacemakers,' Warren laughed.

'*Gettt* fucked,' I replied.

'Just kidding. Cheers. It's a pleasure to meet you. I'm a big fan.'

'Cheers,' I said. We clinked Heineken bottles.

I don't know what it is, but with just about everybody that I've ended up having a long relationship with, professionally and personally, I've known from almost the second I met them that it was inevitable. I had that feeling sitting there talking with Warren.

'Want to get up for a jam?' he asked.

He didn't have to ask twice and I joined him and the others doing 'Kansas City' and 'Stormy Monday'. The band was great and I was impressed by the guitar player's slide technique, but it was Warren's playing that interested me the most. I could tell he was playing to impress and he did. His rhythmic Hammond playing, soloing, and his piano playing did just that. He was bloody great. Much too good to be playing in a local band in some sweaty armpit in Perth.

'You ever thought about coming over to the big smoke?' I asked him.

'Of course, but Sydney and Melbourne are a bloody long way from here. And I don't really know a soul that can help me.'

'You do now, mate. If you come over, look me up. I'm not that hard to find.' I wrote my phone number on a napkin.

'Thanks, Billy.' He looked at the number and smiled. 'What're you doing later?'

I looked at my watch. It was 1.30 a.m. 'Nothing much . . . Why?'

'Aw, got a bit of a party going if you feel like a beer or two.'

'You're on, mate.'

A beer or fifty was more like it. Warren was a maniac. I got back to my hotel at 11 the next morning. Still pissed. And woke up at 6 that night sick as a dog with the hangover from hell. Jesus, he could drink! I'd never seen anything like it. And eat! We'd stopped at a pie shop on the way and he savaged four pie floaters in eight gulps. He was full of jokes and laughed continually, breaking me up with his dry Aussie sense of humour. It was obvious that Warren was the quintessential real Aussie good bloke. No bullshit. Loved a good time. Everybody loved him and he could play the hell out of anything with keys on it. That night he told me a bit about himself and the band. It was called the Beaten Tracks and was very popular in Perth. Of course the guitar player that night, Dave Hole, is now a world renowned Australian blues man and slide-guitar player extraordinaire, and drummer Ace Follington went on to play with many successful rock and blues bands. I'd been right about Warren's fitness. He told me he used to surf ski and paddled from Perth to Rottnest Island in races a few times. That's about twelve miles each way. I had the feeling that Warren didn't do anything by halves.

Our chance meeting that night was close to the end of my Perth stay and I didn't see him again before I left. When I returned to Sydney from that trip I was in a cab from the airport when I noticed newspaper placards outside milk bars with a red headline, 'Pop star bankrupt'. *Wonder who that poor bastard is,* I thought. It turned out to be me, but that's a whole other rave . . .

It was after my return from Perth that I started doing shows at the Whiskey Au Go Go, which was owned by my manager John Harrigan. It started out as a temporary thing, mainly to get me back into the scene after my extended break in Perth. It soon became obvious that the Whiskey gig was something special and it was at that point that I decided to start another band. I recruited Jimmy Thompson, the young drummer from Tony Worsley and the Blue Jays, and a young English guitar player named Mick Lieber, and used a number of bass players. The Whiskey was starting to cook big time and presented a golden opportunity for me to launch something new, so I was constantly on the lookout for a permanent bass player. I decided to hold auditions over a couple of days at the club and Mick, Jimmy and I ran them through. All sorts and varieties of hopefuls turned up. Over the two days, none of them had been any good but I had one more guy coming in. His name was Paul Wheeler. Paul was the only one that had been recommended to me. Mick had heard him audition for Python Lee Jackson and he seemed to think he was right for the gig. I hoped he was because he was my last hope and it's impossible to get a band off the ground when you know that one of the members is tempo-rary. I'd never heard of him but I'd never heard of any of the others, so what the hell.

'G'day, Billy. Paul Wheeler,' he said confidently, shaking my hand.

Paul was a young guy about my age, real clean-cut, with short blond hair, thick-rimmed accountant's glasses, five seven or eight, dressed English cool and with a big grin on his face. I liked him instantly. He'd come out from England with his parents in the early sixties and had been playing around Sydney with a band called the Affair that also fea-tured the jazz guitarist Jimmy Kelly. Auditioning is always a funny process. Everybody who turns up thinks they can play, but of course very few can.

'What sort of stuff are you doing?' Paul asked in his soft English accent.

I told him I'd be doing five nights a week in the Whiskey and I needed to cover a lot of musical ground from my hits to the kind of R&B that most of the American crowd wanted to hear every night. We started with Joe Tex's 'Show Me a Man that Loves a Good Woman' which was an R&R favourite. From the first bass note I knew that Paul was it. He played a finger style that was both fluid and confident, melodic and strong. When we played a ballad he adapted instantly and had no problem following the changes.

Halfway through I stopped and said, 'OK, that's enough.' I don't think he could believe his ears.

'What do you mean?' he said, scowling, knowing he'd played great.

'The gig, mate. You've got it. Can you start rehearsals tomorrow?'

'Oh shit . . . great. Yeah, I can start today if you want.'

I didn't realise it then, but I'd just found the first link in the chain that became the Sunbury Aztecs. Paul's powerful bass style and gentle personality were without doubt major contributing factors to that band's eventual success. Among other things Paul could play the best bloody rock shuffle in the country. Still can. Without his important contribution to the band I don't think it would have done anywhere as well as it eventually did. Paul also became the quiet between Gil's and Warren's mania. He was a gentle soul and a perfect catalyst, both musically and personally. The crowds loved him, and so did I. By 1969 we had both metamorphosed into very different people from the two greenhorns who went to Melbourne for two weeks. Paul had changed 180 degrees from the young Mod I had met. He was still quiet, but gone were his accountant's glasses and tailored clothes, replaced by a pair of John Lennon specs, overalls and shoulder-length hair.

A year after that audition Paul and I walked into the

Thumping Tum in Melbourne to see some female blues singer everyone was raving about. Her name was Wendy Saddington. She sang her little arse off and the crowd loved her. More importantly, to me that is, the keyboard player in the band was Warren Morgan. Turns out that the Beaten Tracks had won the Perth Hoadley's Battle of the Bands and part of their prize was a trip to Melbourne. Dave Hole had left and had been replaced on guitar by another legendary Australian blues man, Phil Manning. That night was the first time I ever saw Phil play. Wendy Saddington took the word 'chain' from Aretha Franklin's 'Chain of Fools' and the first incarnation of one of Australia's greatest ever blues bands was formed. In July 1970 Warren 'Pig' Morgan, as he had become known, joined Lobby Loyde, Kevin Murphy, Paul Wheeler and myself and the second link of a killer new band was in place. Lobby and Kevin left in January 1971 and three months later I met the 'Rat Man'.

Gil Matthews' full title eventually became Julius, Rat-boy, Flatbread, Crapinpants Matthews. To his closest friends, Rat Magnum Pee-eww! Rippers, I know, but believe me that's exactly who he was. Still is today when he's let loose. An absolutely unique, one-of-a-kind character. I've never known another like him. He is the funniest, most irreverent person I've known. Didn't give a fart what people thought of him. And speaking of farts, Ratboy has got a machine-gun arse and can fart on cue no matter how many times you tried it, even twenty times in a row. And stink? Where do you think 'Rat Magnum Pee-eww' came from? He's fucking rotten. Makes my eyes water just writing about it. After Jimmy Thompson, Kevin Murphy and Lobby Loyde left the Aztecs, Pig, Paul and I continued performing with a number of temporary drummers. In February 1971 we were playing one of our many Saturday night gigs at the fifteen-hundred capacity Coburg Town Hall in Melbourne.

The hall sits directly behind the now-defunct, infamous Pentridge Prison which for over a hundred years was the hard-core maximum-security home for all kinds of convicts. I had ex-Pentridge cons tell me that they looked forward to our Saturday night gigs at Coburg because we played so loud. Evidently they could hear us plain as day and would kick back rocking in their cells and be back in the world. I had a couple of mates doing time for an ounce of grass and after I found out about the volume I would talk to them on the PA and dedicate songs 'to the boys next door'. Then crank the volume past its already ear-splitting level just to make sure they could hear. But the coppers eventually got wise to what was happening and told me in no uncertain terms one night to 'knock it off you fuck'n little smartarse or you'll be singing on the other fuck'n side of the walls!'

That February night at Coburg a second stage had been set up at the other end of the hall for Grantley Dee and his band. Grantley was a blind Aboriginal pop singer and DJ who was well known around Melbourne at that time. The place was jam-packed and we swapped sets during the gig. A couple of times during our breaks I stood in the wings at our end and watched them play. The band was good but I was particularly impressed by the drummer, who had great chops. The best I'd heard in a long time. I could see him grinning at me from the opposite end of the room as I stood and watched. After the gig the band and I were waiting backstage for Norm to pack the gear. I was in the dressing-room by myself when Norm shouted, 'Thorpie, the drummer from the other band wants to talk to you.'

I guessed him to be early twenties. Dressed in black jeans, black shoes and a black roll-neck sweater. About my height and as skinny as a rake with jet black hair and sparkling eyes. A long nose dominated his long happy face, which had a cheeky grin plastered all over it. There was something familiar about him but I couldn't place it.

'G'day, I'm Gil Matthews,' he said, shaking my hand.

'Hi Gil, what can I do for you, mate?'

'I'm your new drummer,' he said without missing a beat.

'Oh yeah, how's that?'

'Well, I can play better than that cunt any day of the week,' he said matter of factly, nodding his head.

'Can you now?' I tried my best not to crack up. What fucking balls! 'What makes you think so?'

Without another word he pulled a pair of drumsticks from his back pocket and started playing the tightest single-stroke roll I've ever heard on the dressing-room bench. He held it for about thirty seconds, fanning and tightening it until his hands became a blinding whir, all the while grinning at me like a loon. That's when I picked where I'd seen him before. He was a dead ringer for Jughead from the Archie and Jughead comics. I didn't speak as I watched him slowly move the roll across the counter top and up across the mirror which stretched to the far wall. Without missing a lick he rolled off the mirror and jumped it across the corner and onto the wall. It was fantastic. He held the tight roll across the side wall, jumped onto the back wall, keeping it going to the open door. He held the roll effortlessly for another thirty seconds, then grinned and—*bluurrttt!*—he ripped off an enormous fart that sounded like somebody throwing wet liver against a bathroom wall. Jesus it sounded bad and—Pee-eww! Never missed a single stroke when he farted. Held it around the door jamb. Grinned and left, continuing to play. I was furiously fanning the air, trying to escape the horrendous pong, when I heard the press roll fading off in the wings. He was still playing.

'We're at Sebastian's on Thursday,' I shouted. 'Come in and have a blow.'

Blurrrttt! Another atomic fart. 'See ya there, cunt!' he shouted back, his voice disappearing with the press roll.

I sat with one hand over my nose, the other holding my gut as I tried not to laugh so I wouldn't have to breathe dead dinosaur fumes. And that was just the beginning.

I've always loved quality drumming. In another life I think I could have been a good drummer. I played drums as a kid in the school military band and loved the power and tribal rhythm. From seeing some of the greats like Louie Bellson and Buddy Rich, and from working with some really fine players, I understood the rudiments and both recognised and appreciated great technique. But I'd never heard or seen anything like this in my life. The technique required was nothing short of awesome. It was a phenomenal stunt. Not to mention the balls he had doing it. I think I loved that even more.

'Who was that?' asked Paul, fanning the air and throwing a backward glance at the press roll that was still disappearing across road cases and walls into the distance.

'Our new drummer, mate.' Paul and I looked out the door. He was still going. 'Scary, isn't it?' I laughed.

Thursday night rolled around. I hadn't heard anything from this Gil maniac and put the episode down to lairising. We were about to finish the second set to a packed room and there at the back of the crowd was Jughead's unmistakable grin. I took the break and the audience moved upstairs to the lounge area. Gil came strolling confidently over.

'Well, you ready for me or what?'

'Next set, mate. I'll just check with Steve if it's cool to use his drums.' Steve Innis had been filling in with us since Murphy had left the band.

'Ah, it's cool, Thorpie. It was Steve who suggested I come and talk to you the other night.'

'How come you want to play drums with me?'

'I'm sick of fucking around, Thorpie. I've played drums since I was four years old. Got sick of playing in shitty bands, so I took up guitar. Played it for the last four years, then got sick of that too. I'm a drummer but there are no decent bands around I want to play in.'

'So you like us then?'

'Yep. This is the band for me.'

I couldn't help but like him. He had a cheeky confidence and a grin on his face the whole time. No arrogance. Just the demeanour of a player who knew he could play and wasn't scared to tell me about it. That kind of confidence is rare. Confidence without arrogance, I mean. He hung with me during the break and I introduced him to Paul and Pig.

'How you going?' said Paul, shaking his hand.

'Like a rat up a drain pipe,' Gil laughed.

'In that case,' I grinned, 'Warren "The Pig" Morgan, meet Gil "The Rat" Matthews.'

I didn't realise it but I'd just witnessed the birth of a lunatic legend. And the name Rats stuck forever.

The break was over. Gil made his way down and re-organised the drum kit. He didn't play anything. Just tap tap ding boing as he adjusted the drums and tuned the skins. We went on stage. I realised he hadn't asked what we

were going to play. Tempos . . . endings . . . intros . . .
nothing. So I thought, *Okay smartarse. Keep up with this.*
The room filled to the rafters again and we were ready to
play the next set.

'People, we've got someone sitting in on drums for this
set. I've never heard him play but he reckons he's pretty
good. So please put your hands together for Gil the Rat-
head Matthews.' Polite clapping. Rat atat! . . . ding! . . .
doing! . . . favy doo bop! . . . favy baaaang! Gil cut into a
heavy medium rock feel and straight into a solo.

From the second he hit the first drum I knew. He slowly
built the intensity and complexity of the feel, playing some
outrageous combinations of feels and licks. Gradually
increasing the tempo as he went, he played a legit under-
handed style and obviously came from the old school. His
style and approach was Buddy Rich to a T, and he played
it like it was second nature. We stood with our mouths
open. Looking at the crowd who had their mouths open,
back to Gil, at each other. It was a great moment. He
played for about five minutes, never repeating the same
thing twice. Did phenomenal rolls on the toms which he
effortlessly slid to the snare and cymbals. Even played the
bottom of the toms and cymbals. Never once dropped a
beat. He had the whole room by the balls. Us included. We
were all applauding when one or another great burst of
playing blew us away. And they were all blowing us away.
He was a magician. I'd never seen anyone like him. Except
maybe Buddy Rich himself.

The intensity built. Gil's hands were a blur as he moved
them around the kit in blinding combinations of paradid-
dles, triplets and rolls. Ending on his snare drum in the
full-on version of the incredible press roll that had put him

on the stage in the first place. He swelled and subsided. Swelled and subsided. Exhibiting unbelievable effortless control, his bass drum pedal going double time, perfectly synchronised with the roll. After bringing it to a massive crescendo he rolled the press roll off the kit, rolled up the side of my amp, across the back wall, down Paul's amp and back to the high hat. Then he stopped dead, bent over and—*Bluurrrttt!*—dropped a monstrous tearing fart into the high-hat mike. Amplified by the PA it sounded like somebody ripping a giant wet buffalo skin at 150 dB. I mean dinosaur skin because it stank like something that had been dead in the wet for a million years.

'Holy shit,' yelled the Pig, holding his nose as the pong hit him. 'Payeeew . . . Jesus fucking Christ.'

I'm not kidding, it reeked like a combination of burning wet cabbage and old tyres. People's eyes in the front row started to water but Ratboy just sat there grinning and bopping his head and shoulders from side to side. We all looked at each other, then fell on the floor laughing. The crowd went crazy with laughter and cheering. Without missing a lick Rats went straight into the feel of a slow blues we played around that time called 'Gangster of Love', playing the musical intro that I usually played on guitar. He played the melody by pressing with one hand on the tom skin as he hit it to make the notes. 'Good enough for the gig, cunt?' he yelled, and we went into the song. The place shook with cheering applause. We had our drummer!

After the show we went upstairs to the little club bar for a drink and to talk about the future. 'Hello, William. Fine drummer,' said the elegantly-dressed man in a black cape and fedora as I walked past. I didn't recognise him at first, but it was none other than the acclaimed author and actor

Barry Humphries who was a regular visitor to Sebastian's.

A band had come together that night. We all knew it and jabbered away about how great it had been. Gil was in and we excitedly told him about this upcoming gig and that. He'd blown us all away and there was no being cool or holding back our enthusiasm. What I'd just witnessed was virtuosic. I asked him about his background. Where he'd learnt to play and the like, and why I hadn't heard of him before. He told us he was a Melbourne boy and that he'd been playing since he was a kid. A few things about switching from drums to guitar for a while and playing with Barry Macaskill's Levi Smith Clefs. And that's it. I didn't find out until we'd worked together for years just how modest Rats had been. He'd started as a kid all right, but what he hadn't said was how. Gil was a child prodigy and six years old when he'd opened the show as 'Australia's Wonder Boy' for Buddy Rich at the Melbourne Town Hall in the early '50s. Buddy Rich returned some years later and asked Gil to perform on his shows around Australia. He was so impressed by Gil that he took him back to the States. Buddy Rich and the other legendary drummer, Gene Krupa, regarded as probably the two greatest show drummers of all time, invited Gil to tour the USA with them on their upcoming tour. The tour took in thirty-eight states. Mainly drum exhibitions in sold-out auditoriums. Gil was set up between Buddy and Gene and they swapped eights all night. Ending with the three of them in a no-mercy drum showdown. Gil was fourteen years old!

During that trip he went to LA and became friends with Cubby O'Brien, the drumming Mouseketeer, and Cubby invited him on the Mouseketeer show. Gil is the only Australian drummer ever to have been granted the unbelievable privilege of being asked to tour with Buddy Rich and Gene Krupa, and perform on the same stage, as well as being inducted as an honorary Mouseketeer. He has the video, Mouseketeer ears and scroll to prove it. And typical of the Australian music industry's total disregard for the historical side of our musical heritage, hardly anybody in this country knows about it. Until now.

We had our drummer all right. It was another match made in heaven. Somehow another magic combination of personalities had been brought together. It was a real band again. No disrespect to the band when Jimmy, Lobby and Murphy were in it. They were all exciting, stimulating line-ups, we had some fantastic times and any one of them could have gone all the way. But the group personality never quite gelled into that magic combination that makes a band a band. This was it. The same feeling I knew so well from the early Aztecs. Same inexplicable cosmic combination of personalities, lunacy and talent that has a combined energy that can be neither suppressed nor denied. It simply is. From that night on, the new Aztecs line-up just rocketed. The whole musical personality of the band changed. Songs that we'd played for ages took an unbelievable left turn into this fresh high-energy sound. The crowds swelled. Offers doubled and six weeks later we did our first major concert in Melbourne to 5000 cheering people at the Melbourne Town Hall.

One year later, in front of 250,000 screaming fans at the Myer Music Bowl in Melbourne and in the middle of a blinding drum solo, Gil 'Rats' Matthews stopped dead. That's right—*Baluuurrrttt!*—he ripped off an enormous wet tearing fart into the high-hat mike that reverberated through the gigantic PA. It sounded like somebody tearing the wet sound barrier and it echoed across the crowd, then across the Yarra River and shattered shit-covered windows a mile away. He grinned, switched on a fan he had behind him, and blew the stench of rotting elephant guts all over the stage. We all ran into the wings screaming with laughter from the stink and the first ten rows fainted. That was recorded, by the way. We've got it somewhere. Like I said, Rats didn't give a fuck. He's one of a kind.

Beep, beep, beep, beep! . . . I was back in Bellevue, still holding the photo of us all. Smiling at things I hadn't thought about in years. Then the words Toorak Black came into my head. The dreaded Toorak Black! Oh shit, that's right. Melbourne . . . Pig and Momma's 1971 . . .

18
Toorak Black

Two weeks after Warren 'Pig' Morgan joined the Aztecs in July 1970 he married the love of his life, Nene, in one of the most outrageous weddings ever. Out of respect to them I'll leave that one for them to tell in detail some day. And it has to be told. It's enough to say that at the reception Pig and Nene's relations got a first-hand close-up and personal look at Melbourne's music scene. Everybody got so out of it that Pig ended up playing his own bridal waltz and Nene danced it with her dad Clive. At one stage in the outrageous reception, Pig's new mother-in-law was jiving, spinning, weaving and going for it big time when suddenly she shot across the dance floor on her back, her light blue silk evening gown up over her head, and slammed into the piano. The night was total lunacy.

A fortnight later Paul and I moved out of Gipps Street and Paul found a house in Mount Martha on the Mornington Peninsula. I was at a bit of a loose end after my break-up with Jackie a few months earlier and Pig and Nene, or 'Momma' as she was affectionately known, asked me to move in with them until I found a place of my own. I stayed a couple of months. My bed in the living room of their tiny flat off St Kilda Road consisted of an old leather chaise with a boogie board sitting on an old TV at the end for my feet. As ridiculous as it sounds, I had some of the best nights' sleep of my life on that contraption. One day a girlfriend of Nene's from Bendigo named Kelly came to see her. They were out all day and got home late, so Nene invited her to stay the night. Pig and Momma went to bed and left us to talk for a while. 'Niiightt,' said Nene, smiling at me. I offered Kelly my sleeping contraption but she wouldn't have it, preferring to use a sleeping bag of Pig's that she spread out on the living-room floor about six feet from my bed.

We talked for a while and it got quite late. She went off to the bathroom and I got into my surfboard. A few minutes later Kelly came out wearing the shortest see-through nightie I'd ever seen. It was completely transparent and she was totally naked underneath. The bottom of her nightie barely covered her naked arse. She acted like nothing unusual was happening and went about folding her clothes up with the lights still on. I couldn't believe it. I just lay there gawking. *Oh boy! Oh boy!* sang my dick.

Kelly paraded around, fiddling with her clothes, getting herself a glass of water, doing nothing. All the time stretching and bending over for my benefit. There was no doubt where this was going. Kelly was a big girl. Twenty-two or three, maybe five ten, brunette, beautiful, with a gorgeous body and a forty-inch set that pushed out the front of her nightie like two huge melons with noses on them. She didn't say a word, just kept fiddling with her stuff and

285

bending over on her hands and knees on the floor six feet away, with her quim smiling right at me. She didn't look at me or say a word. Then without warning she got up, turned out the lights, came and sat on top of me with her pussy an inch from my grinning face, and jumped my bones on the spot. The action got hot and heavy and the surfboard was banging like a piece of corrugated iron in a high wind. And Kelly was a noisy one. Moaning and screaming as she rode me like a bareback rider. She nearly broke my back, the chaise and the TV when she reached a shuddering, moaning climax. I could hear Pig and Nene killing themselves laughing in the other room.

Norman E our bad roadee had been living alone for about a year in the upstairs of a converted stables not far from Pig and Nene's. The loft, as he called it, had become the party house for the band and the landlord, who lived downstairs, loved all the late-night activities. Especially the young spunks who regularly tramped up and down the stairs outside his window dressed in miniskirts and tight jeans.

Norm offered me the place out of the blue, and out of respect for Warren and Nene's privacy I reluctantly left my sturdy surfboard/TV bed and moved into the loft. From the first night it was a party. I knew that Norm always pulled good sorts. It was the quantity that amazed me. After gigs they would be banging on the doors at 3 a.m. in groups of four and more and of course we had to show them nothing but the finest rock 'n' hospitality. I'd just come out of a monogamous five-year relationship with Jackie Holme and I hadn't slept around in all that time. It took about five minutes to get back into the swing of it! Hey, I had to do something to heal my broken heart.

The loft was a sort of crash pad for anyone who was lost

for the night. Over the next month and a half we had all sorts of overnight guests, amongst them a bunch of musos who had escaped from behind the Iron Curtain. Called Syrius, they were from Hungary or Czechoslovakia and had been one of the leading fusion bands in Europe, winning major European jazz awards. They spoke little English and for a long time after the one word they could pronounce perfectly was 'brandy'. Forever after, to them I became 'Brandy Billy Thorpe'. Their leader and bass player was the now famous Australian funk/jazz bass player and arranger Jackie Orczaksky and their then young manager Charles Fisher recently produced the Savage Garden smash CD that took the world by storm. But for the most part our guests were female. They treated the place as their own. In some cases coming and going as they pleased. At any one time we'd have a couple of young spunks wandering around wearing only their panties. Hated it! The loft was essentially one big, open space with a tiny bedroom and bathroom at one end. The bedroom was so small that, other than the rare occasion when special privacy became necessary, it was used mainly as a storeroom. Norm and I had our beds, which consisted of four mattresses each, laid out on the floor at opposite ends of the loft some fifty feet apart.

I didn't have a steady girlfriend during that time. Norm and I were in male heaven and it reminded me of the ridiculous days of the original Billy Thorpe and the Aztecs mania in the early '60s when the only determining factor as to how many girls you had in one day was the twenty-four-hour limit and the fact you had to sleep sometime. There's no future in it, and it's a total waste of time, but sleep is nevertheless necessary. But for a while the loft had me back in the old rock 'n' roll lifestyle.

One night at a gig Pig told me he and Nene had found a great little terrace house for rent in Hawksburn Road, Toorak. It was tastefully furnished and there was a bedroom in the front for me if I wanted it. As much as the loft had been fun, I'd had enough. I wanted some privacy and jumped at their offer. I loved them both dearly, like family. Pig was such a character and Momma was a ballsy country girl from Bendigo who doted on him. I adored Nene and wrote a song for her, 'Momma', which appears on the *Live at Sunbury* album. We were great mates and Momma could cook! Pig was in hog heaven. I'm not sure who'd given Warren the moniker but it stuck, and never was a man more adequately described. For his eating habits that is! When Pig ate you didn't interrupt or reach across the table for fear of losing an arm. His eyes rolled back like a white pointer when he took a bite and a dreamlike expression filled his face. Pig's grazing prowess was so well known that a reviewer once wrote that 'the Aztecs have taken a month off so that Pig can go to the country to do some serious eating'.

It was December 1970 when we signed the lease and in we moved. The house was a comfortable one-storey terrace in all-white stucco. The oak front door with lead glass inlays was off a small courtyard behind a six-foot white stucco wall. A black-and-white tiled entrance way led past the first bedroom which was mine, down past Pig and Momma's room, then through a stained-glass door into a graciously proportioned living room. Beyond the sit-down kitchen was another hallway which led down three carpeted steps, past the bathroom and into a large den at the back where Pig put his upright piano. Party room!

The place had some great furniture, artefacts and art-works that the owners had graciously and trustingly left. There was also a wonderful collection of books. I read Dostoyevsky, Tolstoy, Proust, Kipling, Ibsen, Freud, Prahamyansa Yogananda, Hemingway, Chekov, J. Krishna-murti, Darwin and many others during my stay there. The one thing that freaked us out and anyone who came to the house was a twelve-foot bearskin rug with a giant bear head still attached to it. It sat in the middle of the living-room floor with its mouth open, grinning giant teeth, and there was no physical or psychological way to avoid it. Somebody was always tripping over the bloody thing and many a stoned night somebody would freak out over it and run screaming into the night. It was huge and must have been worth a small fortune, but we hated it. The owners insisted it stay so we were stuck with it. Later, we disguised it with a Groucho Marx nose, moustache and glasses, a long silver cigarette holder, a false beard and a turban. We named him Herman. Now, *we* thought it was ridiculously funny but it ended up freaking people out even more. After a little mishap you'll learn about in a minute we rolled Her-man up and left him standing against the living-room wall. A Groucho-looking, turbaned, bearded, cigarette-holding bear's head forever scrutinising the room and guests.

But bear rug or not, we settled in and had a great time. The house was always full of people. Phil Manning, Big and Little Goose from Chain, and Jiver their faithful roadie, Wendy Saddington, Reno from Compulsion, Pete Wells, Molly Meldrum, Michael Chugg, Christy Eleisor, Michael Gudinski, Bon Scott, Paul Wheeler, Kevin Murphy and far too many others to mention all partied in that house in Toorak. Pig's piano became the centre of all entertainment and groups of us with acoustic guitars would sit all night making spontaneous music until daybreak. They were fantastic times and I wish to God I had recorded some of them. Some nights were as good as it gets by any standard.

Then came The Plant. Like I said, Momma was a country girl. Her father Clive was a one-of-a-kind bull of a man. He was a hard-drinking, cursing, chain-smoking carpenter with the sunburned, weatherbeaten face of an eighteenth-century whaler and a voice so loud and deep it rattled my balls and made my eyes water when he spoke. His hands were like ham hocks. We all loved him and he us and many a night he'd turn up out of the blue at Gipps Street with two dozen bottles and party us all into the ground. Clive, who also had a market garden in Bendigo, knew we smoked dope and didn't give a shit. Even tried it a couple of times. He knew it for the harmless thing that it was and after his experiences in the infamous Changi prisoner-of-war camp where he escaped at nineteen years of age, had a hell ride on a raft in the Pacific where there was cannibalism, and then watched his mates taken by sharks, he reckoned that 'any bloody thing that makes people laugh and talk about peace and love is a bloody good thing'. A wise man, the old Clive!

Anyway, we'd collected a serious amount of rare seeds from various dope plants and when I first moved into Pig and Nene's little flat in St Kilda we decided it was time to plant some and grow us a plant for our private consumption. Although we knew quite a few dealers I never liked buying from them or them being around us and knowing about our personal lives and habits. Our own free supply of grass seemed like a great idea. But where to plant the seeds? Getting busted was a reality we couldn't overlook. Then Nene got the bright idea to ask her dad if she could plant them in the garden in Bendigo. 'No bloody worries,' he replied without so much as a blink.

So off Pig and Momma trotted one Saturday arvo and planted some seeds from the finest dope known to man. One of them took and every few weeks they'd go up and check on the progress. In their absence the plant was dutifully cared for by Clive's old Chinese gardener. He even wrapped it in plastic in the frost. The months passed. We moved into Hawksburn Road. Pig and Momma stopped going up to check on the plant and after a while I sort of forgot all about it. Then one Saturday evening, it must have been around February or March 1971, I heard all this commotion at the front door. I opened it and all I could see was this gigantic dope plant. It was huge—about the height and girth of a large Douglas fir. Pig and Momma had wrapped it in plastic, tied it to the top of the old blue Valiant and driven all the way from Bendigo and right through the heart of Melbourne to Toorak. And they were whacked out of their living minds. I couldn't see either of them. All I could hear was uncontrollable giggling coming from behind the shaking plant out in the front courtyard. I squeezed my way through the door and saw them both on their knees, crying, laughing, trying to keep the plant from falling on them.

'Thorpie . . . heee . . . hee . . . Thorpeee . . . Thorpie, can you hear me?' Pig sang like the *Tommy* theme.

'Oh fuck!' . . . Cackle, laugh, scream, giggle. 'Oh shit,' giggled Momma.

'Thorpeeee. Look . . . look. Ah, oh shit! . . . Look what we've got.' . . . Snigger . . . cackle, cough . . .

'Oh God, Momma . . . Momma . . . you hoo hoo . . . te-tell him . . . Oh Jesus . . . Helpp . . . Helppp. We need . . .

helpppp . . . Gotta . . . oh fuck ha ha . . . gotta get it . . .'
More gut-wrenching hysteria.

'Inside. Get it inside!' Momma finally managed to get out.

Their hysterics had me in hysterics as well. On their knees, tears streaming down their faces, trying desperately to hold the huge plant up and talk at the same time, they were a bloody riot. After much 'oh shitting', laughing and falling around we got the plant on its end and struggled to get it through the front door. But it wouldn't go! I had to get a saw and cut some of the lower branches off and even then we only just managed to squeeze it through. We half-carried, half-dragged it down the passage into the living room where Pig and Momma collapsed on the floor in another fit of laughter. They were as whacked as loons. And the plant reeked of resin. It was sticky to the touch like treacle and smelt like someone had boiled a skunk. This was without doubt the most serious dope plant I've ever seen in my life. In fact, it's not doing it justice to call it a plant. What Pig and Momma had grown was a ten foot tall, six foot in diameter dope *tree*.

They were leglessly stoned, but it turns out they hadn't smoked a thing. Essentially the plant was one giant, solid, ripe Buddha head, so full of resin that it had gotten into their pores when they loaded it. They were zonked just from carrying the bastard to and from the car. After they'd dug it up and tied it on the roof, they were so hopelessly bent from the resin they couldn't even get it together to call me and tell me they were bringing it home. God knows how Pig drove! So here we are with a bloody dope tree in the middle of our rented living room in Toorak. If the coppers had run through the door at that moment we'd just be getting out now. Despite all the humour, grass was no laughing matter in 1970. We knew plenty of people who'd been busted and, pathetic as it sounds in today's fucked-up world, a couple of them were doing two years in Pentridge for a one-ounce bag. Imagine what they'd have given us for this. It was pounds.

I made Pig and Momma some strong coffee and they drank gallons of water, but it still took about an hour before either of them got it together. We had to get the thing stripped and put away because the old paranoias had hit and the realisation of what was now covering the bearskin rug became all too real. Freak out! So we put on some rubber gloves and began stripping the heads off the plant. The big ones at the top were over two feet long and six inches in diameter and I had to cut them in half with a carving knife to get them into the garbage bags. The gloves didn't help much. There was so much resin that it got on our arms and in our hair and before long we were laughing like idiots again, covered in sticky brown dope resin from our knees to the top of our giggling heads. It took until 3 a.m. to get it all bagged. We cut the remaining trunk and branches with a hand saw and decided to burn them in the big open fireplace. Wrong!

I threw a match in and—Waaaawooomppp! A six-foot fireball shot up the chimney and out into the living room. I turned instinctively when I saw the flash, but I wasn't quick enough. The flames caught the back of my jeans and set my arse on fire. At the same time the rug in front of the fireplace caught fire. Freak out! I was jumping around 'owing' and 'oh shitting', desperately trying to put my flaming arse out, and Pig and Momma were frantically stomping on the burning rug. The three of us looked like stoned Indians at a pow-wow doing the dope dance! We were so whacked we'd never considered that the resin was highly inflammable. The branches burnt like I'd thrown a can of kerosene in the fireplace and thick blue smoke poured up the chimney and into the room. It took about sixty seconds for the whole house to fill with choking, pungent smelling, dope smoke . . . another freak out!

Like a stoned idiot I made things worse by throwing water on the fire. Then it really got bad. We couldn't even see the walls on the opposite side of the bloody room. It was so ridiculous that we just gave up and lay on the floor, coughing and holding our stomachs from the pain of laughing so hard, and waited for the sirens outside. But none came. The smoke reeked of dope and they must have smelt it five miles away in St Kilda. Eventually the fire burned down to a smoulder. The house smelled worse than a Kowloon dope den on Chinese New Year but we didn't dare open the doors or windows. There was so much smoke if we'd let it out I swear a twenty-foot atomic mushroom dope cloud would have risen over Toorak and somebody would have seen and smelt it for sure. We just had to choke, grin and bear it. When it finally cleared, freak out number three. The bear rug in front of the fire was ruined. It was as sticky as if we'd poured gallons of honey on it, and the carpets where the plant had sat had turned a sticky deep browny green. It was a mess. When we counted the garbage bags we freaked again. They were the full-size, green plastic variety, all packed to splitting. And there were eight of them!

There was a tiny tool shed in the bricked back courtyard and we stored the bags, the rest of the stripped branches and trunk there, deciding to sort it all out later that day. It was now 7 a.m., we'd been laughing for twelve hours straight and we were all totally exhausted. It's hard work being that whacked. The carpet was a wreck but nothing a good professional shampoo couldn't fix. We could probably replace the burnt rug. And a good scrub would clean the once-cream walls which had taken on a dull blue-grey smoky tone. It was the bearskin rug that was the real worry. I could just see Pig and me shuffling into the Toorak dry cleaners like Cheech and Chong with the bloody thing over our heads . . .

'Oh, it's just resin, Madam.'

'What kind?'

'Oh just plain old dope resin, madam.'

'Excuse me?'

'Yes, that's right, madam, marijuana resin . . . What? You'd like to make a quick phone call . . .'

Yeah right. Why not just go and give ourselves up now? 'No need for cuffs, officer. And you can get that shotgun outta my arse. I'll go quietly!'

We took the bearskin outside, hung it on the clothesline, hosed it, shampooed it with hair shampoo, and left it to dry in the sun. Late that afternoon we finally got ourselves together and checked on it. Freak again! There were about ten billion ants and bugs, some of which belonged in the Melbourne museum, stuck all over it, stoned as maggots, and that's not the worst of it. It stunk worse than an old drunk's fart, and apart from its head it had shrunk to about a third its size. It looked ridiculous! We cleaned it off again but it still looked ridiculous so we hosed it down and tried to stretch it. Riiiiip! The bloody thing came to pieces in our hands. The next day after it dried we stapled and taped the pieces back together, stuck Herman's disguise back on, rolled what was left of him up and stood him in the corner of the living-room. And there he remained for the rest of the year, resplendent in the turban, Groucho Marx moustache, nose and glasses, cigarette holder firmly between his teeth.

We also had another permanent guest at Hawksburn Road. My young boxer puppy Buster, whom you met stiff as a board at Wallacia. In 1966 I bought my girlfriend Jackie a pedigree boxer that she named Sonny. One day in Gipps Street Sonny got out after a boxer bitch on heat that lived directly across the road. I heard loud yelping and a woman screaming her lungs out. I ran over to find Sonny and the bitch knotted, with Sonny facing backwards having twisted himself 180 degrees trying to get off. They were both howling in agony and, as strange as it sounds, looked embarrassed. We finally separated them by hosing them and my dog Buster was the result. One lazy afternoon I was driving through the Brighton shopping centre and stopped to buy something in a local shop. I took Buster with me on a leash. He was only nine or ten months old. On the way back to the car a huge, black German shepherd-Werewolf cross grabbed him, dragging him and me all over the footpath. After giving Buster a terrific hiding he ripped half of one of Buster's ears clean off. I finally got him off with a kick in the nuts that sent him yelping off and rushed Buster, ear streaming blood, to the local vet.

Eighteen months later I was driving through the same shopping centre with Buster in the front seat when he started to growl, which he rarely did. Without warning he leapt out of the window. I was doing about 45 mph when he jumped but Buster didn't give a shit and hit the ground running flat-out up the street ahead. About 200 primary school girls from the local Catholic school came streaming out of the school gates and across the road in front of me. Some headed for the local milk bar, others to the bus stop. It was one big, chattering, laughing swarm of navy blue school dresses and white hats, and Buster shot straight at them like a laser-guided missile. He disappeared amongst them and I heard a couple of screams. Then I heard what sounded like the end of the world. The sound of dogs viciously fighting and 200 eleven- and twelve-year-old schoolgirls screaming their terrified lungs out.

I ran over to find Buster beating the shit out of some big dog right in the middle of the little girly swats. I tried to separate them but they were going at it big time. I'd never seen Buster like this and then I realised the dog he was hammering was the same black mongrel that had torn his ear off eighteen months before. Buster had changed a bit since their last bout, now tipping the scales at over ninety pounds, and he was literally killing this big mutt. He had him by the throat, shaking him like a rag doll. Blood was running from the tear in his throat and all over Buster's face. I couldn't get him off. Boxers get a jaw lock like bull terriers and he was locked on tight and killing this dog.

They were thrashing about in a wide arc on the footpath, scattering the terrified children in every direction. Girls were screaming hysterically. The bus driver who had just pulled up was screaming. The passengers were screaming out the windows. Shop girls were screaming. The parents who had come to pick up their daughters were screaming. It was pandemonium. I was taking a terrific verballing from some old girl. 'You should be ashamed of yourself, young man, having a savage dog like that out on the street. I'm going to call the police . . .'

Suddenly, silence. Buster just stopped and the word 'poliiiice' reverberated through the eerie quiet. Nobody moved or said a word. Then it happened! Buster could have killed this dog, but he'd thought of something way worse. He stood over him with his fangs bared, growling, pinning the poor shaking mutt on the ground with his muscled chest and powerful forearms. Then he slowly manoeuvred himself around and, bingo! . . . Buster started fucking him. It was *not* a pretty sight. That's when the screaming really began. Screaming girls, parents and shopgirls took off in every direction, but I could have kissed the little bastard. Talk about adding insult to injury! There he was, ears back, grinning, going at it like a bull in springtime. I could hear him thinking 'bite' . . . stroke . . . 'my' . . . stroke . . . 'fucking' . . . stroke . . . 'ear' . . . stroke . . . 'off' . . . stroke . . . 'will' . . . stroke . . . 'ya' . . . stroke . . . 'you' . . . stroke . . . 'fucking' . . . stroke . . . 'black' . . . stroke . . . 'cunt' . . . stroke . . .

The big black mutt had no choice but to lie there in disgrace, quivering with shock and take it. Buster finished with a shuddering climax, got off, shook himself, then nonchalantly wandered over and sat at my feet, panting. Grinning his silly big grin up at me, with his tongue out, saying, 'I fixed him, Dad, didn't I? He won't bully no more kids, will 'e, Dad?' The big mongrel took off limping, wailing and yelping down the street, disappearing around the corner presumably to find a quiet spot to lick his wounds and smouldering arsehole. Well, that's the dog that lived with us at Hawksburn Road. He was mad as a hatter but the greatest friend and companion ever. Everybody loved Buster and Buster loved everybody. At some stage someone must have blown some dope smoke up his nose because all of a sudden whenever anyone lit up a joint, over he'd bound for a hit then stroll back to his couch to dream his dog dreams.

So back to the dope tree. We had a nice supply to say the least but it was fresh and way too green to smoke. Of course we dried some out in the oven for a sample. It blew our heads off and we realised that it would be magic stuff if it was cured properly. It needed drying, which had to be done by hanging it so the resin ran down into the heads and leaves to get the best and strongest grass. But where could we hang eight full-size garbage bags of grass without alerting the neighbours or the coppers? We could ask someone else to do it for us but that would have put the word around that we had it, and either it'd get ripped off or we'd be busted. They were both no-nos. Then came the stroke of genius. Or so we thought. And the idea was so simple. We'd give a bag each to a couple of close friends we trusted, let them cure it themselves, and keep a bag for ourselves to smoke. Now here's the genius . . . ready? We'd turn the rest into hashish! The champagne of all smoke! No problem. Somebody's got to have a book on how to make hash. If the bloody Turks and Nepalese can do it, so can we! No worries. And so a book on the ancient art of hashish making was acquired. Without going to the lengths that the ancients did and mixing it with steer dung, we decided on a combination of recipes that we were convinced would produce perfect hash with a kick like a mule. We had much serious debate over a label name and went through all the best name brands. Let's see, there's Afghani Brown, Durban Poison, Nepalese Opiated Temple Balls, Lebanese Red, Thai Buddha Sticks. I know, I know, we'll call our own private stock Toorak Black. Yeah, that's it! That's got a bell-like ring to it. We must have been out of our minds. What am I saying? We *were* out of our minds.

We cured our smoking bag. It was the strongest grass I'd ever had. You couldn't talk, walk or think on it. All you could do was laugh, so it became known as laughing grass and was without doubt the happiest high I've ever experienced. We kept the cured grass stored in several large gladbags, each holding close to a pound. One morning we got up to find Buster lying flat on his back in the middle of the living room . . . eyes spinning, tongue hanging, hardly breathing. He couldn't move and his stomach was three times its normal size. It stuck out the sides of his ribs like a goat that had just been swallowed by an anaconda. I was about to give him the 'what have you done you baaaddd boy?' routine when Momma pointed to the remains of one of our gladbags on the floor in the corner. He'd been busted big time!

'Oh fuck, Pig! Where did he get that? He's going to die, mate. No-one can eat a pound of that dope. Not even Buster.'

'No worries, Thorpie,' replied Squire Morgan confidently—that's what Murphy called him. 'It's Buster, mate. Nothing can kill him. He'll be sweet. Why don't you call Dr David and ask him if there's anything we can do.'

'Dr David? oh, David . . . Yeah. Great idea.' I found his number and dialled.

'Hi David, it's Billy Thorpe . . . Oh fine, mate . . . Yep, band's going great but listen, I've got a small problem . . . Well, you see my dog's just eaten about a pound of grass. That's right, a pound. Yes I know. Unbelievable . . . What's that? Well there's a shitload of resin on this stuff. It's stickier than shit. We got stoned just looking at it. Yeah, lots of resin . . . Excuse me . . . oh, he's about ninety pounds. Real big . . . Yes he's breathing OK. His heart's steady as a rock. Slow as an agent's cheque, but steady . . . Should I take him to a vet or what? . . . Will he die? . . . Is there anything I can do for him? . . . I see. Whaaat? . . . OK, David. Thanks mate.'

'What did he say?' asked the Pig.

'Ah . . . ah you're not going to believe this one, Pig.' I grinned.

'What . . . what?' He started to laugh, seeing my grin.

'Well, mate, David said to put on some Pink Floyd and call him in the morning!'

We collapsed laughing. We often did. The neighbours must have thought they'd opened a funny farm next door because all that came out of that house was the sound of uncontrollable gut-wrenching laughter. It was ridiculously strong grass and quite a few people wanted us to sell them some. But dealers, us? Never. We were musicians, not bloody dope dealers. Grass was for fun, not profit. We eventually gave most of our smoking stash away save a few ounces for private consumption. But we still had the supply for the Toorak Black, which went into earnest production.

Without turning this book into a recipe for hash-making, suffice it to say that our recipe involved boiling the grass with a few secret ingredients, letting the residue dry, grinding it with a mortar and pestle, mixing it with honey, then wrapping it in cheesecloth and twisting it in a vice to squeeze the excess honey out and turn it into a solid block of hash. We did this dutifully. The result being four blocks of Toorak Black, each roughly the size of a large briefcase. According to the ancients, the next step was to bury it in the ground to let the honey ferment and, bingo, in six

weeks a killer supply of Toorak Black. But where to bury
it? We couldn't ask or tell anyone. The word would get out
for sure. So we hunted around for the right spot. Another
stroke of genius! Not far from Hawksburn Road on Toorak
Road was a large empty lot. It had been vacant for years
and was grown over with all sorts of lantana and tall
weeds. As the crow flies it was about a quarter of a mile
from our front door and nobody would ever suspect that
about thirty pounds of hash was buried on Toorak Road,
smack dab in the heart of the most affluent suburb in Melbourne. It was genius, all right. So we waited for the first
cloudy night and buried it on the corner lot.

We had a six-week tour coming up and Momma was
going to go home to Bendigo for that time. If the hash was
discovered, no matter how remote the possibility, we would
be nowhere in sight and there was no way of connecting us
to it. So it was done and a week later we went on the road.
Talk of the resulting stash of dreaded Toorak Black dominated our conversation, and it took on legendary status
before we'd even dug it up. The excitement grew as the day
of our return approached, and the exhumation and sam-
pling ceremony took place. The last gig of the tour was in
Albury. After the show we hastily packed the van and off
we shot like giggling children on Christmas Eve, all abuzz
with anticipation. Rather than dropping everyone at their
respective abodes, the whole band would come back for the
ground-breaking ceremony. Such an auspicious occasion
surely must be shared by all for storytelling in the quieter
days of later years.

By the time we approached Toorak Road the atmosphere in the van was palpable, and when we turned into it
a mumbling buzz drifted through the van. As we crossed

Chapel Street we were chattering like Rhesus monkeys, and a cheer went up as we approached the corner of Toorak and Hawksburn Roads. Then silence. A stoned, stunned, disbelieving, mind-boggling, incomprehensible, freaked-out, 'Oh sweet Jesus this can't be real', mouth-gaping, 'tell me it's not fucking happening' silence.

On the corner of Hawksburn Road and Cromwell Street, where our stash of the already legendary Toorak Black lay like a ripe young virgin waiting eagerly for the fire between her naked thighs, was the shell of a brand new building. And there's more! On the front of the building hung a large hand-painted sign with the words, 'Toorak Library'. The despicable fiends. Hang the low-life bastards! Someone's built the Toorak fucking library right smack on top of our legendary Toorak Black!

Oh heartbreak! Oh woe! Is there no God? Is there no God . . . no God . . . no Gooood?

'Wake up, son,' said Sister Bertha. 'It's time for your bath.'

19
A Light in the Tunnel

'**H**ave you had a bowel movement since you were admitted?' asked Bertha, shaking the Toorak Library from my head.

'Er . . . what?' I was still in the van, crying.

'A bowel movement. Have you had one?'

'A bowel movement?' I asked, not really understanding. If she'd asked if I'd been to the bathroom it probably would have computed. Bowel movement sounded like a part of a classical symphony to my fuddled head.

'Well, have you?' she asked patiently.

I thought for a second. *Have I?* I wondered. *Nah, I'd remember that.* 'Sister, I've hardly had an eyelash movement since you first hit me with that bloody needle of yours.'

Bertha threw back her head in the first real laugh I'd heard from her in the whole time I'd been there. 'Well, son, they was my instructions like I told you. Hey, anyway, you ain't had any heart trouble or head pain have you?' I shook my head. 'See,' she smiled.

'You see, morphine has a tendency to freeze up the bowel, like heroin, and a hard movement is a normal symptom of opiate withdrawal. You haven't been on it that long but you've had quite a lot. A hot bath should help. Would you like to take one, son?'

'Kiss me, Sister,' I laughed.

'Okay, I'll just give them their shots and be right back.' Bertha went over to the Severinos and did what she had to do. Then she came back and disconnected the cables from the heart monitor, prised the suction cups and about half a pound of hair from my chest, pressed a button that lowered the metal bed about a foot and went to get an orderly to help me to the bathroom. This time when the locks clicked and creaked, Bertha and Idi were accompanied by a mountain with legs wearing a white, full-length hospital coat. No kidding, he had to stoop to get his massive body under the door frame. This guy was about seven feet six, wide as a door and at least 350 pounds of solid muscle. He made Arnold Schwarzenegger look like Billy Bardy.

'This is Carl,' Bertha said, nodding to the mountain. The mountain just nodded and grunted a deep guttural 'Urrgghh'. The Severinos lay blissed to the gills, staring in stoned disbelief at the man mountain. Mouths gaping. Loose bottom lips hanging like two front porches. Eyes blinking in slow motion.

'OK, ready?' Bertha asked.

'Yep,' I said confidently and slid my legs over the side of the bed. The floor felt refreshingly cool against my feet and my brain told them that they were ready for a stroll around Central Park. I put all my weight down. The blood rushed from my brain. Tremble . . . splaat! I collapsed like a sack of wet cement on the cold floor before Carl could get one of his massive hands on me. My legs were completely useless. The Severinos broke up and started going at it in Spanish.

'Cool it, scumbags,' ordered Idi and they went silent.

'You OK?' Bertha asked, kneeling down and taking my hand. Luckily I'd fallen on my right side and hadn't hit my head or broken arm. Apart from a surge of pain up my left side and a shooting pain in my skull when I fell, I felt fine . . . Stupid with my bare arse hanging out, but fine.

'Carl, would you please help Mr Thorpe to the bathroom.'

In one effortless motion, he bent down, scooped me gently off the floor and carried me out the door as if I was a week-old baby. I felt like sucking my thumb. But I immediately felt dizzy. The horizontal movement was unnatural. Weird. Disorienting. Like I was experiencing motion for the first time. After three days practically motionless on morphine in a white room I couldn't focus on the hall that sped past. The walls of the passage ahead came at me at a hundred miles an hour like two atomic-driven roller doors. The ceiling rolled over me in nauseating white waves, their backs encrusted in blurred light from the bulbs.

'Stop. Stop . . . Please stop for a moment,' I mumbled. 'I'm going to be sick.'

My heart was pounding in my ears. Carl went 'Urrggghhh' and stopped. The passage continued to whizz by at a blinding speed, then it turned on its side and went into a blinding spin. I passed out.

Beep, beep, beep, beep. I came to back in my bed with Bertha and Carl standing over me and my heart monitor boogieing.

'You right, son? You white as a sheet,' Bertha said, feeling my pulse. 'Get your heart rate down, son. Come on, relax.'

The ceiling spun in slow revolutions. I felt like I had that first morning. Couldn't focus. Nothing to hold on to. Steel waves crashed on crystal beaches again. Shattering them into a million grains of glass. The sound of boiling white water thundered in my ears.

'Er . . . I, er, think so,' I mumbled through the nausea. Fighting not to hurl.

'Well I been tellin' you you ain't nowhere near fixed. Now perhaps you'll believe me.' Bertha placed the back of her hand against my forehead. It felt cool. Soothing. Reassuring. 'You've had a major shock, son. Being dead ain't no cakewalk. Gonna be some time yet 'fore you strummin' and wailin'.' She smiled. 'Now you rest up for a bit. We'll try it in a wheelchair this time. Okay?'

They left me still fighting for focus. Something for my brain to grab hold of and force the ceiling to stop.

When my eyes finally took hold the first thing I saw were the beaming moustaches. 'Morpheeno, morpheeno,' they grinned. I just lay there zombied. My heart rate had come down and I slowly slid back. It had been a shock. A very real shock. It scared the life out of me. I couldn't understand it . . . I'd felt fine. Still groggy from the medication, but apart from being out of it I genuinely thought I was OK. Ready to rock. I obviously wasn't. That little stroll brought my cold hard reality rocketing home for the first time since Bertha had told me about it all. I had been critical with a heart attack and a concussion just seventy-two hours earlier. All the bravado in the world couldn't change the terrifying fact that I'd been dead for sixty seconds and it would take more than a few days in bed to make that right. Cold sweat ran down my face and back. I looked around me and noticed the guy in the bed next to me. I'd forgotten all about him. The last couple of days there had been a screen between us most of the time. He looked like he hadn't moved. Still in the half sitting position with his arms straight out in front of him. His head wrapped like an Egyptian mummy with just his eyes and mouth holes. Oh shit, now I've got the Cuban mafia and fucking Tutankhamen as neighbours. *Whatever it is that I did, God, I'm sorry*, I thought. *Please get me out of here.*

The door opened and in walked Dr Harrison and Bertha. This time the doctor was smiling. 'So how are we?' he asked me cheerily. 'Sister Beatrice tells me you had a little turn. Well, we are in a bit of a predicament, eh?' He laughed.

I tried my best at a smile.

'What happened exactly?'

'I just got giddy, doctor. It was motion sickness, I think. Felt weird to be moving again.'

'Sister said your heart was racing. Any chest pain?'

'No doctor, none.'

'All right, I'm going to give you a check out just to make sure everything's in place.' He listened to my heart with a stethoscope, checked the readout on the heart machine, my eyes, my tongue. The works. Writing his findings on his clipboard.

'I was feeling fine until my little walk,' I told him. 'That came as a bit of a shock and I realise that I'm not superman after all.'

'Well your heart seems to be fine. The elbow has multiple fractures but it set in a normal position. Should be as good as new in a couple of months. It's your heart you should be happy about. You've got the heart of an ox.' Dr Harrison looked over at the cardiovascular machine as it monitored my ticker and pulsed its green luminous sine wave across the screen. 'My prognosis is no problems. You're a very lucky young man. Seems it could have gone either way. If it hadn't been for the interns you'd probably have been a goner.'

Christ, what a twist. If I hadn't tried to headbutt one of them he wouldn't have hit me and my heart probably wouldn't have stopped in the first place. But if he hadn't been there I wouldn't be here thinking about it now. So work that one out.

'Thank you, God,' I said.

'Amen to that,' said Bertha.

'Any history of heart trouble in your family?' the doctor asked.

'No, not to my knowledge.'

'Have you ever had any problems with it before this?'

'No, never. Why?'

'Oh, standard question, but I didn't think so. We took a look at it over on the MRI and it looked fine. Do you have an addiction to cocaine or any other drugs?'

'No doctor, I don't.' He gave me a quizzical glance over the top of his glasses. 'No, really. I haven't done it that much. It's just that over the last couple of days I was celebrating with a few people who had pure Colombian cocaine and, well, it was really goo-hood,' I laughed. 'But addicted to coke or anything else . . . absolutely not.'

'Well that's good to hear. You see in my opinion it was probably the combination of such high amounts of cocaine and alcohol that caused your heart to seize. According to the intern's report it was doing about 280 beats a minute before it stopped.'

'What happened exactly?' I asked.

'Well, evidently you lurched at them in the dark and ran straight into the wall.'

Wall my arse! I thought. *It was a fist!* I might have been spinning but I know the difference between a wall and a fist. Walls don't have knuckles.

'It seems they put you back on the gurney and were loosening your clothes and trying to take off your boots when you came to and started to struggle with them. You were adamant about not letting them have your boots. Anyway, that's when your heart stopped. One of them went for emergency help and the other gave you mouth to mouth and massaged your chest when it started. Evidently it stopped again for a full minute before the emergency team arrived. They injected adrenalin straight into your heart. My God, it's lucky we didn't do the blood test first. If we'd known what was in your system, we probably wouldn't have administered the adrenalin.'

'Jesus! But I wasn't that out of it. I wasn't falling around drunk and stoned or anything like that. I was in a lot of pain and I was ripped, but not a mess.'

'That's what they said when we checked with emergency room records. But if the cocaine was as pure as you say you'd have no idea of how high you were. Trust me, you must have been flying. It nearly killed you.'

There were no words to argue with that. Jesus H. Christ, how do I get myself into these things? More to the point, how do I get out of them?

'Is there anything I can do for you, son?' the doctor asked.

'Did you manage to make that call?'

'Well, I didn't personally, but I know it's been made and your manager and family should know you're OK. As soon as I hear anything I'll have sister let you know. Now, do you think you're ready for another try at a bath?'

'I'd like to rest for a while if you don't mind.'

'Fine. When you're ready. I probably won't need to see you again today, but don't worry, you'll be out of here in no time.'

'So that answer your questions?' Bertha asked when Dr Harrison had left.

'Yes ma'am.'

'And how do you feel?'

'Very happy to be alive, ma'am.'

I was exhausted. My first venture into the outside had been a severe jolt to a nervous system that was already shot. Although I'd only moved a hundred feet down the corridor, something had changed in me. I could feel it. I felt weak. Not from the medication, literally weak. For the first time in my life I felt the fragility of my own existence. There are moments in life when your myths evaporate and you enter another phase, wondering how you deluded yourself for so long. It can happen over a woman, a business partner, or just some benign event that triggers the personal realisation that you've been kidding yourself for a long time. I think it was at that very moment that my delusion of immortality left me. I wasn't bulletproof after all. Just flesh and blood like everybody else. No more. No less. I looked around the room. Nothing had changed. There were the Severinos. Eyes glazed, mouths agape, safe in the arms of Morpheus. I looked over at Idi and my eyes skimmed the faces of Warren, Paul and Gil laughing at me from an old snapshot on the bedside table. Their smiling faces made me smile. Took me back. *What fantastic characters*, I thought.

A thunderclap boomed outside the windows, shaking the building, its rumble echoing through the skyscraper canyons of Manhattan Island. Lightning flashed, followed by the sound of heavy rain. *A storm*, I thought. *How beautiful. God, I'd love to be out there getting soaked.* I started to drift, the images of lightning and rain melding with the grinning faces at my bedside table.

A storm . . .

20
Aztec Air

Shape-shifting giants on white velvet horses . . .
drifting like galleons on a dark swirling sea.
Gods hurling handfuls of blinding white lightning
ride chariots of fire pulled by black onyx steeds.

Whirlwinds of flame from vapourised monoliths
Arc in blue veins through down-covered dragons.
Cannons resound from ghostly grey turret tops.
The ramparts lie burning from fire-laden wagons.

Electric blue banners on billowing battle tents.
The phalanx retreats, the die has been cast.
Banners blood red on a golden horizon.
The battle is over, the storm has now passed.

Massive turbulence buffeted Aztec Air flight 101, tossing
the plane like a feather on the surface of a violent black

ocean. Up sideways down. Then the next giant wave. Then another. Up 1000 feet. Down 500 in one screaming Kamikaze dive after another. The reverse twin engines screaming like giant outboard motors leaving the water at full throttle. The storm had been no secret. We could see it from seventy-five miles away. It was off to the west, nowhere near our intended flight path, but it slowly wrapped around us on all sides. Monstrous swirling towers of electric vapour challenging our air vehicle to a one-sided joust. Seeing no escape, our pilot had taken the plane to its limit of 15,000 feet somewhere over north-western NSW. But the thunderheads towered over us like mutant cotton-wool chess pieces, seeming to touch the stratosphere, and we found ourselves in the belly of a terrifying storm. Helpless. Our lives in the hands of a relative stranger who fought with the controls to keep us level. One second the nose was up at forty-five degrees, the next down at forty-five. Scary shit, even for the seasoned light air traveller. 'Strap yourself in, get out the vomit bag, and hang on to your arse,' the pilot yelled as the storm hit us broadside like a vapourised tsunami.

'You're going to die!' screams the voice. 'Scattered to the four winds. They'll find your dick in Goondiwindi and your nuts in Cairns. The only thing they'll bury will be what's left of your seat with your arsehole still stuck to it.' Then terror reaches a silence inside you and you wait. When you think the plane can't possibly take another second of it . . . it's over. Morphed back into the silent somewhere whence it came. The skies clear. God strikes the set, ending another savage reminder of who's really the boss. He dresses the sky in a radiant golden cape suspended from the heavens by ribbons of magenta light. Free as a bird.

On Aztec Air flight 101 from Melbourne, the four happy pranksters, pilot and road crew say an emotional hello to their arseholes, having kissed them goodbye several times in the last hour. It had been one hell of a storm but the twin-engined Piaggio had handled it well.

'Three cheers for cap'n Jim,' shouted Warren.

'Arggh Jim . . . Arghh . . . Arghh,' we responded.

Sick of the continual 600 mile drives to play the smaller Australian country towns, we decided there had to be some alternative. And there was. Our manager Michael Browning pulled off a coup with a local Melbourne air company and negotiated a one-year lease on a twenty-seater ex-World War II Italian troop transport called a Piaggio. Eventually the lavish expense nearly broke us, but it was a blast while it lasted. This luxury afforded us every freedom and convenience, and allowed us access to many hitherto inaccessible country towns that, apart from the odd Slim Dusty and Chad Morgan shows, had pretty much been denied live entertainment, particularly rock 'n' roll. Over the years as a soloist, and with the various Aztecs, I'd played most of the more significant dots on the Australian map, but by the early '70s they seemed to have been largely ignored by the agents and lay fallow, bereft of any entertainment other than the local bands and the pub on a Saturdee night. Their only connection to Australia's popular culture and rapidly developing modern society came through radio and television—and not all of them had television. We realised that there was a large audience out there that was not being tapped. Because of their isolation from the bigger smokes, the punters in these outback towns would be willing to spend their hard-earned dollars to see someone like us play, and we decided to go for it.

The plane of course came with a pilot. Within thirty seconds of meeting him Pig had nicknamed captain Jim Davidson 'Arghh Jim'. Jim was a small man with a big set of balls. After retirement from flying with the military, Jim had gone into various branches of civil aviation from crop-dusting to delivering medical supplies to remote areas of New Guinea by literally dropping a DC3 on jungle mountain ledges. Jim had fought the dreaded Rising Sun in the air over the Pacific and lived to tell the tale. He was an old war dog, and if you put wings on a toaster, Jim could fly it. Although a good thirty years our senior, he fitted into our lunacy like a dick in a rubber. A quiet man when we met, Jim was all about the business of flying. No drinking or fun and games after the shows for him. Straight to bed at 8 p.m. sharp.

The Piaggio was very comfortable, and roomy enough to let you walk around without having to duck your head. One of the design features was a small private cubicle at the back that comfortably sat six people. You entered it through a door in the rear of the cabin. We decorated the cubicle with gig posters, Turkish cushions and drapes, and it became the band's private bar and smoking room which we named the Manoonah Bar after the rhythm of a pumping boogie. Manoonah, manoonah, manoonah, manoonah. In a stroke of travelling genius Paul Wheeler suggested we maximise our comfort by adding a hookah. I guarantee that Aztec Air boasted the only six-pipe, Scotch-filtered, Turkish bubbly bolted to the floor on any airplane in the world. The Manoonah Bar also had its own air filter, to keep the dope smoke out of the cabin so that Arghh Jim didn't wig out on dope fumes and start sky dancing whenever he got a lungful. But like all the best laid plans of mice and rock hooligans it didn't work and pretty soon Jim was flying us around Australia whacked out of his brain. We all took turns to fly it at times. Gil had had some flying lessons and I had accumulated about fifty hours over the years. When the horizon was clear and the weather like the surface of a lake we all flew it. Of course Gilbert the Rat never did anything normally and you'd come out of a deep sleep in a terrifying dive with your head in your lap, with Rats at the controls wearing a handkerchief knotted on his head like a flying helmet and aviator goggles, yelling 'Kill the yellow bastards.'

'We'll be in on the ground in twenty minutes,' Jim yelled over the racket that day of the storm. 'Better fasten your seat belts. They haven't had anything like us on this strip before.'

'You can say that again,' Paul yelled over the din.

Just in case they repeal the statute of limitations, I will call this town Redville. Suffice it to say it's somewhere in the Australian bush. The seemingly endless expanse of uninhabited, treeless red desert that rolled out to an endless horizon on every side started to narrow. To focus. Lifeless patches of grey became trees. Black dots livestock. Brown dust, a million brilliant golden starbursts as sunlight from our silver fuselage bounced across the surface of a muddy billabong. Fences. Bush corrals. A plume of dust from a vehicle on a dusty bush track. Farms. Houses. Dirt, green lawns. Life. People. Strong tough people full of bush spirit and heart. The true Australians. Living and dying by the unyielding unforgiving will of the land. Born from generations of stock with red dirt in their veins. We could see the little town ahead. Tiny toy houses with grey tin roofs laid out from a centre that had been established for God knows what in God knows when by God knows who. The seemingly random pattern of the buildings like so many corrugated McDonald's cartons strewn across a red desert landscape. Thrown from the sky by some giant hand, blown by a desert wind, then left to dry for a hundred years in the scorching sun.

If it wasn't for the tall grove of trees at each end, the red dirt landing strip was barely distinguishable from the red desert dust. It looked more like a grimy bandaid on Ginger Meggs' grubby knee. Jim pulled a lever and I felt a dull thud. Nervous eyes darted around as the landing gear locked into place. Phew! The tiny airstrip was covered in spinifex and weeds. No control tower. No landing markers. No landing instructions for Jim. Just a tattered orange windsock hanging like a flaccid sunburned dick waiting patiently for the next travelling breeze to tease it into an erection. Just put the bastard on the deck. Outback flyin' style. Two thousand feet. A thousand. Five hundred. Two hundred.

'Fuck meeee!' yelled Jim, fighting the plane up.

'Fuck what?' screamed ten arseholes.

'A high tension wire,' he yelled. Sure enough, stretched across the approach to the runway, between two poles and not a hundred feet ahead, was a thick overhead power cable.

'Hang onnnn!' Jim yelled.

'You're fucking kidding!'

He hit the throttle and the engines screamed, then Bang—the rear wheel hooked the wire and the rear of the plane shot up in the air, throwing us all against the seats in front. Our faces pushed in like kids in a cake shop window. 'Fuuuuuck!'

Jim forced the nose up. 'Come onnn you bastard,' he yelled, but it wouldn't go. The plane hung in the air for a heartbeat, shuddered like a wet dog shaking water off its back, then dived at the dirt airstrip a hundred feet below at 150 miles an hour.

'Ohhhh . . . shiiittt!' ten voices silently screamed.

'Come onnnn you bastard,' Jim yelled, fighting the controls. 'Come onnnnn! . . . Come onnnnn you bludger.'

Baaaangggg . . . Urghhh . . . Bounce . . . 'Fuuuckkk' . . . Bounce . . . 'Oh shiiiit' . . . bounce . . . 'Fuuuuckk meee!' . . . bounce . . . baaaang . . . bump, screeacch . . . thump . . . shudder rattle . . . sliiide . . . The eagle has landed.

We had arrived in Redville. Seemingly in one piece. I looked around. Nobody spoke. We were all still hanging onto whatever we'd been hanging onto when we hit. A cloud of red dust fanned by the whirling propellers surrounded the plane. Jim switched the engines off and the props slowed to a dull pulse and stopped. 'Fuck, what about that?' 'Oh shiit.' 'Jeeesus Charist.' Everybody got off an expletive. What else were we going to say? 'Jolly gee, Quince Moreton, that was a bit bumpy, what?' No, 'Fuuuuck' did it very nicely. Everybody was jabbering at once. But everybody appeared to be in one piece.

'Everyone OK?' Jim yelled.

Apart from Rats who was trying to get his head out of Pig's arse, everybody seemed fine. Shaken but not stirred.

'Don't light any smokes!' yelled Jim. 'Just in case we've got fuel leaks.' *Smokes!* Jesus, our arses were still smoking from the landing. 'Let me out first, then all out.'

Now we didn't need to hear that twice. 'Fuel leaks' has a certain ring to it. Jim opened the door at the back and pulled the lever to let the stairs down. The second he hit the ground ten sets of arseholes and elbows were standing next to him on the dirt runway, chattering like a women's Rotary. It was midday and a stifling, scorching hot day. The temperature had to be in the hundreds and the choking red dust stuck to our faces and hair like shit to a blanket. We followed Jim around while he examined the plane. The rear wheel housing was slightly buckled but the wheel itself was fine. A deep gouge ran from the rear undercarriage to halfway down the belly, but it hadn't torn the metal. And that was it. It seemed OK.

'You little whore!' As smiling Jim patted the Piaggio's belly like an old friend. 'You little beauty,' he laughed. It had done well, but Jim deserved the Medal of Honour. It was an amazing bit of steel-balls flying that put us on the ground. There's no doubt Arghh Jim had saved all our lives. I could tell by the faces that we'd all had that same thought.

'Three cheers for Cap'n Jim,' I shouted. 'Arggh Jim . . . Arghh . . . Arghh.' And we crowded around him patting him on the back and shaking his hand.

Norman E and the crew began pulling our bags and gear from the hold when two speeding dust plumes appeared at the far end of the runway, headed in our direction. They pulled to a skidding halt, covering us in dust again, and a body floated out of the cloud.

'G'day boys. Jack Miller. Me friends call me Jacko,' the body said. 'Saw yers comin'. See yers 'ad a bit a trouble with the bloody wire. Bloody thing. Someone's always 'ittin' the bastard . . . Any'ow, yers are all right eh?' We just stood looking at Jacko, amazed by this bush nonchalance.

'G'day, Thorpie.' He came over and shook my hand. 'Boys.' He nodded. Jacko was a deadset cocky. Mid-forties, five foot five, round sunbaked face, skinny legs, muscular arms and with a huge beer gut that hung over his blue stubbie shorts like a dripping globule of dough escaping over the side of a donut vat. With black curly hair, blue eyes, thongs and a blue singlet, Jacko Miller was straight out of the Ettamogah pub bar. He shook hands with the rest of the group.

'Eh, Chooka,' he yelled to the truck that had now become visible after the dust cleared. 'Eh, cunt, get yer arse over 'ere and say 'ello ta the boys. He's been dying to meet yer, Thorpie.' Jacko grinned and nodded his head excitedly. 'Bin in the pub since 8 tha smornin' pluckin' up the bloody courage. E's gonna give yers an 'and settin' up yer gear an' that.' The door to the battered flatbed slowly opened and Chooka fell out face down in the dust with a splat. 'Ah shit, Chooka,' Jacko said. We just stood there staring.

Give us a hand with our gear? I thought. Chooka's hand couldn't find his own arse. Christ knows how he'd managed to get into the truck, let alone drive.

He dragged himself to his feet on the open door, pirouetted and fell back on his arse again, mumbling incoherently. He sat there for a moment, then pulled himself up the door again and hung there, dusting himself off, sending a new dust cloud into the air. The door swayed back and forth with Chooka hanging off it, staring around the airstrip and into the distance. He finally realised where he was, got a bead on us and came staggering over. Chooka was late fifties, sunbaked red, maybe six feet, built like a wet whippet with a battered Akubra, a dead rolly stuck to his bottom lip, and except for the old R.M. Williams boots and short blue socks he'd been dressed by the same tailor as Jacko. He stood, or I should say swayed, with his eyes spinning, trying to get a handle on anything that would keep the world still. Finally locked onto me. 'Fugg's Forpie. For-pie . . . Ow ya fuggin' goin' maaate? . . . Fuggin' beaudy,' he grinned. 'Pud it there, mate.' He put his hand out about a foot to my right and fell face down at my feet. We all broke up. Chooka was a classic.

'Ah shit, Chooka,' said Jacko. 'Get up orf the bloody ground.' But Chooka was out. 'Oh Jesus, give us an 'and to get 'im into the back of the flamin' truck will ya, boys? He's a bit pissed.'

A bit pissed! Chooka was shitfaced blind at midday. Norm and a couple of the crew helped get Chooka onto the open flatbed and Jacko came back over to us.

'Where's the promoter, Jacko?' I asked, hoping like crazy that his answer wasn't going to be . . .

'I'm puttin' on the show tonight, Thorpie. An yers are stayin' at me motel as well. Any of yers fancy a coldie and a feed?' He looked around the group. 'Me missus threw some snags on the barbie when we 'eard the plane. Should be goin' like a bottler by now.' He grinned and rubbed his hands enthusiastically. After the landing and the heat, nothing could have sounded better than an ice cold beer and some country snags.

'Snags sounds great. Beer . . . Yeah, great,' went the response.

'All right, why don't we get yer stuff onto the truck and we'll go straight over. It's only 'alf a flamin' mile from 'ere. Eh, Norm, yer don't mind drivin' the truck do yer?' Norm nodded his OK.

The crew got our gear and bags onto the flatbed and secured it with ropes. Chooka was snoring like one of the Piaggio motors and Jacko tied him down as well. 'Silly old bugger,' he said, fixing the rope around Chooka's waist to the back of the cab. Pig and Paul got into the front with Norm and the crew jumped on the back. Chooka, Rats and I got into Jacko's beaten-up Holden ute and he took off like a front-runner at Bathurst. Of course every time we hit a bump Rats made a sound like Japanese chicken, which freaked poor old Jacko right out. Rats did that a lot in cars and we'd also nicknamed him the Samurai Shock Absorber. Five minutes later we pulled up outside a country motel in the middle of a green paddock just down the road from the airstrip.

''Ere we are, boys. This is me motel.' Jacko nodded proudly at the place. 'The dance is in town but yers are stayin' 'ere. So leave yer stuff on the truck. It'll be sweet. I'll get some 'elp fer Norm this arvo. 'S too bloody 'ot fer work. Let's 'ave a beer first. Come and meet the missus. She's yer biggest bloody fan, Bill. Doreen and her girlfriends 'ave been getting titivated all flamin' mornin'. Jeez, yer'd think it was the bloody Queen comin',' he mumbled to himself.

The motel stretched the boundaries of the word to its absolute limit. A flat-roofed rectangular block of gleaming white fibro with a flat corrugated-iron roof, twenty doors and some windows was more like it. But this was the bush and a bed is a bed. Norm pulled up behind us thirty seconds later. We were standing there taking it all in when five big country boilers came waddling over. Faces aglow. Giggling like kids.

'Aw ace it up, Doreen,' Jacko said to one of them. They were pink with excitement and swarmed around us clucking like hens. 'Doreen, this is Billy Thorpe.'

'Oh gawd. It's so bloody exciting to 'ave yers 'ere,' giggled Doreen. 'It's real luverly ter meet yer. I've followed yer fer years.'

'Nice to meet you too, Doreen.' I shook her hand and she went scarlet.

'Oh gawd,' she said again.

'This is the Aztecs and our crew.' I introduced them all.

'Pleased to meet yers all I'm sure,' she said. 'And this is Florrie, Beryl, Marge and Raylene.' We all shook hands. 'Come on, me snags'll be burnin',' Doreen said, and we followed the group around the back of the building.

Doreen was early forties, close to six feet tall, as round as a rain barrel and looked as strong as an ox. She and Jacko made a real odd couple. Doreen wore a bright yellow mumu with red galahs all over it, R.M. Williams boots with yellow ankle socks and the brightest, bluest perm I've ever seen. It looked like somebody had thrown a bottle of light blue ink on her head, rolled her hair in toilet roll centres, sprayed it with a whole can of hair spray and plugged her into a wall socket to dry. The crowning glory was the yellow and pink flowered hat that sat precariously on top, looking like a combination of a drag queen's swimming cap and a fruit salad. The others were all big country women who looked like they could arm wrestle a hippopotamus into a willing submission, and all suitably attired in their Sundee best. And talk about bright colours. They glowed like a fashion statement in Cairns in the late '50s, but they'd obviously taken a lot of time to get decked out and we all respected it. Well of course Rats had to say something.

'Jesus, Thorpie, look at that arse,' he whispered, nodding at Doreen as she swayed along in front of us. 'Imagine her taking a shit—'

'Shhh,' I whispered. 'Don't start—'

'Eh Thorpie,' he went on. 'Imagine them in the cot. The poor little bastard must have to tie a plank across his arse and wear a crash helmet and flippers. I'll bet he ties himself to the bed in case she farts.'

Oh Jesus, I thought. I knew the Rat and he was just getting started.

The unmistakable smell of barbecuing sausages hit us as we turned onto a small patio at the back of the motel. Several grinning cockies stood around the brick barbie, beer cans in rubber coolers in hand. All traditionally attired in faded blue stubbies, blue singlets and battered R.M. Williams boots. We were introduced and then dished up enough country snags, potatoes and salad to kill a horse. 'Go for it, boys,' smiled Jacko, playing the proud country host. The feed and a cool beer brought us all back to earth. A short time later we were joined by another half dozen locals and their wives and kids, and the barbie was raging like a country wedding reception. About an hour in we could hear this 'Ehh whistle . . . Ehhhh,' coming from around the other side of the building.

'Oh shit! Chooka,' Jacko yelled, and ran off.

What with meeting the local chapter of the Hawaiian women's club and the feed, we'd all forgotten poor old Chooka was still tied to the back of the truck. He appeared no worse for wear from his bondage, or any soberer, and got straight into the piss. Half an hour later he was making a second attempt at conversation with us when he fell face down in a vegetable patch and no-one took a blind bit of notice. The beer and Scotch and Cokes had been flowing and by this time Rats was wearing a big flat loaf of bread on his head like an admiral's hat, Raylene's white sunflower-shaped glasses, a teddy bear that he'd pinched from some little kid and a flower in his teeth. He looked like a gay conquistador but nobody gave a shit. They loved him. Pig started calling him 'Big Julie' and that's when Rats got another nickname, Julius Flatbread Crapinpants Matthews.

The party looked like it was ready to kick on into next week and Norm grabbed Jacko and some of his mates before they were too blind to stand. They left to set the gear up in the local hall. We thanked Doreen for the barbie. She got us our room keys and we went to our rooms. If that's what you can call them. They were tiny. The door opened inwards and I only got it half open when it hit a cupboard. I had to squeeze around it to get inside. The room might have been small but it was immaculate and clean, with a single bed each side of a console with a radio built into it. To the left of the door was a bathroom and shower. A small table with two chairs stood near a sliding door that opened up onto an extension of the patio. The fibro walls were paper thin and I could hear Pig and Rats talking as plain as day. I walked out onto the patio to find the others standing there scratching their heads. I had my own room but for some unknown reason the others had been doubled up, with Pig and Rats sharing the room next to mine.

'Jesus, Thorpie, you can't swing a bloody cat in there,' said Pig. 'What's your room like?'

I told them it was the same and that I'd go and ask Doreen for separate rooms, which I did. Unfortunately the motel was booked out for the big gig and we were stuck the way we were. Anyway, it was only for one night.

The gig was in a typical little country hall. We'd been on the road for several weeks doing small towns and the small PA we carried had been adequate for the gigs so far. Anyway we had our faithful sound man Barnie Deutche with us, so we didn't bother doing a sound check. We didn't have to start until 9 so we all crashed for the rest of the afternoon. Sometime later I was woken by Pig's voice from next door.

'Dah! . . . This fuckin' air-conditioner is giving me the shits.'

I went next door and Rats was laughing at Pig, who was pacing around the room.

'What's up, mate?' I asked.

'This bloody air-conditioner is fucked. It keeps going on and off. I've been trying to get some sleep and every time I get off the bloody thing starts to conk out and sounds like a bloody Mack truck coming through the wall. When I turn it off it comes back on by itself. The bloody thing's driving me insane.' Rats was laughing his arse off. 'Christ, Thorpie, I can't sleep with that going all night. It'll drive me bloody mad.'

'Why don't you get Jacko?' I suggested. 'Maybe he knows how to fix it.' With that Pig was out the door and back a minute later with Jacko and a still-pissed Chooka in tow.

'Now let's 'ave a look 'ere,' Jacko said, turning the switch on the console between the beds.

'Yeaaah . . . yet's haf a loog,' mumbled Chooka. He squinted his eyes trying to see what we were all looking at.

Doog . . . doog . . . doog . . . dooog . . . rattle . . . rattle . . . clang bup . . . bup . . . bup, bup, bup . . . The air-conditioner came on like an over-choked grader. 'That's the bloody noise,' Pig said. 'It does it when it's turned off as well.' He glared at the console.

'Ah, they all make that noise when they come on,' said Jacko. 'It'll settle. Ya just 'ave ter leave it warm up fer a bit and it'll be sweet.'

'Shweeeeeet,' yelled Chooka as he fell over a chair and speared himself out the door onto the patio with an 'Ah fuuuggg.'

'Shit, Chooka,' said Jacko. We fell about laughing. 'Listen, let it run fer a bit 'n' leave it on when yers go to the show tonight. It'll be sweet.'

'Shwweet,' mumbled Chooka, falling back through the curtain.

'Come on you silly big bastard.' Jacko grabbed Chooka and off they went, leaving Pig staring in disbelief at the air-conditioner. I went back to my room and drifted off again.

Doog . . . doog . . . doog . . . clang . . . rattle . . . ping bup, bup, bup, bup . . . 'Dahh . . . fuck!' I heard through the wall as the air-conditioner did its thing again.

'It's not that bad, Piggy,' laughed Rats. 'Just ignore it. It doesn't bother me.'

'Ignore it . . . Igfuckingnore it! The bloody thing's driving me mad. I bloody can't sleep and the bloody thing keeps coming on by itself.'

This went on and on until Norm came to get us for the gig. Pig was ropable and threatening to tear the air-conditioner out of the wall and 'stick it up Jacko's fucking arse!'

The country hall was just that. Wooden. Small stage. And about as much atmosphere as a confessional. Our stage gear and lights had dressed it up quite a bit and we arrived to the sounds of laughing and punters dancing to Neil Sedaka's 'I love, I love, I love my little calendar girl' blasting through the PA. We always carried some oldies tapes for country gigs and the country folk always loved them. The place was packed to the rafters and it seemed like the whole town was there. It probably was. They hadn't had a show there in over nine months and this was a major event in a country town of that size. The audience was a ripper. All decked out in their best suits and frocks.

Yes, frocks. I hadn't seen a frock at a gig since the Catholic Hall in Moorooka when I was eleven years old. And the dance styles were great. Some were twisting, some jiving, some doing variations of the swim and a surf stomp, and some of the oldies were doing their best at some sort of Pride of Erin. All at the same time! It was a classic, but they were already having a country ball. Jacko came back into the dressing-room behind the stage to see if we were ready.

'Christ, the whole bloody town's 'ere,' he said, rubbing his hands. 'So I 'aven't done me money. Right, I'm goin' to announce yers. I love this bit,' he grinned.

'Ladies and gentleman, can I 'ave a bit a quiet.' The drone from the hall continued. Tap! tap! tap! went Jacko's finger on the mike. 'Can I 'ave a bit a quiet please,' he yelled over the din. Nothing changed.

'QUIETTTT!' he screamed with a whistle and screech as the mike fed back. 'That's bloody better. Now . . .'

'On ya Jacko', 'Eh Jacko, sing us a bloody song', 'Take it orf' went the wags in the crowd.

'All right, quieten down. And you bloody shut up, Wal, or I'll flatten ya.'

'In ya bloody dreams,' yelled Wal.

'All right, all right . . . Now you all know why we're 'ere. It's been a bloody long time since we've 'ad a show up 'ere and we've never 'ad anybody like this before. So put yer 'ands together and give a big country welcum ter Billy Thorpe and 'is band the Aztecs.'

A cheer went up and we walked out on stage. 'Play bloody "Poison Ivy"' . . . ' "Over the Rainbow"', they started before we'd even plugged in. I counted in 'Be Bop A-Lula' and when we hit the first atmosphere-tearing chord the crowd literally fell backwards on each other from the shock of the volume. They'd never heard anything that loud in their lives. They stood there with their hands over their ears and their mouths wide open for about a minute. Little kids ran for their mothers and some of the oldies were blinking so hard I thought they were going to fly away. It was hilarious. The shock slowly subsided and they began to get into it. Chooka and a group of pissed mates had congregated at the front of the stage to my right, yelling out and mumbling between songs in a language only they could understand. One by one everyone in the hall came down the front for a close up look at someone they'd only ever seen on TV and in magazines. They shouted out for favourites and we played some of my early '60s stuff like 'Poison Ivy' which we rarely did but it was the right thing to do for this audience and they loved it.

They got right into the hard rocking blues as well, enjoying themselves in the uninhibited and unaffected way that only country folk can. The beer had been flowing from three eighteens out the back but there was no trouble of any kind and the night turned into a ripper. One of Doreen's girlfriends won the hamper in the raffle which I announced during a break. We went out and drank with the locals around the kegs and they loved the fact that we weren't up ourselves and mixed with them. Lots of autographs and photos with Donga and missus, Raylene and her boyfriend Wal, and just about everyone there. There were no hassles of any kind. Just incredibly polite, friendly and respectful Aussie country folk who were genuinely grateful that someone like us had taken the time to fly into their little bush town and perform for them. It was only a little town and some of them must have travelled miles. There wasn't one drama or complaint and everybody, including us, had a ball. It was a pleasure to play to them and see their response to a music which for the most part they'd never heard before. The sounds of Muddy Waters and Howlin' Wolf mixed with our brand of rock must have been quite a culture shock to these people in the early '70s.

In the middle of a rocking second set Warren did an impromptu rocking solo piano version of 'On the Road to Gundagai' which brought the house down and Rats farted into his high-hat mike in the middle of a blistering drum solo which completely freaked them out and brought cheers from the crowd. It wasn't so much a gig as a town party and they wouldn't let us off. We ended up playing every bloody song we knew and a few that we didn't before the show wound down at midnight and everybody drifted home to their little country houses and back to their bush reality for another nine months. Jacko was beside himself happy. The night had been a raging success and I think he saw himself as the future of bush entertainment. He was a hero and he'd made some money. He ran us back to the motel and told us there were drinks and some tucker ready and that he'd invited a few mates over to ''ave a drink with yers, if that's all right, Billy'.

What was I going to say? Fuck you, Jacko. Of course it was all right. By 1.15 the party was raging and the barbie area out the back of the motel started to really take off. Rats had the bread on his head and the teddy bear again, and had found a water pistol from somewhere, which he filled with beer and was squirting at everybody from the bushes. I'd gone to my room a little earlier for something or the other and on the way back I passed him, grinning, trying to get a fire hose loose from the wall. Thank God he hadn't and the water pistol had to do. A Gene Vincent record scratched away on an old portable record player and five foot five Jacko was doing his level best to jive with six foot Doreen. Instead of letting go of her hand every time he spun her, he held onto it and she had to duck to her knees to go under his arm. She came out of the spins at a terrifying speed and Jacko's feet shot off the ground, his eyeballs flew out, his hair stood straight up and the pressure nearly tore his arm off. Chooka had a go at jiving as well, if that's what it was called. He was still as pissed as a newt but a real happy drunk who obviously didn't bother a flea. He grabbed one of Doreen's girlfriends and cut into it like Fred Astaire on speed. His feet were flying in every direction and at some stage in his life I could see old Chooka had been the dancin' lad. He was cutting all sorts of stuff, spinning Beryl and whooping and hollerin' with his left hand in the air like a buckjumper. Suddenly he cut into a spin that would have made Michael Jackson look for a new career. But Chooka was out of control and he shot across the patio, flattening Beryl as he went, bounced off a Hill's Hoist with a resounding doiiinggg and pirouetted down an embankment with a 'Fuuggg meeeeee!' Buster Keaton turned in his grave. Jacko picked Beryl up and she dusted herself off. 'Silly old bastard,' said Jacko and went back to spinning big Doreen.

Other couples were dancing and bopping along to the music and everyone was having a great old time. Paul and I had blown a small number and we sat quietly by the barbie, drinking and killing ourselves laughing. It looked like the Muppets' country cousins on acid, with Rats and Pig leading the band. The party raged for a while and one by one people said their goodnights and drifted off. We sat around with Jacko, Doreen, Chooka and some of his mates before saying good night too and heading off to our rooms.

We had no intention of going to bed, but had had enough of the country comfort. We wanted some of our own brand of lunacy. I went back to my room and had no sooner closed the door when I heard 'Spirit . . . ooooooh . . . spirit . . . oooo. Spirit can you hear meee?' coming through the wall from Pig and Rat's room. It was Ralph and Zelda.

We all ran into their room at the same time. Ralph and Zelda didn't appear that often but when they did they were usually accompanied by Dig, Doug and Dan the Dig It Brothers, and that combination was just too good to miss. Sure enough the room was dark except for a candle burning on the table. Next to it sat the mysterious Zelda with a pillowcase tied over her head like a Polish peasant, and a bedspread wrapped around her. It was Piggy. Ralph Rotten, who was Rats, sat on a chair in the centre of the room.

'Spirit, can you hear me?' sang Rats in his favourite *Tommy* melody. 'Spirit . . . I'm calling you who who who who,' he sang like the Indian love call.

Zelda just sat staring at the candle, mumbling incantations.

'Spirit, can you hear me? . . . Spirit, are you there? . . . Oh wise Zelda will you summon the great spirit?'

More mumbling from Zelda.

'Spirit, oh spirit. It is I, Ralph Rotten, with Thorpie and the boys. We need your words of wisdom. Oh spirit, spirit . . . can you hear meee?'

'What d'ya want, cunt? Don't dig it,' shouted Zelda, channelling one of the Dig It Brothers.

'Which one are you, spirit? Dig, Doug or Dan?' asked Ralph.

'It's Dan. What d'ya want?'

'Where's Doug and Dig, Dan?'

'Ah Dig didn't Dig Doug not digging it when I, Dan, didn't dig Doug not digging Dig's dirty fucking landing this morning.'

We all roared. Pig was as pissed as we were. Getting that out was a miracle.

'Dan, can you give us some words of wisdom?'

'Don't dig it,' said Dan.

'Aw come on, Dan, Dig and Doug will dig it if Dan digs it.'

'Don't dig it,' laughed Dan. Zelda pulled the pillowcase around her, trying to keep a straight face in the candlelight.

'Will you show yourself, Dan?'

'Dan's gone. This is Dig. Dig it?' channelled Zelda in a deeper voice.

'What happened to Dan, Dig?' asked Ralph.

'Ah Doug didn't dig Dan not digging it and sent me Dig to dig it instead of Dan. Dig it?'

We're all on the floor by now.

'Will you show yourself, Dig?'

'Ah, Dig's a cunt. This is Doug. Dig it?' Zelda channelled in a high voice this time.

'Wh . . . what happened to Dig, Doug?' laughed Rats.

'Dan and I, Doug, didn't dig Dig not digging Dan not digging it and I'm here to dig it instead of Dig. Dig it?'

'Will you show yourself, Doug?'

'Don't dig it,' said Zelda, cracking up. It was ridiculous.

'Aw come on, Doug.' No answer. 'Doug . . . Doug . . . Are you still there, Doug?' Ralph wailed.

Still no answer.

'Where are you, Dig?'

'Ah Dig, Doug and Dan didn't dig it und I haf un ozzer shpirit vaiting to come srough, Rolf,' laughed Zelda in the worst European accent known to man.

334

We all called the new spirit. 'Spirit, can you hear me?'

The lights came on and a piece of white cloth shot around the room about six feet from the floor and disappeared out the door. Rats and Pig had rigged a pillowcase to some elastic and tied it to Pig's chair. When he loosened it the pillowcase fired around above us like a ghost on speed. We all knew it was coming but the lights going on and the pillowcase freaked us all the same. The whole room went into hysterics. Pig stood up and the bedspread he had around him slowly started to rise in front of him. He had two brooms underneath with a shoe on each end and it looked like his body was levitating. Pig's going 'Oooh . . . oooohh' and we're all dying. He blew the candle out, and then, Whooosh!—the unmistakable sound of a flying pillow.

'Pillow fight,' yelled the Rat and the room went silent. Then sniggering and whoosh . . . whoosh as those who had found pillows swung them in the dark. Whoosh. 'Ah fuck,' as somebody connected. Whack . . . bang. 'Dah.' Whoosh. Thud. 'Shit!'

I heard somebody run out of the room and the fight continued. Just then there was a knock on the door on the patio side and the room went silent.

'Eh . . . eh Forpiee. Forpie. S'mee . . . Chooka. Carn let us in maaate. Carn led's haf a dring, maaate . . .' Knock, knock. 'Carn 'smee. 'Sbloody Chooka maate. Led's haf a beer maate. Carn.'

The door opened and there was Chooka's silhouette swaying in the doorway. Just then the door behind me opened and a solid jet of water shot across the room and hit Chooka square in the gut. His feet left the ground, he shot backwards off the patio and arse over head down the same embankment he'd pirouetted off in his Michael Jackson spin. 'Arghh fuuuuggg!' he screamed, disappearing over the edge with a splat. Then a burst of water hit us. It was fucking Rats and the bloody fire hose I'd seen him fiddling with earlier. I'm not talking about a trickle from a garden hose. I'm talking the real, hundreds of pounds of water pressure deal. The water went off and I could hear Rats killing himself laughing outside. I got up off the floor and turned on the light. The floor was soaked. The walls were wet. The lamps were over, the beds soggy, and we were all dripping like we'd just come out of a pool.

'You cunt,' somebody yelled and we took off after him. Somebody grabbed the hose and turned it on. Lights came on in the other rooms and heads came out of doors. Nobody said a word, just watched as Billy Thorpe and his sopping Aztecs chased a screaming Rat around the car park with a fire hose. We finally cornered him and gave it to him until he begged for mercy. By then we were being cheered on by our admiring audience. We carried Rats back to the room. A few faces came to the door and had a laugh but everybody was cool. Everybody that is except for Jacko, who hit the proverbial roof when he saw that one of his rooms was now ready for the 800 metre freestyle.

'Look at me fuckin' room. Jesus, me fuckin' room,' he said, checking it out.

Nobody said a word. Then, 'Eh Thorpie, led's haf a beer maate. Carn Jacko have a beer maate.' It was Chooka back from his flight. The sight of him broke us all up, including Jacko. His boots were gone. He was dripping wet and covered in mud and leaves from head to toe. The only discernible feature was his bloodshot eyes.

'Carn Thorpie. Led's 'ave a beer, eh?'

Somebody got Chooka a towel and we had a beer or

twenty and the party kicked back on in the wet. Pig jumped off his bed onto the floor and a gallon of water shot up into the air. He got on the floor and lay there doing the backstroke. Rats started wringing out pillowcases and Zelda's cape which had gotten soaked and we hung them on the Hill's Hoist out the back. It was still very hot and a dry wind was blowing. They'd be dry in no time. It was the carpet and the walls that were the worry. The carpet squelched with every step and the walls, Jesus! I noticed Rats fiddling with something on the wall over the console beside his bed and the next minute he poked his finger straight through it. The fibro had turned into wet paper. He quickly grabbed a lamp from the floor and stuck it in front of the hole, grinning at me like a kid who'd just farted. Which he did at that very second. It was a Rat fart which is like no other fart in the known universe. The sound is somewhere between a rotten wet tractor trailer tyre being torn in half and an elephant doing a head dive into a vat of warm cheddar cheese. And the pong is fucking horrific. I swear he has a secret recipe that he boils up and feeds himself, because no combination of foods that I know of can produce the sound and stench of a dinosaur with diarrhoea. Rats' farts do. They're unbelievable. Everybody ran for the door holding their faces. One breath of a Rat fart and you're stone dead and your body just turns into dust as it hits the floor. We're all outside gasping and the Rat's inside sniggering to himself. We walked back in and he ripped another one off. Once he gets started it's all over, and he was started. This went on for five minutes until Rats got bored with farting and we all came back. The farts had taken the edge off the soaked room and after a while Jacko was drinking and laughing with the rest of the group.

Chooka had a stubbie in each hand and a rolly hanging from his mouth. He'd never been happier in his life. Then he spotted a bottle of red on the console between the beds.

'Ah . . . luff a glazza red maaate. Carn. Led's av a glass a red. What d'ya think, Forpie. A glazza red or what? Carn.'

There was no stopping him. He had the cork out of the bottle and was swigging it before anyone could say anything. The party kicked on for a bit. Jacko got some more grog and another couple of bottles of Scotch and pissed wasn't the word. Ratshit was the word. Then Paul produced a couple of giant hash joints, just to put a capper on the evening before we crashed. We all had a hit, including Chooka. Big mistake. His eyes actually stopped spinning for a minute and that was the problem. It was the first time in years that he could see anything clearly and he freaked right out and went into a spin-out. I could see he was going to chuck and Pig and I started to carry him into the bathroom. But we didn't make it. Baaarrrrfff! Red wine, snags, about six cases of beer, and what looked like four roast dinners and three pizzas hit the floor, the walls, the ceiling, and me and Pig.

'Dah, fuck,' shouted Pig. I was gagging so bad I couldn't say anything. I just ran out of the room and hosed myself from head to toe. Oh Jesus I hate the smell of vomit. Especially when it's as exotic as Chooka's. Pig hosed himself down as well and we stood there laughing our arses off. Jacko came out. He was blind staggering drunk but he grabbed the hose, fell back through the door and turned the hose on. All the guys bailed out the other end. We all stood at the door and watched as he fell about hosing Chooka's surprise out the far door onto the patio. The floor filled up with water again and it reeked.

'Well that's it for me. I'm off to bed, boys. See ya in a few years,' I laughed and left. I could hear the party going on next door like it was in my room. I had a shower, packed my bag and got into bed. I forced myself to sleep and was just drifting off through the laughing when, Caraaash! Something came crashing through the wall above my head, covering me in dust. I turned on the light and looked up. It was a fist with a glass of Scotch and Coke in it.

'Hey, cunt, you forgot your drink,' laughed Piggy. The room next door cracked up. I put my eye up to the hole. Big mistake. Rats had his arse over it and farted right in my face. I nearly passed out. I lay there for a bit listening to it all and it slowly quietened down and the others left, leaving Pig and Rats to sleep in a soaked room that smelt worse than the Kings Cross public shitter at 5 a.m. on a Sunday. But they were so pissed it didn't matter. The quiet was beautiful until . . . Doog . . . doog . . . doog . . . clang . . . rattle . . . ping bup, bup, bup, bup, ting rattle doog doog doog doog . . .

'Dahh . . . fuck!' Pig yelled as the air-conditioner did its thing again. Rats broke up. They talked for a bit and I could hear the squelch of water as Pig stormed around and Rat's evil laugh. Then it went quiet. I was just about out and Doog . . . doog . . . doog . . . clang . . . rattle . . . ping bup, bup, bup, bup . . . 'Dahh . . . fuck!' And more laughing from Rats.

This went on for another hour or so. Silence for a while, then Doog, doog, doog . . . bup, bup, bup, bup, 'Dah . . . the fuckin' thing' and Pig squelching around the room while Rats laughed. I was beat but their voices always made me laugh and the way they interacted was always hilarious.

The sound of Pig raging and doog, doog, doog, 'Dah fuck' had me in hysterics.

I woke up with Norman E standing over me. Daylight streaming through the window nearly blinding me. 'Billy, come on, mate. We better gotta get out of here.'

'What who . . . I . . . what?' I sat up and a lightning bolt split my head. 'Oh shit, who? I?'

'It's Norm, mate . . . Come on get up. Jim's out at the plane already,' he said, shaking me awake. 'Let's get out of here before Jacko sees the bloody mess when he's sober. Come on, mate.'

The room was spinning and I wanted to die but I forced myself out of bed and got dressed. Thank God I'd already packed. I heard Pig and Rats stirring next door and then Doog . . . doog . . . doog . . . clang . . . rattle . . . ping bup, bup, bup, bup, ting, rattle, doog doog doog doog . . . 'Dahh . . . fuck!'

Then, Caaraashhh! Norm and I ran in and Pig had the air-conditioner out of the wall and it hit the floor just as we walked in. 'Fuckin' thing,' he said and went into the bath-room, squelching on the carpet as he walked. 'Dah fuck,' I heard again and the three of us went to have a look. There was Chooka out cold on the floor and the sink was full to overflowing with carrot and pizza speckled red wine vomit which was dripping all over the floor. Pig calmly sat down and took a crap, mumbling like a crazed Nazi to himself in the midst of the pong.

'Look, a Pig in shit,' said the Rat and we cracked up cry-ing, holding our stomachs. It was a ridiculous sight. We got ourselves together and looked at the room. It was wrecked. There was a gaping hole in the back wall where the air-conditioner had been and another where Pig had stuck his hand into my room. The opposite wall was melting in soft flakes. The carpet had two inches of water on it and was purple where Chooka had hurled. The lamps were wrecked and the soaking drapes hung from the windows like sad faces.

'Come on, guys. Let's get the fuck out of here,' said Norm. 'The gear's already on the plane and I've got the keys to the truck. Let's fucking go! Come on, Pig, you silly bugger. Hurry up.'

'Dah fuck . . . Bluuurttt, riiipp,' replied Piggy.

Ten minutes later we were taxiing down the runway. Jim took off in the opposite direction from the one we'd landed in, avoiding the wire, but just missing the treetops as we took off. The plane banked to the left and we went right over the top of the motel. There below us on the lawn were Jacko, Doreen and a couple of maids all shaking their fists at us as we flew over them. It was like a scene from a Charlie Chaplin movie and we went hysterical. Before long the rave started again. A quick trip to the Manoonah Bar got us all right back on track, and off soared the happy pranksters into the wild blue yonder. Pig was still ranting about the doog, doog, doog and all the while Rats had this evil grin on his face. Finally he put his hand in his pocket and handed something to Pig. Pig looked at it for a second and said, 'Dah fuck. You cunt, Rats, Youuu cuuunttt!' and started chasing Rats up and down the aisle, pummelling him with a rolled-up newspaper.

None of us had any idea what it was all about so we just sat there until they finally collapsed in a screaming laughing heap on the floor. I knelt over them and asked Pig what was happening. He tried to speak but he was laughing so hard he had tears rolling down his cheeks and all that came out were little squeaking sounds. He held up his hand and opened it, and the penny dropped. In his palm was the black plastic on-off knob from the console between their beds in the motel room. Like the crazed maniac he was, Rats always looked for your button and when he found it he pushed it relentlessly until you went insane. And he had literally found Pig's button the first time Pig had reacted to the doog, doog, doog. Rats had been lying there all that time switching the air conditioner on and off and driving Pig crazy. It had been him every fucking time, the maniac. I couldn't breathe for laughing and when the word went around the plane I swear the fuselage nearly burst its seams. Arggh Jim wanted to know what all the laughing was about and Rats went up the front and told him. Jim laughed so hard the plane lost trim and shot to the left for a few seconds before he righted it.

'Whoaaa,' we all yelled and burst out laughing again.

'Hey Rats,' I shouted over the laughter.

He came back, grinning from ear to ear. 'What d'ya want, cunt?'

'Hey Rats, did you ever tell Paul about that time we . . .'

'Wake up, son. You dreamin' again? Come on, we gotta get you into that bath. You ready?'

21
The Bath

'Well are you ready for that bath now?' the voice
asked.

'What? I, er . . .' I had no idea where I was.

'Your bath, son. Carl's got you a wheelchair. Come on,
let's get you up.'

The room came into focus. 'A bath? What bath?' I said.
'There's no bath on the plane, Rats. What do I need a bath
for?'

'Honey, I know you get high on your medication, but
this ain't no airplane and there sure ain't no rats here,'
Bertha laughed. 'Is there, Carl?' she asked.

'Urrrggg,' replied Carl and I was back. There was Bertha
with Carl towering over her shoulder, looking down at me.

'You with us now?' asked Bertha.

'I, er, I think so,' I mumbled, shaking the cobwebs away.

'Good. Carl's got the wheelchair. This time no more
bare-assed leaps,' she laughed.

Bertha lowered the bed and Carl effortlessly lifted me into the wheelchair with his huge arms, then off we went. The chair felt much better. No nausea this time. Idi unlocked the door and I was out of my cell! We followed Bertha down the passage and this time I got my first real look at where I was. There were no rooms on the opposite side of the passageway, but we passed at least twenty medical cells exactly the same as the one I was in. All barred with steel. All with armed guards. And all full of ailing maniacs. Their crazed icy stares as I passed them chilled me to my soul. It was scary shit. They looked like caged ghouls and vampires, spotting some new fresh flesh. Waiting for the keeper to make one mistake so they could escape and devour the first innocent fresh blood they came across. It was a long corridor and I guessed the Mental Hospital covered the entire top floor of Bellevue. God only knows what existed in the actual asylum. I didn't want to know.

The further we got from my room the noisier the inmates were and I figured I had been in the quieter and less violent section of the ward. Then my mind flashed to the Severino brothers. *Jesus Christ*, I thought. *If the Severinos are regarded as quiet, what the fuck kind of weirdness do these rooms hold?* Carl was moving too fast for me to get more than a glancing shot into them, but just as he slowed down to make a right turn I heard screaming and howling coming from a room at the very end of the corridor. Through the barred windows I saw several orderlies and a couple of guards trying to get at a naked patient who was standing on his bed, smeared from head to toe with what looked like wet shit. He was free, and crazily swinging the loose chains attached to his wrists at their heads. They were ducking and weaving, trying to avoid the handcuff nunchakas. As we turned the corner I heard the unmistakable sound of fists on flesh and the screaming subsided.

I couldn't believe it. I was out of my claustrophobic cell and actually going somewhere. Actually making what felt like my first real move towards getting out of this terrifying place. It was Tuesday and I'd only been there about three and a half days but the morphine had heightened the sense of lunacy and of helplessness. Time had freeze-framed and it felt more like six months. We went right through a large shower room and into a smaller room which contained two jacuzzi-sized baths sunk side by side into the tiled floor. One of them was already full of steaming water. The steam rose in clouds to the ceiling where it condensed, forming large clear droplets that hung like liquid stalactites.

The steam hit my lungs and I took the first real breath of my second life. I felt instantly human.

'Well, I think you'll be all right in here for a while,' said Bertha as she carefully slipped a long, clear plastic cover over my cast. She unwound the bandage from my head. 'How's your head feel, son?' she asked, touching the back where I hit it when I fell.

'Feels OK, Sister,' I said, feeling it. 'A little tender but it's fine.'

'Good. That's one thing we don't have to worry about, eh?' She smiled and I nodded. 'I'll have a guard on the door. If you need anything, just holler. OK? Carl, would you put Mr Thorpe in his bath please?'

Carl knelt down and laid me in the steaming water as gentle as a mother with her newborn baby. I still had my back-to-front cotton gown on but I didn't care. Didn't feel much like waving my willy at the crowd anyway. There are no words to describe how good that steaming hot water felt to my bed-weary bones. Tears were streaming down my cheeks and I just lay there drifting on the high. The last thing I heard was, 'Bye, Mr Thorpe. Enjoy yourself.'

Enjoy myself! I'd never felt so good in all my life. The steaming hot water sucked all the ache, pain, fear and tension out of me. I lay there motionless with my head against the side in half-conscious bliss, letting the soothing hot water do its stuff to my body and brain. I was still bent on the codeine but it was nowhere near as severe as the morphine. The steaming bath seemed to ease the stone away and my head started to clear.

My body was tingling with pleasure when I heard, *Psst . . . eh . . . psst.* I looked down and Roger Ramjet was trying his best to reach the ceiling, throbbing from the stimulation of the hot bath and the sense of freedom. *Eh, come on,* he cajoled.

Oh OK. If you insist. I had the biggest biff of my life. Flames came out of my ears, my eyeballs hit the ceiling, swallows flew out of my arse, and now I know how Gigantor feels when he comes. The release was unbelievable. All the tension left my body and my mind drifted in the warm shallows of an ocean beach. I stayed like that for a full half hour, almost scared to move in case the feelings disappeared. I finally pulled myself together and washed myself, 'Owing' and 'Oh shitting' every time I moved or bumped my left arm. My long hair was knotted and it took me ages to get it untangled with one hand. It was a struggle but I got myself out of the bath, dried, and into the clean backless gown that Bertha had left neatly folded on a plastic chair in the corner. Then I sat on the chair and waited.

'You feeling better, son?' Bertha asked when she returned.

I sighed and nodded. 'Could you dry my hair, please? I can't manage with this arm.'

'Sure,' she said, taking a towel. 'Damn, you got some hair! Don't it drive you crazy?' she asked as she pulled a comb through my waist-length locks.

'Oh, you get used to it,' I laughed.

'Now, what about a bowel movement?'

'No Sister. I don't feel like it at all.'

'Well it might be a good idea to try. Can you make it to the bathroom in the next room or would you like Carl to help you?'

'No I can walk. I'm a bit shaky but I can walk.'

'Okay, off you go.' She said it like I was a five-year-old. This was a completely different Bertha from the one who had been freaking me out with her dreaded needle for the past three days. I knew her name was Beatrice but I'd come to think of her as Bertha. She had a radiance I hadn't noticed previously and I realised that I hadn't really looked at her before. She was a big woman but attractive in her own way. Her skin was blue-black and smooth as a duckling's down. Big brown eyes sparkled out of a smiling round face. Her teeth were perfect, white as pearls, and her features seemed to have been created while her face was still wet. Her big cheeks and jelly roll lips meticulously moulded with a lot of TLC by some loving artist's hand. Her nurse's uniform glowed shocking white against her dark skin and stretched the limits of the manufacturer's endurance guarantee, fighting to fit around a huge bust and onion butt. To top it off her tiny sister's hat teetered high atop a huge shock of gericurled, black nappy hair like a dixie cup on a tumbleweed.

I struggled over to the loo and sat down. Nothing. Not even a whistle from a lonesome fart. Ten minutes later I was still sitting there, straining till my eyes bulged. Nothing. My stomach was rock hard and felt like I'd swallowed a bowling ball. *Oh boy, this is going to be fun*, I thought, squinting at the pain I knew would follow my first triumphant dump after a morphine-filled long weekend. I'd heard about the pain that heroin addicts go through when they take their first dump after withdrawal. As Bertha had said, opiates freeze the bowels up and they stop functioning. But the shit's all still in there and it has to come out, one way or another. The resulting excretion has become known as 'the Yenshee baby' because that's the face you pull when you're screaming a rock-hard bowling ball that tears your arse apart as it comes out. *Oh boy*, I thought. *It's always good to have something to look forward to.*

'How you doin' in there?' asked Bertha.

'No good, ma'am. I think I'll burst an eyeball if I strain any harder.'

'OK, OK. But we had to try. If you don't pass anything in the next twenty-four hours then we'll hit you with the kamikaze wash.' I didn't even ask! I was too stuck on that 'in the next twenty-four hours'!

Five minutes later I was back in murderers' row. The morpheeno brothers' glassy stare was still fixed on some poppy fantasy on the ceiling. Mouths still hanging open. Eyes slowly blinking. God knows what goes through the minds of someone who's committed such depravities. I didn't want to know. I felt 100 per cent better. Alive for the first time in three days. Ready to get out.

'Come on, Rob!' I said.

Screech. Clang. The door opened but it wasn't Rob who strolled in. It was Detective Jack Cirello. The door locked behind him.

'Mornin', brother. I hear you had a bit of a spin out. You OK?' As soon as he walked through the door the Severinos tried to crawl up their arses and disappear. Squirming in their beds. Eyes darting at one another. 'Morning, cocksuckers,' spat Cirello. 'Where's that scumbag brother of yours, huh?' Their stoned eyes were blinking so fast I thought they were going to blow the sheets off my bed. 'Fucking scumbags!' Cirello said, then turned back to me. 'So what exciting things you bin up to? A few games of squash and a couple of drinks at the Plaza?'

'I wish, Jack,' I smiled back. I liked this guy. He was real. Got right down to it. His positive energy made me feel better immediately.

'So you gonna tell me another one of your crazy stories or what?' Cirello picked up the photos. 'You should write a damn book, Bill.'

'If I ever get out of here, maybe I will. But nobody would believe it, Jack. It's just too fucking weird.' We both laughed. 'Jack, I'm a bit fucked, mate. Why don't you tell me about yourself. You said you were married. You got kids or what? What's your wife's name?'

Cirello's face lit up. His mouth in a closed smile that wrinkled the corners of his eyes. His head nodding in a 'yeah, I got a wife and kids' reply.

'Christine and I met at NYU back in '65, the year before I went to Nam.' He drifted for a second, putting the pieces in place. 'We got married when I got back in '70. Fuck, man, I was a mess. You wouldn't believe it was the same guy sitting here. I was fucked up pretty bad, man. She saved my damn life.'

'Kids?'

'Just one. Josephina. My pride and joy. Fifteen months old. Born August 17th, last year.'

'You're kidding, Jack. My daughter Lauren was born August 19th in Cedars Sinai Los Angeles. I don't fucking believe it.'

'Soul sisters, brother. Fucking soul sisters. Put it there.' Cirello beamed as we shook hands. 'Your second?' he asked.

'Yeah, my oldest daughter Rusty is seven. Born in Melbourne.'

'What is she, a country singer?' He laughed.

'No, Jack. She was born with a full head of bright red hair. Freaked Lynn and me out. All the girl names we picked went out the window. She was so tiny we called her "Mrs Mouse" for a year, then my dad started calling her Rusty and that's her legal name.'

We sat looking at each other. No words. Thinking about the real world. The only thing that's real in this world. Family.

Clang! Creak! The cell door opened, jerking me back. Bertha stuck her head round. 'Telephone for you, detective,' she said, holding the door.

'Gotta go, Bill. Be back in a while.' Cirello smiled and left. 'Soul sisters,' I heard him say as he went through the door.

Family, I thought. Lynn, Rusty and Lauren. Oh shit, I forgot to ask him about making the phone call. God, Lynn will be completely freaked out by now, back there in LA with a baby and I'm in this fucking joint. The tears started to roll. I hadn't thought much about Lynn and the kids. I'd tried not to. There was enough emotional drama going on in my head without freaking myself out with more 'what ifs'. I'd purposely asked Cirello and Dr Harrison to call Rob and not Lynn. I didn't want some doctor from Belle-vue Mental Hospital or a New York City police detective calling and freaking her out even more. I'd thought that the call coming from Rob would be a lot easier on her. My short conversation with Jack Cirello brought them right there into the room. Pictures of Lynn just twenty-two years old sitting in the delivery room at Brighton Hospital in Melbourne. Alone. Waiting to have her first baby. They wouldn't let me stay, then an hour later rushed in to ask permission to save Rusty's life with a caesarean.

Lauren had been born by caesarean as well and images of her in my arms, so tiny and fragile, just minutes after she was born filled my mind. I collapsed when the doctor gave her to me and only just missed dropping her on her beauti-ful head. I looked at the Severinos and it was strange. But somehow they knew! I could tell by the looks on their faces. Maybe they'd picked up on our conversation, who knows, but for the first and only time we were just patients sharing a hospital room. I guess murderers have kids too.

I felt the strain of the day creeping over me. The bath had made me drowsy and if Jack Cirello hadn't arrived I'd have fallen asleep. Suddenly I felt totally exhausted. My eyelids got heavy, the Severinos faded and I drifted off. Images of Lynn and the kids washed across a cloudy white screen. Lynn . . . My beautiful Lynn . . .

22
Follow that Bike

'**F**ollow that bike!'

    'Mate,' the cabbie said. 'I've always wanted to hear someone say that.' He grinned at me in the rear-view mirror.

    It was late May 1971, around 5.30 on a blustering, cold Melbourne autumn evening. It was raining lightly, as usual. I'd been in Sydney for the day and was headed home to Hawksburn Road. The peak-hour traffic jam was snaking its way along Punt Road just south of the Melbourne Cricket Ground. Like all the other helpless commuters, we were being pulled uncontrollably all the way to the Punt Road Bridge over the ever-muddy Yarra River. I was pretty tired from a long day and the flights. Just sitting in the back seat, daydreaming. Mulling over the day as you do. Not taking that much notice of anything. I happened to glance sideways and—*Pow!*

    Just ahead of me, to my left, in line with the cab's passenger-side door, was a yellow 125 cc Yamaha dirt bike with rally tyres. Sitting on it a young beauty. I couldn't quite see her face for the helmet and big silver sunglasses she wore, but from the gentle angle of her jaw, the way her damp blonde hair fell from under her white crash helmet, the cream woollen scarf wrapped stylishly around her neck and throat, and the confident line of her body I just knew she was a stunner underneath. And I knew I had to meet her.

She was wearing a brown suede jacket with little silver clasps at the sides that pulled it in at the waist, highlighting the contours of her upper body. Her riding gloves were brown suede and matched her jacket perfectly. Strong hands gripped the handlebars as she revved the throttle to keep the bike alive, ready to sprint for the finish line when the light changed to green. Tight black jeans were tucked into high-heeled, knee-high, lace-up brown suede boots. She wasn't tall. By the size of the bike I guessed her to be maybe five three or four, but in perfect proportion. Her slim but muscular legs were planted squarely, strongly, almost defiantly on the ground as she confidently straddled the stationary bike mid-traffic . . . And her arse! . . . Oh, what an arse! I've always been a butt man. Now I don't bat for the other side—cleavage is wonderful—but I just *lurve* a heart-shaped arse, and this girl had a tail on her like the cover of a Valentine's Day card. I couldn't take my eyes off her. The lights changed and she took off in the wet like a champion rally rider, gunning the little dirt bike full throttle in a whining 125 cc scream up Punt Hill.

She stayed ahead of us by about five or six cars all the way to the St Kilda junction, where she disappeared in the traffic.

'I've lost her, mate,' said the cabbie. 'Which way do you think?'

'Probably gone down Fitzroy Street,' I replied, my eyes straining to find her.

The lights changed and the traffic started to move. We were just approaching the intersection of Fitzroy Street and the Nepean Highway, about to head towards the beach, when I caught sight of her speeding up the highway.

'Left . . . left,' I yelled. 'Don't lose her whatever you do.'

The cabbie was caught up in the chase and wrenched the wheel to the left, cutting off three honking cars. We sped through a light that had just changed red and headed up the Nepean in pursuit, but she was nowhere in sight. We drove for a couple of miles and then doubled back, but she was gone. I realised that I was almost outside Ray Evans' office, which was in the old *Go-Set* offices. One of Australia's first music papers, *Go-Set* had been started by Peter Rafael in the late '60s. Peter now managed Max Merritt and the Meteors. Ray Evans was a manager-cum-agent who later went on to co-found the Consolidated Rock booking agency with my then manager Michael Browning and Michael Gudinski. As well as the Evans/Gudinski booking agency and Mushroom Records, also with Michael Gudinski, Ray handled some of my bookings for Michael Browning and booked me from time to time. It was Ray who had arranged the TV show that had taken me to Sydney that day and I was planning to visit him in the morning, so I figured I may as well do so now. He was always there so I paid the cabbie off.

'Sorry we lost her, mate,' he said, sounding as disappointed as I was.

I walked around the corner and into the building. Sitting in the hallway at the bottom of the stairs was the yellow Yamaha trail bike! I couldn't believe my eyes. I ran up the stairs and into Ray's office. 'What are you doing here?' he asked me. 'I thought you were staying in Sydney.'

'Decided to come back, mate. Listen, that yellow trail bike outside. Does that belong to someone in this office? Do you know how can I find out who—'

'Ray, sorry I'm late,' said a voice behind me. 'The traffic was really bad. Can you please sign these?'

I turned and it was her! I couldn't speak. Just stood there staring at her. Mouth open like a kid in a lolly shop. 'Hello,' she said with a smile. I still couldn't speak.

'Billy,' said Ray. 'I don't think you've met my new secretary. Billy Thorpe this is Lynn McGrath . . . Lynn, Billy.'

'I'm pleased to . . . um . . . meet . . .' I mumbled as I extended my hand.

'Pleased to meet you too,' she said with a big smile.

Pow! The touch of her silky warm hand sent a twinge of excitement from my stomach to my crotch. My heart skipped a beat. I was speechless. She was gorgeous, sporty, vivacious, warm, charming, shy, polite, maybe nineteen or twenty years old, and small like I'd thought. Even smaller, actually. I measured her at five feet one, maybe two, and perfect as a china doll. I stood staring like a dill and she must have thought I was an idiot. Her jacket and helmet were gone and she wore a cream roll-neck sweater that highlighted perfect breasts. Her shoulder-length blonde hair was still wet and parted down the centre. Her eyes a dreamy light blue and her mouth! She had a perfect mouth with sensuous lips and big white teeth shaped in such a way they pushed the front of her mouth slightly forward so I could see them most of the time except when her mouth was tightly closed. She reminded me a bit of Catherine Deneuve. No, Brigitte Bardot. No . . . I was dumbstruck.

My stomach knotted and I knew right then and there that this was the one. 'This is the one,' the voice in my brain kept saying. I realise that it sounds like a clichéd line from a cheap Louis L'Amour novel but that's what was going through my head. Over and over . . . This is the one! With the first love of my life, Pepper, I recognised something special when we met. The same with Jackie Holme, who had overwhelmed me with her grace, style and beauty. I'd been hopelessly in love with them both, but I'd never heard this voice in my brain before. I knew then that I would spend the rest of my life with this beautiful stranger standing in front of me.

All this is going through my head and I'm standing there with a dumb shit-eating grin all over my stupid face. Although she was warm and friendly she didn't seem all that impressed at meeting Billy Thorpe. No ego intended, but most people usually react in one way or another. She was very nonchalant about it like she really didn't give a damn, and that was an even bigger turn-on.

'Ray, OK if I take off?' she asked. 'I'm all done. Those just have to go out first thing in the morning.' She gestured to the papers Ray had just signed.

'Fine, Lynn,' he replied. 'See you later.'

'Bye, Billy. It was nice to meet you.'

'Me too,' I replied and she turned and left the office. There was that arse again. Oh God!

'Ray, who is that? She's fantastic. I've got to—'

'Slow down, mate. Lynn's a Portsea girl. She ran the booking office for Flag Motels, then worked for Gudinski for a while. She didn't have much to do and got bored, so I offered her a job and here she is.'

'She's fantastic, mate. I've got to meet her.'

'You just did,' Ray replied.

'No, meeet heerr. You know. Can you set it up or what?'

'Well, it's her twenty-first tomorrow and there's a bit of a party at the Catcher. Some of the staff and her friends are going. Nothing elaborate. Just an informal get-together. Why don't you stick your head in?'

'Great, mate. Thanks.' I turned and ran out of the office. 'Nice talking to you,' I heard Ray yell as I took the stairs three at a time on the way down. I hit the street just in time to see her disappearing with a roar up the Nepean Highway. 'Ah shit,' I said.

'Easy, son,' said Norman E the bad roadie, whom I hadn't seen pull up in our van.

'What are you doing here, Norm?'

'Just passing and saw you run out, me ole. What are you "ah shitting" about?'

'Ah, I just missed the new secretary Lynn. She's fantastic.'

'I told you,' he grinned.

'Told me what?'

'I told you to come and check her out. How many bloody times have I told you about her? I thought you weren't interested. Decided I'd 'ave a go meself, son,' he grinned.

Just passing, my arse, I thought.

'You mean that's the girl you've been on about?' I realised that Norm had told me about a dozen times that I had to come and check her out. 'Why the hell didn't you tell me she was that good?'

'I did, you silly prick. I did!' And he had, I realised. I just hadn't listened.

'Where can I get some flowers around here?'

Norm caught my drift immediately and gave me that

twisted smile of his, cocking his head down and to the right, one eye half-closed. 'Floweeerrrs! . . . Jesus, this is serious. You're bloody gone!'

It turned out everything was closed and I'd have to get them in the morning. That night I couldn't get Lynn out of my head. Over dinner Momma Nene noticed me playing with my food and asked me what was up.

'Nothing Momma. I'm fine.'

'Oh yeaaaah.' She smiled knowingly. 'Oh-oh, look out,' she said, winking at the Pig.

Munch . . . chew . . . stuff . . . gnaw . . . swallow . . . chomp . . . snort . . . Pig replied.

First thing the next morning I went straight to the florists and sent three dozen long-stem, yellow roses, the best they had, to Lynn at Ray's office. On the card I wrote:

Dear Lynn,
    Have a wonderful 21st,
    Billy.

The Catcher had been one of the roughest and toughest gigs in Melbourne in its day. Taking up three floors of a huge old granary down off Flinders Lane in the heart of the city, it'd been closed for some time but in its heyday in late 1969 it became the unofficial inner-city headquarters of the newly emerging skinheads. They were fine. I played regularly to 500 of them every Thursday night at the infamous White Horse Hotel in Box Hill. It was the White Horse skinheads who coined the term 'Suck More Piss' which later became synonymous with the Aztecs when thousands of people chanted it at the Sunbury Music Festival.

The Catcher was always a bloodbath on a weekend and

bands like Rick Springfield's Zoot, whose slogan was 'Think Pink' and who dressed in pink silk suits, played there at the risk of their lives. But it had been a popular joint and I'd played there a lot. The skins never bothered us. We'd had a couple of stinks with speed-crazed mugs, but all in all it was another one of the many great Melbourne gigs that were flourishing at that time.

Norm and I arrived at about 10.30 p.m. It was a private party with some of Ray's new bands providing the entertainment. We made our way up to the second floor. Some young arty pop band was on stage playing as we entered. I don't remember who they were. It was pretty poofy stuff and sounded a lot like many of the young bands some people seem to regard as the fresh new wave in 1998. I didn't know many people and Norm and I wandered around until we found a makeshift bar and got ourselves a drink. But I wasn't there for the beer or the bands.

Norm ran into some young spunk he knew and we split up for a while. I wandered around with my solitary beer, looking for the girl of my dreams. And there she was sitting on the floor with her back to the wall to the left of the stage, with about a dozen other girls, sipping beer from a can. My feet froze. I couldn't move. I'd played in front of hundreds of thousands of people and been on live TV since I was eleven years old but I couldn't get the balls together to take another step. Norm spotted me and came over, saying, 'Well, mate, now's your chance. What are you waiting for?' I didn't answer and we walked over together. Lynn was throwing her head back and laughing loudly as we sat down with the rest of the group. I could tell right away that she was a little tipsy. But beautiful as I'd remembered. Anyway, it was her twenty-first birthday party. She was entitled to get a bit pissed.

It was one of the few times in my life I was lost for words. 'Happy twenty-first, Lynn,' I yelled over the music. 'You having a good time?'

'Yes thanks,' she said. 'Are you?'

'Yes thanks,' I replied.

'Great.' She smiled that smile and then went back to talking to the girl next to her. Not a word about the flowers. Nothing but these polite pleasantries. And no real acknowledgement of my presence at her party. I was devastated. I sat there for a couple of minutes, then stood up to leave. 'Bye,' she shouted to me as I walked away. 'Bye,' I replied and that was that. I got Norm and I left a shattered man. But shattered or not, I was determined to get her on side and swore to myself that I would pursue this girl like she'd never been pursued in her young life.

Norm and I went up to the International Club, ate some schnitzels, played some pool, drank a few Scotches and he dropped me home. I slept quite late the next morning, got my act together at about 11.30 and started my day. Pig and Momma weren't home and I'd just eaten a late breakfast when the doorbell rang. Nobody we knew was up and making house calls at that time.

'Who is it?' I yelled. The bell rang again.

I checked the house quickly to see if there was any grass or roaches lying around, then checked the stash in the secret hole. Yep, everything shipshape. Hey, that was the routine in those days. I opened the front door and nearly fell over. It was her! I was speechless again.

'Oh, hi . . . How a . . . er?' I asked like an idiot. She had taken me completely by surprise.

'I'm great thanks,' she smiled, lighting up the street. 'Oh this is Kay. Kay Halley,' she said, gesturing to the girl standing beside her whom I hadn't even noticed.

'So, um . . . er . . . what brings you both around here?'

'I wanted to apologise,' Lynn said.

'Apologise for what?'

'Apologise for not—'

It was only then I realised they were still standing on the doorstep and I rudely cut Lynn off mid-sentence. 'Oh I'm sorry . . . Please come in . . . come in. I didn't mean to leave you standing outside like that. Please come in.' I showed them down the hall into the living room. Lynn wore a black poncho over black trousers that were tucked into her suede knee-length boots. On her head a big black felt hat. She looked fantastic. I have no idea what the other girl even looked like. She wasn't there. They sat down on the couch and I saw them both give Herman the bear a strange look. His shrunken body was still propped up in the corner with his Groucho disguise on.

'What's that?' Lynn asked.

'Oh, just Herman,' I replied like an idiot.

'Oh,' she said and gave Kay a strange look.

Jesus, this is going well, I thought.

There was one of those long pregnant pauses where your whole life seems to pass before you and then my brain got it together. 'Can I get you something to drink?' I asked. 'A soft drink, water, a beer, a joint?' *Oh Jesus, why did I say that?*

'Just a glass of water,' she smiled and her girlfriend nodded.

I went off to the kitchen, fighting with voices in my head. 'Christ, what's wrong with you, you dumb shit?' 'Don't know. I'm tongue-tied.' 'Well untie the bastard, you silly little prick! This is her! Remember?' I was never like

361

this around girls. I wouldn't think twice about going up to someone I fancied and saying something romantic like "Scuse me, can I bite your arse?' and here I am can't even get two words together. I gave them each a glass and sat on the chair opposite. They both looked at the empty glasses and then at me. 'Oh shit I'm sorry,' I said, grabbing the glasses and running to the kitchen. This time I brought them some water.

'So what can I do for you?' I asked, breaking another seemingly endless silence.

Lynn blushed nervously. 'I'm really sorry, Billy. I didn't know . . .'

'Didn't know what?'

'That it was you who sent me those beautiful roses. I had to come around to apologise and thank you.'

Her voice had me. It had a slight hoarseness to it. Gentle, soft, caring, deliberate of vowel, gentle of consonant, and very loving. This was the same girl I'd met two days earlier, but I hadn't had the chance to experience this gentle side. She was so personal with her delivery and I had that churning in my stomach as she spoke. 'Oh joy, she didn't snub you last night!' said the voice. 'Shut up and listen,' said the other.

'I had no idea it was Billy Thorpe who had sent them. We only met for a second. I've been ringing everyone I know called Billy, including Billie Halley, Kay's mum.' Lynn gestured to her friend. 'It wasn't any of them. Then I ran into Norm Swiney and he asked me how I liked the roses. Then I knew.' She blushed red. 'I feel awful. It was such a lovely thing to do and I didn't even say thank you. You must have thought I was awful.'

I didn't speak. I couldn't. I was gone. Head over heels.

Mesmerised by the way her mouth moved. The little brown freckles on her nose. The way she cocked her head to me, favouring her left eye. The way her eyes glistened, opening and closing ever so slightly in her apology. The way she sat, vulnerable yet proud. Knees together, calves apart, toes pointed in, her delicate porcelain fingers interlaced, palm up, thumbs touching, resting gently in her lap. That slow-motion blink as she licked her bottom lip a millisecond ago. Lynn was all about beautiful and beautifully sincere. I had the feeling that nobody had ever done anything like that for her before and I detected just a hint of something in her voice. A sadness. A slight breaking in her 'sorry' and 'thought I was awful'. Her eyes moistened ever so slightly as she spoke the words. Her inner beauty radiated out of her, filling the room. Touching me. This was a deep, caring, vulnerable, innocent and sweet young girl. I wanted to hold her close to me and tell her it was all right. There was a silence for a moment and we sat looking at one another.

I went over to her and took her hand, lifted it gently to my lips and kissed it. There was *the* scent. That natural body scent, I mean. I wanted to breathe her in. Lynn had my flavour of the ancient aphrodisiac blended only by Gods to attract one specific mortal to another. That instant recognition of someone I'd loved since before I was born and was born to love. A slight shudder coursed through her body at my kiss and her eyes met mine with a look that melted my heart. They were moist again.

'Thank you,' she said.

'Thank you,' I replied, gently moving a rebel piece of wild hair from her face.

She shuddered once again. We didn't know it then but two souls that had been drifting a long time through God

363

knows how many galaxies, worlds and millenniums recognised each other at that moment. Soul mates. The one!

'Can I take you to dinner tonight?' I asked. My fear was gone. 'Let me buy you a birthday dinner.'

She looked into my eyes. Her steady gaze searching back and forth, moving slowly from my left eye to my right and back again. Her eyes fixed on mine. 'Yes,' she replied in a half whisper.

'You pick the place. Anywhere you like.'

'Peanuts.' She smiled.

'Excuse me,' I asked, not understanding.

'Peanuts. It's a restaurant in the city. I know the owners. It's not too expensive and the food is good. What do you like?'

'You,' I said, looking into her eyes. 'I like you very much.' She blushed and smiled. Now she was lost for words and she sighed. It was then I caught the scent of her breath. It was a beautiful scent. Beautiful. It made my head spin. It was a sweet, almost a peach or apricot scent, and I had the urge to kiss her. It wasn't a breath freshener, it was her. Her natural scent was enticing and this time I shuddered and stood looking at her. Drifting in silence until the ticking from the old wall clock brought me back.

'Peanuts it is. I'll pick you up in a cab at 7.30. Is that OK? Where do you live?'

'Oh just around the corner off Williams Road. But I'll pick you up. We can go on my bike. There's no need for a cab,' she smiled. 'You'll be safe with me.'

'I know I will.'

Part III

23
I Shall Be Released

I was awakened by the clang and screech of the door being opened. In burst Jack Cirello followed by Detective Moore, with Bertha and Idi in tow. They were all smiles. 'We've got the son of a bitch, you greasy sons o' bitches,' Cirello spat at the Severinos as soon as he was through the door. 'We got him!'

'Yeah?' smiled Idi, nodding his whole body.

'They gonna fry the lot of you,' Cirello spat at the Severinos. 'Ah shit, we got him.' Cirello was ecstatic. He was pacing from one end of the room to the other, clapping his hands together saying, 'We got him . . . We got him.' Not a word from the Severinos. Blank black eyes and gaping mouths fixed in their poppy glaze.

'Mmmuhhh may Shhhackkk . . . Shhhackkk . . . Er fise ake et bee outha meeerr!' said a voice. The room went silent. I couldn't believe my ears. The Mummy was talking! Jack and Detective Moore burst into hysterical laughter.

'Err uck uuu Shaaack! . . . et bee outha meeerr!' the
Mummy mumbled again. Cirello and Moore were killing
themselves. I had no idea what was happening and the Severinos just gaped at the talking Mummy beside me.

'Et bee outha meeerr . . . ssstts ot ers fugg n meeeer!' the
Mummy said, standing up and zombieing over to Cirello
who was up against the wall holding his gut crying. The
thing looked ridiculous walking, like something out of the
Three Stooges with a bandaged head and both its arms stiff
out in front. The Severinos shit themselves and ducked
under the covers. I couldn't believe my eyes.

'Ah, Jesus . . . Itchy balls?' Cirello laughed, scratching his
own. The penny dropped and I started to break up as well.

'Cmmmnnn Shaaaack. Urnt phuggg eroun! Fleese!
Ssstt's gillig meee.'

'Sister, would you please do the honours,' Cirello said to
Bertha.

'Ma pleasure, detective.' She took a pair of scissors from
her pocket. 'Now come and sit on the bed,' she said to the
Mummy who zombied back and obediently sat down.

'He's one of ours,' Jack cackled. 'Oh Jesus, I think I've
pissed myself.'

Bertha was beside herself. She'd been trying to be sister
but it was too much. 'Bit hot in there, son?' she asked the
Mummy, cutting his bandages away.

'Ah shit, thpptt! . . . thpptt! . . .' he said, spitting the lint
from his mouth. 'Ah Jeezuz. My balls. My balls, sister.
They're killing me.'

'Well I sure ain't gonna scratch 'em for ya, son. What
about you, detective? You wanna ease this man's pain?' she
asked, laughing. Cirello and Moore had tears streaming
down their faces. They couldn't talk beyond, 'Ah . . . oh

shit . . . Ahhhh.' 'Let me get these off a you arms.' Bertha cut through the thick bandages around both arms and removed the half plaster casts.

As soon as they were free the detective frantically started scratching his nuts like a Mummy with crabs. He looked hilarious sitting on the edge of the bed, bandages trailing off him, thrashing away at his itchy nuts.

'Ah . . . oh. Oh Jesus,' he moaned. 'They been killing me, Jack, you son of a bitch. You didn't have to tell them to do me up this bad. I haven't been able to move, you son of a bitch.'

Cirello was still laughing his heart out. 'We got him, Frank . . . we-hee got him,' was the first thing that came out.

'Where?' the Mummy asked.

'In a crack house over Harlem. Stoned as a mother-fucker. No resistance. Walked straight in and out.' The Severinos were out from under their covers. Eyes wide. Taking in every word.

'Great, Jack. That's fucking great!' The three detectives hugged like long-lost brothers. They were overjoyed and Jack Cirello knew that maybe he could get a little sleep at last.

'Detective Frank Costello. This is Sister Beatrice Rose, Samuel Craddock, and my good friend Bill over there,' Cirello gestured to Bertha, Idi and me.

'Pleased to meet you, sister. Hi Samuel,' Costello said. 'And Bill, I feel like I already know you. I nearly blew my cover and choked pissing myself over that goddamned dog of yours. How they hangin', Bill?'

'Just fine thanks.' I laughed because Costello was still frantically scratching his.

'Ah, you son of a bitch, Cirello,' he laughed and everyone broke up again.

'Now, sister, I think you need these.' Cirello handed Bertha some documents. 'I'm supposed to give them to the front desk but maybe you could do that for me if you'd be so kind.'

'What are these, detective?' she asked.

'They're the release authority for those two scumbags. They're being transferred today. A prison medical van will be over sometime this afternoon. Can you have them ready?'

The Severinos stared at the ceiling, showing no emotion.

'I'm not sure they're ready to be moved, detective,' Bertha said.

'They're ready, sister. Oh, they're ready. Says so right on there.' Cirello smiled at Bertha, then threw a hand-grenade stare at the Severinos.

'Okaaaay. If you say so. I'll just check this with admissions,' she said. 'Now, gentlemen, the party's over. I'm going to have to ask you to leave.'

The Mummy and Detective Moore came over and shook my hand.

'Great to meet you both,' I told them. 'Take it easy.'

I smiled as they left. That had been one of the funniest minutes of my life. The fact that the detective had been lying there for three days undercover with itchy nuts pushed every button on my trolley. It was hilarious.

Cirello went over to the Severinos and stood looking down at them. Staring fireballs. They looked up at him sheepishly, holding the tops of their sheets, waiting for the fist in the face, but it didn't come.

'You're all gonna be one big happy fuckin' family in the

joint by tonight, you scumbags. Party's over. Ain't a whole
lotta sympathy and no more morph for you sons o' bitches
in there. When the general population finds out what you
did, if your greaseball throats ain't cut first, you'll be fish-
ing your balls outta your cereal bowls and your arses will
be smokin' from all the big black dicks. Don't worry, they'll
heal up just in time to burn 'em to a crisp in the chair.'
Cirello hawked back and spat in both the Severinos' faces,
then pulled his finger across his throat.

'Morte!' he laughed. 'Fuckin' dead!'

Cirello came over to me and his anger subsided. 'That's
all she wrote, Bill. Now maybe I can get some sleep for the
first time in a week.'

I just nodded and we looked at one another for a long
beat. In a small way our experience had created a bond of
sorts. The Cross and R&R. The Whiskey Au Go Go. Pam
Redding the stripper. You can't fake that kind of fate. It had
been a real pleasure to meet him, and in a way I was sorry
to see him go.

'Well, kid, I'm goin' home to my girls. Ain't seen a
whole lot of me for a while. Listen, I put another call into
that hotel this morning and left another message. They said
your pardner had checked out but was calling in for messages. Heard anything?'

I shook my head.

'You will, kid. Don't worry. Well, it's been a real pleasure
to meet you, Bill. I'll give my particulars to the sister. When
you get out of here drop me a line one day. Maybe we can
bullshit about the old times like civilised men over an ice
cold beer and a steak. And our soul sisters have got to meet.'

I was choked up and he could see it. 'Take it easy, pal,'
he said and gave me a big hug.

'Thanks, Jack. You kept me sane,' I said in his ear.

'Shit, kid, you must be in trouble if Jack Cirello kept you sane . . . Later.' He smiled, nodding his head with his bottom lip out. 'You're all right, kid.' He stuck his pork-pie hat on his head, then turned and left with Bertha and Idi.

It was so quiet it was loud. Here we were again, just one big happy trio. Me looking at them staring at me looking at them. The Bellevue rock 'n' roll revue. Step right up, ladies and gentlemen. It's show time.

I guess the difference between me and most people I know who aren't crazy is that I've lived the wild ride. Too crazy to stand back and buy a ticket and watch, I had to be, needed to be, had no choice but to be at the centre of the jester's wheel. Feel its gyroscopic gravity pulling the things around me to its glitter-ball centre. Roll up. Roll up. Who wants to watch the crazy man dance? Cost you ten bucks to see the greatest show on this stage tonight. Watch him do his stuff. He'll brain ya, drain ya, and entertain ya. Take ya mind off. Have a beer. Get down, get up. Go home.

Being a singer's a crazy fucking life. D'ya ever wonder? Spinning the big dreams night after night through the words and the changes. Playing the notes. Acting the fool. Roll up. Roll up. It's show time. It can all get to you sometimes. Smile, son, the camera's rolling.

That face in the crowd that reminds you of the mealy mouthed bank clerk when you were a kid. That one a definite prospect to do ten years for armed robbery. That one groping that jerk a future hooker. Easy to pick the punters' odds. Years of practice. Different spaces. Same old mould. Look at 'em nodding. Slaves to the moment. To the thundering pulse from a bank of amplifiers with enough ball power to split a granite heart at 500 feet. Oh you want to talk while I'm busting my arse? Talk over this, cunt! Concentrating and not concentrating. Some nights as good as it gets. Some nights just going through the paces. A one-trick pony fucking a woman you can't stand in a cold wet bed. But that's what I'm paying for, son. So fuck me again and harder this time.

An easy gig for an old lag who's ploughed the field so many times the familiar sweating juice-filled cavities feel as warm and comforting as a broke barfly at 3 a.m. Know the seasons and the reasons. The shape and the sides. Another night in the lights. Another dollar in the kick. Another dance in the glorious ego-filled warmth of your own sunshine. Play them hits, boy. Play them hits . . . Suffocating in an airless room . . . Drowning in an ocean of your own success. It's just a song. Not real pain. Never mind anyway. Dance for us, jester. We paid for the right. Higher, jump higher. We saw that trick the other night. Do something new. Stick to what you know. Smile. Act like a star kid and people will treat you like one. Same ole same ole. No quarter given, no matter the circumstance. Just play it again, son. My girls wants to dance.

Sometimes it gets you. You know what I mean? Right here between the cheering and the sound of your heart breaking. Don't bring me down, son. That's not your gig! Help 'em forget all that shit for a couple of hours. Dance, boy. Make 'em happy. 'Most people I know think that I'm crayzee. And I know at times I act a little hastee . . .'

Right then and there, that's how I felt about my life. My blues couldn't get any fucking bluer. Locked in an insane asylum with two murderers. Can't get much better than that. *You've really made something of yourself, you idiot!* Your wife and children on the other side of America. No idea where you are. Freaking. Helpless. Shit, I gotta get a job or something when I get outta here. *Did I just say that?* Jesus, I must belong in here! My head was going around in circles. I lay there watching the ceiling fans turn their slow hypnotic loops. Don't know for how long. An hour. Two, maybe. Sinking down . . . down . . . I hated myself and the world. Bertha had been cutting my doses and the drugs were starting to wear off. I guess I was Jonesing. But Jonesing or not, I had reached the very bottom.

'Wake up. You've got a visitor.' Bertha's voice roused me from my nightmare. I opened my eyes and Rob was beaming down at me.

'Rob. Rob . . . How . . . er . . . what . . . ?'

'I've come to get you out,' he said. I'd never been so glad to see anyone in my life. 'Are you OK, mate?'

'How do I look?'

'Like shit, mate. Like shit.'

'Jesus, it's good to see you. When can I get out? How did you manage? What about someone to sign for me? Where are we going to get—?'

'Slow down, Billy. I've been staying at Yvette's for the last few days but checking with the hotel. And I got two messages this morning, from a Dr Harrison's office and a Detective Jack Cirello. What's a detective got to do with this? Are you in some sort of trouble?'

'You're fucking kidding aren't you, Rob. Do I look like I'm in fucking trouble?' Rob just laughed. 'No, mate. Apart from this shit, no trouble. Cirello was here because of them.' I nodded at the grinning Severinos. 'Nice guy. I asked him to call you.'

'Oh shit,' said Rob, taking his first real look at the Bobbsie twins. I'd gotten used to their mania, but I guess fresh from the outside world the Severinos looked as insane as they really were. 'Who are they?' he whispered.

'Tell you 'bout it later, mate. When can I get out of here?'

'As soon as the letter from Ed Abraham arrives,' Rob said. Ed Abraham, or I should say Dr Edward Abraham, was Rob's business partner in LA. At one time he was team doctor to the LA Raiders football team and then specialised in lower back surgery, developing many of the techniques and surgical instruments used by specialists today. More importantly, he was a highly respected surgeon and a great friend.

'What's Ed got to do with this?' I asked, a little confused.

'Well, you're not going to believe this. When Dr Harrison told me that a condition of your release was that an outside doctor take responsibility for you, I mentioned Ed. It's unbelievable but he and Harrison went through Harvard Medical School together. They haven't seen each other in years but they've spoken on the phone and it's all being organised as we speak.'

I was speechless. See what an insane role fate plays in my crazy life. On the heads of everyone I hold dear, that's true. Ed Abraham had gone through medical school with the doctor in charge of the Bellevue Mental Hospital's intensive care ward. Unbefuckinglievable!

'Oh thank God,' I yelled.

'I've brought some fresh clothes and your shaving kit. The sister has them. You're checked out of the Salisbury and we're on tonight's red-eye to LA. If Ed can get the documents here in time you'll be out this afternoon.'

Out this afternoon . . . Out this afternoon . . . The sweetest words I've ever heard rang like Christmas bells in my head.

375

'Have you spoken to Lynn? How is she? Is she freaked out?'

'Well, she was, mate. I've talked to her twice a day since you disappeared. We've had a missing persons out on you since Saturday. Jesus, I was bloody frantic. We checked every hospital in the city, but what are the chances of guessing you were in this place? How in the fuck did you end up in here?' Rob looked at the grinning Severinos. 'Jesus, mate!' He shivered.

'It's a long story, Rob. I'll tell you on the plane.'

'When you didn't call her on Sunday like you said you would, Lynn called the hotel and they put her through to me. I didn't know what the hell to say so I told her you'd gone to Toronto to do some stuff with one of the radio stations up there. I was lying through my bloody teeth. When we hadn't heard anything by Monday I called and told her you were missing. I couldn't tell her much because there was nothing to tell. She freaked out but she was real cool about it. She's strong as an ox, mate, you know that . . .'

I just stared at him, nodding my head. *She must have been frantic*, I thought as I watched Rob talk. *Oh shit! She must have been frantic.*

'I called her this morning when I found out where you were. She had a good cry but she's fine, mate. Don't worry, you'll be home soon.' Home soon . . . home soon . . . The bells were chiming again.

'What about Rusty and Lauren? Are they OK? How's little Lauren doing? Oh Jesus, Rob, I really fucked up this time. Oh shit.' I burst into tears. It all came rushing out. Rob took my hand but said nothing. There was nothing to say. I sobbed my heart out for five minutes, then it was over. Money couldn't buy the relief those tears brought me.

I guess they were long overdue but the morphine, codeine and trauma of the place had held them at bay. 'God, I thought I'd never get out of here, mate,' I said, wiping my eyes.

'Are you sure you're OK? What's the heart monitor for?'

'He had a bit of a turn but he's going to be fine,' Sister Bertha's voice cut in. 'Now I'm going to have to ask you to leave, sir. This is highly irregular in this part of the building, but considering the circumstances Dr Harrison got approval for your visit. But we gotta get back to business.'

'OK,' said Rob.

'Now Dr Harrison has informed me of your release papers, and as soon as I hear anything I'll call you. No point waiting around here, Mr Raymond.'

'Well that's the plan then.' Rob smiled. 'I'll wait by the phone. So keep them crossed. Oh, by the way, I brought you these. He handed me my travelling wallet. 'Thought you might like to refresh your memory until you get out. I looked inside and there were four small family photos. One each of Lynn, baby Lauren and Rusty plus a family shot. My hand started shaking and tears welled in my eyes.

'Thanks, mate,' I sobbed.

Tears welled up in Rob's eyes as well. 'See you soon, mate.' He patted my arm, then left with Bertha. Idi locked the door behind them.

Some time passed. I don't know how long. I was lost in my family. But the door creaked open. Bertha and Idi walked in, accompanied by four huge orderlies in white coats led by Carl the giant killer. They looked like the front row of the Hulk's football team, except two of them were pushing wheelchairs. A couple of burly plain clothes jacks followed them. Then four NYPD uniformed coppers each the size of a barn. And each with a Mossberger pump-action in his hands. The cavalry had arrived. It was Severino show time.

Bertha disconnected some tubes and cables from the Severinos' beds. The detectives undid the shackles on their hands and feet. Carl and one of the orderlies each picked up a groaning brother and sat him in a wheelchair. That quick. No velvet gloves. No 'how are your .357 magnum bullet holes?' Just plain 'get their goddamned murdering Cuban arses in them chairs and let's get 'em outta here.' The NYPD cops stood with their shotguns pointed at the Severinos while the detectives shackled their legs and arms to the chairs and they were ready to party.

'Okay, Sister, we're all ready,' one of the detectives said. He handed her some documents. 'Here's a copy of the release order. The master copy is with your supervisor at the front desk. I think you'll find everything's in order. I've already signed their condition report. If their wheelchairs should accidentally roll under a bus, it won't be down to you. They were in perfect electrocuting condition when they left here, so you're cool.'

Bertha glanced at the papers. 'I'm sure they are,' she said. 'They're all yours. Take good care of them. They're still in need of medical attention.'

'Oh we will, Sister. The very best.'

Carl and another orderly started pushing the wheel-chairs and as they got to the door Joachim, the brother who had been opposite me, turned to me and said, 'Me voy al transbordador a decarga la caretta. No hallegado la hora fatal mir compadrita. Adios amigo.' Which roughly trans-lated as, 'I am going to the crossing to unburden my soul.

Your reckoning is yet to come. Goodbye my friend.' He grinned and they were gone.

Clang. Creak. I was alone. Just me and the walls. It scared me even more than the Severinos had. It was a strange feeling. The morpheeno brothers had been the first thing I'd seen when I came to that first morning. In a way it had been their insanity that had kept me occupied for the first couple of days. They were scum. I knew that. But without their grinning 'morpheenos' the room seemed empty of more than their physical presence. Just me and the walls. 'That's enough of this shit. Snap out of it. What are ya?' the voice said. And the voice was dead right.

I pulled the suction cups from my chest and got out of bed. The heart monitor went dead. My legs felt fine. Still groggy from the codeine but no shakes this time. I was going to be fine and already mentally out of there. I walked around the room for the first time in over four days. *Walking. Now this is a buzz you take for granted*, I thought as I took the first steps of my newborn life. It was just a room. A room like any other room. Not scary. Not frightening. No ghosts. No horrors. Just a room. And a lot smaller when I paced it than it had felt from the morphined exaggeration of my bed. I reached the window and Idi was gone. So was his chair.

I took the photos from the bedside table and got back into bed. I spread the four family photos out, then lay the old photos in a square around them . . . Lynn, Rusty, Lauren, Pig, Rats, Paul, Lobby, Jimmy, Murphy, Momma, Buster, Mum and Dad. All wonderful, kind, loving, giving people. And there they all were. It was all right there. My life. I looked at the shots one at a time, savouring the memories they evoked. Bathing in the comfort of their smiles.

What fantastic people. What great times. Great friendships. Enduring. For life. Bonds so strong not even death could erase them. Love as deep as the soul will allow.

How crazy can you be if these are the people who love you? I thought. *Don't ever get sane, Thorpie. There's no future in it* . . .

I heard tapping on the window and looked around. There was Rob. And he was grinning from ear to ear.

24
Free at Last

The freezing cold December night air almost burst my lungs when I took my first outside breath. The unfiltered atmosphere licked my face like a seal's tongue. Icy and wet. Slamming my pores shut. Making my face itch and my nose scream. Eyes couldn't focus on what my ears couldn't decipher. Nose unable to greet any but the tenderest of odours with anything more than a stunned sniffle. Too much. Way too much information for a man on his first steps back from the dead. Outside hit my senses like a battering ram. A heavy body swimming through its first tentative steps into a frightening world. I was so excited at the prospect of getting out that I hadn't really considered any of this. *Back to normal,* thought I. *A few days in the rat house. So what? Back on deck. Carry on. Take it all in stride. Stiff upper lip. Start where you left off. Nothing to it. Jolly ho. Everything's the same.* But it wasn't the same. It was like I was experiencing everything for the first time. An emotionally naked alien dropped into a well-dressed world. Senses reeling. Body slammed by the sheer enormity of the dynamic.

We take so much for granted, waffling aimlessly through our everyday lives. So much. Unaware of the miracle of life. Unquestioning. Just another night. Just another snow flake. Just another breath. Just another heartbeat! But after my incarceration in the dim netherworld of a Bellevue mental ward the world was a new and scary place. There were people and things out there. Lots of them. Everywhere. Moving. Honking. Glowing. Yelling. Hustling. Beautiful. Ugly. Noisy. Monstrous. Things moving in so many directions at once that I couldn't focus them into the tapestry that we normally associate with the modern bustling world. My senses couldn't compute. Against the reality that my room had become, the scale of outside was staggering.

Light snow fell like fine icing sugar on a neon cake. New Yorkers trudged silently along the clamouring sidewalks. Earmuffs, gloves, scarfs and collars braced them against the sting of the early winter chill. I stared out the cab window like a turn-of-the-century Russian peasant straight off the boat. What is this place? Who lives here? And there and there? What's that? Like I'd never seen it before. In a way, I guess I hadn't. Not like this. Cars, lights, buses, policemen, magazine stands, cart vendors selling bagels, coffee, chestnuts, hot dogs, pastrami. The smells. The vibe. The sounds. The music. The life. The people. Free. I was free. Looking out the rear window of the cab as it pulled away and headed down First Avenue, Bellevue Hospital looked like any other building in Manhattan, or the world for that matter. Red bricks stacked hundreds of feet in the air held together by mortar and gravity. Nothing special. Nothing to attract your attention. You pass buildings like them every day of your life, without so much as a thought for what goes on inside. What lunacy they may contain. Who lives there. Who's dying there. Bellevue disappeared across a sea of lights, bobbing cabs, sidewalks and Manhattan traffic. A dull red monolith lost in a sea of neon and headlights snaking their way through the winter snow. I watched Bellevue shrink, slowly disappearing from view into a distant Lego construction, and all the insanity, fear and helplessness I'd experienced there disappeared with it. It had been an ethereal experience. Detached. Like a psychotic voyeur peeping through a venetian blind. Once removed. Spatial. Unreal. Like it wasn't me. Like it never happened. But it had happened all right. The dull ache inside my plaster cast made the point every time the cabbie ran over a manhole as he sped New York style towards Kennedy Airport. Los Angeles. Lynn and my girls. Home.

'Can I get you anything, sir? I notice that you've been having some trouble sleeping with your arm. If it's paining you some we probably have something in the galley you can take for it.'

'No thanks, miss. I like the pain. It let's me know I'm here.' I smiled.

The hostess just shook her head and walked back down the aisle.

Pan Am flight 16, the red eye out of Kennedy, departed right on time at 12.30 on Thursday morning. With the three hours time difference, that would put me back on the ground in LA around 3.30 and home by 5 a.m. The second I hit the first-class seat, pressed recline and put my head back, I was out. If I'd seemed restless to the hostie, it was probably because I'd spent the last couple of hours wrestling with the Severino brothers and Jack Cirello over Buster's bone, while Rats and Pig chased each other around

Lauren's cot, and Rusty rode on the back of Lynn's bike while she did wheelies around the Whiskey Au Go Go dance floor. I was still dreaming the big dreams. This time everyone I'd ever met was in them. But I felt good. Ragged as a Bowery bum's arse. But good. It was over.

I reached into my bag and felt for my photo wallet. Oh God, look at them. Lynn and the girls. The centre of my life. My stomach churned at the thought of seeing them again. Their scents. Their smiles. Their touch. But did I have some explaining to do! How am I ever going to explain this without looking like a complete idiot? *No reprieve on that front, mate. You'll be in shit up to your ears for the next six months.*

'Where are you going?'

'Oh just out for a quiet one with the boys.'

'Yeah, right.'

I'd busted myself big-time with this little caper. No amount of Billy bullshit was going to talk me out of this. I looked at the photo of Lynn. I felt the cool shadows of the trees by the pool in our house on Mulholland where the shot was taken. Laughing friends in the background. Kids and dog in the pool. An empty wine bottle by the barbecue. The sounds and scents came back. LA came back. Life came back. What a woman she was. First child at twenty-two. Not married. Took it in her tiny stride like a 90 mph curve on her trail bike. Suffered my outrageous slings and arrows for years with a smile and the occasional kick in my arse. Five foot two of hand-packed dynamite with a Belgian lace fuse. The one.

I dozed off with my life in my hands. Thinking about our wedding just a few short months before. A wedding that, like everything else in my life, seemed to have been choreographed by some acid-crazed Disney cartoon director.

25
The Amazing Tina

Who doesn't love Vegas? The kitsch by which all other kitsch is measured. The ultimate plastic. The quintessential neon monument to the American dream. One big score . . . Yeah . . . That's all it takes . . . Just *one big score*. If LA is tinsel then Vegas is vinyl. Soft and slippery as the back seat of a hooker's Chevy on a Saturday night. Touch me. Feel me. Lick me. Worship me and you will be saved . . . Hallelujah! . . . Mine is the power, the sex and the glory. I'm the best goddamned religion your money can buy! So bow your head and open that wallet, motherfucker!

Down every palm-lined neon boulevard . . . from every rat-infested back-street nook and cranny, through the gaming rooms, the showrooms . . . from the sticky wet tips of every dip and moll's fingers drip the echoes of glories past. Of the great days. Of booze and broads. Of Frank, Deano and Sammy sprinkling their golden daydream bulldust at the feet of every starstruck, dream-filled sucker who believed his time at the big table had finally arrived. That one in a million bite at the golden apple. This time . . . This time . . . Just one more roll of the dice and I'll be a goddamn American hero the whole world will respect. Just like Frank . . . Come on . . . Seven the hard and fast way . . . My kingdom in one night . . .

'Snake eyes. Place your bets,' yells the craps boss. There goes another sucker who would be king.

It was 10 a.m. on Valentine's Day 1979 when our battered yellow cab pulled up outside the Las Vegas Hilton. The ride from the airport through the dust and grime of the trailer-park trash-filled desert suburbs gave no hint of the neon paradise beyond. In their weatherboard and stucco houses, dealers, cooks and showgirls conceded a sad and lonely defeat. Disillusioned, sweat dripping, they sit in front of rattling air-conditioners in the sweltering desert heat. Victims all of a siren's voice that had called each lonely soul with the promise of a dream fulfilled. But there are no winners here. Just the hands that grind the fodder that feeds the hungry beast.

'God it's hot,' said Lynn, taking my arm as we followed the Mexican bellboy. No old world New York class here. From his unpressed grey polyester pants and vest to the off-white shirt with the croupier's armbands to stop the cuffs from slipping over his hands, nothing fit. Well nothing, that is, except the scuffed black loafers, burgundy bow tie and velvet bellman's box hat. Even the hat size was a bit suss. He looked like he was wearing his big brother's clobber.

'Check in, señor. I bring ze bags. Si?'

We went over to the front desk. 'Can I help you, sssir?' the polite desk clerk inquired, giving us both the once-over. His eyes peering over the top of his glasses to see if we looked like money. 'How long are you planning to ssstay with usss, er . . . Missster Thorpe?' he asked, checking my name on the registration slip.

'Oh, just a couple of nights. Until Monday,' I replied, signing in.

'Oh what a charming accent, if you don't mind me saying so. Are you English?'

'No, Australian, mate,' I said, catching Lynn's sideways glance.

'Ohhhh . . . how adventurousss. Did you bring me a Koala bear?'

'Yeah, it's in my bag. Can you ask room service to send up a gumleaf casserole. He's probably a bit hungry. Hasn't eaten since Woolloomooloo.'

'Woolloollooloo! Oh what an exssotic name. So much nicer than Lassss Vegassss!' I liked this guy. He was a crack-up. He was being genuinely friendly, which is rare in any hotel in the States let alone in a town like Vegas. 'Just a bit of relaxation for the weekend?' he asked.

'No. Actually we're getting married.'

'Oh, how romantic. Oh congratulationsss to you both.' He smiled, clapping his hands together in front of his chest like he'd just found out he was a bridesmaid. 'Can I come and throw some rice?' He went into a high-pitched cackle after that one. 'Well, in that case . . . in that case, let me seee . . . We'll have to do our very best to find you something comfortable, won't we my dearssss?'

He winked at Lynn and she blushed. I could never understand how somebody who had lived with me for seven years and heard and seen just about every mania there is could get embarrassed at the silliest little things. But she always did. It's one of the million things I love about her. She's real! Still a Portsea girl at heart. No side, and Aussie to the core.

'Errol. Oh *Errollll*,' the desk clerk shouted to someone in the room off the front desk.

'Yes, Raymond,' answered the voice.

'Errol, is 2525 free? Hold on, dears,' he said to us.

'Yes. All ready,' came the voice from the deep.

'Twenty-five twenty-five it is then. You'll just love thisss room,' he said, handing me the key. 'I see Carlosss has your bags. He'll show you up. Have you chosen a venue for your wedding? There's some lovely little spots around town, you know.'

'Well, no we haven't. We thought we'd just take our chances. Can you suggest anywhere?'

'Not really. Just look in the yellow pages. There's hundreds of them. Enjoy your ssstay in Las Vegasss and congratulations again . . . Oh, you're both sssso sssweet.' He smiled, clapping his hands enthusiastically. Then he hit the desk bell, gave me my key and we followed Carlosss up to our room. I tipped him a twenty.

Raymond was an even nicer guy than we'd thought. I'd signed for a normal room and he'd given us a great suite on the twenty-fifth floor for the same price. It had a large living room and separate bedroom with a jacuzzi that looked out over a fantastic view of Las Vegas and the Nevada desert beyond. Although the Hilton isn't on the strip, we could see it easily. When the neon curtain rose at sunset we'd have a hell of a light show. It was perfect.

'Well, here we are, mate. When do you want to get married?' I asked Lynn, hugging her close.

'Tomorrow. Let's have our last single night in Las Vegas and do it in the afternoon.'

'Let's do it right now!' I said, pulling her towards the bedroom. 'Got any stockings?'

'You lech!' She grinned.

'Well, have you?'

'Have I what?'

'Got any stockings?'

'Only the ones I'm wearing.'

'Come heeeere!'

Why the wedding bells? And why Las Vegas? Lynn and I had decided a long time ago that we didn't want to get married unless it became necessary for legal reasons or for the sake of our children. I guess we were hippies at heart when we first met. Marriage seemed like so much bullshit to both of us. Just about everyone we knew who had gotten married had their relationships disintegrate. So many of them seemed to have been pressured into it by family and it just didn't seem important to us. We were all that mattered to us, not some piece of paper saying the government or church recognised our rights as man and wife. We were the happiest couple and family we knew. Still are. How was a marriage certificate going to improve that? Like the man said, 'If it works, don't fix it.' Why mess with a great thing? We loved each other for life. End of story.

It turned out that the legal reason came along when my application for a US green card was approved. My lawyer called to say the government wouldn't recognise Lynn's immigration status as an unmarried woman and she and our daughter Rusty weren't eligible for a green card. Our newest daughter Lauren, who was six months old, was fine because she had been born in LA and was an American citizen. But there was a real chance they would deport Lynn and Rusty and force me to battle it out in the courts. I'd done everything by the book and I was furious, but there was nothing we could do about it. So here we were in Vegas. We'd thought about a formal ceremony with family and friends but it just didn't feel like us. A Las Vegas wedding was the perfect choice.

Vegas is more than neon and concrete. She's the ultimate seductress. From every orifice in her tempestuous body drips the juice from the apple in the garden of Eden. Seven twenty-four, the plaintive mating call of a million lonely silver dollars echoes through that neon desert oasis. As tempting as a siren's call and sadder than a street girl's dreams. Vegas is like any other red-light town. The workers in the casinos, clubs and showrooms were the same carney, show-biz, street-wise types that I'd cut my bones with in Kings Cross back in the early '60s. My first impression of Vegas was exactly that. A glamorous, expensive Cross. Except here the gambling was legal and less fun. I felt right at home as we strolled the strip that first night. The old night-shifter mentality slips back. It's so easy to pick the grifters, hookers, pimps, flim-flams, would bes, dips and undercover cops from the straights who stick out like hogs' balls. At that stage in 1979 Las Vegas hadn't become the family-oriented resort that it is today. It still had the old-time veneer of the '50s and '60s about it and I loved the chintz. It was America personified. Disneyland for big kids.

We'd done the usual round of places like Caesar's Palace, Harrah's, and Circus Maximus. It was still pretty early for Vegas and we didn't really feel like crashing, but we were sick of the casino rooms. Lynn had turned into a casino's dream. After weeks of telling me how much she hated gambling and, 'I'm not wasting any of my money on those machines, they're all rigged,' she pulled a three-aces jackpot on a one-armed bandit at Harrah's and won a grand. I practically had to drag her screaming out of the casino with her heels dragging and her right arm still going at 100 mph. She was a scream. Hooked in a heartbeat. I love to play baccarat and while Lynn tried to buy us another house I played a little and won a couple large. So we were well ahead. The weekend was free.

We'd stopped outside some restaurant on the strip about to have a coffee and some spruiker type came over to me and said, 'Hey man. Psst. Hey . . . Yeah you, brother. You and your lady looking for a little action or what? . . . Here take this. It's the greatest fuckn' show in town, brother. Guaran-fuckingteed to blow your goddamned mind.' Then quick as a flash he was onto the next sucker with the same rave.

I looked at the leaflet he'd given me and it read:

(THE CHICKEN SHACK INTERNATIONAL)
Presents
THE GREATEST SHOW IN LAS VEGAS
STARRING
THE AMAZING TINA
Come see Vegas's leading lady. (6 shows nightly 9 till 4 am)
Too raunchy for the rooms
Too spectacular for the theatres
Too mind boggling for words
TINA'S GUARANTEED TO BLOW YOUR MIND
125 East Admiral Drive, Kennelet
Just grab any cab and ask for the Amazing Tina's show.
Everybody knows about Tina's show!
Just 8 minutes from the strip
(Under 21 not permitted. Must have ID)

'Ah ha, some kulcha,' I laughed.

'What? Show me. What did that guy give you, Ferdie?'

'Ferdie?' you may well ask. Well Ferdie is the nickname Lynn gave me when we first met. She said I reminded her of Ferdinand the Bull in the cartoons. You know, the one that's always scuffing up dust with his front feet and charging head-first into things. Never understood that association myself.

'What *is* that?' she grabbed the flyer from my hands. 'The Amazing Tina, eh? What can she do that I can't, you dirty bugger?'

'Probably nothing at all,' I smirked, looking up and whistling to myself.

'What is it? A sex show or something?'

'No idea, mate. Doesn't interest me.' Whistle whistle.

'Do you want to go?' Lynn paused. 'You do, don't you?'

'You never know, Tina might give you some good tips.'

Lynn punched my arm. Ten minutes later we pulled up outside one of the funkiest looking joints I'd seen in a long time. I paid the cabbie and we stood outside looking at it. The area was funky too, but OK. I didn't feel any threat here. It was just the joint had paint peeling off it and the neon sign outside read

HE ICK N AK

'God, what a dump!' said Lynn.

'Yeah,' I agreed. 'Let's grab a cab.' I didn't feel much like dealing with a bunch of weirdos in some lowlife shithole ten minutes off the Vegas strip, and, besides, I had Lynn with me. With the guys maybe. But my future wife? Nah!

Just then two couples came out of the joint. The guys

were pissing themselves and the girls were giggling their heads off with their hands over their mouths, whispering to one another.

'Hey, excuse me . . . Excuse me,' I called out to them. 'What's the show like? Is it worth the hassle?'

They all looked at each other and started laughing again.

'Go in, buddy,' one of the guys said. 'She's a goddamned genius.'

'It's worth a look, buddy,' said the other and they all walked up the street cackling to themselves and going 'buck . . . buck . . . buck . . .'

Lynn and I looked at one another and said 'Okayyy!' And in we went.

The entrance to the club was a short narrow passageway. A classic example of a strip-joint doorman sat on a stool at the far end, in front of a pair of tattered red velvet drapes. He was dressed in white polyester pants, white socks, white patent leather loafers, black belt and a black shirt. His hair was slicked back with enough grease to lube a truck and his pockmarked face shaved as smooth and slimy as a snake's back. His skin had that wet slick glow that only reads one word. Speed. He sat there undressing Lynn as we approached, a dead Havana hanging in his mouth, bopping his head and bouncing his knees in time to 'Saturday Night Fever' as it crackled through two little black plastic speakers mounted above the drapes. The ceiling was painted flat black. Or had been about thirty years ago by the look of the peel. Faded burgundy fleur-de-lis wallpaper covered the walls and looked like it had been hung by the same guy that painted the ceiling. This joint obviously hadn't seen a cleaning rag since Mo Greene's days. Along one side of the narrow passage hung a half dozen black-and-white framed posters, each containing the photo of a beautiful young Asian girl in sequined high heels and bikini. In the photograph she was blowing out a book of matches and winking at the camera.

'Got some ID, honey?' the doorman asked Lynn, snake-eyeing her up and down and featuring on her boobs. Rolling the Havana from side to side in his mouth as he mentally groped her. Because of her size Lynn looked like a cute little schoolgirl and was always being hassled for her ID. She handed him her licence. He checked the photo. 'Cool,' he slimed. ''At'll be twenty simolians a piece, ma' man,' he said, sliding his black reptile eyes over to me. I paid him. 'Cool,' he said again and stamped the backs of our hands. 'Go ride on in, folks. Sit wherever yo lak. Next show start in ten. Cocktail waitress will git yo dranks.' His head started bopping again as his eyes followed Lynn's arse through the drapes and into the club. *Cool's going to get my fist in his fuckin' mouth if he doesn't cool it*, I thought, shooting him a look. He just sleazed me a Havana grin.

The stage was about thirty feet away, with black velvet drapes that were closed as we entered. To our right, red leather booths sat along the club's curved back wall. In the centre of each booth was a flickering yellow candle in a small red jar. There were more booths along the curved wall opposite, around the room and down either side of the stage. On the floor area itself were about a dozen round cafe-style tables, each with four chairs and a flickering yellow candle in a little cut-glass jar. The walls were painted flat black and in much better condition than the entrance. Posters of dancers, strippers and unknown celebrities hung in large groups at various places. A mirror ball spun from the centre of the ceiling, refracting beams of dancing disco light from small coloured spots that were fixed to the walls. The sound system was also in better nick than the one outside and 'Saturday Night Fever' continued its hypnotic pulse. As rough as it had looked from the outside, the club actually wasn't that bad. Christ, I've played in places that made this joint look like the London Palladium. It smelt a bit of stale booze and sweat, but what old club doesn't? It was fine.

There were about twenty-five people already in the place. Mostly couples in the little booths and a few of the usual contingent of sleazeball barflies with slicked-back hair, gold chains and polyester flowered shirts who sat huddled together in a couple of the booths in the far back corner. Probably working out which old people's home to rob next or where to fence a truckload of crutches they'd just thieved. The bar slimes all looked our way as we entered. Lizard eyes flicking over us. A couple of them obviously said something about Lynn. I guessed they didn't get many young beauties like her in a joint like this. But that was it. No threat perceived, the lounge lizards went back to bidness.

'Come on, let's get down by the stage.' I took Lynn's hand.

'Why down there?' she asked, pulling against my arm.

''Cause that's where the stage is. Come on, we're fine. This place is no worse than the Pussycat and about half as rough as the Catcher. Don't freak out. They're all just folks like us.'

Lynn didn't look too sure but we went down and sat in an empty booth about ten feet away from the stage. A cute blonde cocktail waitress in high heels and a huge set tucked precariously into a skimpy see-through blue teddy came wiggling over.

'What can I get you, honey?' I didn't hear her. Her tits got in the way. Lynn kicked me under the table.

''Scuse me?'

'Y'all won a drink?'

'Oh right. I'll take a double Jack on the rocks and a Heineken for the lady, please.'

'Honey, y'all don't look old enough to be in here.' Lynn flashed her stamp and it was sweet. 'Too cool,' she said and swung her half-naked arse across the room.

'Hey,' said Lynn, elbowing me. 'Y'all keep yo hands in yo pants.' I didn't even realise I was gawking.

About twenty servicemen, some with girls, came bouncing into the club. The vibe lifted immediately. The cocktail waitress started doing massive business and before long the joint was jumping.

Tits came back with the drinks. I was paying her when a voice came over the PA.

'Ladis an genlemen. I lak ta welcum y'all to the internationally famus Chicken Shack where the ladies rule an thuh dranks're cool.' It was slimeball. 'Thuh amazin' Tina gonna be on shotly. Won yo plead pud yo hants toageder for our fust attracsheonn. Thuh sweet 'n' sassy Barbie Doll.'

'Disco Inferno' came pumping out of the PA. All the servicemen started whistling and clapping and the place started to resemble one of the bar scenes from *From Here to Eternity*. The curtains pulled and there, as naked as a jay except for her high heels, stood the sweet and sassy Barbie Doll, a giant feathered fan in each hand. Now Gypsy Rose Lee made a pretty good case for keeping the fans covering her body. That's the whole idea of a fan dance. This girl stood there stark bollickers with them down by her sides. She was so out of it she couldn't lift the things up, she just stood there swaying like an old drunk for a wobbly vacant minute, squinting into the white spotlight coming from the back of the room.

'Come on honey . . . Yeyaaahhh! Do it babe,' one of the soldiers shouted.

'Yeah, jiggle them jiggy jugs honey,' shouted another.

Somewhere in Barbie Doll's brain some fried receptors must have connected and she began to shake her shoulders, which made her huge boobs bounce from side to side like two water-filled balloons.

Then she got rhythm. Well, sort of . . . The soldiers were clapping to the beat and Barbie started to go for it. She made a gallant attempt at some form of blissed-out erotic moves but they mainly consisted of stumbling around the stage occasionally kicking her foot up in time with the disco beat. The feather fans were still hanging lifeless at her sides, dragging on the stage. Why the hell would anyone straight or bent want to try a fan dance to the pumping beat of 'Disco Inferno' in the first place?

Barbie Doll braved a couple of staggering steps towards the front of the stage, tried a couple of exotic moves with the fans while shuffling her feet like a pissed tap dancer, took a shot at a three-sixty spin, tripped on one of the fans and—Sparoiingggg!—pirouetted head-first off the front of the stage into the air, did a complete somersault and landed with a splat on a front table full of cheering soldiers. Flattening it. Still clutching the huge fans.

It was fucking great. I couldn't contain myself. I was laughing so hard I nearly choked. Lynn's going 'Shhh . . .

shhhh . . . the poor thing.' I'm crying. Soldiers, beer bottles, candles and hats all shot up in the air when Barbie landed, like someone had hit a seesaw with a giant hammer. But they took it real well and stood around clapping her magic acrobatics as she sat at their feet on the floor.

It was a bloody classic and worth the twenty bucks right there. I'd have gladly paid another twenty to see it again. The servicemen at the back were whistling and laughing. One yelled out, 'Do it again, honey.' 'Yeah . . . do a flip on this . . . Let's get it on.' I was starting to have a great time. I love joints. Slick is always boring. 'Cause slick means pose. And any mug can pose. There's no art to that. The joints are where the real stuff of the night life happens. You see people as they really are. Maybe not your everyday people but nevertheless it's the funny, sad stuff that makes you laugh, or tears your heart out. And it makes for great memories.

Barbie Doll obviously hadn't felt a thing and sat where she landed amongst the debris and soldiers. I think she thought she was still on stage because she raised her arms a couple of times like a circus act taking what she took for applause. A couple of the big soldiers lifted her up by her arms and a huge bouncer I hadn't noticed before arrived out of nowhere. He scooped her up, put her over his shoulder fireman style and carried her backstage. She just hung there like a limp chicken. Legs spread. Her naked arse and pussy bouncing all the way up the steps and behind the curtain. I looked at Lynn and she burst into laughter.

'It was pretty fucking good, wasn't it?' I tried to get out through my tears.

'Yes,' she cried. 'What is this place?'

'The best night out we're going to have for a while,' I laughed. 'We've still got the Amazing Tina to go yet.'

'Oh God,' Lynn said and we both cracked up again.

The club went back to normal buzzing and private laughter, before Slimeball's voice came over the PA. 'Laayydis an gen'lemen. We here at thuh Chick'n Shack woult lak to 'pologise for thuh unfortunat acciden'. Miss Barbie ain't feelin' so good this evinin' and we gonna move ride on along wud thuh show. Won yo plead pud yo handts togeder for thuh eight wonna o' thuh worl. Thuh mazin' Miss Tinaaaaa.'

The lights dimmed and an exotic Arabian Nights theme flowed out of the sound system. The curtains parted and a spotlight hit the Amazing Tina as she entered the stage wearing spike silver sequined high heels and a floor-length blue velvet cape. Everybody clapped her entrance. Now this was definitely the same Amazing Tina that was featured out front, except she was at least twenty years older than the one on the posters. If I'm any judge of age, this Amazing Tina was in her late forties. But very well preserved and still very beautiful.

She danced slowly from the wings with movements that were somewhere between a flamenco and a belly dancer's. Hands turned gracefully on supple wrists. Fingers playing imaginary castanets or finger bells. Occasionally she twirled a slow three-sixty which lifted her cape and revealed her naked body underneath. The servicemen all whistled and clapped their enthusiastic appreciation. Her movements were precise. Purposeful. Well balanced and professionally executed. She had the body language and stage mannerisms of a circus high-wire act. Very sure. Very graceful. Very well practised. Tina wasn't some old-hack stripper. She had obviously graced a far better stage at some stage in her life.

A male figure wearing a dark kaftan and a velvet fez

appeared mysteriously in a cloud of smoke from the wings, carrying a large round tray on which was a large round object covered with blue velvet. Around it were some other items I couldn't see in the dim light. Tina's assistant placed the tray theatrically in the centre of the stage and exited. As he passed through the curtains into the wings, Tina whipped the cape off, which brought cheers from the servicemen. She placed it ceremoniously by the tray and continued to dance. Lynn and I looked at one another. This woman had an amazing body for someone her age. Her beautiful Eastern face had aged but her body hadn't and she still had the slim, fit, tight figure of a twenty-year-old with large firm breasts. She was really quite stunning.

As her hands continued their slow fluid turns in the air, Tina slipped down in a slow, full splits on top of her velvet cape. More whistles. She gracefully assumed a kneeling position facing the audience, and took a large book of matches from the tray to her left. She held it theatrically above her head for the crowd to see. The boys in uniform screamed and whistled as Tina tore off a single match, struck it, and set the whole book alight. Pushing herself off the floor with her other hand so that her back arched and her pussy faced the audience, the Amazing Tina spread her legs, held the burning match book two feet from her crutch and, Whoooosh—blew the burning matches out with her pussy. It gave a whole new meaning to the burning bush. *And this is the opening to her act*, I thought. *Oh boy!* I looked at Lynn who had her mouth wide open, staring in disbelief. The place broke into a combination of clapping and yelling which she acknowledged with a pearl-white smile. Lynn just looked at me and shook her head. I was whistling like a New Yorker hailing a cab in rush hour. Tina let the applause subside and slipped the velvet cloth off the tray, revealing a large glass bowl containing about two dozen, peeled hard-boiled eggs. Lynn looked at me again.

'Oh no,' she laughed.

'Oh yes,' I laughed back.

With the same ceremony she'd used with the matches, Tina took one of the eggs in her hand, displaying it above her head, then brought it slowly down to her crutch and—*suuuckk*—sucked it up her pussy in one move. Gone! Lots of cheering, including me. She held it in for a few seconds for effect then, *Splat!*—fired it back into her hand. She repeated this a few times and I could hear *Suuuckk . . . Splat . . . Suuuckkk . . . Splat . . . Suuuuck . . . Splat . . . Suuuckkk!* This time the egg stayed inside. Tina placed her hands on the floor behind her and raised herself into a sort of reverse crab with her legs spread and pussy facing the room. The music stopped and the place went silent. Then *Kaaapoww!* . . . she fired the egg over the gaping crowd and clean across the room to the back wall.

The place went crazy. It was amazing. This woman had taken the Kagel technique to a whole other dimension. She got another egg and *Suuckkk! . . . Kapowwww!* Another chicken missile shot across the room. Then another and another and another, all in rapid succession until she'd fired about a dozen salvos into the amazed crowd. The whole joint was clapping and cheering. Tina was taking her bows from the floor when her assistant appeared from the wings. He walked out into the crowd and headed straight to a table full of whistling servicemen in the centre of the room, about twenty-five feet from the stage. Selecting one of them, he stood him up facing the stage and put an empty, regular-size spirit glass upside down on his head.

Utter silence!

Tina took another egg . . . *Suuuckkk!* . . . positioned herself . . . lined the soldier up in her pussy sights and *Kapowww!* The egg left her pussy like a torpedo, shot more than twenty feet and knocked the glass clean off the top of the flabbergasted soldier's head.

Well, it was lunacy. The soldiers were on their feet cheering. People at the back were on their feet and I was whistling and cheering my head off. It was the most amazing thing I've ever seen. Even Lynn was applauding excitedly. No-one could deny it was a remarkable feat, no matter how crude it may seem to some. To my bent sense of humour it was pure magic.

'Jesus, I hope I never have to follow her on a show,' I yelled at Lynn and she broke up.

But the show wasn't over. El Kaftan repeated this with other soldiers who eagerly volunteered. Each time moving them further from the stage and to different points in the room. Every time, *suuckkk* . . . aim . . . *Kaapowww!* A direct hit. She never missed once.

I mean where did she ever come up with the concept in the first place? I want to be in show biz, right. What will I do? Let's seeee? . . . I'll be a dancer . . . Nah . . . Be a juggler . . . nah . . . A singer . . . Nah . . . I *know*, I'll fire eggs out of my pussy and knock glasses off the audience's heads! Yeah, that's it! Fuck, how do you practise an act like that? The mind boggles! Tina was down to her last egg when one of the soldiers in the middle of the room started whistling to get her attention. He stood up, opened his mouth wide and pointed to it. The only thing missing was a drum roll. The place went deathly silent. Tina took her last egg . . . *Suuckkk* . . . position . . . aim . . . *Kaapowww!* The final chicken missile left her power-packed pussy at 100 mph, banked left in a slightly curved trajectory, dropped at the very last second and . . . *Paaalopp!* . . . shot straight into the soldier's mouth from twenty feet away. He chomped on it and swallowed, then threw his arms triumphantly up in the air.

'Now have you ever seen a chicken do that?' he yelled.

The club went orbital. I'd seen a few things up until then, including the donkey sex shows in Bangkok and a freak in a club on the Rehperbahn in Hamburg who took his dick in both hands and batted tennis balls thrown at him by the audience. But donkey fucking and dick batting were nothing compared to this.

This was Art with a capital A. Her accuracy was staggering. This woman was literally a vaginal howitzer. God, it brings a whole new concept to combat, doesn't it? Guys would be clawing over each other to get to the front line! 'Any volunteers?' 'Me sir, me.' 'No, me. I'll go . . . I'll go!' They'd be charging admission to get on the firing range. And her husband? Whoa! He wouldn't be hard to pick. He's the guy staggering around mumbling with his eyes spinning and a dribbling mouth. God, it must be amazing. Nah, that's not a good enough word. I've got half a mongrel just writing about it!

After the final mouth assault the Amazing Tina took several bows. The crowd clapped wildly for her to come back on stage but no-one shouted 'More'. There was nothing that could follow that.

Lynn was in shock! 'Well, did you learn anything, mate?' I asked, laughing. 'I wonder if she gives lessons? We could stay an extra week or two. What do you think?' Lynn kicked me under the table and went scarlet. Like everyone else in the club we sat there jabbering away and laughing about it. Had another drink. And made our way out of the club. Tina was signing autographs just outside the curtains in the passageway.

'I've got to get one,' I said.

'Oh no.'

'Why not?' I waited my turn in the line and finally reached her. 'Hi, Tina. That was amazing. I'm in show business and I've never seen anything like it.'

'Oh really, what do you do?' she asked in a well-educated Asian voice.

'I sing, make records. You know.'

We stood there like old stage buddies for five minutes, having a great old rave. I was honestly impressed. Entertainment is just that. It's meant to entertain you. Regardless of the concept, a show either entertains or it doesn't. And Tina had definitely entertained everyone in that club. The way she presented herself on stage there was nothing crude about her performance. She was a pro. She told me she'd been raised in a peasant village in Thailand. Her mother had taught her the art as a child. As a teenager she had fed her family by it. Not literally, of course. Now she had two young kids going through private school in LA and some apartments in the Hawaiian islands. All financed by her egg show. She also told me that she was opening her own club in Hawaii.

Many years later, my dear friend and fellow Aussie John Farrar of The Strangers, *Grease* and Olivia Newton-John fame, told me about this club in Honolulu that I had to see the next time I was there. Honolulu was a regular holiday spot for our family and one bored night Lynn and I went to a club called the Spot Light in the Bowery section. Lo and behold, it was Tina's club. She did the exact same show to a packed house and we talked again. John and I actually discussed filming her live when we got the time, but she retired in 1989 and closed the club before we got it together . . . Meanwhile, back in Las Vegas I hailed a cab outside the Chicken Shack and we headed back to the Hilton. As we drove through a rainbow sea of flashing neon and chrome, I looked at my prized autograph, which I still have.

> *To Billy with egg*
> *love*
> *The Egg Lady. xxxx*

'I *wonder*,' I said.
'What?' Lynn asked.
'I wonder if there are any shops open this time of night.'
'What for?'
'I want to buy a gross of eggs.'
Lynn punched me hard on the arm. 'Stop it,' she said.
'Buck . . . buckk . . . buckk buck buck . . .' Punch!
'Ow!'

26
The Hitchin' Post

W e woke about 10 a.m. and ordered breakfast. The view from high up in the Hilton was of another sun-drenched desert day. Same as the last. Same as the next. As we ate we scoured the yellow pages for listings for wedding chapels. We had no real criteria in mind, just something that might take our fancy. There were hundreds of them. The Naughty Naked Nuptial Nest where you can do it in the raw . . . The Celestial Chapel of Heavenly Bliss where you can get married in a 'genuine replica' of a Gemini space capsule . . . It went on and on.

'Close your eyes and run your finger over the next page,' I said. 'Whatever it lands on is it.'

'Okay,' Lynn replied. I turned the page. Lynn wrinkled her nose, held her eyes as tight as a four-year-old at a birth-day party and ran her finger slowly across the page, settling on an ad halfway down.

'Open your eyes, mate,' I said. We both looked.

The Hitchin' Post

Come on you love birds . . .
Mosey on down to the ole nuptial corral
Get yo'self hitched at the best little ole hitchin' house
in Vegas.

Open twenty-four hours a day.
Las Vegas 9210 . . . 54 Hitchings Avenue . . .

'Yippeee kai yai,' I laughed. Lynn giggled nervously.
'OK, you ready?' She nodded. I called the number.

A woman answered. 'Hi y'all, this is The Hitchin' Post.
Best little ole hitchin' house in Vegas. What can I do for you
on this beautiful Las Vegas mornin'?' Her voice was young
and sexy.

'Er hi . . . I . . . er, we saw your ad in the yellow pages
and we'd like to get married today.'

'No problem, pardner. To whom am I speaking?'

'Billy Thorpe. Oh, William Richard Thorpe . . . Excuse
me? . . . No, not Phillips, Thorpe. T.H.O.R.P.E . . . That's
right Thorpe, William Richard . . . Oh that's OK . . .'

Then I went through the whole routine again with
Lynn's name, after which I fielded some questions about my
accent. It seems the woman at The Hitchin' Post didn't
know the difference between Australia and Austria.

'You have to go to the Las Vegas County Courthouse
before the actual ceremony and pick up your hitchin'
licence,' she told me once she had our particulars. 'They'll
be lines so it will take bout an hour and a half. You both
got some legal form of ID, hon? . . . Yep California drivers'
licences are A-OK aroun' here. Now, you tell them that

407

you're getting hooked at The Hitchin' Post. They'll put that on your licence. 'Scuse me? . . . Honey, you just mosey on down to the corral. Be here by three-thirty, hon. We'll take it from there. 'Scuse me? . . . Oh honey, we ain't gonna break yo' bank. We're pretty standard. You can check anywhere. Oh a hundred and a quarter for the ceremony. Will you be wanting a priest? . . . OK, a priest will be another fifty.'

And so the plans were laid. I explained all the details to Lynn and we sat looking at each other, at Vegas and the desert, then each other again. Not saying much at all. It was a strange feeling. Here we were getting married after so many great years together. I think we were both hoping it wouldn't break the spell.

'It's eleven now,' I said at last. 'You want to have some lunch on the strip then go and get the licence? Let's not come back here.'

'Let's go back to bed,' Lynn purred. 'I want to make love to a couple of guys today.'

'What?'

'A single guy and a married one.' She laughed and let her robe slip to the floor.

Lynn was such a turn-on. Twenty-eight years old and she didn't look a day over seventeen. So tiny. So fragile and perfect. A woman child. I could never imagine her any taller than her 5 feet 2 inches. It wouldn't be right. It's as if God had purposely packed as much love and beauty as he could find into that one tiny girl to see if anyone could handle that much bang in something so small. Lynn is the perfect size for me in every way. Our bodies fit like two halves of the same puzzle. No ragged edges. No adjusting to a new partner. Perfect. Her small size had spawned an iron will to win and Lynn could outswim, outdance, outparty and outplay just about anyone I knew at tennis and pool. Including me. She'd been a local swimming and tennis champion when she was a kid and only her size had stopped her from going all the way. She'd played every sport, including footy, rode a trail bike, rode a horse like a jockey and won ribbons in Portsea gymkhanas. She grew up in the bush and always had a bit of a Ginger Meggs tomboy about her. Had to be able to be one of the boys. Especially when she didn't get to five feet two inches until she was sixteen. With her freckled face, blue eyes, blonde hair, tight athletic body, and the mixture of her gentle beauty and a selfless, loving personality, she was irresistible. The first time we made love she was very nervous and inexperienced. But her innocent, enthusiastic sexuality grabbed me like no other girl I'd ever been with. The scent of her body that first night! I couldn't get enough. Still can't.

I stood admiring her as she turned and walked naked into the bedroom, the Nevada morning light bouncing off her silky white skin. She looked like a champion gymnast. So strong and full of life. And her heart-shaped arse! Oh Lawd! *God, I love you*, I thought, watching her. The great surrealist Salvador Dali once wrote about his beloved Gala, 'When we make love I feel like I am making love to every woman in the universe.' I know he meant to the very spirit of woman. That's how it felt the first time with Lynn. And that's how it's always felt. The one.

'Well, are you going to look or are we going to dance?' Lynn turned around, laughing, as I perved at her.

'I like to look *and* dance.' I went over and hugged her.

Lunch was a goner but by 1 p.m. we were showered and getting dressed.

'What do I wear to my Las Vegas wedding at The Hitchin' Post?' Lynn asked as she went through the closet yet again.

'What you've got on will be fine.' She was in flesh-coloured lace panties and bra and her high heels.

'Lech,' she laughed.

'No, seriously.'

'Stop it! I'm serious. I don't know what to wear,' she said, getting all verklempt and going through her things for the twentieth time.

'Whatever feels right, mate. What about that new dress I bought you?'

'This one?' she asked, pulling it out and holding it against herself in the mirror. It was a sleeveless, high-necked cotton number with an over the knee skirt and a belted waist. Burgundy, sheer, with little flower motifs woven into the fabric. She slipped it over her head. 'How's it look?'

'Go and stand by the window so I can see it properly,' I said. She went over. 'Mmm, it looks great from here.' I smiled as the light silhouetted her body through the fabric.

'Lech,' she said again.

'Hey, you want me to stop leching after you?' She laughed and shook her head. 'What am *I* going to wear?' I asked.

'Oh your usual, I suppose,' Lynn said.

I put on a pair of fresh jeans, a denim shirt, cowboy boots and a light cotton jacket. Hey, it's The Hitchin' Post in Vegas! 'How do I look?' I asked.

'Go and stand over by the window.'

'Lech.'

'Hey, you want me to stop?'

We hugged and kissed. Lynn had one more fuss around

the room on a woman's usual last-minute hunt for stuff, and we were out the door to our wedding. We'd ordered a cab and Raymond yelled 'Good luck, darlingsss' as we walked through the lobby.

The Las Vegas County Courthouse was not what I'd imagined. No horses, no hitchin' rails. No injuns. Not a bloody gunfighter in sight! Just an uninspired grey concrete bunker with concrete steps up to two glass doors. We stood in line with about fifty other about-to-bes, all smiling nervously at each other. Chinese, Mexican, Texans, French, Germans and two Australians. Total strangers momentarily connected by one of life's greatest adventures. If you're lucky.

We eventually got to the desk and went through the formalities. Once again Lynn was hassled about her age. Even when she showed her driver's licence, the guy behind the desk wouldn't believe she was the legal age of consent. Luckily she'd brought her Australian passport. I paid the twenty-five dollars and we had our marriage licence with 'The Hitchin' Post' typed in big black letters across the top. Now all we had to do was get married.

Our cab pulled up outside The Hitchin' Post at 3.20 p.m. The building sat back from the street on a small corner lot in a semi-residential street in a semi-funky neighbourhood. On the opposite corner was a Texaco service station, across the road a 7 Eleven and a joint named Gerry's. We stood looking at the building, not sure exactly what it was we were looking at. The Hitchin' Post looked somewhere between a turn-of-the-century western barber shop, Little Red Riding Hood's cottage and a whorehouse. All decorated by a half-pissed Greek on acid. Four candy-apple red and white striped poles supported a large white canopy that led up the candy-apple red stairs to the candy-apple red door. From the roof of the short verandahs either side of the door hung candy-apple red and white striped awnings and the railings on the verandah were painted in candy-apple red and white striped high-gloss enamel. On each side of the canopy was a horse hitching post also painted in . . . you guessed it! The entire front of the house was candy-apple red and the windowsills and door jambs high gloss white enamel. On the top of the canopy and the awnings, embroidered in candy-apple red, was a giant horseshoe and the words The Hitchin' Post.

All the paintwork, the canopy and awnings were immaculate. Someone had taken a lot of care with the decor. Lynn and I stood there staring at the place like it might go away if we wished hard enough . . . but it was still there five minutes later.

'Come on, mate, it's late. We're getting married in just over an hour.' Lynn didn't say a word, just followed me under the canopy and up the candy-apple red stairs to the door. I knocked. No answer. I knocked again. No answer.

'Oh thank God,' Lynn said. 'Nobody's home.'

I knocked again . . . still no answer. We figured it was divine intervention and walked back down the stairs. We were at the bottom when a voice crackled through an intercom. 'Come round the back, hons. The entrance is in the rear.' We looked at each other and broke up.

'Oh what the fuck,' I laughed and we trudged around to the back of the house. What there was of it!

The entire back of the building had been burnt off and bits of it were still smouldering. We just stood there with our mouths open. 'In here, hon,' the voice said, shaking us back into our nightmare. 'In here . . . Watch your step. We've had a little accident.' *A little accident*, I thought.

Christ, half the joint has burnt down. The outside walls of the back rooms were gone and there were a burnt mattress, scorched clothing, furniture and debris hanging out. All drenched. Stepping over charred timber we found a pair of charred stairs and went up, careful not to slip in the stream of water that was running down them from inside the house. 'Come on in, hons,' repeated the voice.

I pushed what the firemen had left of the door . . . And there she was! Six feet, late fifties, 250 pounds of cellulite and a forty-five inch set crammed into a pair of luminous pink stretch tights and a white T-shirt. Her face was garishly plastered in make-up with enough false eyelashes and bright blue eye shadow to do the entire drag show at the Albury, and of course candy-apple red lipstick. On her head, looking like a fresh baked Navaho pot, was a two-foot-high platinum-blonde beehive. On her feet a tiny pair of clear plastic, backless high heels with a fluffy pink pom-pom on each toe, and silver sparkle heels.

'Hi, hons. Welcome to The Hitchin' Post.' We stood there gaping. There were no words. 'Sorry bout the mess. The water heater 'sploded this mornin' just after you called and we had a bit of a burn.' We still couldn't speak. She dead set looked like Frankenstein in drag . . . and we were standing in his burnt-out laboratory. It was wrecked. All the cabinets were burnt beyond repair. Some of the floorboards had been pulled up. The windows, glasses and crockery had exploded from the heat and the sink was piled to overflowing with sopping food.

Neither Lynn nor I dared open our mouths because the only thing that would have come out would have been uncontrollable laughter. 'Why don't you come into the vestry?' she said, turning and walking down a short passageway. *Vestry?* I thought. It hit Lynn too because she started to crack up. 'Don't you fucking laugh. I'll shit myself,' I mumbled, fighting off hysterics. 'This is where we'll take care of all the formalities before we go into the chapel for the ceremony.' *Chapel?* I thought. *Can't wait to see the bloody chapel. Oh dear God don't let me laugh. Please.* Frankenstein's arse was at least three pick handles across and packed into her luminous pink tights like twelve dozen hard-boiled eggs. She wobbled along in front of us, teetering on those tiny high heels. The vestry occupied the front left half of the house and as we entered she turned theatrically. *An old showgirl*, I thought. *There's no mistaking it.* She waved her hand around the room like a display girl at a car show. 'This is our exotic aquarium. We find the atmosphere in here calms even the most nervous couples.'

Calms? The room was lined wall to wall with grimy fish tanks full of the most raggedy, half-arsed, sorriest looking bunch of fish I'd ever seen. No self-respecting cat would have touched them. I walked over to look at one of them and it came up to the glass. 'Throw a fucking hook in,' it pleaded with its eyes. It was unbelievable. The carpet was a threadbare burgundy and yellow Persian copy with all sorts of stains on it. Wherever there wasn't a fish tank there were black velvet artworks with Las Vegas motifs on them. The kind you buy at carnivals with pictures hand-painted in bright green luminescent paint. From the ceiling in the centre of the room hung a small cut-glass chandelier with most of the glass missing. Only three of the six flickering artificial candle globes worked, and one lonesome glass teardrop hung precariously from the bottom edge, begging for a truck to go by so it could commit suicide on the rug below. To our right was a door painted in white high-gloss enamel with the word 'Chapel' stencilled on it in black.

414

'Well, hons, you all ready for the big day? Your first time, hon?' Frankenstein asked. I looked at Lynn. She couldn't speak. Just nodded her head. 'Thought so.' She grinned, showing tobacco-stained teeth with candy-apple red tips. 'You look a little nervous. I can always pick first-timers, hon. Smile, you're gonna love it.' If Lynn had even moved her lips we both would have pissed ourselves. 'I bin hooked eight times. Lurved every one o' them ta death,' she said with a 'yesiree Bob' nod of her head. *I bet you did*, I thought. *Sucked the life right out of the poor bastards.*

'And what about you, hon?' she asked. 'First time too?' I nodded. 'Ah knew it,' she smiled, supremely confident in her antennas which were sticking out the front of her skin-tight white T-shirt like two Boeing 747 engines. Thumb-sized nipples strained like whippets' noses to bust out of a bra that belonged in the brassiere hall of fame. 'Well, hons, we have a few formalities to attend to before the priest arrives. Let me get my husband. He always acts as witness and likes to take care of business. Be right back.'

She did another showgirl turn and patted the back of her two-foot beehive as her elephant arse rolled out of the room. Lynn and I looked at one another. Looked around the room. Looked at one another again and lost it. Lynn nearly pissed herself when I said, 'How the fuck do I get into these situations for Christ's sake?' It's ridiculous. It's never the norm.

'Oh God, I have to pee. Don't make me laugh any more. I'm going to wet myself,' Lynn said as she wiped the tears from her eyes. 'I have to go to the bathroom!'

'I bet the shitter is a ripper,' I said.

'Don't! . . . Don't . . . I'll pee my pants,' Lynn pleaded, standing up and holding her stomach. She was looking around when Frankenstein came back in. 'Er, I need a bathroom,' she said.

'Mr Thorpe, my husband Hugo will be with you in a second. OK, girl. This way . . . Little nervous, hon?' I heard her ask Lynn as they disappeared down the passage. Lynn's shoulders went up and she just nodded her head.

Now Hugo was something else again. Things were getting weirder by the minute. Five foot three. Built like a toothpick. Seventy years old with a thick Polish accent and false teeth that clicked when he spoke. He wore a pair of battered tan patent leather shoes and light blue socks, a pair of brown wrinkled polyester pants, a red and white checked shirt with a navy blue tie and a light blue seersucker jacket that hung off him like a scarecrow. And the crowning glory . . . the worst toupee known to man! It looked like a cow had shit on top of his head and someone had sprayed it with black shellac. It was outrageous. What a ripper Hugo was. Their wedding photos must have been bloody pearlers!

'Mishta click Zorpe. I yam click pleased to meet ju.' Hugo extended his frail white hand.

'How do you do,' I replied.

'Vell click mishta click Zorpe. Ve are gradeful zat click ju choos us at click ze Hitchink click Potz click.' *Oh Jesus!* I thought. *I'm not going to get through this.* 'Vhat short of click rink do ju haf int click mindz?' As he spoke Hugo pulled out a drawer in the small, litter-covered desk by the chapel door.

Rings! Thank God! We'd completely forgotten about the rings. 'Oh, I don't know.'

'Vell click ve haf a goot click selegshun 'ere,' he said, pushing some clutter aside and laying a ragged, red velvet-covered jeweller's tray on the desk top. On it were rows of different types of gold wedding bands. 'Dis kindt click ten click dollar. Dis click vun fivteen. Dis click twenty . . . und click za top off ze line click, dis vun twenty click five dollar.' Hugo breathed on a 'top of the line' ring and polished it on his jacket lapel before handing it to me.

'Well I think I'll take a twenty-five dollar one,' I said, trying it on. 'But I'd like to let my wife make her own choice.'

Just then Lynn and Frankenstein walked back in. 'She's all better now, hon. Just a little nervy, that's all.'

I looked at Lynn. She looked at Hugo. Then at me. She couldn't believe it either but didn't say a word. Her eyes were riveted on Hugo.

'I see you've met my husband,' Frankenstein said and patted Hugo on top of his black cow turd. He blinked furiously and his head bounced down into his jacket. 'This is Hugo,' she said to Lynn.

'How click do ju click do,' went Hugo.

Lynn shook his hand and nodded her head, trying to keep it together.

'Oh, we haven't really been formally introduced, hons, what with bein' a little embarrassed by the little mess and all. I'm Loralita Von Dolmerer. Pleased to make your acquaintance.' She extended her hand like a duchess waiting for us to kiss it. *Loralita Von Dolmerer?* It was complete lunacy.

'Nice to meet you,' I said, shaking her hand. Lynn just nodded, still staring at Hugo.

'Lynn, we can choose our wedding rings.' Her look flashed that she had forgotten all about them too. 'Which one do you like?' I asked her, pulling us back.

Hugo went through his click price click routine and Lynn managed to keep her cool. She chose the same model I had, and we both tried on different rings until we found the right size.

'Now we have to fill out the licence, hons, and take care of the bill if that's okay.'

'Sure. How much is it?'

'Let's see. Fifty for the rings. A hundred and a quarter for the service and fifty for the priest.'

I handed Loralita two hundred and twenty-five dollars cash.

'Muchabliged, hon,' she said, fanning it like a croupier and counting it in a flash. We signed the wedding licence and some other Las Vegas County forms and Hugo and Loralita Von Dolmerer left so that 'You two lurve birds c'n be 'lone together in the vestry.' We waited for the priest.

'I don't believe this is happening,' I said.

'Oh it's happening,' Lynn said, trying to control her laughter. 'What about his toupee? It looks like a cow turd!'

'I know, I know,' I screamed, and off we went again for the next ten minutes. I looked at my watch. It was 4.35 p.m. and in came the Von Dolmerers.

'The priest has just pulled up, hons. He'll be right in. We can start a little early if you like.'

'Great,' I said, still trying to take the pair of them in. They looked like a Fellini circus act.

Bang . . . crash . . . ploing . . . crash . . . dinggg tinggg ting . . . ting ting! It sounded like someone throwing pots and pans around in the kitchen. 'Goddamn!' Boing . . . crash. 'Shit!' Crash. 'Goddamn!' And in came our priest. Sixty-five years old. Five feet five. Two hundred pounds. Ruddy Irish complexion with a three-day-old grey stubble.

Curly unkempt grey hair. Black scuffed shoes, the right one with the laces undone and dragging on the floor. A wrinkled black suit, black bib and reverse white collar. And pissed as a fart.

'Sheesushh Loralita. What the goddamn happened out there?' he asked, shaking a pot from his foot.

I thought I was going to die. The only one missing was Curly from the Three Stooges. 'I goddamn nearly broke ma goddamned neck on that goddamned pile of shiiit, Loralita.'

'Er, Reverend Hale, this is the future Mr and Mrs Thorpe,' Loralita said, gesturing to us.

'Oh my shildren,' he said, pulling a pair of glasses from his pocket and mishooking them on one ear so they half hung off his face. 'How wonerful to shee . . . ah, you young love birts.' He was blind!

'Excuse me, Mrs Von Dolmerer, can I speak to you for a second?' I asked and led her into the passage. Lynn was sitting in a chair, her eyes as big as saucers.

'Yes, hon,' Loralita said.

'Listen, mate. This priest is pissed as a fart. Christ almighty, he can't do the ceremony like that.'

'Look, I'm sorry, hon, but our regular priest is sick and I only got Reverend Hale a while ago at home. Everyone else is booked for the evenin', bein' Valentine's an' all. The town is packed. Now we can use him or reschedule. What you wanna do? I assure you the reverend can handle it. He's been like that for twenty years. He drove here didn't he?' I hated to think how many poor innocent tourists he flattened on the way. 'Anyhow, I seen him a lot worse than this. He'll be fine, hon. It's a real short ceremony.'

How short can it be? I wondered. Christ, the reverend couldn't find his arse in the dark! Lynn was still sitting in the chair, staring at Hugo and the reverend. I called her over.

'The situation is their regular priest is sick and they got this silly old bastard half an hour ago. The town's booked out because of Valentine's. So it's this guy or reschedule. What do you want to do? I'll go with your decision.' Lynn looked at me dumbfounded. 'I know, I know. But we can call it off or go with it. It's up to you.'

'I'm not going through this again. It would kill me. Let's go for it.'

'You sure?'

'Yep.'

I hugged her. 'We'll remember this one, mate. Wait till we see the chapel.'

'Don't make me laugh. I'll pee myself.'

We went back into the vestry. The fish with the death wish was still doing backflips in his tank, trying to get my attention.

'Everything OK, hons?' Loralita asked.

'Yep. Let's do it,' I replied.

'Hot dawg, that's the dang cowboy spirit ain't it, Hugo?'

'Yep click.'

The reverend was hanging off a chair in the corner, trying desperately to stop the room from spinning.

'Hons, I'm going to make the reverend a strong black coffee. He's had a hard day. You don't mind do you? You like one too?'

'No, go ahead. That's a real good idea.'

Hard day killing three bottles of scotch, I thought.

Time seemed to stand still. Loralita made the coffee and the reverend got most of three cups down. I say most because his hand was shaking like the proverbial shitting dog and a lot of it ended up on the floor. But it seemed to kick some life into the poor old bugger. We sat there watching it all without saying a word. It was like a sitcom but no-one can write that funny. Ten minutes later the reverend seemed a little steadier on his feet but he was still well pissed.

'Can I pleashe have your full namesh?'

I started to tell him. He fumbled a pen from his jacket and took about a minute to unscrew the top, closing one eye and licking his lips in concentration as he swayed on his feet. When he got to the last twist he gave it one final twirl and it spun off into the air and dropped into a fish tank with a plop. We looked at one another. He staggered over to the desk and opened a leather-bound book. His hand shook so badly it shot off the page onto the desk. 'Goddamn pen,' he cursed.

'Now now, Reverend Hale,' Loralita scolded. 'They'll be no cussin' in the vestry.'

'Ma pologisss folgs,' he swayed. 'It's my medication. Didn't expeck ta be out tonight, you undersssshtand.'

'Here, let Hugo do it for you,' said Loralita.

'Letz click zee . . . dat ees click Zorpe click . . .'

'No. No, Thorpe. T.H.O.R.P.E. . . .'

And on it went. Click. Lynn and I were dying. Five minutes later we were registered in the Reverend Hale's register of marriages.

'OK, hons, you ready?' I looked at Lynn and we both nodded, hardly able to wait for whatever lunacy happened next. 'The reverend will go into the chapel and prepare the service, won't you, reverend? Er, reverend . . . reverend,' she yelled. The reverend was out there with the birds, dreaming of his next drink.

'Er . . . what? Yedshh. Yeshh. The shapel. Go into the shapel. Gotta get into the shapel.' He launched himself out of the chair, got a bead on the door, pointed his feet in the right direction, fired himself across the room and walked face first straight into the fucking door. He ricocheted off it into Loralita's cushioning tits. 'Goddamn thing shut on me,' the reverend cursed.

That was the end of my undies. I blew the arse right out of them. Lynn sat there with an astonished look on her face, mouth open, slowly shaking her head. Meanwhile Loralita got the reverend in the door, careful not to let us see the 'shapel' before we entered. 'It's always a big surprise. We're very proud of our little chapel, aren't we Hugo?'

'Yep click.'

'Surprise!' The only thing that would have surprised us then would have been for the earth to open up beneath our feet. And after what we'd just watched for the last forty-five minutes even that wouldn't have fazed us that much. Loralita came back. 'Right. Hugo will give the lovely bride away and I'll be the witness. As soon as the Wedding March begins you both walk down the aisle together and Hugo will give you away. OK, hon?' Lynn nodded. 'Hugo likes that bit of the ceremony, don't you, Hugo?'

'Yep click.'

'Hugo, you can start the music.' Hugo went down the passage and . . . Da screetch da-da screetch. Da screetch da-da screetch. Da, da da-da screetch da-da screetch da-da screetch. Here screetch comes the screetch bride. The record sounded like an old 78 rpm and scratched is not the word. Fucked is the word. It was unbelievable.

We could only just hear the music through the scratching and hissing, but we kept our cool. We were going to go through with this even if it killed us. I took Lynn's arm and followed Frankenstein into our wedding, crossing a passageway and passing through two musty blue velvet drapes and into the chapel. An aisle ran down the centre of the converted master bedroom which had four rows of old wooden church pews that looked like they'd been auctioned from the set of *The Grapes of Wrath*. There were no windows and at the end of the aisle was a rickety-looking trellis arch draped in white cotton.

Swaying precariously beneath it, holding desperately onto a lectern that looked like it came in the same auction lot as the pews, was the Reverend Hale. Da screetch da-da screetch. Da screetch da-da. On into the breach. If there had been a window I think we would have dived out head-first, run across the street and hit Gerry's joint. But there was no escape now. No turning back. Loralita and Hugo walked around the side of the pews and joined the rev under the arch. The sight of them standing there beaming at us was classic. The rev was fighting the spins. Loralita hoisted her arse into her tights and patted her beehive. The cow turd on Hugo's head was gleaming in the two little spotlights above his head. Lynn and I were left to walk the plank alone. Da screetch da-da screetch. Da screetch da-da. On went the scratching symphony and down the aisle we went.

'You OK, mate?' I said, hugging Lynn to my side.

'I think I've peed my pants,' she whispered.

'Come on, not long now.' We reached Larry, Curly and Frankenstein.

Da screetch da-da. Da screetch da-da screetch da-da screetch da-da screetch da-da screetch! The bloody record was stuck.

'Oh Lawd, Hugo,' Loralita said. 'We gotta get that damned player fixed.'

She ran around the pews and out the door. The whole place rocked as she passed. I thought it was going to collapse. Da da screech da-da screech da scarrrreeeeech! Scaareecchhh . . . riiiip! da-da. Loralita got it and came rolling back in. She patted her beehive, got the wedgy out of her arse, hoisted her tits and the ceremony continued. We were beyond laughing. It was insanity!

'Dearly beloved, we are gaffered here today in the shight off God to wet this man and thish woman in the bonts of holy matrimony. Ish there anyone here who objects to thish marriage? If sho let h'm shpeak now or for heffer hold hish peashe.' I heard the fish yell, 'Throw me a fucking hook. I'll object to anything you like!' The reverend waited for about thirty seconds. Hugo was looking around like somebody was going to object. There was nobody there but us. Of course no-one was going to object. The silly old prick. 'OK then . . . Who givesh thish younk lady away?'

'Me click,' said Hugo and he took Lynn's arm.

'Do you, Lynn er, MacNamaramaranonon,' the reverend mumbled, squinting at the page.

'McGrath,' Loralita corrected.

'Yesh, yesh. McGranth. Take thish man to pee your lawfly whetted hushbant?'

'I do,' said Lynn, looking into my eyes. My knees went.

'Do you, Willumm Risshrd Thorne . . .' squint . . . 'er, Thorpe.' He took his glasses off and glared at them like it was their fault. 'Willumm Rishrd Thorpe . . . take thish woman t'be your lawfly whetted wife?'

'I do,' I said.

Lynn looked so radiant at that moment. Glowing. Alive.

My wife. It felt wonderful, and the look on Lynn's face told me that she felt it too. I fell in love with her all over again.

'Pleashe take the ringsh and plashe them on eash other's finkers.' Hugo fumbled the rings from his pocket and handed them to us and we slid them onto each other's hands. 'I now pronounshshoo man an'uuurppp! wive. You may kishh the brite!' We kissed and the reverend fell back into a chair, went 'Pheew!' and wiped his face with the curtain over the trestle arch.

I looked over Lynn's shoulder as we kissed and there were Loralita Von Dolmerer and Hugo. Tears streamed down their cheeks and her blue eye make-up ran into a purple puddle where it met her candy-apple red lipstick. As bizarre as they were, they were also truly sweet. Oblivious to the lunacy that had gone on around them. Completely absorbed in their little Hitchin' Post. They loved it.

'I love you, Mrs Thorpe.'

'I love you, Mr Thorpe,' Lynn whispered and the greatest wedding ceremony ever came to an end. A million-dollar wedding couldn't have beat it.

'Well, what do you want to do to celebrate?' I asked Lynn as we headed back to the Hilton in a cab.

Lynn pulled me closer. 'Nothing can top that, Billy,' she whispered. 'Let's go straight back to LA and be with Rusty and Lauren,' she said, kissing me. 'We've got our whole lives to celebrate.' It made me cry.

Lynn was right. Our life together with our girls, who have now grown and gone out in the world, and with our dear friends has been nothing short of the greatest celebration of love and life. Oh, a few crazed ups and downs. But never about us. Never once. When I got back to LA after Bellevue, Lynn and Rusty hugged and kissed me like I'd just returned from outer space. And little Lauren peed in my lap. 'If you ever do anything like that again I'll kill you,' was the only thing Lynn said about it. She never mentioned it again. It wasn't until I started writing this book that we spoke about it.

In 1999 it will be twenty years since that amazing afternoon at The Hitchin' Post in Las Vegas. And twenty-seven years since Lynn knocked on the door at Pig and Momma's the day after her twenty-first. Apart from when I've had to be on the road, we've been inseparable since the day we met. Rock 'n' roll and marriage don't mix, huh? Bull! You just got to be lucky enough to find 'the one'.

It's a mad and crazy world out there, ain't it? But you gotta love it. It'll kill you if you don't. If you ever need any help with all the craziness, just call. I'm just as sane as I ever was. And I've got my Bellevue Mental Hospital release form to prove it!

Not even close to the end.

Billy Thorpe
Sex and Thugs and Rock 'n' Roll

Billy Thorpe is an Australian rock legend, but in 1963 he was a
seventeen-year-old singer fresh out of Brisbane, who arrived in
Sydney's Kings Cross ready to crack the big time. Through his eyes
we see the Cross at a unique moment in its history, and Australia on
the threshold of an astonishing new wave of youth culture.

For Billy it's a tantalising and dangerous new world and he soon
finds his life turned upside-down by an erotic ménage à trois and a
murder. And as if that's not enough, he joins a group called the
Aztecs and within twelve months they have a national No. 1 hit.

Sex and Thugs and Rock 'n' Roll is a rollercoaster ride through this
amazing year of Billy's life. Take the trip.

AVAILABLE FROM PAN MACMILLAN